Great Recipes for Good Health

READER'S DIGEST

Great Recipes
for
Good Health

Published by The Reader's Digest Association Limited

LONDON · NEW YORK · SYDNEY · CAPE TOWN · MONTREAL

GREAT RECIPES FOR GOOD HEALTH
was edited and designed by
The Reader's Digest Association Limited,
London.

First Edition
Copyright © 1993
The Reader's Digest Association Limited,
Berkeley Square House,
Berkeley Square, London W1X 6AB.
Copyright © 1993
Reader's Digest Association Far East Limited.
Philippines Copyright © 1993
Reader's Digest Association Far East Limited.

Printed in Belgium

ISBN O 276 42104 3

The typeface used in this book is Perpetua,
designed in 1929 by Eric Gill.

Editor Judith Taylor

Art Editor Mavis Henley

CONTRIBUTORS

Consultant Editor Pat Alburey

Nutritional Consultant Editor Cynthia Robinson, BSc

Nutritional Consultant Moya de Wet, BSc, SRD

Recipes created by

Pat Alburey, Valerie Barrett, Jackie Burrow

Carole Handslip, Petra Jackson, Meg Jansz, Angela Kingsbury

Danielle Nay, Louise Pickford, Jane Suthering

Judith Taylor, Hilaire Walden

Photographers	*Home Economists*	*Stylists*
Martin Brigdale	Berit Vinegrad	Penny Markham
Laurie Evans	Maxine Clark	Lesley Richardson
Vernon Morgan	Kathy Man	Antonia Gaunt
Clive Streeter	Lyn Rutherford	Maria Kelly

Title pages and section openers

Devised and photographed by Gerrit Buntrock

Artist Charlotte Wess

Some of the recipes have been adapted from
'Great Recipes for Good Health', published in 1988
by Reader's Digest, USA.

CONTENTS

Eating for health and pleasure 10

Basic recipes 16

BREAKFAST AND BRUNCH

Filled avocados with strawberry dressing 22
Spicy beans on toast 23
Potted beef 24
Cheese salad in pitta bread 25
Citrus and mango salad 26
Courgette and tomato omelette 27
Scrambled eggs Benedict 28
Orange French toast 29
Hummous savoury slices 30
Double haddock kedgeree 30
Kidneys in tomatoes 32
Smoked mackerel pâté 33
Melon refresher 34

Muesli 35
Fruit pancakes 36
Pizza muffins 37
Pork and pheasant pie 38
Porridge and dried fruit compote 40
Potato cakes with bacon 41
Cheese rarebit 42
Fish rarebit 43
Pork and bean tacos 44
Marinated tuna and tomato sandwiches 46
Hot vegetable baguettes 47
Waffles with Stilton topping 48
Homemade yoghurt with pear sauce 48

SOUPS AND STARTERS

Apple and carrot soup 52
Aubergine and sweet pepper soup 53
Broth of chicken and Chinese leaves 54
Chicken and courgette soup 55
Minted chicken soup 56
Chilled cucumber and walnut soup 57
Crab soup 58
Lentil soup 59
Minestrone 60
Mulligatawny soup 62
Mushroom soup with barley 63
Split pea and potato soup 64
Provençal soup 65
Sweetcorn chowder 66
Chilled cream of tomato soup 67
Fresh vegetable soup 68
Chive vichyssoise 69

Artichokes with creamed bean filling 70
Asparagus and mushroom omelettes 71
Chicken liver croustades 72
Duck and apple with orange dressing 73
Wild mushroom tartlets 74
Mussel salad 75
Pears with piquant cheese filling 76
Grilled peppers 77
Pheasant terrine 78
Salmon and asparagus ramekins 79
Marinated scallop brochettes 80
Smoked trout pâté 81
Baked tuna tomatoes 82
Turkey and tarragon loaf 82

FISH AND SHELLFISH

Sea bream and vegetable parcels 86
Steamed cod with ginger 86
Haddock and goat's cheese soufflé 88
Grilled halibut with red pepper sauce 89
Baked monkfish 90
Fish pie 90
Stuffed plaice with nutmeg sauce 92
Plaice and vegetable parcels 93
Skate vinaigrette 94
Lemon sole with sesame seeds 94
Stuffed whiting 96
Oatmeal herrings 97
Soused herrings 98
Fisherman's mackerel 99
Mackerel with hot sour sauce 100
Red mullet with leeks and tomatoes 100

Salmon with cucumber and dill sauce 102
Salmon fish cakes 102
Grilled salmon with horseradish sauce 104
Lemon-marinated sardines 105
Gingered swordfish steaks 106
Trout in herb and wine jelly 107
Trout with orange and mint stuffing 108
Curried tuna and fruit 110
Devilled crab 111
Souffléed Brixham crab 112
Spiced prawns 113
Scallops with creamed celeriac 114
Stir-fried squid and vegetables 114
Seafood gumbo 116
Californian seafood stew 116

POULTRY AND GAME

American captain's chicken 120
Chicken biriani 120
Caribbean lime chicken 122
Chicken and vegetable curry 123
Roast chicken with a stuffing of figs,
rice and thyme 124
Fricasseed chicken with onion 126
Gardener's chicken 127
Poussins with garlic 128
Chicken with pink grapefruit 129
Chicken and mushroom hotpot 130
Chicken with onion and herb stuffing 130
Oven-fried chicken 132
Pan-fried chicken with cucumber 133
Chicken breasts Provençal 134
Sweet and sour apricot chicken 134
Tandoori chicken 136
Chicken and vegetable stew 137

Roast duckling with lime sauce 138
Duck satay 139
Stir-fried duck and vegetables 140
Turkey balsamico 141
Turkey burgers with soured cream 142
Rolled turkey with mint 142
Turkey escalopes with sherry sauce 144
Turkey with sweet potato stuffing 144
Pheasant casserole with apple and cabbage 146
Roast pheasant with prunes 147
Pigeons braised with orange and rice 148
Braised quail with mushrooms 150
Calabrian rabbit 151
Grilled rabbit 152
Rabbit pie 152
Roast venison parcel 154
Venison stew 155

BEEF, LAMB AND PORK

Beefburgers Scandinavian style 158
Beef wrapped in cabbage leaves 158
Beef parcels with chestnuts and red wine 160
Beef kebabs with courgettes and tomatoes 161
Spanish-style spiced beef 162
Beef stir-fry 163
Sweet and sour braised beef 164

Beef stew with tomatoes and basil 165
Roast beef with Yorkshire puddings and
mushroom gravy 166
Sirloin steak with basil sauce 168
Fillet steak with wild mushrooms 169
Oriental steak 170
Peppered sirloin steak 171

Osso bucco 172
Stuffed escalopes of veal with mushroom sauce 173
Lamb and asparagus stir-fry 174
Lamb baked in aubergines 174
Lamb and barley stew 176
Lamb stew with carrots and runner beans 177
Lamb curry 178
Braised lamb chops with flageolet beans 179
Herbed lamb cutlets 180
Lancashire hotpot 181
Kidneys creole 182
Lamb's liver with orange and onion 183
Stuffed leg of lamb with orange sauce 184

Lamb and lentil shepherd's pie 186
Pork and chickpea stew 187
Indonesian-style pork kebabs 188
Stuffed loin of pork 188
Normandy meatballs and cider sauce 190
Pork with roasted peppers 191
Pork and red-cabbage casserole 192
Spicy pork loin 193
Pork and vegetable stir-fry 194
Southern bacon and beans 195
Gammon and lentil loaf 196
Gammon in plum sauce 196

PASTA AND GRAINS

Cannelloni with chicken and walnuts 200
Cannelloni with ricotta and spinach 200
Farfalle with broccoli and nuts 202
Fusilli with bacon and mushrooms 203
Vegetable lasagne 204
Linguine with peas and tuna 205
Linguine and tomato pie 206
Macaroni with leeks and tarragon 207
Ham, pea and noodle gratin 208
Chinese noodles with nuts and apricots 208
Penne with spinach and cheese 210
Pasta shells with chickpeas 211
Stuffed pasta shells and watercress sauce 212
Pasta shells with sardines and pesto 214

Spaghetti with prawns and capers 215
Tagliatelle bolognese 216
Armenian bulgur pilau 216
Bulgur and lentils with pepper sauce 218
Rabbit couscous 219
Polenta with tomatoes and artichokes 220
Chicken liver risotto 221
Paella 222
Rice with egg and prawns 224
Jambalaya 225
Lamb and courgette risotto 226
Kidney bean risotto 227
Nutty brown rice with eggs 228
Spiced seafood and coconut pilau 228

VEGETARIAN MAIN DISHES

Aubergine and cheese gratin 232
Stuffed aubergines 232
Bean and aubergine moussaka 234
Broccoli and cheddar soufflé 235
Butter-bean hotpot 236
Cabbage noodle casserole 237
Carrot and rice terrine 238
Cheese and potato pie 239
Cheese and vegetable pudding 240
Chilli with rice 241
Cottage cheese and basil quiche 242
Courgette and carrot quiche 243
Curried vegetables with cucumber sauce 244
Falafel in pitta bread 245
Fennel and potato hotpot 246
Gougère ring filled with ratatouille 246
Lentil cottage pie 248

Lentil dhal and spiced cabbage 249
Lentil, split pea and nut rissoles 250
Lentil and potato stew 251
Noodle and tofu stir-fry 252
Nut roast 253
Vegetable paella with eggs 254
Pancakes with Mexican stuffing 254
Pancakes oriental style 256
Layered pease pudding 258
Peppers with artichoke stuffing 259
Peppers with bean and mushroom filling 260
Pizza with three-pepper topping 262
Spinach ring with white-bean sauce 264
Spiced vegetable stew with couscous 265
Tofu and vegetable stir-fry with rice 266
Two-layer tortilla 267

VEGETABLE SIDE DISHES

Asparagus baked in white wine 270
Aubergine and pumpkin gratin 270
Aubergine and tomato slices 271
Broad beans in parsley sauce 272
Green beans with dill dressing 272
Runner beans with cherry tomatoes 272
Beetroots with horseradish sauce 274
Broccoli with basil sauce 274
Broccoli with sweet pepper 275
Brussels sprouts with garlic crumbs 276
Baked cabbage wedges with cheese 277
Braised red cabbage with cranberries 278
Carrots and peppers in onion sauce 278
Carrots glazed with orange and ginger 278
Cauliflower in red pepper sauce 280
Cauliflower in spicy tomato sauce 280
Courgettes and cherry tomatoes 281
Braised fennel and potatoes 282
Jerusalem artichokes braised in wine 283
Leek stir-fry with herb croutons 284
Mangetout with carrots and red pepper 285

Marrow with ginger and almonds 286
Mushrooms in red wine 287
Mushrooms with yoghurt and dill sauce 288
Onions in herb sauce 289
Red onions in raisin sauce 290
French-style peas 290
Green pea purée 290
Baked garlic potatoes 292
Curried potatoes 293
New potatoes with creamy mint sauce 294
Sesame potatoes 295
Potato slices 295
Two-potato cake 296
Spinach balls in tomato sauce 297
Sautéed spinach with lemon and garlic 298
Spinach and rice cakes 299
Swede, carrot and potato purée 300
Sweet potatoes with apples 301
Tomato gratin 302
Mustard-glazed turnips 303

SIDE SALADS

Artichoke, broccoli and cheese salad 306
Aubergine salad 307
Avocado, bean and cucumber salad 308
Green bean and courgette salad 308
Mixed bean salad 309
Bean sprout salad 310
Pickled beetroot salad 310
Italian-style bread and tomato salad 310
Broccoli and sesame salad 312
Marinated carrots 312
Cauliflower and mushroom salad 312
Celeriac salad 314
Citrus fruit and watercress salad 314
Coleslaw 315
Cottage cheese and fruit salad 316
Cucumber and fruit salad 317
Spicy cucumber and red pepper salad 318

Fennel and cabbage salad 318
Fusilli salad with peppers and basil 318
Greek salad 320
Lamb's lettuce and beetroot salad 320
Oriental mushroom salad 320
Pasta salad with salmon and spinach 320
Summer pasta salad 323
Pineapple salad 324
Potato, artichoke and red pepper salad 325
Prawn and fetta salad 326
Prawn and spinach salad 327
Rice, orange and walnut salad 328
Spinach and bacon salad 328
Spinach and orange salad 330
Syrian herb and wheat salad 330
Roasted vegetable salad 332
Waldorf salad 332

DESSERTS

Almond and raspberry meringue 336
Apple and raisin crisp 338
Mixed berry ice cream 339

Black Forest gâteau 340
Chocolate berry parfait 342
Chocolate pudding 343

Crème brûlée 344

Fruit salad 345

Gooseberry pancakes 346

Lime and ginger cheesecake 347

Mango choux ring 348

Melba summer pudding 350

Orange soufflé 351

Orange and strawberry flan 352

Peach and almond strudel 354

Peach sorbet 356

Pears in white wine 357

Plum cobbler 358

Rhubarb and date crumble 359

Strawberry charlotte 360

BREADS, CAKES AND BISCUITS

Cheese and onion bread 364

Crumpets 364

Crusty breads and rolls 366

Wholemeal muffins 368

Olive and tomato focaccia 369

Pitta breads 370

Pretzels with cumin seeds 371

Soda bread 372

Banana spice loaf 373

Date and walnut tea-bread 374

Spicy maple tea-bread 375

Prune tea-bread 376

Fruit and nut cake 376

Swiss roll 378

Chocolate cookies 380

Date and oat slices 381

Savoury biscuits 382

Sesame snaps 382

COCKTAIL SNACKS AND DRINKS

Chickpea and rosemary dip 386

Cottage cheese and basil dip 386

Guacamole 386

Courgette and cheese wheels 388

Mushrooms with watercress stuffing 388

Spicy toasted nuts 388

Freshwater prawns in spiced dressing 390

Stuffed radishes 390

Sardine and rice parcels 392

Spinach soufflé squares 392

Tomatoes with prawn stuffing 394

Tuna and cucumber rings 394

Turkey bouchées 396

Iced apple-mint tea 397

Banana milk shake 398

Hot chocolate and banana 398

Iced coffee 399

Mulled cider 400

Spiced cranberry shrub 401

Gingered lemon and lime fizz 402

Ginger tea punch 402

Grapefruit and mint spritzer 402

Herb tea 404

Amber orange-tea punch 405

Orange and pineapple crush 406

Orange-yoghurt drink 406

Passion fruit citrus sodas 408

Pineapple-mint yoghurt drink 408

Hot redcurrant punch 410

Mixed vegetable juice 411

Index 412

Acknowledgments 416

EATING FOR HEALTH AND PLEASURE

This is a book that shows you how to eat and cook in a way that promotes good health. It is not about food fads or crash diets, but about a wise, long-term pattern of enjoyable eating.

The recipes do not involve giving up good food. They are designed to create dishes that you would choose to eat – and all the more readily because they observe the rules for a healthy diet. They follow the 1991 recommendations of the Department of Health's Committee on Medical Aspects of Food Policy (COMA).

Knowing what to aim for is crucial in checking whether your diet is healthy. Equally crucial is knowing what you are eating, so there is a chart with each recipe to show what nutrients a single serving contains. The nutrients are given in grams since this gives whole numbers for the small amounts involved; using ounces would involve a great many fractions and make comparison of recipes difficult. The recipes, however, give the ingredients in both ounces and grams.

The recipes require no special equipment or unusual ingredients. Although grouped in particular chapters, many of the recipes are versatile. Some breakfast dishes or starters, for example, could suit you equally well as a light supper, while one of the breads or side salads could make part of a packed lunch.

There are dishes not just for everyday fare, but for special celebrations and family get-togethers, for when friends come for summer tea in the garden, and for when they come to a buffet party. There are drinks for these occasions, too, so that drivers, children and others who do not want wine or spirits are not condemned to sugary squashes or insipid juices.

Clear step-by-step instructions are given for all the recipes, and these are based on tests carried out by ordinary people cooking in their homes as well as by trained home economists. Every dish is illustrated, and the photographs give many ideas for attractive presentation at the table.

Changing eating habits

Habit is the main factor in most people's diet. Eating habits are often formed in childhood and can be hard to change. Parents providing the food during these habit-forming years had known postwar austerity, and then in the 1960s revelled in providing increasingly available rich foods.

In recent years, the range of available foods has changed dramatically. Items that were once seasonal are on sale all year. There are processed and deep-frozen foods, ready-made dishes and a seemingly infinite variety of snacks.

Not only the food in shops but ways of life, too, have changed dramatically. Many people in Britain now can spend more on food than their grandparents or parents could. They live in warmer houses, so have less need of a thick insulating layer of fat; they work indoors in greater comfort, sit down more to work, and sit down to be taken to work. They walk less, and the work done to make a living or to run a home uses less physical energy. Many leisure pursuits are far from strenuous – and may consist of going out for a meal or watching television.

The failure to adapt eating habits to present energy needs is showing up in diet-related health problems, including obesity, heart attacks and high blood pressure. It is not that people cause all their own health problems by a poor diet; inherited conditions, upbringing, the needs of work, and economic circumstances all affect health. But diet can be the final straw, and once a medical problem has arisen, eating wisely can be the best long-term way of dealing with it.

What is food for?

The body uses food and drink as its fuel supply for growth, maintenance and energy. Carbohydrate is converted into glucose which is carried by the blood to where energy is needed. A small amount of glucose is stored for a time in the muscles and liver, and the rest is converted into body fat.

Small amounts of fat are vital to maintain the structure of body cells and to enable vitamins A, D, E and K to be absorbed. The fat we eat provides energy for activity, protects delicate tissues such as the kidneys and forms a layer of insulation under the skin. It is particularly high in calories; excess intake is converted into body fat.

Protein provides the materials for the body to build and repair cells, muscles, bones and organs.

Fibre, from the cell walls of plants, has no nutrients and is indigestible, but it adds bulk to food and, as it makes its way undigested through the system, it carries away waste products.

Vitamins enable the body to make use of other nutrients. An adequate supply of vitamins helps to give good skin, resistance to infection, a healthy nervous system, well-maintained cells and blood vessels, and prompt healing of damage.

Minerals help to give healthy bones and teeth, efficient carrying of oxygen and waste by the blood, effective muscle function, the breakdown of food to usable energy in cells, maintenance of the nerves, and the proper balance of fluids.

Planning a healthy diet

A good diet should supply just enough nutrients for growth, repairs and chemical processes, and give ample energy for daily tasks. The energy derived from food is measured in calories.

To maintain a stable weight, 15 calories a day are needed for every pound (0.45kg) of body weight – rather more for people doing physical work, and rather less for those who sit a good deal. Among adults in their most active years, between 19 and 50, men of average height and build need about 2550 calories a day, and average women about 1940 calories. Older people need fewer calories and growing children and adolescents need more. Many people, however, eat more than enough for their daily needs and have an excess store of body fat.

CARBOHYDRATES Nutritionists now advise that about half the day's calories should come from carbohydrates. Carbohydrates come in the forms of starch (complex carbohydrate) and sugar (simple carbohydrate), both of which provide 4 calories per gram (about 115 calories per ounce). Sugar, however, is something to be wary of – not natural sugars, for example the fructose and lactose in fruit and milk, because these are accompanied by valuable nutrients such as protein and vitamins. Refined sugar (sucrose)

does not come in a natural package with other nutrients; because of this, the calories it provides are often called empty calories. Honey and syrup are virtually the same as refined sugar.

Starch is the form of carbohydrate to eat in greater quantities. Bread, cereals, oats, potatoes, grains, pasta, peas, beans and lentils are all high-starch foods which should be a regular part of the diet. Not many years ago, starchy foods were thought of as fattening; they were the first item to be cut by people wanting to lose weight. Eating less fat is a far healthier alternative – and makes a much bigger cut in calories.

PROTEIN A healthy diet must include protein, but most of us eat far more than we need. About 2oz (60g) a day of pure protein is enough; about one-fifth of meat is protein, and about one-tenth of bread. Like carbohydrate, protein provides 4 calories per gram. Animal protein – beef, lamb and pork, poultry and game, fish, and eggs, milk and cheese – is called complete protein because it contains the right combination of some 20 amino acids to make the protein accessible to the body. Proteins from plants are known as incomplete proteins; certain combinations are needed to make their protein available to the body. For example, pulses – beans, peas and lentils – should be combined with grains such as rice, or with cereals such as wheat.

FATS Fat should provide a maximum of 35 per cent of the daily calories, not the present British average of 40 per cent. Fat, the most concentrated calorie source, provides 9 calories per gram. Cutting down fats will help to prevent obesity and heart ailments.

It is not just reducing fat that improves the diet; the type of fat is also important. You should cut out as much as possible saturated fats, high amounts of which are in meat, milk and dairy produce, coconut and palm oil, and the hydrogenated vegetable oils in, for example, hard margarines. Saturated fats stimulate production of cholesterol which furs up arteries, impeding circulation and causing extra work for the heart.

Small amounts of polyunsaturated fat are vital for cell structure. This kind of fat is derived from vegetables, seeds, nuts and fish; polyunsaturated oils include corn, sunflower and sesame oil.

The third type of fat, monounsaturated fat, is present in large amounts in olive oil, rape seed oil (sold as vegetable oil), nuts and avocados, but is present also in smaller but significant amounts in all other fatty foods. Monounsaturated fats have not been linked with any harmful effects.

FIBRE You should eat 18g (about ⅔ oz) of fibre a day. This is a lower figure than once recommended, because of a new method of analysis; fibre has a new name too – non-starch polysaccharides (NSP). Fibre can be insoluble or soluble. Insoluble fibre is found in whole-grain cereals, wholemeal bread and pulses. Soluble fibre is found in fruits and vegetables.

To increase fibre intake, eat brown rice rather than polished, and wholemeal bread rather than white; replace some meat with beans, lentils and other pulses, and eat good helpings of leafy vegetables and fruit daily. There is no advantage in exceeding the daily target; too much, or a sudden increase in, fibre causes discomfort.

VITAMINS AND MINERALS The foods that provide protein, carbohydrates and fibre also give a plentiful and varied supply of vitamins and minerals. Take care about sodium (eaten mainly as salt), which can be a factor in high blood pressure. At the moment the average intake in this country is 3600mg a day. Nutritionists recommend a reduction to 2000mg (2g) a day – and just 500mg would probably be enough.

What the charts tell you

To help you keep track of what you eat, every recipe in the main body of this book has alongside it a chart of nutritional information. The chart does not detail every component in the recipe but only those you need to take care about. A varied diet has enough protein, vitamins and minerals, so no figures are given for them – except for sodium, which is often eaten to excess.

The number of calories provided by one serving of the dish is shown first. Then the chart shows how much carbohydrate there is altogether in a serving; a separate entry shows how much of the total carbohydrate comes from sugar, that is from deliberately added refined sugar (or occasionally honey), not the natural sugar in fruits and vegetables. The figure for added sugar is often zero, and in that case it is emphasised by being printed on a shaded strip. In the recipes using yeast, the sugar used to start the yeast fermenting is converted to carbon dioxide and none of it remains in the finished dish.

The chart shows the total fat in a serving, and also has a separate entry to show how much of the total is saturated fat. Where this is particularly low – 11 per cent or less of the calories per serving – the figure is on a shaded strip so that a flick through any chapter shows at once the recipes that are low in saturated fat.

A shaded strip also shows which recipes make a useful contribution of fibre. The shading is used when the fibre content per serving is 3g or more, that is one-sixth of the daily target.

The sodium content of a serving is shown in milligrams not grams, since the amounts are so small. You can spot the low-sodium (low-salt) recipes quickly because of the shaded strip. This is used when a serving has one milligram or less of sodium per calorie; many have much less.

Why the recipes are healthy

In the creation, testing and selection of recipes for this book, all the latest nutritional targets and guidelines have been borne in mind – plenty of complex carbohydrate and fibre, moderate amounts of protein, and very little saturated fat, refined sugar and salt. With all the groundwork done, you can simply eat and enjoy the dishes – and learn from the choice of ingredients and cooking methods a great deal about healthy eating to apply to some of your old favourites.

The carbohydrate content in main dishes varies widely because some have rice, pasta, or potatoes as an integral part of the dish. Others have starch in a supporting role. Where this is not so, there is often a suggestion to serve bread, potatoes or some other carbohydrate food with the dish.

Starchy foods, such as cereals, potatoes, grains, pasta, peas, beans and lentils, are varied and filling. How you cook them makes a difference to the diet. Potatoes should generally not be creamed with milk and butter, or fried, although the occasional helping of creamed potatoes or chips does no harm. Rather than mash potatoes with fat, you can steam them or bake them with other vegetables to make them moist. If you do fry potatoes, cut them in thick slices so there is less fried surface in proportion to the inside. There are very simple recipes that give you the roast potato taste without lots of fat (see p.295).

Pasta in itself is a very good thing to eat, but do not serve rich sauces with it or sprinkle on too much cheese. It is simple to make your own sauces based on tomatoes or other vegetables and avoid the saturated fat, salt and even sugar that some ready-made sauces contain.

Grains, another excellent carbohydrate source, are the staple of some of the world's healthiest diets. Rice is at its most nutritious when it has its brown bran coating, which also gives it a satisfyingly chewy texture and a nutty flavour; it is an excellent base for salads. However, some dishes, fish for example, require the softer texture and less pronounced flavour of white rice.

Many of the recipes include beans and other pulses, all excellent starchy foods. The recipes are based on using home-cooked pulses (see p.17) since most tinned varieties contain salt. Dried pulses take some time to prepare at home but they need supervision for very little of that time.

The majority of the recipes have no added sugar. Some desserts, and drinks with sour ingredients make use of it, and a few savoury recipes contain a small amount to produce a sauce or glaze. A little sugar now and again will do no harm, but it is better to gain sweetness from fruits (and some vegetables) which also contribute fibre, vitamins and minerals to the diet.

Even in dishes where sugar is used to give a particular effect or to make special-occasion desserts it has been kept to the minimum needed to make the recipe work well and taste good. There are carefully adapted recipes for several old-fashioned tea-breads, which are also excellent for packing to eat at work or school as a change from straightforward bread. The aim has been to give recipes for breads that taste good on their own without fatty or sugary spreads.

Ways of cutting down fat

Besides having a reduced fat content overall, the recipes generally use olive oil, but occasionally other fats are used. Polyunsaturated vegetable oils or virtually tasteless corn oil, for example, are used in desserts, cakes and biscuits. Sesame's flavour is welcome in stir-fries, walnut oil is delicious in salads, and butter (used only in small quantities) has a particular creamy taste that improves delicate sauces.

Dishes are kept low in fat by skilful adaptation of ingredients, as well as by reducing quantities. For example, low-fat yoghurt replaces egg yolk and oil to make a thick salad dressing. Skimmed or semi-skimmed milk replaces full-fat milk in sauces, puddings, pancakes and other dishes.

Helpings of red meat are smaller than some people may be used to because the meat contains invisible fat even after all you can see has been trimmed off. Poultry and game helpings are larger because their flesh is lower in fat – but the skin is not low in fat and where the skin is left on to keep the meat moist during cooking, there is a reminder to remove the skin before serving or before eating.

Cheese is prudently reduced to keep down the saturated fat, but its flavour and protein make cheese invaluable. In some dishes, reduced-fat Cheddar is used, in some a small amount of high-flavour mature cheese is the choice, while in others low-fat cottage cheese, fromage frais and quark (made from skimmed milk) are used.

There is no deep-frying in this book, but the benefits frying offers – sealing in the juices of food and enhancing its flavour – are achieved by browning or lightly tossing food in a small amount of oil. The Chinese method of stir-frying with a small amount of oil is also used.

Scares about cholesterol from egg yolks have subsided; the cholesterol level in blood does not result solely from the diet. The body makes cholesterol independently of what is eaten. For most people, keeping down saturated fat will control cholesterol. Medical treatments will help anyone whose body produces excess cholesterol.

The recipes include desserts, biscuits, cakes, party snacks and some brunch dishes which have been adapted to reduce saturated fat and make healthier snacks than crisps, biscuits, cakes and ice-creams. Some special-occasion dishes have a total fat content higher than the norm, but it is expected that such items will not be eaten often.

Keeping a check on protein

The main-course recipes all contain an adequate amount of good quality protein. The focus in creating the recipes has been to avoid excessive amounts of protein which will simply be turned into body fat. For red meat, the suggested serving is 4oz (115g). It is better to move away from serving large slabs of meat and make the most of the smaller, but adequate, 4oz by cutting it into fine strips or slicing it thinly. In fact, 4oz of meat is not all that small a helping. It takes quite a large lamb or pork chop to provide 4oz of meat after trimming away all the fat. And although a 4oz steak may look small, the same weight of lean roast beef, cold and thinly sliced, looks a much more ample helping.

Poultry and game, which are lower in fat, are used in larger amounts of about 6oz (175g). White fish provides high-quality protein while being particularly low in fat, and oily fish (generally fish with darker flesh) contains particular types of polyunsaturated oils that help to improve the balance of fats in the blood.

It is easy to get enough protein without eating meat or fish; eggs are another source of high-quality protein. If you do not want to eat meat, fish or eggs, you can get high-quality protein from low-fat cheeses, low-fat yoghurts and skimmed or semi-skimmed milk. Without eating any protein from animal sources you will still get enough protein from plants if you combine pulses with grains, cereals or nuts.

Cutting down on sodium

The main source of sodium in the diet is salt, and most people take far too much of it. Many foods – fish, shellfish, meat, milk and spinach, for example – contain a natural supply of sodium. Without adding any salt during cooking or to food on the plate, you can get all the sodium you need, but savoury snacks, tinned soups and vegetables, prepared sauces and relishes, cured meats such as bacon and ham, bread and cheese, even sweet foods such as cakes and biscuits have salt added. The daily requirement is very small – the equivalent of one level teaspoon of salt.

Adding salt has become such a habit for many people that without it food seems insipid at first. Within a short time, however, it becomes plain that salt often masks the flavour of food, and only the salt can be tasted, while the individual subtleties of other ingredients are lost. To enhance these true flavours, the recipes use herbs, garlic, ginger and other spices, but not to excess.

Bacon, ham and cheese are used sparingly. Several recipes include raw prawns to be cooked at home; this is to keep the sodium level down, since ready-cooked prawns have invariably been boiled in brine. To help you to avoid the high sodium content of some ready-cooked ingredients, there are recipes (see pp.16-19) for no-salt or low-salt home-cooked tomato sauce, tomato purée, pulses and stocks. Methods of cooking rice without salt and pasta with a minimum of salt are also given.

When salt is occasionally added to a dish, it is in a very small amount, often ⅛ level teaspoon. A 'pinch' is a very variable measure and may be more than ¼ teaspoon; a few such pinches a day could double the daily sodium count. The easiest way to measure ⅛ level teaspoon is with a standard measuring spoon. Fill the ¼ teaspoon, level it off with a round-ended knife, then press the knife tip down into the salt across the middle of the spoon and push the unwanted half out.

Vitamins and minerals

A varied diet gives most people all the vitamins and minerals they need. Vegetarians and vegans need to take care to get enough vitamin B12, which most people get from meat. Alternative sources are egg yolk, milk, cheese, and yeast extract supplemented with B12.

Vitamin overdose has become a slight worry. Vitamin pills containing vitamin D and nicotinic acid can have serious effects if taken in excess. An increase of vitamin A in liver has occurred, from supplements in the feed for livestock, it is thought. Pregnant women are advised against eating liver since there is a small risk to the unborn child from a high intake of vitamin A.

A much more frequent occurrence is the loss of minerals and vitamins by keeping or cooking food too long. Eating fruits and vegetables at their freshest ensures the highest vitamin content. Frozen vegetables and fruits are processed quickly after gathering and retain their vitamins; indeed, they contain all the nutrients of fresh vegetables. Only their texture is different; they lose the distinctive crispness of fresh vegetables.

You should eat fruits and vegetables as often as possible, and when cooking them, do so for the shortest possible time. To retain the nutrients in vegetables, steam them, stir-fry them, bake them, or sauté them in a minimum of oil. When you cook meat in a casserole, cook the vegetables with it, adding those that need short cooking for the last few minutes. When you do boil vegetables, use as little water as possible and do not throw it away but add it to stock, soups or sauces.

Handling food safely

Food poisoning is on the increase in Britain, and some cases are caused by food prepared at home. A few precautions will reduce the risks. Once you have bought food, take it home quickly and store it in a cool place or a refrigerator. Cover foods before storing in the refrigerator, do not let them touch and do not fill the refrigerator so full that the cold air cannot circulate. Put meat on a large enough plate, so it will not drip, and raised on an upturned saucer to keep it clear of blood that runs out; cover it with a large upturned bowl. Keep raw or cooked meat for only 2-3 days.

Use a refrigerator thermometer to test that the refrigerator is cold enough. It should be at 5°C (40°F) or less to minimise the growth of bacteria. If it is not an automatic defroster, defrost it about every eight weeks. Check the door seal often. Keep the refrigerator clean, wiping up spills at once, and wiping it out regularly using a boiled cloth and a bowl of hand-hot water with a teaspoon of bicarbonate of soda added.

Always wash your hands with soap and warm water before handling food. Keep work surfaces clean and boards well scrubbed. Use clean knives and other utensils, and wash anything used to prepare meat, poultry, fish, raw eggs and vegetables that may have any soil on them before using it for another ingredient.

Rinse the inside of poultry before cooking. Make sure that meat, especially pork and poultry, reaches a high enough temperature during cooking, so bacteria that could cause food poisoning are killed. When dishes are cooked, eat them piping hot or cool them quickly and put in the refrigerator. Do not keep dishes or part-cooked ingredients just warm so that bacteria proliferate; 5-63°C (40-145°F) is the danger zone.

Raw or under-cooked eggs (which are included in some mayonnaise and desserts) should not be given to the elderly and frail or to infants and pregnant women.

There is a small danger of listeria infection associated with mould-ripened cheese, and cheeses made with unpasteurised milk. Pregnant women should not eat them because the unborn child could be infected with listeriosis (which can be fatal). There is no danger with pasteurised cottage cheese, fromage frais and hard cheeses.

The simplest and cheapest way to store food is to put it in a china or glass dish and cover it with its own lid or a plate. Unless specifically stated on the label, do not wrap fatty food such as cheese directly in PVC-based cling film, because of the slight danger of cancer-causing agents entering the food. When you wrap food for cooking, use baking paper or greaseproof paper rather than foil whenever possible to avoid tainting the food.

Fruits eaten without peeling need particular care before eating or cooking to remove the chemicals so often used to get them to the shops in prime condition. Fruit such as apples should be well washed under hand-hot water, then rinsed and dried to remove any residue from sprays. Citrus fruits are frequently given a thin coating of antifungicidal wax to make them keep better. If you are going to use the rind, you should first scrub the fruit gently under running water, using a boiled nylon pan scrubber – unless you are certain the fruit is unwaxed, as organic fruit is.

You should not eat any green parts of potatoes as these contain the poison solanine. To prevent potatoes from turning green, keep them in a thick brown paper bag in a cool, dry, dark place.

Using the recipes

All the recipes give at the beginning a preparation time, based on the experience of those who have tested the recipes. This includes the time needed to prepare the ingredients and to assemble the dish, including the browning of vegetables and meat, for example, before the dish is put in the oven or left to cook in a saucepan. It is the time you can expect to be working on the dish before leaving it to cook. It cannot be an exact time since people differ in the speed at which they carry out

tasks. Some cooks have many gadgets to help them, others do most tasks manually. Tips are included to give practical advice that will save time or make the dish work better.

When you choose a recipe, be sure to read all the ingredients and instructions before you start making it. You may need to soak beans or prepare a stock or tomato sauce in advance. Follow the imperial or the metric measurements all through. Do not mix the two. Where ingredients are given in spoonfuls, they have been measured with standard measuring spoons. You should use a level spoonful when this is listed; a rounded spoonful can be twice as much as a level spoonful and would affect the taste if the ingredient is ginger or basil, for example, and the consistency if the ingredient is flour for thickening a sauce.

Sets of British standard measuring spoons are sold quite cheaply in kitchen and hardware shops. It is also cheap to buy stacking bamboo steamers, and adjustable fold-out metal steamers resembling umbrellas. Nonstick frying pans and roasting tins cost more but are worth having because you can then use a minimum of fat.

The cooking time given for a dish is again based on the experience of those who tested the recipes but, as with the preparation time, there will be some variability since ovens vary. Most cooks know the quirks of their own oven and make adjustments.

At the end of a main dish recipe, alternative ingredients are sometimes suggested to use in place of foods that are not always available or to vary the dish, and there is often a suggestion of side dishes to serve with a main dish to complement the taste, add colour or improve the nutritional balance. These alternatives and serving suggestions are not included in the nutritional chart. The chart includes only the items listed in the ingredients.

Some of the recipes are very quick to prepare, some take longer, and some require a little preparation the day before. Choosing and preparing meals is worthy of thought, planning and effort. Speedy cooking is necessary on occasions but cooking is a rewarding and creative challenge, and time should be spent on something so vital in caring properly for ourselves and for others. It is worth taking time not just over cooking but over eating itself if the most benefit is to be derived from it. Do not gobble or eat on the run; make a meal an occasion even if it is at an office desk. Devote time to it, eat slowly and relish your meal. Food is not a weakness, a fad, an obsession or a sin, but one of life's necessities and one of its most enduring pleasures.

BASIC RECIPES

Fruit juice

It is easy to make your own fresh-flavoured juice from soft fruits. Use the fruits when they are fully ripe, if you can, and they will not usually need to be sweetened. Very acid fruits such as blackcurrants, redcurrants and cranberries, however, need sweetening to be palatable. Weigh the fruit after hulling or removing the stalks.

Berry fruit juice

MAKES ¾ pint (425ml)
PREPARATION TIME: 20 minutes
COOKING TIME: 20 minutes
TOTAL CALORIES (unsweetened): 115

1lb (450g) prepared raspberries, loganberries, blackberries or strawberries, washed
4 tablespoons water (¾ pint/425ml for strawberries)
0-½ oz (0-15g) sugar

1 Put the fruit into a heatproof bowl that will sit firmly on one of your saucepans. Crush the fruit with a potato masher, or the back of a spoon. Add the water.
2 Sit the bowl on the saucepan, half filled with simmering water, for 20 minutes or until the juice runs freely from the fruit.
3 Scald a large square of muslin in boiling water, and wring it out. Place a nylon or stainless steel sieve over a bowl and line it with the wet muslin.
4 Mash the heated fruit again to press out as much juice as possible, then pour the pulp and juice into the sieve. Fold two opposite sides of the muslin securely over the fruit, then twist the ends tightly in opposite directions to force out the juice until no more comes out. Discard the pulp in the muslin.
5 Stir the sugar, if used, into the juice until it has dissolved completely.

You can make the same amount of juice using redcurrants, but you will need to use ¼ pint (150ml) water with the fruit and add ¼ -½ oz (7-15g) sugar. With blackcurrants and cranberries, 1lb (450g) of fruit needs ¾ pint (425ml) water and

makes 1 pint (570ml) juice. Stir ½ -1oz (15-30g) sugar into blackcurrant juice and 1-1½ oz (30-45g) into cranberry juice.

For the fullest nutritional benefit, drink the juice as soon as it is made, either as it is or diluted with up to 3 times its volume of soda water, mineral water or skimmed milk. Alternatively, let the juice cool, then put it in a covered jug and keep it in the refrigerator for up to 2 days.

Instead of straining the juice through muslin, you can turn the fruit pulp into an unlined sieve and press it gently with a wooden or stainless steel spoon, but the juice will not be quite as clear. Use only a nylon or stainless steel sieve; other metal sieves will react with the acid in the fruit and taint the juice.

Sauces and dressings

Sugar, salt and fat are cut down or cut out in these recipes. The analysis charts for all dishes including tomato sauce or purée are based on using the recipes below.

Tomato sauce

MAKES 1 pint (570ml)
PREPARATION TIME: 15 minutes
COOKING TIME: 55 minutes
TOTAL CALORIES: 295

1 tablespoon olive oil
1 medium onion, peeled and chopped
1 clove garlic, peeled and crushed
1 level teaspoon each chopped fresh thyme, oregano and rosemary, or 1 level teaspoon dried mixed herbs
1lb (450g) ripe tomatoes, skinned, de-seeded and chopped
14oz (400g) tinned tomatoes
Freshly ground black pepper

1 Heat the oil in a stainless steel or enamel saucepan and cook the onion in it

gently for 8 minutes, stirring from time to time, until softened but not browned. Stir in the garlic and cook for 1 minute.
2 Mix in the herbs, fresh tomatoes, and tinned tomatoes with their juice. Bring to the boil, then partially cover the saucepan and simmer for about 45 minutes, until the sauce is reduced by about one-third and thickened. Stir occasionally to break up the tomatoes. Season with pepper.

This chunky sauce goes well with pasta and vegetables. For a smoother sauce to serve with fish or meat loaves, cool it slightly and blend in a food processor or pass through a food mill. It keeps in a refrigerator for 3 days, or in a freezer for 12 months.

Tomato purée

MAKES 28 tablespoons (¾ pint/425ml)
PREPARATION TIME: 10 minutes
COOKING TIME: 1 hour 50 minutes
TOTAL CALORIES: 155

1½ lb (680g) ripe tomatoes, chopped
1¾ lb (800g) tinned tomatoes

1 Put all the tomatoes, and their juice, into a stainless steel or enamel saucepan. Bring to the boil, lower the heat, cover and cook gently for 20 minutes.
2 Cool slightly, then blend in a food processor. Pass back into the saucepan through a nylon sieve to remove the seeds.
3 Bring the purée to the boil, then let it bubble gently for 1¼ -1½ hours, stirring frequently, until it becomes so thick that it remains in two halves when a wooden spoon is drawn through the centre.
4 When the purée is cold, turn it into a clean jar and cover with an acid-proof lid. Store in the refrigerator for up to 4 weeks. Alternatively, spoon into ice-cube trays and freeze. Turn out the cubes and pack them in plastic containers or polythene bags to keep frozen for up to 12 months.

Use the purée to improve the flavour and colour of sauces, soups and stews. Make several batches during the summer when tomatoes are cheap. When plum tomatoes from Italy are available, or other fresh tomatoes have good flavour and colour, use them instead of the tinned tomatoes.

Vinaigrette dressing

MAKES 4 tablespoons, to dress a salad for 6
PREPARATION TIME: 5 minutes
TOTAL CALORIES: 230

1 level teaspoon Dijon or whole-grain mustard
Freshly ground black pepper
1 clove garlic, peeled and crushed
2 tablespoons chopped fresh parsley
1 tablespoon cider vinegar or wine vinegar
2 tablespoons extra virgin olive oil

1 Mix all the ingredients in a bowl with a small wire whisk or wooden salad server, until blended and slightly thickened.

For the best flavour, make the dressing just before you need it. Use balsamic or raspberry vinegar for a mellower flavour. For a delicately flavoured salad, you can use a light olive oil or corn oil instead of the distinctively flavoured virgin olive oil. For a more strongly flavoured dressing, use half walnut oil and half olive oil.

To vary the flavour, use lemon or orange juice instead of vinegar and add different herbs – basil, chives, marjoram, fennel, dill or lemon balm. Do not over-chop them or the colour and taste will be spoiled. To give a spicy edge, add a little grated nutmeg, or ground cardamom seeds or cinnamon.

Yoghurt dressing

MAKES 12 level tablespoons (6oz/175g), to dress a salad for 8
PREPARATION TIME: 5 minutes
TOTAL CALORIES: 130

4 level tablespoons Greek yoghurt
6 level tablespoons low-fat natural yoghurt
2 tablespoons lemon juice
1 level teaspoon Dijon or whole-grain mustard
Freshly ground black pepper

1 Mix the yoghurts, lemon juice and mustard in a bowl and season with pepper. Serve immediately, or cover and refrigerate for up to 3 hours before using.

Use the dressing plain and simple, or flavour it with chopped fresh herbs, spring onions, watercress, ground cardamom or freshly grated nutmeg. Use it to dress leafy salads, grated or chopped vegetables, cooked potato slices or pasta.

Dried beans, peas and lentils

Although preparing dried beans and peas at home takes time, only about 10 minutes needs your attention; you can leave them unattended for the rest of the cooking. You can make sure that home-cooked beans and peas do not go mushy and you know that no salt has been added as it has to most tinned beans. All the analysis charts for dishes containing dried beans and peas are based on using salt-free ones.

All dried beans and some dried peas have to be soaked before cooking; soaking allows them to re-absorb water and return to their natural size.

Soaking doubles the weight of dried beans or peas, so when a recipe lists, for example, 8oz (225g) cooked haricot beans in the ingredients, you will need to soak and cook 4oz (115g) dried beans.

Beans

To prepare dried beans, spread them on a plate and remove any discoloured ones or grit. Put the beans into a colander and rinse under the cold tap, or wash them repeatedly in a bowl, until the water becomes clear, then drain well.

The beans must then be soaked. Put them into a large bowl with enough cold water to come at least 4in (10cm) above the beans. Cover and leave for at least 5 hours or overnight if more convenient.

Drain the beans and rinse well again. Put them in a very large saucepan and add water, allowing 3 pints (1.7 litres) for 8oz (225g) soaked beans (half this weight before soaking). Bring to the boil, uncovered, and boil briskly for 10 minutes; this is essential for all beans to rid them of substances that can upset the digestive system. Then turn down the heat, partially cover the saucepan with a lid and simmer very gently for 1-1½ hours, until tender.

The cooking time will vary according to the type and age of the beans, and on the water they are cooked in. Soft water cooks them faster than hard water. Drain the beans and use in any dish.

Peas and lentils

Pick over and rinse dried peas and lentils in the same way as beans.

Whole peas and chickpeas must be soaked as dried beans and then be cooked like beans before being used in dishes.

Split peas and lentils do not need soaking or pre-cooking. To cook them on their own, rather than using them in a recipe, cover with unsalted water or, for extra flavour, stock (see p.19), allowing about 3 pints (1.7 litres) of cooking liquid for 4oz (115g) dried peas or lentils. Bring to the boil, then partially cover and simmer. Split peas will take 40 minutes to 1 hour; they break up as they cook and so are used mainly for soups and purées. Split red lentils will take 20-25 minutes, and green and brown lentils 25-30 minutes.

Rice

In cooking rice, you should keep as much as possible of its nutritional value. Cooking it by the absorption method is the best way to achieve this; in other cooking methods nutrients and flavour are thrown away with the cooking water. In the nutritional chart for a recipe that has rice as an ingredient, the analysis is based on rice cooked by the absorption method and without salt.

Allow 2oz (60g) of rice per person, which provides an ample 6oz (175g) serving (and 220 calories) of cooked rice. Pour the weighed rice into a measuring jug to see how many fluid ounces (millilitres) it makes; you will need 1½-2 times that amount of liquid, depending on the type of rice. For example, 8oz (225g) of ordinary long-grain white rice measures 10fl oz (285ml) and needs 15fl oz (425ml) liquid. Generally it needs cooking for 15 minutes.

Easy-cook long-grain white rice needs double its volume of liquid and takes 18-20 minutes to cook.
Long-grain brown rice needs double its volume and takes 25-30 minutes.
Easy-cook brown rice needs double its volume and takes 30-35 minutes.
Basmati rice needs 1½ times its volume and takes 10 minutes.
Wild rice needs double its volume and takes 45-50 minutes.
Risotto rice, such as arborio, and paella rice, such as Valencia, need at least three times their volume of liquid and take 20-40 minutes, depending on whether the liquid is added all at once or little by little. These times are only a guide; different brands and batches of rice vary.

There is no need to rinse the rice before cooking. Rice is clean enough now to use straight from the packet. Put the rice into a heavy-based saucepan with the measured, unsalted water or stock (see p.19). Bring to the boil, stir to separate the grains, then cover and turn the heat very low.

Simmer for the cooking time without lifting the lid, which lets out steam and lowers the temperature. The rice should be tender and all the liquid absorbed. Fluff up the rice with a fork and serve immediately, unless it is basmati rice. Leave basmati rice in the covered pan, off the heat, for 5 minutes before serving.

Pasta

Serve this Italian speciality slightly firm in the centre, or as the Italians describe it 'al dente' – literally 'to the tooth'. Cooking times depend partly on size and mainly on whether the pasta is fresh or dried.

To cook any pasta, use plenty of water. For every 8oz (225g) of uncooked pasta, allow 3 pints (1.7 litres) water, and ½ level teaspoon of salt to prevent sliminess.

Put the pasta into water at a full rolling boil to keep the pieces or strands separate. Swirl the pasta with a fork as the water returns to the boil. Boil fresh pasta for 2-3 minutes and dried pasta for the time recommended, then lift out a piece of the pasta, nip off a fragment and eat it. If it is

still too hard, cook a little longer, testing about every 30 seconds.

As soon as the pasta is ready, drain it in a colander, shaking gently. Serve at once.

Cooking time for dried pasta

The time depends on the size, shape and age of the pasta, and on the brand.

LONG
Linguine (narrow ribbons) 8-10 minutes
Lasagne (sheets) 8-10 minutes
Spaghetti (strings) 10-12 minutes
Tagliatelle ribbons or nests 10-12 minutes
TUBULAR
Cannelloni (large tubes) 5-6 minutes
Macaroni (small, short tubes) 8 minutes
Penne (pointed quills) 12-14 minutes
SHAPES
Conchiglie (shells) 10-12 minutes
Farfalle (butterfly bows) 10-12 minutes
Fusilli (short spirals) 10-12 minutes

Homemade fresh pasta

MAKES 12oz (340g)
PREPARATION TIME: 30 minutes
TOTAL CALORIES: 1215

7oz (200g) pasta or strong flour, or a mix of 4oz (115g) plain and 3oz (85g) wholemeal flour
2 eggs, size 2, lightly beaten
2 tablespoons olive oil
1-2oz (30-60g) fine semolina for sprinkling

1 Sift the flour into a bowl, tipping any bran left in the sieve into the bowl. Make a well in the centre and pour in the eggs and oil. Mix to form a slightly soft dough.
2 Knead on a very lightly floured surface for about 5 minutes, until even-textured. Do not flour the surface too much or the dough will become tough.
3 Roll out the dough in two halves to make each about 16×13in (40×33cm). Trim the edges with a sharp knife and cut the sheets in half lengthways and across to give 8 large sheets for cannelloni (see p.200). Cut each sheet in half again to give 16 small sheets for lasagne (see p.204). Use at once, or stack between waxed paper sheets lightly sprinkled with semolina and refrigerate for up to 24 hours.

To make pasta strands, roll out the dough in two halves as above and trim the edges.

Sprinkle each half very lightly with semolina and roll up loosely. Using a sharp knife, cut the rolls into strips ⅛-½ in (3-13mm) wide to make narrow linguine or wider tagliatelle. Immediately unroll the strands and put them on a large baking tray, sprinkling them with semolina so they do not stick together.

For orange pasta, add ⅛ level teaspoon saffron powder to the flour. For green pasta, add 2oz (60g) cooked, squeezed and finely chopped spinach with the eggs.

You can reduce the preparation time to about 15 minutes by using a pasta machine to roll and cut the dough. If you are using wholemeal flour, discard the bran after sifting. It would make the pasta tear as it passed through the machine.

Ready-to-use pasta

Sheets of lasagne and cannelloni tubes are now sold in forms that need no cooking before being layered or packed with a filling. When making a sauce to coat such lasagne and cannelloni dishes, add about one-third more liquid to it than usual. The pasta absorbs liquid from the sauce as it cooks. If you are short of sauce, boil the pasta for 5 minutes before use, so that it will absorb less liquid from the sauce.

Chinese noodles

Use the same quantity of water as for Italian pasta but add no salt, as Chinese noodles already contain salt. Add the noodles to boiling water and remove the pan from the heat. Cover and leave fine noodles for 4 minutes, medium noodles for 6 minutes. Drain and serve at once.

Stocks

Making stock is slow but requires little effort and you know that your homemade stock contains no fat, no salt and no additives. The stocks here have been used in the analysis charts of all recipes that include stock. They are so low in calories that the number per serving is negligible.

When you are making beef or veal stock, ask the butcher to chop the bones; this cannot be done at home. For the best chicken stock use a boiling fowl with its giblets (except the liver), but wing tips and drumsticks make a good stock and are cheaper. For fish stock, save and freeze the heads and bones of fish you fillet at home or have filleted by the fishmonger. Label and date stock before freezing it. Bring the frozen stock to the boil just before use.

Beef stock

MAKES 6 pints (3.4 litres)
PREPARATION TIME: 20 minutes, plus
3-4 hours to cool and overnight to chill
COOKING TIME: 7 hours 30 minutes
OVEN: Preheat to 220°C (425°F, gas mark 7)

7lb (3.2kg) chopped marrow bones
1lb (450g) unpeeled onions, wiped
6lb (2.7kg) shin of beef, cubed
9 pints (5 litres) water
4 large carrots, peeled and sliced
6 sticks celery, trimmed and sliced
2 leeks, trimmed, sliced and washed
1 whole unpeeled bulb of garlic
Sprig thyme
2 bay leaves
4 sprigs parsley
20 black peppercorns
6 allspice berries

1 Put the bones and onions in a roasting tin and cook in the heated oven for 1 hour 30 minutes, until well browned.
2 Lift the bones and onions into a stockpot or a very large saucepan. Add the beef and 8 pints (4.5 litres) of the water. Bring slowly to the boil, then pour in ¼ pint (150ml) of the remaining water, turn down the heat and skim off the scum.
3 Meanwhile, pour off the fat from the roasting tin. Pour the remaining water into the tin and bring to the boil, stirring to loosen the brown residue. Boil for 2-3 minutes, then strain the liquid through a sieve into the stockpot or saucepan.
4 Add the remaining ingredients, partially cover and simmer for 5 hours 30 minutes, skimming the surface from time to time.
5 Immediately after cooking, strain the stock into a large bowl through a large colander lined with a scalded and wrung out piece of muslin or linen; discard the meat, bones and vegetables. Cover the bowl with a food net or a clean teacloth, making sure it does not touch the stock. Cool for 2 hours, then refrigerate overnight.

6 Next day, discard the solidified fat. The stock keeps for 3 days in a refrigerator. To keep longer, spoon measured amounts (¼, ½ or 1 pint – 150, 285 or 570ml) into rigid containers or polythene bags. Seal, label and freeze immediately.

To make veal stock, use knuckle of veal and stewing veal in place of beef marrow bones and shin. There is no need to roast them.

Chicken stock

MAKES 6 pints (3.4 litres)
PREPARATION TIME: 20 minutes, plus 3-4 hours to cool and overnight to chill
COOKING TIME: 4 hours 30 minutes

6lb (2.7kg) boiling fowl and giblets (except the liver), washed and chopped, or chicken drumsticks and wing tips, washed
8 pints (4.5 litres) water
12oz (340g) onions, peeled and quartered
12oz (340g) carrots, peeled and sliced
Whole unpeeled bulb of garlic
4 sticks celery, trimmed and sliced
1 leek, trimmed, sliced and washed
Small branch lovage
Sprig thyme
2 bay leaves
2 large sprigs marjoram or oregano
3 cloves
20 black peppercorns
2 large pieces blade mace

1 Put the fowl and giblets, or drumsticks and wing tips, into a stockpot or very large saucepan. Pour in all but ¼ pint (150ml) of the water and bring slowly to the boil.
2 When the stock comes to the boil, pour in the remaining water, lower the heat and skim all the scum from the surface.
3 Add all the remaining ingredients, partially cover and simmer for 4 hours, regularly skimming off the scum.
4 Straight after cooking, strain and cool as beef stock. Next day store as beef stock.

You can make turkey and game stock in the same way. These stocks will keep for 3 days in the refrigerator.

Vegetable stock

MAKES 4½ pints (2.5 litres)
PREPARATION TIME: 30 minutes, plus
3-4 hours to cool
COOKING TIME: 4 hours 30 minutes

1lb (450g) swede, peeled and diced
1lb (450g) carrots, peeled and sliced
1lb (450g) onions, peeled and sliced
1lb (450g) leeks, trimmed, sliced and washed
Whole unpeeled bulb of garlic
Small branch lovage
Sprig thyme
2 bay leaves
Large sprig parsley
24 black peppercorns
7 pints (4 litres) water

1 Put all the ingredients into a stockpot or very large saucepan. Bring very slowly to the boil then reduce the heat, partially cover with a lid, and simmer gently for about 4 hours.
2 Immediately after cooking, strain as beef stock. Cool for 3-4 hours then store in the refrigerator for up to 5 days before use. For longer keeping, pack it as beef stock and freeze immediately.

Fish stock

MAKES 2½ pints (1.4 litres)
PREPARATION TIME: 20 minutes, plus
2-3 hours to cool
COOKING TIME: 40 minutes

2½ lb (1.1kg) white fish trimmings (bones, heads with gills removed), washed
White part only of 1 small leek, thinly sliced and washed
2 sticks celery, trimmed and thinly sliced
1 medium onion, peeled and thinly sliced
1 small lemon, thinly sliced
Sprig dill
Sprig parsley
12 black peppercorns
1 bay leaf
½ pint (285ml) dry white wine
2½ pints (1.4 litres) water

1 Put all the ingredients into a large stainless steel or enamel saucepan and bring slowly to the boil.
2 As soon as the stock comes to the boil, turn down the heat and skim off the scum that has risen to the surface.
3 Partially cover the saucepan and simmer for 30 minutes, then immediately strain as for beef stock.
4 Use the stock at once, or cover and cool it for 2-3 hours. Keep fish stock in the refrigerator for 1 day only before use. For longer keeping, pack and freeze it in the same way as beef stock.

BREAKFAST AND BRUNCH

The first meal of the day may be taken with the dawn or much nearer midday, and may vary from a mere nibble and a drink to a hearty spread. Often it is a quick bite before work or school, but it can be a dawdling treat as you read the newspapers, or a sociable feast with guests. There is a recipe here to suit any morning, whether your choice is simple fruit and yoghurt or real old-fashioned porridge, savoury potato cakes with bacon or a splendid feast of kedgeree.

Filled avocados with strawberry dressing

SERVES 4
PREPARATION TIME: 25 minutes

4oz (115g) strawberries, rinsed, dried and hulled
2 level tablespoons low-fat natural yoghurt
Freshly ground black pepper
1 large orange, peel and pith removed, segments
freed of membranes and cut into small pieces
3oz (85g) cucumber, diced
Seeds from 4 green cardamom pods, crushed
1 tablespoon raspberry vinegar
2 ripe avocados
Curly endive, lamb's lettuce, watercress and mint
sprigs to garnish

1 Blend the strawberries and yoghurt in a food
processor, or pass the fruit through a nylon sieve
and whisk into the yoghurt. Season with pepper.

2 Mix the orange, cucumber, crushed
cardamom and vinegar.

3 Halve the avocados and remove the stones.
Arrange the halves on serving plates and
surround with the endive, lamb's lettuce and
watercress. Fill the avocados with the orange
mixture. Spoon on a little of the strawberry
dressing and garnish with the mint sprigs.
Serve the rest of the dressing separately.

ONE SERVING	
CALORIES	170
TOTAL FAT	14g
SATURATED FAT	3g
CARBOHYDRATES	8g
ADDED SUGAR	0
FIBRE	4g
SODIUM	15mg

*Fresh orange and
cool cucumber, spiked
with cardamom and
raspberry vinegar, are
bathed in a smooth
strawberry dressing to
make an unusual filling
for buttery avocado.*

TIP
*To ensure that
each avocado half
remains steady on
the serving plate,
cut a thin sliver
from its rounded
side.*

Mild, mashed beans gain a hot edge from curry spices in this savoury, fibre-packed topping for toast. Fresh tomato slices moisten the dish.

Spicy beans on toast

ONE SERVING

CALORIES 280

TOTAL FAT 8g

SATURATED FAT 1g

CARBOHYDRATES 42g

ADDED SUGAR 0

FIBRE 6g

SODIUM 205mg

SERVES 4
PREPARATION TIME: 10 minutes
COOKING TIME: 10 minutes

2 tablespoons olive oil
2 green sticks celery, trimmed and finely chopped
1 medium red onion, peeled and finely chopped
1 clove garlic, peeled and crushed
2 level teaspoons curry powder
1 level tablespoon chopped fresh savory or thyme
14oz (400g) cooked borlotti, cannellini or haricot beans (see p.17), drained and mashed
4 slices crusty bread
Tomato slices and coriander leaves to garnish

1 Heat the oil in a frying pan and cook the celery and onion in it over a moderate heat for 6-8 minutes, stirring frequently, until softened but not browned.

2 Stir in the garlic, curry powder and savory or thyme, and cook for 1 minute. Mix in the beans and cook gently for 3-4 minutes, until heated all through.

3 Meanwhile, toast the bread on both sides. Spread the bean mixture on the toast and arrange the sliced tomatoes on top. Sprinkle with the coriander and serve at once.

Lean, hearty beef braised in red wine and blended with fromage frais is transformed into a light-textured spread with a rich, meaty taste.

Potted beef

ONE SERVING

CALORIES 195

TOTAL FAT 7g

SATURATED FAT 2g

CARBOHYDRATES 5g

ADDED SUGAR 0

FIBRE 0

SODIUM 90mg

SERVES 4
PREPARATION TIME: 25 minutes, plus 4 hours to cool
COOKING TIME: 1 hour 45 minutes
OVEN: Preheat to 160°C (325°F, gas mark 3)

2 teaspoons olive oil
1lb (450g) shin of beef with bone and fat removed,
cut into large cubes
¼ pint (150ml) red wine
1 clove garlic, peeled and sliced
1 level teaspoon dried marjoram
1 bay leaf
8oz (225g) low-fat fromage frais
1 level teaspoon mixed peppercorns, crushed
Fresh coriander leaves to garnish

1 Heat the oil in a frying pan and brown the meat in it on all sides over a high heat. Lift the meat out of the pan with a slotted spoon and put it in a small, ovenproof casserole.

2 Stir in the wine, garlic, marjoram and bay leaf. Cover with a tightly fitting lid and cook in the heated oven for about 1 hour 45 minutes, or until the meat is tender enough to cut with a spoon. Stir once or twice during cooking.

3 Turn the meat and liquid into a shallow dish, discarding the bay leaf. Leave to cool, then refrigerate for at least 2 hours. Lift off any fat from the top and remove and discard any membranes and gristle from the meat. Blend the meat and the cooking juices in a food processor until smooth, or mince very finely, passing it twice through a mincer.

4 Add the fromage frais and blend again for 1 minute or beat with a fork. Spoon the

mixture into four ramekin dishes, sprinkle the crushed peppercorns on top and chill in the refrigerator for 1 hour. Garnish with the coriander just before serving.

Melba toast makes a light and crisp accompaniment to the smooth potted beef.

Cheese salad in pitta bread

ONE SERVING	
CALORIES	270
TOTAL FAT	9g
SATURATED FAT	3g
CARBOHYDRATES	36g
ADDED SUGAR	0
FIBRE	1g
SODIUM	250mg

Peppery radishes and crisp carrots combine with Cheddar in a filling for pitta bread; alfalfa sprouts add a crunchy finishing touch.

SERVES 4
PREPARATION TIME: 15 minutes

1 level tablespoon Greek yoghurt
1 tablespoon white wine vinegar
½ level teaspoon dried oregano
¼ level teaspoon paprika
Freshly ground black pepper
4oz (115g) reduced-fat Cheddar cheese, cut into thin strips
1 medium carrot, peeled and coarsely grated
4 radishes, trimmed and sliced
4 pitta breads
4 cos lettuce leaves, washed and dried
2oz (60g) alfalfa sprouts

1 Combine the yoghurt and vinegar and stir in the oregano and paprika. Season this dressing with pepper, then mix in the cheese, carrot and radishes.

2 Split open the pitta breads along one side and put a lettuce leaf in each, hollow side up. Spoon the cheese mixture into the lettuce, and top evenly with the alfalfa sprouts.

You can use ricotta or well-drained cottage cheese in place of the Cheddar. For a change of flavour, use a de-seeded and chopped tomato and 1 level teaspoon chopped fresh basil instead of carrot and oregano.

Citrus and mango salad

SERVES 4
PREPARATION TIME: 20 minutes

1 ripe pink grapefruit, peel and pith pared off
1 ripe yellow grapefruit, peel and pith pared off
1 large ripe orange, peel and pith pared off
1 large ripe mango
Lemon balm or mint leaves to decorate

ONE SERVING

CALORIES 105

TOTAL FAT 0

SATURATED FAT 0

CARBOHYDRATES 25g

ADDED SUGAR 0

FIBRE 5g

SODIUM 10mg

1 Holding the pink grapefruit over a bowl to catch the juice, cut down both sides of the membranes with a very sharp knife and as each segment of flesh is freed, put it in the bowl. Squeeze the remaining tissue to extract all the juice. Prepare the yellow grapefruit and the orange in the same way.

2 Using the sharp knife, cut down each side of the mango and trim the halves of flesh away from the stone. Cut a deep cross in the flesh of each half. Holding one half of the mango with the flesh uppermost, press the skin with your thumbs so that the flesh bulges up. Trim the flesh away from the skin and slice it into the bowl. Treat the remaining half of the mango in the same way.

3 Gently mix all the fruit and spoon it into chilled glasses. Decorate with the lemon balm or mint leaves.

You can prepare this salad the night before and leave it in the refrigerator, covered, overnight.

Pink and yellow grapefruits, orange and tropical mango make a brilliant, bitter-sweet salad to bring the taste buds alive in the morning.

Courgette and tomato omelette

SERVES 6
PREPARATION TIME: 10 minutes
COOKING TIME: 10 minutes

1 tablespoon olive oil
6 spring onions, trimmed and chopped
2 cloves garlic, peeled and crushed
8oz (225g) courgettes, halved lengthways and cut into thick slices
14oz (400g) tinned tomatoes, drained and chopped
½ level teaspoon each dried basil and dried thyme
Freshly ground black pepper
3 eggs, plus 3 egg whites, size 2
2oz (60g) grated mozzarella cheese
Sprigs of fresh thyme to garnish

1 Heat the oil in a large, nonstick omelette pan and cook the spring onions in it over a moderate heat for about 1 minute, until softened but not coloured. Mix in the garlic and courgettes and cook for 3 minutes, shaking the pan from time to time.

2 Stir the tomatoes, basil and thyme in with the onions, and season with pepper. Cook for about 2 minutes more, or until the courgettes are tender and the liquid from the tomatoes has almost evaporated.

3 Meanwhile, heat the grill and beat the eggs and egg whites lightly with a fork. Pour the mixture over the vegetables and stir gently for 2 minutes, pushing the set mixture to the centre and tilting the pan to let the unset mixture run round the edge.

4 When the mixture is set underneath, scatter the mozzarella over the top, and put the pan under the hot grill for about 2 minutes, until the omelette is set and lightly browned on top. Cut into wedges, garnish with the thyme sprigs and serve at once.

Crusty bread and a green or mixed salad are good accompaniments to this dish. You can vary the omelette filling, using leek, diced cooked potato, red or green pepper, chopped broccoli or chopped mixed fresh herbs. Instead of adding cheese, scatter on 2 rashers of unsmoked back bacon, trimmed of fat and finely chopped.

ONE SERVING	
CALORIES	115
TOTAL FAT	7g
SATURATED FAT	3g
CARBOHYDRATES	3g
ADDED SUGAR	0
FIBRE	1g
SODIUM	165mg

Chunks of courgette and sweet tomato sparked with spring onion, basil and thyme add texture to this light omelette that is simple to prepare. Melted mozzarella tops the pale egg base to give a golden finish to a savoury brunch dish.

Scrambled eggs Benedict

SERVES 4
PREPARATION TIME: 10 minutes
COOKING TIME: 10 minutes

ONE SERVING	
CALORIES	280
TOTAL FAT	15g
SATURATED FAT	4g
CARBOHYDRATES	22g
ADDED SUGAR	0
FIBRE	1g
SODIUM	700mg

1oz (30g) polyunsaturated margarine
½ oz (15g) plain flour
8fl oz (225ml) chicken stock (see p.19)
1 tablespoon lemon juice
Freshly ground black pepper
4 eggs, size 2
2 tablespoons skimmed milk
4 very thin slices boiled ham, about 4oz (115g)
together, fat removed
4 slices wholemeal bread
2 level tablespoons chopped fresh parsley
Fresh parsley sprigs to garnish

1 Heat half the margarine in a small saucepan, mix in the flour and cook gently for 1 minute, stirring. Gradually stir in the stock and lemon juice, then season with pepper and bring to the boil over a moderate heat, stirring all the time. Lower the heat and simmer for 2-3 minutes, stirring frequently until the sauce has thickened. Cover and set aside.

2 Whisk the eggs lightly with the milk and season with pepper. Put the remaining margarine in a small nonstick saucepan and set to melt over a low heat.

3 Meanwhile, heat the grill to medium, wrap the ham in foil and place it in the grill pan under the rack. Arrange the bread on the rack and put it under the grill, toasting it lightly on both sides.

4 While the bread is toasting, pour the egg mixture into the melted margarine and stir continuously over a low heat for about 3 minutes, until it is thickened to a smooth, creamy consistency.

5 Put the toast on warmed plates, lay a slice of ham on top and spoon a share of the egg onto each serving. Pour on the sauce, sprinkle with the parsley and serve at once with a sprig of fresh parsley garnishing each serving.

Instead of serving the eggs on toast, you can spoon them onto warm muffins (see p.368).

> **TIP**
> *Take the scrambled eggs off the heat as soon as they become creamy. They will continue to cook in their own heat while you serve out the ham and, if overcooked, will become rubbery.*

Softly set eggs are piled on crisp toast and wafer-thin ham and topped with a smooth chicken sauce, in a hearty dish for a late Sunday breakfast. For those who like their eggs in a lighter morning dish, French toast offers puffy and crisp triangles of bread that have absorbed the orange-flavoured egg.

Orange French toast

ONE SERVING

CALORIES 135

TOTAL FAT 7g

SATURATED FAT 1g

CARBOHYDRATES 13g

ADDED SUGAR 0

FIBRE 0

SODIUM 175mg

SERVES 4
PREPARATION TIME: 5 minutes
COOKING TIME: 5 minutes

2 eggs, size 2
6fl oz (175ml) skimmed milk
1 level tablespoon finely grated orange rind
4 slices 3-day-old wholemeal bread, ¼ in (6mm)
thick, cut in half and crusts removed
1 tablespoon corn oil

1 Whisk the eggs, milk and orange rind together and pour into a wide, flat dish. Lay the bread in it in one layer and after 10-15 seconds, turn over with a palette knife. Leave for 2-3 minutes to soak up all the mixture.

2 Heat the oil in a large nonstick frying pan and cook the bread over a moderately high heat for 2-3 minutes on each side, until lightly browned. Serve at once while hot and crisp.

Hummous savoury slices

SERVES 4
PREPARATION TIME: 15 minutes

8oz (225g) cooked chickpeas (see p.19)
½ level teaspoon ground cumin
1 large clove garlic, peeled and crushed
2 tablespoons olive oil
2 tablespoons lemon juice
4oz (115g) low-fat fromage frais
Freshly ground black pepper
8 slices from a wholemeal baton loaf
2 rashers unsmoked back bacon, trimmed of fat,
grilled and finely chopped
4 button mushrooms, wiped and chopped
1 level tablespoon toasted sesame seeds
Sprigs of watercress to garnish

ONE SERVING

CALORIES 265

TOTAL FAT 10g

SATURATED FAT 2g

CARBOHYDRATES 31g

ADDED SUGAR 0

FIBRE 3g

SODIUM 450mg

1 Blend the chickpeas, cumin, garlic, oil, lemon juice and fromage frais in a food processor, or pass through a food mill. Season the hummous with pepper.

2 Toast the slices of bread lightly on both sides and spread them with the hummous. Top each slice with some bacon and mushrooms, and sprinkle with sesame seeds. Garnish with the watercress and serve.

Chickpea and sesame spread, served either as an appetising dip or as a side dish in the Middle East, is given an English-breakfast flavour here with a sprinkling of bacon and mushrooms.

Double haddock kedgeree

ONE SERVING

CALORIES 260

TOTAL FAT 7g

SATURATED FAT 2g

CARBOHYDRATES 25g

ADDED SUGAR 0

FIBRE 0

SODIUM 625mg

SERVES 4
PREPARATION TIME: 15 minutes
COOKING TIME: 20 minutes

4oz (115g) long grain and wild rice mixture
8oz (225g) fresh haddock
8oz (225g) smoked haddock

2 eggs, size 2, hard-boiled and shelled
5 level tablespoons Greek yoghurt
1 level tablespoon chopped fresh parsley
Freshly ground black pepper

1 Cook the rice (see p.17) and set it to one side.

2 Meanwhile, put the fresh and the smoked haddock into separate pans, cover with water and bring to the boil. Cover and simmer for about 10 minutes, until the flesh flakes easily. Drain the haddock, remove the skin and bones and break the flesh into large flakes.

3 Cut the hard-boiled eggs in half. Take out and sieve the yolks, then set aside. Roughly chop up the egg whites.

4 Mix the rice, fish, egg whites, yoghurt and parsley in a large saucepan, and season with pepper. Heat gently for 2-3 minutes, stirring until hot all through. Turn the kedgeree onto a warmed serving dish and scatter the egg yolk over the top.

Instead of adding parsley, you can add ½ level teaspoon of curry powder to the kedgeree just before heating it through.

The Victorians adopted this Indian dish for their gargantuan breakfasts, whose descendant, brunch, is now the ideal time to eat kedgeree.

Kidneys in tomatoes

ONE SERVING	
CALORIES	170
TOTAL FAT	7g
SATURATED FAT	2g
CARBOHYDRATES	8g
ADDED SUGAR	0
FIBRE	2g
SODIUM	245mg

Beef tomatoes serve as tender cases for a hearty filling of kidneys and mushrooms, whose juices are the basis of a rich sauce.

SERVES 6
PREPARATION TIME: 35 minutes
COOKING TIME: 15 minutes
OVEN: Preheat to 190°C (375°F, gas mark 5)

6 beef tomatoes, each about 8oz (225g)
1½ tablespoons olive oil
12 lambs' kidneys, skinned, halved and cored
12oz (340g) mushrooms, wiped and chopped
Freshly ground black pepper
1½ level tablespoons wholemeal flour
1 level teaspoon fresh rosemary leaves

1 Slice the top off the tomatoes and set aside. Use a serrated grapefruit spoon or a teaspoon to scoop out the core and seeds without piercing the flesh. Put the tomato cases upside-down on kitchen paper to drain well.

2 Heat the oil in a saucepan, stir in the kidneys and mushrooms, and season with pepper. Cover and cook gently for 10 minutes, stirring occasionally.

3 Lift out the kidneys and mushrooms with a slotted spoon and set aside. Whisk the flour into the liquid left in the pan and bring to the boil, stirring continuously until thickened. Mix in the kidneys and mushrooms. Spoon 2 kidney halves and some sauce into each tomato and push 2 or 3 rosemary leaves into each one.

4 Put the tomatoes in a baking dish, place the reserved tops on them and cook in the heated oven for about 15 minutes, or until they soften.

Serve with toast or muffins (see p.368).

Smoked mackerel pâté

ONE SERVING

CALORIES 220

TOTAL FAT 18g

    SATURATED FAT 4g

CARBOHYDRATES 2g

    ADDED SUGAR 0

FIBRE 0

SODIUM 435mg

SERVES 4
*PREPARATION TIME: 15 minutes, plus 2 hours
to chill*

*8oz (225g) smoked mackerel fillets, skinned, flaked
and any bones removed*

4oz (115g) low-fat fromage frais
Finely grated rind of ½ lime
1 teaspoon lime juice
4 level tablespoons chopped watercress leaves
Freshly ground black pepper
Lime twists to garnish

TIP
*To make a lime
twist, take a thin
slice of lime and
make a cut from the
centre to the edge.
Twist the points of
the cut in opposite
directions and stand
the slice on the pâté.*

*The strong peppery flavour
of watercress offsets the
richness of the mackerel in
this pâté, which is blended
to a soft creaminess with
fromage frais.*

1 Using a fork, crush the mackerel in a mixing
bowl, then beat in the fromage frais well.

2 Stir in the lime rind and juice, and the
watercress. Season with pepper and mix well.

3 Spoon the mixture into a serving dish, cover
and refrigerate for at least 2 hours and up to

4 hours. Serve the pâté chilled, garnished with
twists of lime. Offer crisp rounds of hot toast
with it, or serve it with warmed wholemeal or
white rolls (see p.366).

You can use 1 level tablespoon of soft green
peppercorns in place of the chopped watercress
and ground pepper.

Melon refresher

SERVES 4
PREPARATION TIME: 25 minutes,
plus 30 minutes to stand

2 small ripe Ogen or Charentais melons
6oz (175g) large ripe grapes, peeled, halved
and de-seeded
1 level teaspoon preserved ginger, very finely diced
12 melon, vine or frilled lettuce leaves, washed
and dried

ONE SERVING

CALORIES 45

TOTAL FAT 0

SATURATED FAT 0

CARBOHYDRATES 16g

ADDED SUGAR 1g

FIBRE 2g

SODIUM 15mg

1 Halve the melons crossways and de-seed them. Scoop out the flesh into a bowl without damaging the outer shell. Trim off any stalk or tail from the melon shells so that they stand like bowls. Tie the shells in a polythene bag and put them in the refrigerator.

2 Cut the melon flesh into cubes and gently mix in the grapes and ginger. Cover the bowl and leave to stand for 30 minutes for the juices to run and take in the flavour of the ginger.

3 Set the melon shells on serving plates lined with the leaves. Fill with the fruit and serve.

You can prepare the fruit the night before it is needed. Store it in a dish with a well-fitting lid and refrigerate overnight. Tie the melon shells in a polythene bag and freeze them. Take the fruit out of the refrigerator 1 hour before serving; spoon it into the frozen shells and arrange on the leaves to serve. It is quicker to use green seedless grapes and leave the skins on, but the dish is more enjoyable without skins.

> **TIP**
> *Make sure you cover the melon skins or the melon cubes securely before putting them in the refrigerator or the melon flavour will penetrate other foods that are stored there.*

A little ginger gives a spicy prickle to a sweet and juicy fruit salad for starting the day, whether early or on late and lazy weekends.

Homemade muesli combines the simplest of ingredients in a wholesome dish that achieves a perfect balance of sweetness and crunchiness.

Muesli

ONE SERVING	
CALORIES	235
TOTAL FAT	6g
SATURATED FAT	1g
CARBOHYDRATES	39g
ADDED SUGAR	0
FIBRE	5g
SODIUM	55mg

SERVES 4
PREPARATION TIME: 10 minutes

4oz (115g) rolled oats
1oz (30g) each dried, ready-to-use apricots,
prunes and apples, chopped
1 level tablespoon raisins or sultanas
1 level tablespoon chopped dates
2 level tablespoons chopped toasted almonds,
hazelnuts or pecans
2 level tablespoons wheatgerm
8fl oz (225ml) skimmed milk
4 level tablespoons low-fat natural yoghurt
½ level teaspoon ground cinnamon

1 Mix the oats, fruits, nuts and wheatgerm thoroughly.

2 Divide the muesli between four serving bowls and pour a quarter of the milk on each serving. If you prefer crisp cereal, serve immediately. For soft cereal, let it stand for 10 minutes. Put a spoonful of the yoghurt on each serving and sprinkle the cinnamon on top.

It is usually more convenient to make enough muesli for more than one day. It will keep fresh for 2-3 weeks in an airtight container stored in a cool, dry cupboard.

Fruit pancakes

ONE FRUIT PANCAKE	
CALORIES	70
TOTAL FAT	2g
SATURATED FAT	0
CARBOHYDRATES	12g
ADDED SUGAR	0
FIBRE	1g
SODIUM	35mg

MAKES 16
PREPARATION TIME: 20 minutes
COOKING TIME: 15 minutes

½ oz (15g) caster sugar
8fl oz (225ml) lukewarm skimmed milk
1 level teaspoon dried yeast
3oz (85g) plain flour

2oz (60g) wholemeal flour
1oz (30g) polyunsaturated margarine, melted
3 egg whites, size 2
8oz (225g) fresh raspberries
8oz (225g) fresh blueberries
16 strawberries or cherries

1 Dissolve 1 teaspoon of the sugar in ¼ pint (150ml) of the milk and whisk in the yeast. Cover and put in a warm place for 10 minutes, until frothy.

2 Sift the flours and the remaining sugar into a bowl, tipping in the bran left in the sieve, and make a well in the centre. Mix the yeast liquid with the remaining milk and the margarine. Pour into the well and gradually beat the flour into it to make a smooth, thick batter.

3 Whisk the egg whites until they form soft peaks, then fold them gently into the batter. Cover and leave to stand for 5 minutes.

4 Meanwhile, stand a griddle or large, heavy-based, nonstick frying pan over a moderate heat. Do not let it overheat or the pancakes will burn on the outside before being cooked through. Lightly grease the hot griddle or pan.

5 Pour 2 tablespoons of batter for each pancake onto the hot surface. You will probably be able to cook four at a time, but space them out well and cook fewer together if necessary. Cook for 1 minute, until the pancakes are opaque on top and golden brown underneath. Turn them over with a palette knife and cook the other side for 1 minute. Lift the pancakes onto a clean cloth and wrap loosely while cooking the remaining batches.

Serve the pancakes warm with the raspberries, blueberries and strawberries or cherries. You can use frozen raspberries and blueberries when fresh ones are not available, or vary the fruits according to whatever is in season.

The secret of these delicate pancakes is in folding whisked egg whites into the batter; the result is a fluffy and melting texture with a hint of sweetness that marries perfectly with sharp fresh fruits to create an elegant dish for breakfast guests.

Pizza muffins

SERVES 4
PREPARATION TIME: 15 minutes
COOKING TIME: 5 minutes

6fl oz (175ml) tomato sauce (see p.16)
8 wholemeal muffins (see p.368)

2oz (60g) grated mature Cheddar cheese
1oz (30g) grated Parmesan cheese
4 anchovy fillets, drained and chopped
4 stoned black olives, thinly sliced
1 level tablespoon chopped fresh basil
or oregano to garnish

The soft texture of fresh muffins makes an unusual yet successful base for a pizza topping enlivened by the intense flavour of anchovies.

ONE SERVING
CALORIES 335
TOTAL FAT 13g
SATURATED FAT 5g
CARBOHYDRATES 43g
ADDED SUGAR 0
FIBRE 5g
SODIUM 470mg

1 Bring the tomato sauce to the boil in a small saucepan, simmer for 2 minutes and set aside.

2 Halve the muffins and lightly toast the cut sides only under a hot grill. Sprinkle the Cheddar evenly over the muffins and grill for 1-2 minutes, until the cheese melts.

3 Spread the tomato sauce over the Cheddar and sprinkle on the Parmesan. Return the muffins to the grill for 2-3 minutes, until the cheese is lightly browned and bubbling hot. Scatter the chopped anchovies and olives on top and garnish with the basil or oregano before serving.

Pork and pheasant pie

SERVES 8
PREPARATION TIME: 1 hour, plus 3 hours to cool
and overnight refrigeration
COOKING TIME: 1 hour 45 minutes
OVEN: Preheat to 190°C (375°F, gas mark 5)

For the pastry:
12oz (340g) plain flour
4oz (115g) polyunsaturated margarine
4fl oz (115ml) water
1 egg, size 3, beaten

For the filling:
1½ lb (680g) pork without fat or bone, minced
1 small cooking apple, peeled, cored and grated
1½ oz (45g) fresh wholemeal breadcrumbs
2 level teaspoons dried rubbed sage
2 level teaspoons green peppercorns in brine,
rinsed and drained
1lb (450g) uncooked pheasant meat (from 2 small
birds) without skin or bone, cut into small cubes
½ pint (285ml) chicken stock (see p.19)
2 level teaspoons gelatine

1 Sift the flour into a bowl and make a well in the centre. Put the margarine and water to heat slowly in a small saucepan so that the margarine melts before the water boils.

2 Meanwhile, mix the pork in a bowl with the apple, breadcrumbs, sage and peppercorns.

3 When the water is just boiling, pour the margarine and water mixture into the flour and mix to form a dough. Knead on a lightly floured surface until smooth and pliable. Cut off a quarter of the dough and cover with an upturned pudding basin. Quickly press the rest of the pastry over the base and up the sides of a loose-bottomed tin 7in (18cm) in diameter with a spring-clip side 3¼ in (80mm) deep.

4 Spoon a third of the pork mixture over the pastry base, cover with half the pheasant meat and press down well. Repeat these two layers, then finish with the remainder of the pork mixture, mounding it slightly in the centre.

5 Roll out the remaining pastry to a round large enough to cover the pie. Moisten the edges of the pastry case with a little beaten egg, lay on the pastry top and press the edges together. Trim and crimp the edges.

6 Roll out the pastry trimmings and cut into leaves. Brush the top of the pie with beaten egg and make a hole in the centre for steam to escape during cooking. Arrange the leaves on top and brush with egg; cover the remaining egg and put it in the refrigerator until later.

7 Place the pie tin on a baking tray and bake for 1 hour 30 minutes in the heated oven. Halfway through cooking, cover loosely with foil so that the top does not brown too much.

8 Gently remove the side of the tin and brush the side of the pie with the reserved egg. Return the pie to the oven and bake for about 15 minutes more to brown and crisp the side.

9 Take the pie out of the oven, leave it on the tin base and baking tray and cover it with flyproof gauze or a meat cage. Leave it in a cool place for about 3 hours, then gently replace the cleaned side of the tin.

10 Pour 3 tablespoons of the stock into a saucepan. Sprinkle in the gelatine and leave it for 5 minutes to swell. Stir over a low heat until the gelatine has dissolved, then mix in the remaining stock and leave for 30 minutes, or until the mixture starts to thicken.

11 Carefully pour a little stock at a time through the hole in the top of pie. Let the stock settle and find its level before adding more. Fill until the stock starts to overflow. Refrigerate the pie overnight so that it sets completely.

If you wish, you can stir 1 level teaspoon of finely chopped fresh parsley into the stock just before pouring it into the pie.

ONE SERVING	
CALORIES	485
TOTAL FAT	22g
SATURATED FAT	6g
CARBOHYDRATES	37g
ADDED SUGAR	0
FIBRE	2g
SODIUM	260mg

TIP
To put the stock in the pie, pour it through a small funnel inserted into the hole in the pie lid. First make sure that the way in is clear by putting a teaspoon handle through the hole at an angle and sweeping it all round gently to loosen any meat sealed to the pie lid.

Lean pork, flavoured with apple and sage and enriched with layers of pheasant, fills a grand raised pie that turns a brunch for guests into a sumptuous occasion. Serve it out of doors with a leafy salad, a spoonful of relish and fruit to follow — and the heartiest appetite will be content until evening.

Porridge and dried fruit compote

SERVES 4
PREPARATION TIME: 5 minutes, plus
overnight soaking
COOKING TIME: 20 minutes

4oz (115g) medium oatmeal
3 pints (1.7 litres) water
1lb (450g) dried fruit salad
1 wide strip lemon rind
1 clove
1 stick cinnamon
4 level tablespoons Greek yoghurt

ONE SERVING

CALORIES 345

TOTAL FAT 4g

SATURATED FAT 1g

CARBOHYDRATES 74g

ADDED SUGAR 0

FIBRE 12g

SODIUM 30mg

1 Put the oatmeal in a glass or china bowl and stir in 2 pints (1.1 litres) of the water. Cover and leave to soak overnight.

2 Put the dried fruit in another glass or china bowl with the remaining water, the lemon rind, clove and cinnamon. Cover and leave to soak overnight.

3 The following morning, pour the fruit and water into a saucepan, cover, bring to the boil and simmer for about 20 minutes, until the fruit is tender but not mushy. Remove the lemon rind, clove and cinnamon.

4 Meanwhile, pour the oatmeal and water into a saucepan, bring to the boil, stirring, then turn down the heat and simmer for about 20 minutes, stirring frequently. If the porridge becomes too thick before the oatmeal is tender, add a little more water.

5 Serve the porridge hot in warmed bowls, topped with the warm compote. Put a spoonful of the yoghurt on each serving.

A bowl of steaming, old-fashioned porridge makes a smooth base for spiced, plump fruits poached to tender perfection and topped with creamy yoghurt.

Plain potato and onion, transformed into fluffy little cakes and crowned with crisp bacon rolls, spread an appetising aroma as they cook.

Potato cakes with bacon

ONE SERVING

CALORIES 180

TOTAL FAT 5g

SATURATED FAT 1g

CARBOHYDRATES 26g

ADDED SUGAR 0

FIBRE 2g

SODIUM 480mg

SERVES 4
PREPARATION TIME: 20 minutes
COOKING TIME: 15 minutes
OVEN: Preheat to 220°C (425°F, gas mark 7)

1 ½ lb (680g) waxy potatoes, peeled and whole
1 tablespoon olive oil
1 medium onion, peeled and chopped
Freshly ground black pepper
4 rashers unsmoked back bacon, trimmed of fat
½ level teaspoon paprika
Flat-leaf parsley to garnish

1 Bring the potatoes to the boil in enough unsalted water to cover them, then simmer for 5 minutes. Rinse in cold water, drain, and when they are cool, grate them coarsely into a bowl.

2 Heat half the oil in a saucepan and fry the onion in it for about 5 minutes, until golden.

Mix the onion with the potato and season the mixture with pepper.

3 Spoon the potato mixture into 12 equal mounds well spaced out on nonstick baking trays. Flatten the tops with the back of the spoon and brush lightly with the remaining oil. Bake in the heated oven for about 15 minutes, or until golden brown on top.

4 Stretch out each rasher of bacon thinly with the back of a knife and cut it across into three equal pieces. Roll up the pieces and thread them onto skewers, spacing them out well. Put in a baking dish and cook in the oven for the last 12 minutes with the potato cakes.

Serve the potato cakes on warmed plates. Place a bacon roll on each cake, sprinkle with the paprika and garnish with parsley.

Cheese rarebit

SERVES 4
PREPARATION TIME: 15 minutes
COOKING TIME: 10 minutes

3fl oz (85ml) skimmed milk
½ teaspoon Worcestershire sauce
1 level teaspoon English mustard powder
5oz (150g) grated reduced-fat Cheddar cheese
4 thick slices wholemeal bread
½ level teaspoon paprika
Sprigs of watercress and red onion rings to garnish

ONE SERVING

CALORIES 210

TOTAL FAT 7g

SATURATED FAT 4g

CARBOHYDRATES 21g

ADDED SUGAR 0

FIBRE 3g

SODIUM 505mg

1 Stir the milk, Worcestershire sauce, mustard powder and cheese in a small, heavy-based saucepan over a low heat until the cheese has melted and the mixture is smooth. Remove from the heat and leave to cool and thicken for 10 minutes, stirring from time to time.

2 Toast the bread under a moderately hot grill on one side only. Spread the cheese mixture on the untoasted sides and sprinkle with paprika.

3 Turn the grill up to high and cook until the topping is golden brown and bubbly. Lift the slices onto individual plates, garnish with the watercress and onion, and serve immediately.

The most traditional of British ingredients – English mustard, Worcestershire sauce and Cheddar cheese – melt and sizzle over toast to create this simple snack.

Fish rarebit

ONE SERVING

CALORIES 280

TOTAL FAT 6g

SATURATED FAT 3g

CARBOHYDRATES 24g

ADDED SUGAR 0

FIBRE 3g

SODIUM 585mg

SERVES 4
PREPARATION TIME: 15 minutes
COOKING TIME: 25 minutes
OVEN: Preheat to 190°C (375°F, gas mark 5)

2 level tablespoons plain flour
¾ level teaspoon English mustard powder
¼ pint (150ml) stout or bitter beer

Freshly ground black pepper
4oz (115g) grated reduced-fat Cheddar cheese
1lb (450g) haddock, cod or other white fish
without skin or bone, cut into cubes
4 thick slices wholemeal bread
1 level tablespoon snipped fresh chives or chopped
fresh parsley

Any white fish is suitable for this variation of Welsh rarebit; baking the fish in stout produces a distinctive malty flavour and a rich sauce.

1 Mix the flour and mustard to a smooth paste in a bowl with a little of the stout or beer. Season with pepper and gradually mix in the rest of the stout or beer. Stir in the cheese and fish, and turn into an ovenproof dish.

2 Cover the dish and bake in the heated oven for 15 minutes, then uncover and bake for about 10 minutes more, until the sauce is bubbling and the fish is cooked enough to flake easily when tested with a fork.

3 Toast the bread on both sides and lay it on individual plates. Spoon the rarebit onto the toast, sprinkle with the chives or parsley, and serve immediately.

Pork and bean tacos

MAKES 12
PREPARATION TIME: 1 hour 10 minutes
COOKING TIME: 40 minutes
OVEN: Preheat to 160°C (325°F, gas mark 3)

ONE FILLED TACO	
CALORIES 205	
TOTAL FAT 9g	
SATURATED FAT 2g	
CARBOHYDRATES 22g	
ADDED SUGAR 0	
FIBRE 2g	
SODIUM 40mg	

TIP
To fill and fold a taco, put a spoonful of filling in the centre, turn the bottom third of the taco over it, then turn in the two sides to overlap in the centre and make an open envelope shape.

For the filling:
4oz (115g) dried mixed beans, soaked in cold water overnight
1 small hock or knuckle end of pork, about 1½ lb (680g) including the bone, skin and fat removed
1 tablespoon olive oil
1 small onion, peeled and chopped
1 large clove garlic, peeled and crushed
½ medium green pepper, de-seeded and chopped
1 level teaspoon chilli powder
½ level teaspoon each ground coriander and ground cumin
14oz (400g) tinned tomatoes
4oz (115g) cos lettuce, washed and finely shredded
3 spring onions, trimmed and cut into fine strips

For the tacos:
8oz (225g) unbleached plain flour
¼ pint (150ml) boiling water
1 teaspoon sesame oil

1 Cook the beans (see p.17), putting the pork in to cook with them.

2 Meanwhile, make the tacos. Sift the flour into a mixing bowl and make a well in the centre. Pour in the boiling water and mix to a firm dough, then knead on a lightly floured surface until smooth. Cover and leave to rest for 15 minutes.

3 Knead the dough again and roll it out with a rolling pin on a floured surface until ¼ in (6mm) thick. Stamp out circles with a plain cutter 2½ in (65mm) in diameter, then knead and roll the trimmings and stamp out more circles. There should be 12 in all.

4 Brush 6 circles with sesame oil and lay the remaining 6 circles on top of them. Roll out the sandwiched pairs on a floured surface until the circles are 6in (15cm) in diameter.

5 Cook the tacos one sandwiched pair at a time in an ungreased heavy-based frying pan over a moderate heat. When the sandwich starts to puff with air bubbles, after about 1 minute, turn it over and cook for 1 minute more, or until the underside is freckled with small brown spots. Lift out the tacos and carefully peel apart the two layers. Lay the tacos in an ovenproof dish, put on the lid and set aside. Cook the other pairs in the same way.

6 When the beans and pork are cooked, remove the pan from the heat and drain. Take the meat off the bone and cut it into shreds.

7 Heat the olive oil in a heavy-based saucepan and fry the onion in it for 3 minutes. Mix in the garlic and pepper, and cook for 2 minutes, then stir in the chilli powder, coriander, cumin, tomatoes, beans and pork. Bring to the boil, cover and simmer gently for 30 minutes, then turn into a warmed serving dish.

8 Fifteen minutes before the beans are ready, put the tacos to warm through in the heated oven. Pile the hot tacos on a warmed serving plate to take to the table. Serve the beans, lettuce and spring onions in separate bowls for folding in the tacos at the table.

You can prepare the tacos and bean filling the day before, if more convenient. Store the tacos in a polythene bag in the refrigerator and allow 5 minutes longer for reheating in the oven. Store the filling, once cooled, in a covered dish in the refrigerator and, before serving, bring it to the boil quickly in a saucepan, then simmer it for 10 minutes.

A stack of fresh, warm Mexican pancakes, spicy beans and pork, crisp shreds of lettuce and strips of hot spring onions make a colourful contribution to a spread for entertaining guests or family at brunch. The diners will enjoy the novelty of filling and folding their tacos at the table.

Marinated tuna and tomato sandwiches

ONE SERVING

CALORIES 265

TOTAL FAT 10g

SATURATED FAT 2g

CARBOHYDRATES 29g

ADDED SUGAR 0

FIBRE 2g

SODIUM 455mg

Superbly soggy by design, these unusual and filling sandwiches hold tuna salad in garlic-flavoured bread that has soaked up an oil and vinegar dressing.

MAKES *4 sandwiches*
PREPARATION TIME: *15 minutes,*
plus 45 minutes to stand

*8 slices bread, ¼ in (6mm) thick, from
a 1lb (450g) loaf
4 teaspoons olive oil
2 cloves garlic, peeled, halved and lightly crushed
8 teaspoons red wine vinegar
1 small red onion, peeled and thinly sliced
4 black olives, stoned and chopped
2 medium tomatoes, sliced
7oz (200g) tinned tuna in oil, drained and flaked
4 level tablespoons chopped fresh basil*

1 Cut pieces of waxed or greaseproof paper for wrapping up the sandwiches, and lay 2 slices of bread on each. Trickle ½ teaspoon of oil evenly over each slice, then rub each pair of slices with half a garlic clove. Sprinkle 1 teaspoon of vinegar on each slice of bread.

2 Spoon equal amounts of the onion, olives, tomatoes, tuna and basil onto one slice of each sandwich and top with the remaining slice, putting it oil-side down.

3 Wrap up the sandwiches securely and leave them to stand at room temperature for 45 minutes before eating so the bread absorbs the juices. If you are preparing a packed lunch, keep the wrapped sandwiches in the refrigerator until it is time to pack them, then put them in a plastic box.

A colourful selection of vegetables smothers toasted french bread and glistens with melted Gruyère for satisfying late morning munching.

Hot vegetable baguettes

ONE SERVING	
CALORIES	435
TOTAL FAT	13g
SATURATED FAT	6g
CARBOHYDRATES	64g
ADDED SUGAR	0
FIBRE	5g
SODIUM	740mg

SERVES 4
PREPARATION TIME: 15 minutes
COOKING TIME: 20 minutes

1 tablespoon olive oil
1 medium red onion, peeled and thinly sliced
1 medium red pepper, de-seeded and cut into rings
2 medium carrots, peeled and thinly sliced
2 medium courgettes, trimmed and thinly sliced
8oz (225g) tomatoes, skinned, de-seeded and chopped
1 level teaspoon chopped fresh oregano
Freshly ground black pepper
2 baguettes, each about 12in (30cm) and 7oz (200g)
3oz (85g) grated Gruyère cheese

1 Heat the oil in a frying pan, and cook the onion in it, covered, for about 5 minutes, until it is transparent. Mix in the red pepper, carrots and courgettes, then cover and cook for another 8-10 minutes.

2 Stir in the tomatoes and oregano and season with black pepper. Cook, uncovered, for 2 minutes more to evaporate the liquid.

3 Cut the baguettes in half lengthways and toast them lightly on both sides under a moderately hot grill.

4 Spread the vegetables over the baguettes and sprinkle with the Gruyère. Grill for 1 minute, or until the cheese has melted. Serve the baguettes at once while hot and crisp.

For a picnic, cool the baguettes, then wrap individually in waxed or greaseproof paper.

47

Waffles with Stilton topping

ONE SPREAD WAFFLE	
CALORIES	70
TOTAL FAT	3g
SATURATED FAT	1g
CARBOHYDRATES	9g
ADDED SUGAR	0
FIBRE	0
SODIUM	150mg

MAKES about 20
PREPARATION TIME: 20 minutes
COOKING TIME: 20 minutes
OVEN: Preheat to 150°C (300°F, gas mark 2)

2oz (60g) Blue Stilton cheese, crumbled
4oz (115g) cottage cheese or low-fat fromage frais
6oz (175g) plain flour (white or a mixture of white and wholemeal)
1 level tablespoon baking powder

2 eggs, size 2, separated
½ pint (285ml) skimmed milk
2 teaspoons olive oil
2 level tablespoons snipped fresh chives

1 Mix both the cheeses together, using a fork, and turn the mixture into a small serving dish.

2 Sift the flour and baking powder into a large mixing bowl and make a well in the centre. Pour in the egg yolks and stir with a wooden spoon or wire whisk, gradually drawing in the flour from the sides and adding the milk a little at a time. Beat to form a smooth batter, then beat in the olive oil a few drops at a time.

3 Heat a waffle iron, electric waffle-maker or electric sandwich toaster and brush lightly with oil. Whisk the egg whites until stiff and fold into the batter. Pour about 2 tablespoons of the batter into each waffle shape, depending on size. Close at once and cook for 2 minutes, or until risen, lightly browned and crisp. If you are using a manual waffle iron, turn it over on the heat halfway through cooking.

4 Lift out the cooked waffles on a spatula, lay them on a baking tray, cover with foil and keep hot in the oven. Cook the rest of the batter, putting the batches of waffles to keep hot until all are ready. Serve the waffles topped with a small teaspoon of the cheese mixture and sprinkled with the chives.

Hot golden waffles cry out for a spread to melt into their dimpled top; ultra-savoury blue cheese with chives is an inspired change from the usual syrup.

Homemade yoghurt with pear sauce

ONE SERVING	
CALORIES	135
TOTAL FAT	2g
SATURATED FAT	1g
CARBOHYDRATES	25g
ADDED SUGAR	9g
FIBRE	1g
SODIUM	85mg

SERVES 4
PREPARATION TIME: 30 minutes, plus 6-10 hours to set and 2 hours to chill

1 pint (570ml) semi-skimmed milk
1 level teaspoon low-fat natural yoghurt
1lb (450g) ripe pears
2 tablespoons clear honey
Finely grated rind and juice of ½ small lemon

1 Sterilise the utensils to be used for making the yoghurt – a large saucepan and lid, a lidded, shallow heatproof glass dish, a teaspoon, and a cook's thermometer if you have one. Simply pour boiling water into and all over these utensils, then drain them and leave to dry (or put to dry in a warm oven), touching only the handles or parts that will not be coming into contact with the milk.

2 Pour the milk into the scalded saucepan and bring it to the boil. Put the lid on the pan, remove from the heat and leave to cool for about 20 minutes, until the milk registers 43°C (110°F) on the thermometer, or until it feels warm but not uncomfortably hot when you put the inside of your wrist against the pan.

3 Stir the yoghurt into the milk with the sterilised teaspoon, and pour the milk into the dish. Put on the lid, wrap with a newly washed towel and stand the dish in a warm airing cupboard or near a radiator that will stay hot.

4 Meanwhile, make the sauce. Peel, quarter and core the pears. Cut the quarters across into thin slices, and put in a small saucepan with the honey, lemon rind and lemon juice. Heat gently to dissolve the honey, then cover and simmer for about 10 minutes, until the pears are tender and the juice is slightly thickened. Pour into a bowl, cover, leave to cool and then refrigerate.

5 Look at the yoghurt after about 6 hours. If it is still runny, wrap it up again and leave it for a few more hours. When it is set, use a sterilised spoon to remove any clear whey from the surface. Chill the yoghurt in the refrigerator for at least 2 hours, or overnight if more convenient.

Serve the yoghurt on individual plates with the pears in a side dish for spooning onto each serving. Remember to keep a little of the yoghurt in a small sterilised container in the refrigerator for making the next batch.

Scented pears sweetened with honey make a subtle partner for tart and creamy homemade yoghurt – the ideal start to the day for those who want something nourishing but light.

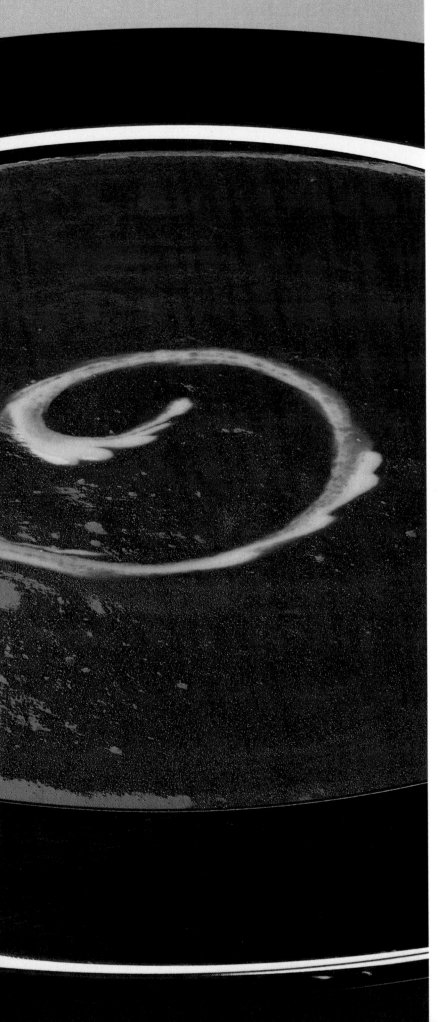

SOUPS AND STARTERS

Hearty winter broths and classic summer soups can please both eye and palate, but the choice of dishes to start a meal does not end there. Try a vivid medley of succulent grilled and dressed peppers, brochettes of tender scallops, little salmon and asparagus pots or a creamy confection of mushrooms held in feather-light pastry flowers. Such appetising, low-calorie treats are the promising preludes to healthy meals.

Apple and carrot soup

SERVES 6
PREPARATION TIME: 20 minutes
COOKING TIME: 35 minutes

1 tablespoon olive oil
1 medium red onion, peeled and chopped
1 stick celery, trimmed and chopped
1lb (450g) carrots, peeled and sliced
8oz (225g) cooking apples, peeled, cored and chopped
1¾ pints (1 litre) chicken stock (see p.19)
½ level teaspoon dried sage
1 bay leaf
Freshly ground black pepper
12 thin slices of red-skinned apple, soaked in lemon juice, to garnish

ONE SERVING	
CALORIES	80
TOTAL FAT	3g
SATURATED FAT	0
CARBOHYDRATES	14g
ADDED SUGAR	0
FIBRE	3g
SODIUM	25mg

1 Heat the oil in a large saucepan, and cook the onion, celery, carrots and apple in it over a moderate heat, uncovered, for about 5 minutes, until the onion begins to soften.

2 Stir in the stock, sage and bay leaf, and season with pepper. Bring to the boil, cover and simmer for about 25 minutes, or until the carrots become tender. Discard the bay leaf.

3 Pass the soup through a food mill, or let it cool for 5 minutes and then blend it in a food processor for 1 minute. Return the soup to the pan and reheat, stirring continuously. Serve in warmed soup bowls, with each serving garnished with 2 apple slices.

Apple is an unusual ingredient in a soup, but its smooth, acid pulp thickens and sharpens this delicate combination of carrot and chicken.

Baking the aubergines concentrates the flavour they bring to this partnership with red peppers in a full-bodied and vivid soup. A hint of vinegar and ginger adds the crucial spark.

TIP
Be sure to bake the aubergines until they are very tender. This rids them of their bitterness and also gives them a distinctive, strong smoky flavour.

ONE SERVING

CALORIES 105

TOTAL FAT 5g

SATURATED FAT 1g

CARBOHYDRATES 13g

ADDED SUGAR 0

FIBRE 5g

SODIUM 70mg

Aubergine and sweet pepper soup

SERVES 4
PREPARATION TIME: 20 minutes
COOKING TIME: 45 minutes
OVEN: Preheat to 180°C (350°F, gas mark 4)

3 small aubergines, about 1½ lb (680g) together
1 tablespoon olive oil
1 large onion, peeled and chopped
2 cloves garlic, peeled and chopped
1 level teaspoon peeled and grated root ginger,
or ⅛ level teaspoon ground ginger
2 medium red peppers, de-seeded, halved and sliced
⅛ level teaspoon salt
1¼ pints (725ml) chicken stock (see p.19)
4 teaspoons red wine vinegar
4 rounded teaspoons low-fat natural yoghurt
Snipped chives to garnish

1 Prick each aubergine with a fork in several places. Lay the aubergines on a baking tray and cook in the heated oven for 40 minutes, or until they are tender.

2 Meanwhile, heat the oil in a saucepan for 1 minute, and gently cook the onion, garlic and ginger in it, uncovered, for 10 minutes, or until the onion softens. Mix in the peppers and the salt. Cover, and cook for a further 10 minutes.

3 Pour in the stock and simmer, uncovered, for 20 minutes, or until the peppers are very soft. Remove from the heat and drain, reserving the liquid and vegetables in separate bowls.

4 Halve the aubergines, scoop out the flesh and chop it. Blend the aubergine flesh, drained vegetables and 7fl oz (200ml) of the reserved liquid in a food processor for 1 minute, or pass through a food mill.

5 Pour into a saucepan and add the rest of the reserved liquid and the vinegar. Stir over a moderate heat for 5 minutes. Serve in warmed bowls and garnish with a spoonful of the yoghurt sprinkled with chives.

Broth of chicken and Chinese leaves

ONE SERVING	
CALORIES 100	
TOTAL FAT 2g	
SATURATED FAT 1g	
CARBOHYDRATES 6g	
ADDED SUGAR 0	
FIBRE 2g	
SODIUM 65mg	

SERVES 4
PREPARATION TIME: 20 minutes
COOKING TIME: 25 minutes

1¾ pints (1 litre) chicken stock (see p.19)
8oz (225g) uncooked chicken breasts without skin or bone
2 medium carrots, peeled and thinly sliced

2 medium sticks celery, trimmed and chopped
1 medium onion, peeled and chopped
3 level tablespoons chopped fresh parsley
Freshly ground black pepper
8oz (225g) Chinese leaves, trimmed and finely shredded
1 large ripe tomato, de-seeded and diced
Celery leaves to garnish

Lightly cooked Chinese leaves retain their freshness and colour, and give a slight flavour of mustard to this clear, shimmering broth of chicken and vegetables.

1 Bring the stock to the boil in a large saucepan. Put in the chicken, carrots, celery, onion and parsley, and season with pepper. Boil for 5 minutes, then turn down the heat, cover and simmer for about 15 minutes, or until the chicken is tender.

2 Take out the chicken and stir in the Chinese leaves and tomato. Simmer, uncovered, for 5 minutes, or until the leaves are tender.

3 Meanwhile, cut the chicken into small cubes. When the Chinese leaves are just tender, put the chicken back in the saucepan and heat through for about 1 minute. Pour into warmed soup plates and garnish with celery leaves.

For a more substantial soup, you can add 4oz (115g) of cooked rice or pasta (see pp.17-18) at the same time as the chicken cubes. Heat through thoroughly before serving.

Chicken and courgette soup

SERVES 6
PREPARATION TIME: 20 minutes
COOKING TIME: 30 minutes

1 tablespoon olive oil
4 tablespoons water
1 clove garlic, peeled and crushed
1 large onion, peeled and chopped
1 small green pepper, de-seeded and chopped
1 stick celery, trimmed and thinly sliced
8oz (225g) courgettes, trimmed and cut into thin strips
2 level tablespoons plain flour
¾ pint (425ml) chicken stock (see p.19)
1lb (450g) plum tomatoes, peeled and chopped
6oz (175g) uncooked chicken breast without skin or bone, cut into small cubes
½-1 teaspoon Tabasco
½ teaspoon lemon juice
Freshly ground black pepper

ONE SERVING

CALORIES 100

TOTAL FAT 4g

SATURATED FAT 1g

CARBOHYDRATES 9g

ADDED SUGAR 0

FIBRE 2g

SODIUM 30mg

1 Heat the oil and water in a large, heavy-based saucepan and cook the garlic, onion, green pepper, celery and courgettes in it over a moderate heat for about 10 minutes, stirring occasionally, until the vegetables are softened.

2 Stir in the flour and cook for 2 minutes. Gradually stir in the stock, then add the tomatoes, chicken and Tabasco. Bring to the boil, stirring, then simmer for 15 minutes, or until the chicken is tender. Stir in the lemon juice, sprinkle with pepper and serve.

When plum tomatoes are not available, use other ripe tomatoes in this soup.

Slivers of courgette, chunks of green pepper and ripe tomato marry well with morsels of chicken in a broth that is subtly enhanced by a trace of Tabasco.

A fresh, minty prickle infuses this cream of chicken soup, which is light yet crammed with tender shreds of chicken. Lemon rind and juice highlight the refreshing flavour.

Minted chicken soup

SERVES 4
PREPARATION TIME: 10 minutes
COOKING TIME: 15 minutes

1oz (30g) polyunsaturated margarine
2 level tablespoons plain flour
1½ pints (850ml) chicken stock (see p.19)
½ pint (150ml) skimmed milk
½ level teaspoon finely grated lemon rind
1 tablespoon lemon juice
12oz (340g) uncooked chicken breast without skin or bone, cut into fine strips
2 level tablespoons chopped fresh mint leaves
Whole mint leaves to garnish

1 Melt the margarine in a saucepan over a low heat. Stir in the flour and cook for 3 minutes, stirring continuously.

2 Gradually mix in about a third of the chicken stock, then add the rest and the milk. Add the lemon rind and juice and bring to the boil, stirring continuously.

3 Stir in the chicken, bring back to the boil, then simmer for 5-6 minutes, until the chicken is cooked through. Scatter in the chopped mint and serve in warmed soup plates, floating the mint leaves on the soup at the last minute.

ONE SERVING	
CALORIES	185
TOTAL FAT	9g
SATURATED FAT	2g
CARBOHYDRATES	6g
ADDED SUGAR	0
FIBRE	0
SODIUM	140mg

Chilled cucumber and walnut soup

ONE SERVING	
CALORIES	90
TOTAL FAT	4g
SATURATED FAT	1g
CARBOHYDRATES	8g
ADDED SUGAR	0
FIBRE	1g
SODIUM	55mg

SERVES 4
PREPARATION TIME: 10 minutes,
plus 2-5 hours to refrigerate

2 medium cucumbers, peeled, halved, de-seeded
and chopped
1 medium red onion, peeled and thinly sliced
2 tablespoons chopped fresh dill
2 tablespoons chopped fresh mint
7fl oz (200ml) skimmed milk

4oz (115g) low-fat natural yoghurt
3fl oz (85ml) chilled vegetable or chicken stock
(see p.19)
1oz (30g) shelled walnut pieces
3 tablespoons red wine vinegar
⅛ level teaspoon cayenne pepper
Freshly ground black pepper
Sprigs of dill and paper-thin cucumber
slices to garnish
4 walnut halves, very finely chopped

Easy to make and a pleasure to eat, this refreshing summer soup is enlivened with mint and dill and enriched with yoghurt and walnuts.

1 Blend the cucumber with the onion, dill and mint in a food processor for 30 seconds, or until smooth. Add the milk, yoghurt, stock and the walnut pieces, and blend for a further 20 seconds.

2 Turn into a bowl and stir in the vinegar and cayenne. Season with black pepper, cover and refrigerate for 2-5 hours. Stir and garnish with the dill, cucumber slices and walnuts. Serve with some crisp pretzels (see p.371).

Crab soup

ONE SERVING

CALORIES 165

TOTAL FAT 6g

SATURATED FAT 2g

CARBOHYDRATES 13g

ADDED SUGAR 0

FIBRE 1g

SODIUM 265mg

This luxury soup made with minimum effort is a cook's delight and a treat for the diners. The gentle flavour of the crab gains a hot undertone from curry powder and basil.

SERVES 4
PREPARATION TIME: 10 minutes
COOKING TIME: 15 minutes

½ oz (15g) slightly salted butter
1 small onion, peeled and finely chopped
1 small stick celery, trimmed and finely chopped
1 clove garlic, peeled and crushed
½ level teaspoon medium-hot curry powder
1oz (30g) plain flour
½ pint (285ml) skimmed milk
1 tablespoon tomato purée (see p.16)
½ pint (285ml) fish or vegetable stock (see p.19)
2 level teaspoons chopped fresh tarragon
2 level teaspoons chopped fresh basil
6oz (175g) cooked white crabmeat, shredded
2oz (60g) cooked peeled prawns, chopped
Freshly ground black pepper
4 level tablespoons low-fat natural yoghurt
½ level teaspoon paprika

1 Melt the butter in a saucepan and gently cook the onion, celery and garlic in it for 5 minutes, without browning.

2 Stir in the curry powder and flour, and cook for 1 minute. Remove from the heat and gradually mix in the milk. Add the tomato purée, stock, tarragon and basil, and bring to the boil, stirring. Simmer for 5 minutes.

3 Mix in the crabmeat and prawns, season with pepper and gently heat through for another 5 minutes.

4 Ladle the soup into warmed soup plates. Swirl 1 tablespoon of yoghurt on each serving, dust with the paprika and serve immediately.

You can use lobster in place of the less expensive crab to make the soup.

Red lentils readily absorb the flavours of the bouquet garni and clove-studded onion in this economical and easily made winter warmer.

Lentil soup

ONE SERVING

CALORIES 285

TOTAL FAT 1g

SATURATED FAT 0

CARBOHYDRATES 51g

ADDED SUGAR 0

FIBRE 5g

SODIUM 50mg

SERVES 4
PREPARATION TIME: 15 minutes
COOKING TIME: 50 minutes

2¹/₂ pints (1.4 litres) water
11oz (300g) red lentils, cleaned and washed
1 carrot, peeled and chopped
1 large onion, peeled and studded with 2 cloves
1 clove garlic, peeled
1 bouquet garni (see p.218)
1 level tablespoon chopped fresh basil
4 level tablespoons low-fat natural yoghurt

1 Pour the water into a large saucepan, add the lentils, carrot, onion, garlic and bouquet garni, and bring to the boil. Reduce the heat, cover, and cook gently for about 45 minutes, until the lentils have softened. Take off the heat, discard the bouquet garni and discard the cloves from the onion.

2 Pass the soup through a food mill, or let it cool for a few minutes and then blend in a food processor. If the soup is too thick, add a little more water.

3 Reheat the soup and pour into warmed bowls. Sprinkle with the basil and serve with a tablespoon of yoghurt to swirl on each bowl.

Serve the soup piping hot with thick slices of crusty wholemeal bread.

Minestrone

SERVES 8
PREPARATION TIME: 30 minutes
COOKING TIME: 40 minutes

ONE SERVING	
CALORIES 190	
TOTAL FAT 4g	
SATURATED FAT 1g	
CARBOHYDRATES 32g	
ADDED SUGAR 0	
FIBRE 6g	
SODIUM 60mg	

TIP
Use farfallini (tiny bows), thin spirals, short macaroni, orecchiette (little ears), or other small pasta shapes that will become very tender after 7 minutes of simmering.

1 tablespoon olive oil
2 medium onions, peeled and chopped
4 cloves garlic, peeled and chopped
2 medium carrots, peeled, cut in half lengthways
and thinly sliced
1 medium potato, peeled and cut into small cubes
3 level tablespoons chopped fresh basil,
or 1 level teaspoon dried basil
1 level teaspoon dried oregano
2 large bay leaves
1/2 lb (680g) ripe tomatoes, skinned and chopped
1 3/4 pints (1 litre) chicken or vegetable stock
(see p.19)
4oz (115g) green beans, trimmed and cut into
short pieces
4oz (115g) small pasta shapes
14oz (400g) cooked cannellini or flageolet beans,
well drained (see p.18)
1 medium courgette, trimmed and diced
4 level teaspoons grated Parmesan cheese
4 level teaspoons chopped fresh parsley

1 Heat the oil in a large saucepan and cook the onions and garlic in it, uncovered, over a moderate heat for 5 minutes. Mix in the carrots, potato, basil, oregano and bay leaves, and cook for a further 5 minutes, stirring and shaking the vegetables occasionally.

2 Stir in the tomatoes, pour in the stock and bring to the boil, then reduce the heat, cover and simmer for 20 minutes. Stir in the green beans, pasta, cooked beans and courgette, and continue cooking for about 7 minutes, or until the green beans and pasta are both very tender. Discard the bay leaves.

3 Serve the minestrone in warmed soup plates and sprinkle each serving with a teaspoon of Parmesan and of parsley.

Minestrone varies from region to region in Italy, but always includes local fresh vegetables and some kind of dried beans. Pasta or rice is added according to whether the cook is from the south or the north. The result is a wholesome and filling family dish.

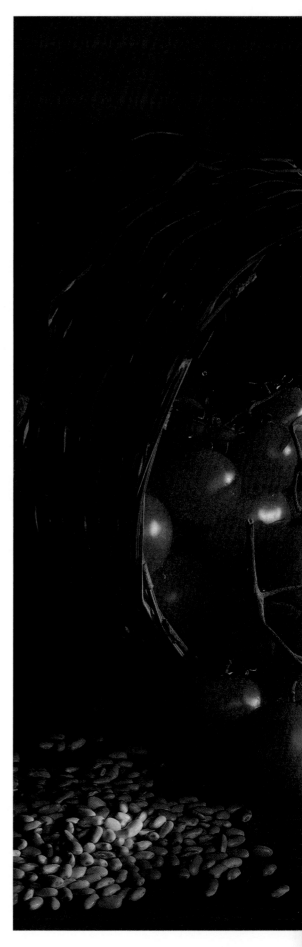

Mulligatawny soup

ONE SERVING	
CALORIES	195
TOTAL FAT	7g
SATURATED FAT	1g
CARBOHYDRATES	25g
ADDED SUGAR	0
FIBRE	3g
SODIUM	95mg

Britons who served in colonial India relished the spicy foods prepared for them there and brought the recipes back home. This lightly curried chicken soup is one of the best.

SERVES 4
PREPARATION TIME: 20 minutes
COOKING TIME: 45 minutes

1 tablespoon olive oil
1 medium onion, peeled and chopped
1 medium carrot, peeled and sliced
1 medium apple, peeled, cored and chopped
1 stick celery, trimmed and chopped
1 small green pepper, de-seeded and chopped
2 level tablespoons plain flour
1 level tablespoon mild curry powder
1¾ pints (1 litre) chicken stock (see p.19)
14oz (400g) tinned tomatoes
⅛ level teaspoon each ground cloves, ground mace and freshly grated nutmeg
Freshly ground black pepper
4oz (115g) cooked chicken, skinned and diced
4oz (115g) cooked rice (see p.17)
4 level tablespoons low-fat natural yoghurt

1 Heat the oil in a large saucepan over a moderate heat and cook the onion, carrot, apple, celery and green pepper in it, uncovered, for 5 minutes, until the onion is softened but not browned. Mix in the flour and curry powder and cook for 1 minute, stirring.

2 Gradually stir in the stock, then add the tomatoes, cloves, mace and nutmeg. Season with pepper and bring to the boil, then turn down the heat, cover and leave to simmer for 25 minutes.

3 Pass the soup through a food mill, or cool it slightly and blend in a food processor. Return the soup to the pan and stir in the chicken and rice. Bring to the boil, turn down the heat and simmer for 5 minutes. Ladle into individual soup plates and top each serving with a tablespoon of yoghurt.

The stout deepens and mellows the flavour of the mushrooms in this delicious soup, which is thickened to a creamy consistency by the old-fashioned method of simmering a handful of pearl barley in it.

Mushroom soup with barley

ONE SERVING	
CALORIES 105	
TOTAL FAT 4g	
SATURATED FAT 1g	
CARBOHYDRATES 12g	
ADDED SUGAR 0	
FIBRE 1g	
SODIUM 35mg	

SERVES 4
PREPARATION TIME: 20 minutes
COOKING TIME: 55 minutes

1 tablespoon olive oil
1 medium onion, peeled and finely sliced
8oz (225g) button mushrooms, wiped and finely sliced
⅛ level teaspoon freshly grated nutmeg
⅛ level teaspoon cayenne pepper
1¼ pints (725ml) chicken or beef stock (see p.9)
¼ pint (150ml) stout
¼ pint (150ml) skimmed milk
1oz (30g) pearl barley
Freshly ground black pepper
2 level tablespoons chopped fresh parsley

1 Heat the oil in a large saucepan, and cook the onion and mushrooms in it over a moderate heat, uncovered, for about 10 minutes, or until the mushrooms are lightly coloured and their juice has evaporated. Stir in the nutmeg and cayenne pepper.

2 Pour in the stock, stout, milk and barley, season with pepper and bring to the boil, stirring. Lower the heat, cover and simmer for about 45 minutes, or until the barley is tender, stirring from time to time. Serve the soup in warmed bowls and scattered with the parsley.

Field mushrooms will give an even better taste but a darker, greyer colour.

Smooth and thick, savoury and satisfying, this surprisingly elegant soup is made from everyday ingredients found in the store cupboard.

Split pea and potato soup

ONE SERVING	
CALORIES	235
TOTAL FAT	5g
SATURATED FAT	1g
CARBOHYDRATES	41g
ADDED SUGAR	0
FIBRE	4g
SODIUM	20mg

SERVES 4
PREPARATION TIME: 20 minutes
COOKING TIME: 55 minutes

1 tablespoon olive oil
1 medium onion, peeled and chopped
1½ pints (850ml) beef stock (see p.19)
4oz (115g) dried split green peas, rinsed
1lb (450g) potatoes, peeled and quartered
Freshly ground black pepper
Watercress leaves to garnish

1 Heat the oil in a large saucepan, and cook the onion in it, uncovered, over a moderate heat for about 5 minutes, until soft. Stir in the beef stock and bring to the boil.

2 Stir in the peas and potatoes, then turn down the heat, cover and simmer for about 40 minutes, or until the peas and potatoes are tender. Leave to cool for 10 minutes.

3 Purée the soup in several batches in a food processor, then reheat in the pan, stirring constantly. Season with pepper, pour into warmed plates and garnish with watercress.

Serve Italian striped bread with the pale soup.

Provençal soup

SERVES 4
PREPARATION TIME: 20 minutes
COOKING TIME: 30 minutes

1 tablespoon olive oil
4 tablespoons water
1 large onion, peeled and finely sliced
1 medium green pepper, de-seeded and chopped
1 clove garlic, peeled and chopped
1 stick celery, trimmed and finely chopped
8oz (225g) small courgettes, trimmed and thinly sliced lengthways
2 level tablespoons plain flour
1lb (450g) ripe tomatoes, skinned and chopped
1 pint (570ml) chicken or vegetable stock (see p.19)
1 tablespoon lemon juice
Flat-leaf parsley to garnish

ONE SERVING	
CALORIES	105
TOTAL FAT	5g
SATURATED FAT	1g
CARBOHYDRATES	13g
ADDED SUGAR	0
FIBRE	3g
SODIUM	20mg

1 Heat the olive oil and water in a large saucepan and cook the onion, pepper, garlic, celery and courgettes in it over a low heat for about 5 minutes, stirring occasionally. When the water has evaporated, stir the flour into the vegetables and continue cooking for 3 minutes, stirring frequently.

2 Add the tomatoes, pour in the stock and bring to the boil, then cover and simmer for about 20 minutes. Take off the heat, stir in the lemon juice and garnish with the parsley. Serve the soup piping hot with french bread.

Olive oil, courgettes, tomatoes and garlic give the authentic character of the French country kitchen to this colourful, fresh vegetable soup.

Sweetcorn chowder

ONE SERVING	
CALORIES 155	
TOTAL FAT 6g	
SATURATED FAT 1g	
CARBOHYDRATES 22g	
ADDED SUGAR 0	
FIBRE 2g	
SODIUM 35mg	

SERVES 4
PREPARATION TIME: 15 minutes
COOKING TIME: 20 minutes

1 tablespoon corn oil
1 medium onion, peeled and chopped
1 stick celery, trimmed and chopped
Small red pepper, de-seeded and cut into small dice

1 level tablespoon plain flour
½ level teaspoon paprika
12fl oz (340 ml) chicken or vegetable stock (see p.19)
12oz (340g) frozen sweetcorn kernels
7fl oz (200ml) skimmed milk
1½ teaspoons lemon juice
Freshly ground pepper
2 level tablespoons snipped fresh chives

The name of this sturdy American soup comes from the 'chaudière', the pot used by French settlers in the southern states for simmering their broths and soups.

1 Heat the oil in a large saucepan and cook the onion, celery and red pepper in it, uncovered, over a moderate heat for about 5 minutes, until the vegetables are tender but not browned.

2 Mix in the flour and paprika, and cook for 3 minutes, stirring continuously. Pour in the stock and continue to stir until the mixture comes to the boil and thickens.

3 Stir in the sweetcorn, cover, and simmer for 3 minutes.

4 Stir in the milk and lemon juice, and season with pepper. Continue cooking over a low heat for 2-3 minutes until the soup is very hot, but take care not to let it boil or it will curdle. Pour into a warmed tureen and sprinkle with the chives to serve.

Enriched with natural yoghurt and chilled to a refreshing degree, this smooth tomato soup is easy to prepare and makes a perfect start to a summer dinner party.

Chilled cream of tomato soup

ONE SERVING	
CALORIES 80	
TOTAL FAT 3g	
SATURATED FAT 1g	
CARBOHYDRATES 10g	
ADDED SUGAR 0	
FIBRE 2g	
SODIUM 50mg	

SERVES 6
PREPARATION TIME: 20 minutes,
plus 2 hours to refrigerate
COOKING TIME: 20 minutes

1 tablespoon olive oil
1 medium onion, peeled and chopped
1 medium carrot, peeled and grated
2lb (900g) tomatoes, skinned and de-seeded
8fl oz (225ml) vegetable stock (see p.19)
2 level tablespoons chopped fresh basil
1 teaspoon lemon juice
Freshly ground black pepper
8oz (225g) low-fat natural yoghurt

1 Heat the oil in a large saucepan and cook the onion and carrot in it, uncovered, over a low heat for about 5 minutes, or until soft. Do not let the vegetables brown.

2 Add the tomatoes, stock and basil, and bring to the boil. Lower the heat and simmer for 10 minutes, uncovered, stirring occasionally. Take off the heat and cool for 10 minutes.

3 Blend the soup in a food processor in three batches, for about 30 seconds each batch. Pour into a bowl, add the lemon juice and season with pepper. Set aside 4 teaspoons of the yoghurt and stir the rest into the soup.

4 Cover and refrigerate for at least 2 hours. Serve in chilled soup plates with a spoonful of the reserved yoghurt on each serving.

Fresh vegetable soup

ONE SERVING	
CALORIES	125
TOTAL FAT	5g
SATURATED FAT	1g
CARBOHYDRATES	16g
ADDED SUGAR	0
FIBRE	3g
SODIUM	35mg

SERVES 4
PREPARATION TIME: 20 minutes
COOKING TIME: 30 minutes

1 tablespoon olive oil
8 button onions, peeled
3 level tablespoons plain flour
1½ pints (850ml) vegetable or chicken stock
(see p.19)

1 medium carrot, peeled and thinly sliced
1½ level teaspoons dried tarragon
1 teaspoon lemon juice
Freshly ground black pepper
3oz (85g) broccoli florets
4oz (115g) button mushrooms, wiped
and quartered
8oz (225g) marrow or pumpkin, peeled,
de-seeded and diced
4oz (115g) low-fat natural yoghurt
1 level tablespoon chopped fresh tarragon
to garnish

1 Heat the oil in a large, heavy-based saucepan
and cook the onions in it over a high heat for
about 5 minutes, shaking the pan from time to
time to brown them all over. Lift the onions
onto a plate with a slotted spoon.

2 Mix the flour into the oil left in the pan
and cook over a moderate heat, stirring, for
1 minute. Gradually blend in the stock and
bring to the boil, stirring continuously.
Simmer for about 3 minutes until thickened.

3 Mix in the onions, carrot, tarragon and
lemon juice, and season with pepper.
Bring back to the boil, then lower the heat,
cover and simmer for 10 minutes. Add the
broccoli, mushrooms and marrow or pumpkin,
cover, and cook for 5 minutes more, or until
the vegetables are tender.

4 Stir in the yoghurt and reheat the soup
without letting it boil or it will curdle. Pour the
soup into warmed bowls, sprinkle with the
fresh tarragon and serve immediately.

For a change of flavour, you can use basil
instead of tarragon in the soup and as a garnish.

*Broccoli, button onions and mushrooms
are among the vegetables of diverse colour and
texture in this chunky soup, but its distinctive
character comes from the tarragon whose flavour
pervades the creamy base.*

Chive vichyssoise

ONE SERVING

CALORIES 155

TOTAL FAT 5g

SATURATED FAT 1g

CARBOHYDRATES 25g

ADDED SUGAR 0

FIBRE 3g

SODIUM 40mg

A generous sprinkling of chives flecks the pale creaminess of this cool, refreshing leek and potato soup and strengthens its flavour.

SERVES 4
PREPARATION TIME: 15 minutes,
plus 2 hours to refrigerate
COOKING TIME: 30 minutes

1 tablespoon olive oil
6fl oz (175ml) water
1 medium onion, peeled and chopped
1 leek, trimmed, sliced and well washed
1 stick celery, trimmed and chopped
1lb (450g) potatoes, peeled and diced
1 pint (570ml) vegetable or chicken stock
(see p.19)
7oz (200g) low-fat natural yoghurt
4 level tablespoons chopped fresh chives
1 teaspoon lemon juice
4 drops Tabasco

1 Heat the oil and 4 tablespoons of the water in a large saucepan and cook the onion, leek and celery in it, uncovered, for 8 minutes, or until the vegetables start to soften. Stir in the potatoes and cook for another 3 minutes.

2 Pour in the stock and bring to the boil, then lower the heat, cover and simmer for about 20 minutes, or until the potatoes are tender.

3 Leave the soup to cool, then blend it in a food processor until smooth. Mix the yoghurt with the remaining water and stir into the soup with the chives, lemon juice and Tabasco.

4 Cover the soup and refrigerate for at least 2 hours before serving.

Artichokes with creamed bean filling

ONE SERVING

CALORIES 160

TOTAL FAT 2g

SATURATED FAT 0

CARBOHYDRATES 27g

ADDED SUGAR 0

FIBRE 8g

SODIUM 245mg

Shallow artichoke cups make exotic containers for a smooth, thick purée of broad beans, potatoes and celeriac. The soft, filled cups have a contrasting base of crisp toast.

SERVES 4
PREPARATION TIME: 25 minutes
COOKING TIME: 15 minutes
OVEN: Preheat to 180°C (350°F, gas mark 4)

3oz (85g) potatoes, peeled and diced
3oz (85g) celeriac, peeled and diced
12oz (340g) frozen broad beans, thawed and outer skins removed
1 level tablespoon low-fat fromage frais
Freshly ground black pepper
4 slices wholemeal bread, lightly toasted
14oz (400g) tinned artichoke bottoms, well rinsed and patted dry
½ level teaspoon paprika
Red and curly endive to garnish

1 Cook the potatoes and celeriac in unsalted boiling water for about 10 minutes, or until they are tender, then drain. Cook the beans in unsalted boiling water for about 5 minutes, until tender, then drain.

2 Rub the potatoes, celeriac and beans through a sieve or vegetable mill. Stir in the fromage frais, season with pepper, and mix well to form a firm purée.

3 Cut the toast into eight triangles and arrange them in a shallow ovenproof dish. Place an artichoke bottom on each triangle of toast and spoon the bean purée onto the artichokes. Cover the dish loosely with foil and cook in the heated oven for 15 minutes.

4 Serve the filled artichokes dusted lightly with paprika and garnished with the endive.

For extra flavour, dip the edges of the toast in chopped parsley before the toppings are put on.

> **TIP**
> **The slightly cupped discs of artichoke bottoms are ideal for this dish. Do not buy artichoke hearts, which are too small and have a crown of leaves attached.**

Tender pieces of asparagus give a luxury flavour and flashes of colour to creamy mushroom omelettes, which make delicate starters to a meal.

Asparagus and mushroom omelettes

ONE SERVING	
CALORIES	180
TOTAL FAT	14g
SATURATED FAT	3g
CARBOHYDRATES	2g
ADDED SUGAR	0
FIBRE	1g
SODIUM	130mg

SERVES 4
PREPARATION TIME: 5 minutes
COOKING TIME: 10 minutes
OVEN: Preheat to 150°C (300°F, gas mark 2)

4 teaspoons olive oil
4oz (115g) button mushrooms, wiped and thinly sliced
5 eggs, size 2
1 level tablespoon snipped chives
2 tablespoons cold water
Freshly ground black pepper
4oz (115g) cooked asparagus, chopped
1 large ripe tomato, skinned, de-seeded and chopped

1 Heat half the oil in a frying pan and toss the mushrooms in it over a high heat for about 5 minutes, until they are lightly browned and the juice has evaporated. Lift them out with a slotted spoon and drain on kitchen paper.

2 Lightly whisk the eggs, chives and water, and season with pepper.

3 Heat ½ teaspoon of the oil in a small nonstick omelette pan and stir a quarter of the asparagus and a quarter of the mushrooms in it over a moderate heat for 1 minute.

4 Turn the heat to high, pour a quarter of the egg mixture on the asparagus and mushrooms, and stir for 30 seconds with a fork, then leave to cook for 30 seconds, or until lightly set.

5 Fold the omelette in three, using a spatula. Turn it onto a hot dish, cover and put in the oven to keep hot. Make three more omelettes, then garnish them all with tomato to serve.

You can use cooked green beans, courgettes or broccoli when you cannot get asparagus.

Chicken liver croustades

SERVES 4
PREPARATION TIME: 15 minutes
COOKING TIME: 15 minutes
OVEN: Preheat to 200°C (400°F, gas mark 6)

½ oz (15g) polyunsaturated margarine
1 level teaspoon whole-grain mustard
1 small clove garlic, peeled and crushed

4 slices wholemeal bread, ¼ in (6mm) thick,
crusts removed
8oz (225g) chicken livers, trimmed, rinsed and
patted dry, and cut into cubes
2 level teaspoons plain flour
3 tablespoons brandy or dry sherry
¼ pint (150ml) chicken stock (see p.19)
2 level tablespoons snipped chives
Freshly ground black pepper
Oak-leaf lettuce, thinly sliced celery and snipped
chives to garnish

1 Mix the margarine with the mustard and
garlic, and set aside.

2 Roll the bread with a rolling pin until its
thickness is about halved. Trim each slice into a
neat square and use half the mustard mixture
to spread thinly on one side of the slices.

3 Gently press the bread slices, mustard side
up, into four deep patty tins about 3½ in
(90mm) in diameter. Cook on a baking tray in
the heated oven for about 15 minutes, or until
the croustades are golden brown and crisp.

4 Meanwhile, heat the remaining mustard
mixture in a nonstick frying pan and cook the
chicken livers in it over a moderate heat,
stirring frequently, for 2-3 minutes or until
lightly browned.

5 Mix the flour into the livers and cook for
1 minute. Pour in the brandy or sherry, and
boil for 1 minute until almost evaporated.
Gradually stir in the stock and bring to the boil.
Turn down the heat and simmer, uncovered,
for 2-3 minutes until the sauce thickens.
Scatter in the chives and season with pepper.

6 Turn the croustades out of the patty tins
and set them on individual plates. Divide the
chicken liver sauce between them, garnish with
the lettuce leaves and celery and sprinkle with
the chives. Serve at once while hot.

*A piquant combination of mustard and garlic
flavours the filling of chicken livers and the crisp
bread cases in which it is served. Brandy gives a hint
of sweetness to the rich sauce that coats the liver.*

Duck and apple with orange dressing

SERVES 4
PREPARATION TIME: 20 minutes,
plus 20 minutes to cool
COOKING TIME: 15 minutes

ONE SERVING

CALORIES 125

TOTAL FAT 6g

SATURATED FAT 1g

CARBOHYDRATES 6g

ADDED SUGAR 0

FIBRE 1g

SODIUM 45mg

The classic combination of duck and orange is fired by a faint trace of ginger and given a subtle crunch by toasted almonds. Apple slices make a sweet contrast.

Thinly pared rind of 1 orange, cut into fine strips
⅛ level teaspoon ground ginger
3 tablespoons water
1 level teaspoon cornflour
Juice of 1 large orange
1 dessert apple, washed in warm water and dried
Juice of ½ lemon
6oz (175g) cold cooked duck breast without bone or skin, cut into fine strips
1 level tablespoon blanched and chopped almonds, lightly toasted
Flat-leaf parsley sprigs to garnish

1 Simmer the orange rind with the ginger and water in a small saucepan for 10 minutes.

2 Meanwhile, mix the cornflour to a smooth cream with 2 teaspoons of the orange juice, then stir back into the rest of the juice.

3 Strain the orange and ginger mixture through a fine sieve and set aside the strips of rind. Pour the liquid back into the pan and stir in the cornflour and orange juice mixture. Bring to the boil, stirring all the time, then simmer for about 2 minutes, stirring frequently, until the mixture is clear and slightly thickened. Pour it into a bowl, cover and leave to cool.

4 Quarter and core the apple. Cut it into thin slices and immediately pour the lemon juice over them. Turn the slices in the juice until they are completely coated, so that they do not discolour.

5 When the orange dressing is cold, toss the duck in it until completely coated, then stir in the almonds. Arrange a share of the apple slices on each of four small serving plates and spoon a quarter of the duck mixture and its dressing onto each plate beside the apples. Garnish with the shreds of orange rind and the parsley sprigs. Serve at once.

Wild mushroom tartlets

SERVES 4
PREPARATION TIME: 15 minutes
COOKING TIME: 15 minutes
OVEN: Preheat to 180°C (350°F, gas mark 4)

ONE SERVING	
CALORIES 145	
TOTAL FAT 7g	
SATURATED FAT 1g	
CARBOHYDRATES 16g	
ADDED SUGAR 0	
FIBRE 1g	
SODIUM 40mg	

A crisp filo pastry case like a golden flower holds spiced choice mushrooms at its heart and gets a meal off to a stylish start.

About 3oz (85g) filo pastry sheets
1½ tablespoons olive oil
2 tablespoons pale dry sherry
1 level teaspoon whole-grain or French mustard
⅛ level teaspoon cayenne pepper
3oz (85g) each fresh shiitake mushrooms and fresh oyster mushrooms, washed and halved
3oz (85g) fresh chanterelle mushrooms, washed
Mixed lettuce and endive leaves
8 level teaspoons low-fat fromage frais
Shredded purple basil or sage leaves to garnish

1 Cut the filo pastry to give twelve 4in (10cm) squares. Brush lightly on one side with oil.

2 Gently press 3 pastry squares, oiled side down, into a Yorkshire pudding tin 4in (10cm)

in diameter, arranging them so that the points are evenly spaced round the rim. Form three more tartlets. Brush the inside of the tartlets lightly with the oil and bake in the heated oven for 10 minutes, until golden and crisp.

3 Meanwhile, heat the sherry gently in a frying pan, then stir in the mustard, cayenne pepper and mushrooms. Cover and cook over a low heat for 4-5 minutes, shaking the pan frequently, until the mushrooms are tender.

4 Arrange the lettuce and endive leaves on four serving plates and put a warm tartlet on each plate. Spoon in the mushrooms, top each tartlet with 2 level teaspoons of fromage frais and garnish with the basil or sage leaves. Serve at once while warm and crisp.

You can use any mixture of mushrooms to fill the tartlets. Wash wild mushrooms thoroughly and dry them with kitchen paper.

Mussel salad

ONE SERVING	
CALORIES 150	
TOTAL FAT 3g	
SATURATED FAT 1g	
CARBOHYDRATES 10g	
ADDED SUGAR 0	
FIBRE 2g	
SODIUM 220mg	

SERVES 4
PREPARATION TIME: 30 minutes,
plus 30 minutes to refrigerate
COOKING TIME: 6-8 minutes

2½ lb (1.1kg) mussels, shells well scrubbed and scraped, beards removed
1 small onion, peeled and chopped
1 sprig each fresh thyme and fresh parsley
1 bay leaf

4fl oz (115ml) dry white wine
2 dessert apples, cored and diced
8oz (225g) celery, trimmed and thinly sliced
1 small red pepper, de-seeded and finely chopped
4 level tablespoons Greek yoghurt
2 tablespoons lemon juice
1½ level teaspoons paprika
1 level tablespoon chopped fresh mint
Freshly ground black pepper
Mixed lettuce and endive leaves, washed and dried

Mussels, which require some care in the preparation, deserve a dish that is worthy of the effort. This salad is such a dish, marrying the silky-soft mussels with crisp pieces of apple, celery and pepper, all swathed in a wine and yoghurt dressing.

TIP
To ensure the mussels are really clean rinse them in several changes of cold water after scrubbing them and removing the beards.

1 Put the mussels in a large saucepan with the onion, thyme, parsley, bay leaf and wine. Cover and cook over a high heat, shaking the pan often, for 6-8 minutes, until the shells open.

2 Line a colander with kitchen paper and place it over a bowl. Pour the mussels into the colander to drain. Discard the thyme, parsley and bay leaf, return the liquid to the pan and boil until it is reduced to about 6 tablespoons. Remove from the heat and leave to cool.

3 Remove the mussels from their shells, discarding any that are not open. Put them in a bowl with the apples, celery and red pepper.

4 Mix the yoghurt with the mussel liquid, lemon juice, paprika and mint. Season with black pepper, pour over the mussels and toss. Cover and refrigerate the salad for 30 minutes.

Arrange a bed of mixed leaves on four serving plates, spoon on the salad and serve at once.

Petals of luscious pear open to receive the tangy cheese and chive filling, creating an ingenious sweet-and-sharp starter for a dinner party.

Pears with piquant cheese filling

SERVES 4
PREPARATION TIME: 15 minutes

4 small, ripe but firm Comice, Packham or
other rounded pears
Juice of 1 lemon, strained
1oz (30g) Blue Stilton cheese
2 level teaspoons snipped chives
3oz (85g) low-fat fromage frais
Curly endive leaves to garnish
2 level tablespoons low-fat natural yoghurt
2 teaspoons balsamic vinegar

1 Using a small, sharp knife, remove a small cone-shaped piece from the base of each pear. Carefully cut out the core, working from the bottom. Cut the stalk off each pear. Peel the pears and immediately brush well with the lemon juice so that they do not go brown.

2 Make four downward cuts in the top of each pear, cutting through the narrow upper part and a third of the way down the rounded part. This will divide the top of the pear into eight segments. Carefully cut each segment again to make 16 thin 'petals'.

3 Mix the Stilton and half the chives into the fromage frais. Pipe a share of the mixture into the top of each pear through a large plain nozzle, pressing the petals apart gently. If you prefer, you can use a small spoon to put the filling in the pears.

4 Place the stuffed pears on individual serving plates and garnish with the endive leaves. Mix the yoghurt and vinegar, and spoon a little of this dressing over each pear. Sprinkle with the remaining chives and serve.

ONE SERVING	
CALORIES	120
TOTAL FAT	3g
SATURATED FAT	2g
CARBOHYDRATES	20g
ADDED SUGAR	0
FIBRE	0
SODIUM	85mg

TIP
If time is short, simply peel, halve and core the pears, then spoon the cheese mixture on top and set two pear halves on each plate with the garnish.

Grilled peppers

SERVES 4
PREPARATION TIME: 5 minutes,
plus 1 hour to marinate
COOKING TIME: 8 minutes

ONE SERVING	
CALORIES	95
TOTAL FAT	5g
SATURATED FAT	1g
CARBOHYDRATES	12g
ADDED SUGAR	0
FIBRE	4g
SODIUM	10mg

The vibrant colours and intense smoky flavour of grilled sweet peppers conjure up dreams of holiday meals beside the blue Mediterranean — with the basil and oregano dressing adding to the illusion.

6 medium peppers, 2 red, 2 green and 2 yellow
1 tablespoon olive oil
1 tablespoon red wine vinegar
1 clove garlic, peeled and crushed
1 level tablespoon chopped fresh basil
1 level teaspoon chopped fresh oregano,
or ½ level teaspoon dried oregano
Freshly ground black pepper
Basil sprigs to garnish

1 Lay the peppers on the grill rack and grill under a moderately high heat for 5-8 minutes, turning frequently until the skins are lightly charred and blistered all over. Put the peppers in a bowl, cover with a clean damp cloth and leave until they are cool enough to handle.

2 Skin the peppers, working over a sieve placed on a bowl, to catch the juices. Discard the skin, seeds and stalk, and cut the flesh lengthways into strips about ½ in (13mm) wide. Mix the different coloured strips together and turn onto a serving dish.

3 Mix the oil, vinegar, garlic, basil and oregano with the juices from the peppers. Season the dressing with black pepper and pour it over the peppers. Cover the dish and leave it to stand at room temperature for 1 hour. Garnish with the basil sprigs just before serving.

You can garnish the dish with nasturtium flowers if you can get them. Serve the peppers with warm wholemeal rolls (see p.366) for mopping up the delicious juices.

Pheasant terrine

ONE SERVING	
CALORIES	215
TOTAL FAT	8g
SATURATED FAT	2g
CARBOHYDRATES	12g
ADDED SUGAR	0
FIBRE	3g
SODIUM	325mg

SERVES 8
PREPARATION TIME: 40 minutes, plus overnight
to refrigerate
COOKING TIME: 1 hour
OVEN: Preheat to 180°C (350°F, gas mark 4)

Oven-ready pheasant, about 1½ lb (680g)
4oz (115g) mushrooms, wiped and chopped
2oz (60g) unsmoked back bacon with fat
removed, chopped
8oz (225g) chicken livers, washed and trimmed
1 red onion, peeled and chopped
2 cloves garlic, peeled and crushed
1 level teaspoon dried thyme
2 level tablespoons chopped fresh parsley
7oz (200g) tinned unsweetened chestnut purée
⅛ level teaspoon salt
Freshly ground black pepper
1lb (450g) large fresh spinach leaves, washed and
dried, thick stalks trimmed off
Fresh bay leaves, red onion rings and mixed lettuce
leaves to garnish

1 Take the pheasant meat off the bone and remove the skin. Cut the meat into small pieces and mince it finely or blend in a food processor until smooth. Mix in the mushrooms, bacon, chicken livers, onion, garlic, thyme and parsley, and mince or blend again. Stir in the chestnut purée and salt and season with pepper.

2 Blanch the spinach leaves for 1 minute in a large saucepan of unsalted boiling water. Rinse with cold water, drain and pat dry with kitchen paper. Lay the bay leaves in a 10×5in (25×13cm) nonstick loaf tin and line the tin with three-quarters of the spinach leaves.

3 Spoon the pheasant mixture into the tin and spread evenly. Arrange the remaining spinach leaves on top. Cover the tin with a double layer of nonstick baking paper and set it in a deep roasting tin. Pour in enough cold water to come halfway up the tin. Cook in the heated oven for 1 hour, or until there is no pink in the juices that ooze out when you push a skewer into the middle of the terrine.

4 Lift the loaf tin onto a board and leave to cool, then put it in the refrigerator until the following day for the terrine to set.

Turn the terrine out and cut it into 16 slices. Garnish it with the fresh bay, onion and lettuce, and serve with crusty bread.

Set a celebration meal off to a grand start with this exquisite blend of pheasant and chicken livers, mushrooms and chestnuts, seasoned with herbs and all meticulously wrapped in dark spinach leaves.

When the longed-for asparagus season arrives in early summer, snap up the thin, cheaper spears to use in this light, irresistible appetiser.

Salmon and asparagus ramekins

ONE SERVING

CALORIES 95

TOTAL FAT 5g

SATURATED FAT 1g

CARBOHYDRATES 3g

ADDED SUGAR 0

FIBRE 1g

SODIUM 320mg

SERVES 4
PREPARATION TIME: 15 minutes
COOKING TIME: 30 minutes
OVEN: Preheat to 180°C (350°F, gas mark 4)

4oz (115g) thin asparagus spears, stems peeled
3 egg yolks, size 3
8fl oz (225ml) skimmed milk
⅛ level teaspoon cayenne pepper
2 level tablespoons chopped fresh dill
2oz (60g) smoked salmon, cut into thin strips

1 Cut off the asparagus tips and slice the stems thinly. Steam the tips and stems for 3-4 minutes, until just tender. Rinse with cold water to cool quickly, then drain well. Set the tips aside.

2 Whisk the egg yolks, milk, cayenne pepper and dill together. Set aside four salmon strips. Stir the rest and the asparagus stems into the egg mixture.

3 Very lightly grease four small ramekin dishes and divide the mixture between them. Stand the dishes on a baking tray and cook in the heated oven for 30 minutes, or until set.

4 Garnish the ramekins with the reserved salmon strips and asparagus tips.

You can serve the salmon and asparagus ramekins warm with hot wholemeal toast, or let them cool, then cover and refrigerate for 2-3 hours before serving.

Marinated scallop brochettes

ONE SERVING
....
CALORIES 110
....
TOTAL FAT 5g
....
SATURATED FAT 1g
....
CARBOHYDRATES 3g
....
ADDED SUGAR 0
....
FIBRE 1g
....
SODIUM 155mg
....

*The exceptionally
smooth yet meaty flesh
of scallops benefits from
a tenderising marinade,
which then adds its herb
and lemon fragrance to
the skewers of grilled
fish and vegetables.*

SERVES 4
*PREPARATION TIME: 15 minutes, plus at least
4 hours to marinate*
COOKING TIME: 5 minutes

*1 tablespoon olive oil
1 tablespoon lemon juice
1 level tablespoon chopped fresh parsley
½ level teaspoon fennel seeds, crushed
1 clove garlic, peeled and crushed
Grated rind of 1 small, gently scrubbed orange
8 fresh scallops, cleaned
1 large courgette, trimmed and cut into
about 12 slices
1 medium red onion, cut into eight segments
4 metal skewers, lightly oiled*

1 Mix the oil, lemon juice, parsley, fennel
seeds, garlic and orange rind in a glass or china
bowl and turn the scallops in the mixture

until well coated. Cover and refrigerate for at
least 4 hours and up to 12 hours.

2 Cover the courgette and onion with cold
water in a saucepan and bring to the boil. Boil
for 1 minute, then drain well.

3 Thread 2 scallops and a share of the
vegetables onto each skewer. You may find it
easier to thread on the scallop corals separately.

4 Lay the brochettes on a grill rack, baste with
the marinade and cook under a hot grill for
about 5 minutes, turning once or twice, until
the white flesh of the scallops is opaque.

Serve the brochettes on warmed individual
plates. You can hand round separately a small
bowl of cooked brown rice mixed with chopped
walnuts and watercress.

Smoked trout pâté

ONE SERVING	
CALORIES	105
TOTAL FAT	3g
SATURATED FAT	1g
CARBOHYDRATES	3g
ADDED SUGAR	0
FIBRE	0
SODIUM	571mg

SERVES 4
PREPARATION TIME: 10 minutes, plus 3 hours
to chill
COOKING TIME: 10 minutes

Large fresh trout, about 10oz (275g)
8oz (225g) low-fat cottage cheese, well drained

6oz (175g) skinned and boned smoked trout,
finely flaked
1 level teaspoon grated fresh horseradish
1 tablespoon lime or lemon juice
Freshly ground black pepper
Radicchio leaves, washed and dried
Wedges of lime and dill sprigs to garnish

The delicate flesh of smoked and fresh trout is sharpened by a prudent addition of horseradish and whisked to a fluffy lightness with low-fat cottage cheese.

1 Line the grill pan with foil, lay the fresh trout on the rack and cook under a moderate heat for 4 minutes on each side, until the flesh is opaque and flakes easily. Skin and bone the fish, flake the flesh and leave until cold.

2 Use a food processor to blend the cheese, fresh and smoked trout, horseradish and lime juice until smooth. Season with pepper, put in a bowl, cover, and chill for 3 hours, or up to 12.

3 Form radicchio leaves into a cup on each serving plate and spoon in a share of the pâté. Garnish with the lime wedges and dill.

Serve the pâté with thinly sliced brown bread.

Baked tuna tomatoes

SERVES 4
PREPARATION TIME: 25 minutes
COOKING TIME: 15 minutes
OVEN: Preheat to 180°C (350°F, gas mark 4)

8 medium tomatoes
2 teaspoons lemon juice
1 tablespoon olive oil
2 tablespoons water
1 small onion, peeled and chopped
1 medium carrot, peeled and finely diced
1 level tablespoon plain flour
7fl oz (200ml) skimmed milk
7oz (200g) tinned tuna in oil, drained and flaked
1 level teaspoon capers, rinsed and drained
3 level tablespoons fine breadcrumbs
1½ level tablespoons grated Cheddar cheese
Freshly ground black pepper
Sprigs of fresh marjoram or oregano to garnish

ONE SERVING

CALORIES 285

TOTAL FAT 17g

SATURATED FAT 4g

CARBOHYDRATES 17g

ADDED SUGAR 0

FIBRE 2g

SODIUM 355mg

1   Cut a slice off the top of each tomato and chop it finely. Scoop out the tomato seeds and cores with a teaspoon, and discard. Sprinkle the lemon juice inside the tomatoes and put them to drain upside-down on kitchen paper for 10 minutes, then pat dry.

2   Meanwhile, heat the oil and water in a frying pan and cook the onion, carrot and chopped tomato in it, covered, over a moderate heat, for about 5 minutes. Uncover and continue cooking until all the water has evaporated.

3   Stir in the flour and cook for 1 minute, then gradually mix in the milk and bring to the boil, stirring continuously. Cook for about 3 minutes, stirring, until the sauce thickens.

4   Take the pan off the heat and stir in the tuna, capers, 2 tablespoons of the breadcrumbs and half the Cheddar until thoroughly blended. Season the mixture with pepper.

5   Fill the tomato cases with the tuna mixture and stand them in a baking dish in which they will fit snugly. Sprinkle the remaining Cheddar and breadcrumbs over them and bake in the heated oven for about 15 minutes, until golden brown on top. Serve the tomatoes at once while piping hot, garnished with the sprigs of marjoram or oregano.

Versatile tuna, blended with cheese and capers, makes a high-flavour filling for tomatoes, while the cheese and breadcrumb topping adds an appetising savoury crunch to this warming dish.

Turkey and tarragon loaf

ONE SERVING

CALORIES 140

TOTAL FAT 7g

SATURATED FAT 2g

CARBOHYDRATES 4g

ADDED SUGAR 0

FIBRE 1g

SODIUM 100mg

SERVES 8
PREPARATION TIME: 20 minutes
COOKING TIME: 40 minutes
OVEN: Preheat to 180°C (350°F, gas mark 4)

2 tablespoons olive oil
1 medium onion, peeled and finely chopped
1 large stick celery, trimmed and finely chopped

6 level tablespoons chopped fresh parsley
2oz (60g) fresh brown breadcrumbs
2 eggs, size 2, lightly beaten
1 level tablespoon chopped fresh tarragon
¼ level teaspoon freshly grated nutmeg
1lb (450g) minced uncooked turkey meat
Freshly ground black pepper
Sprigs of fresh tarragon to garnish

Tarragon is at its best when married to poultry, and the herb's enticing, pervasive aroma contributes much to the enjoyment of this meat loaf whether you serve it hot or cold.

1 Line a loaf tin 7½ × 3¾ in (19×9.5cm) with nonstick baking paper.

2 Heat the oil in a frying pan and cook the onion and celery in it over a moderate heat for about 5 minutes, or until the onion softens.

3 Meanwhile, mix the parsley, breadcrumbs, eggs, tarragon and nutmeg with the turkey, and season with pepper. Mix in the onion and celery.

4 Spoon the mixture into the loaf tin and spread evenly. Cook in the heated oven for about 40 minutes, or until the loaf is lightly browned and there is no trace of pink in the juice that oozes out when you prick it in the centre with a skewer. Take the loaf out of the oven and leave it to stand in the tin for 15 minutes before turning it out.

5 Peel off the paper and put the loaf on a warmed serving dish. Cut it into 16 slices and garnish with the tarragon sprigs.

Serve the turkey loaf with a green salad and french bread and, if you like, a taste of apricot relish. If you are going to serve the loaf cold, leave it in the tin and when it is cool enough, put it in the refrigerator for 3-4 hours, or overnight if more convenient. Turn it out and peel off the paper to serve.

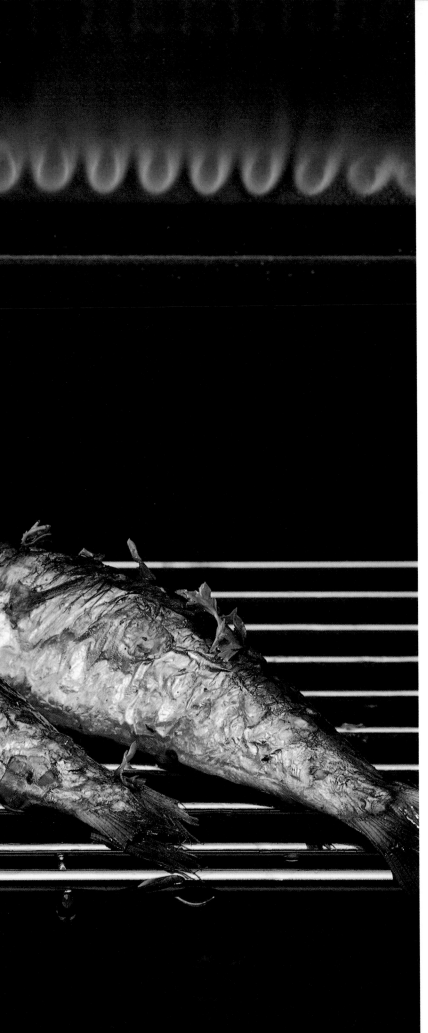

FISH AND SHELLFISH

Quick to cook and easy to digest, fish offers the benefits of animal protein without the overload of saturated fat. The range is wide, from meaty halibut to rich pink salmon, delicate sole to melting mackerel, with prawns and shellfish extending the choice. Sizzling from the grill, chilled in a wine jelly or baked in a paper parcel, they can make healthy family meals and grander dishes for guests.

Sea bream and vegetable parcels

ONE SERVING

CALORIES 180

TOTAL FAT 5g

SATURATED FAT 1g

CARBOHYDRATES 3g

ADDED SUGAR 0

FIBRE 2g

SODIUM 195mg

The paper wrapping seals in the moisture and taste of the bream, while the vegetables remain firm. Rice mixed with lemon zest and chopped fennel makes a subtle accompaniment.

SERVES 4
PREPARATION TIME: 15 minutes
COOKING TIME: 20 minutes
OVEN: Preheat to 200°C (400°F, gas mark 6)

1½ tablespoons olive oil
2 spring onions, trimmed and chopped
1 tablespoon lemon juice
¼ level teaspoon paprika
1 large carrot, peeled and cut into strips
1 large leek, trimmed, cut into strips and washed
2oz (60g) mushrooms, wiped and sliced
2 bream, each about 1lb (450g), scaled and cleaned
Freshly ground black pepper
10 slices lemon

1 Mix 1 tablespoon of the oil with the spring onions, lemon juice and paprika.

2 Blanch the carrot, leek and mushrooms in boiling water for 1 minute, then drain well.

3 Cut 2 sheets of nonstick baking paper large enough to wrap round the fish, and brush with the remaining oil. Place a fish in the centre of each sheet and scatter with the carrot, leek and mushrooms. Trickle half the oil mixture over each fish, season with pepper and lay the lemon slices along the top. Fold the paper sheets closely round the fish and tuck under securely at the ends.

4 Put the parcels on a baking tray and cook in the heated oven for 20 minutes, then open them and see if the fish flakes easily. If necessary, return the parcels to the oven for a further 5 minutes. Lift the parcels onto large, warmed serving dishes to take to the table.

TIP
To divide each fish, run a sharp knife horizontally along the backbone to free the flesh above the bones. Lift off the top fillet carefully and serve. Remove the bones from the remaining fillet and serve.

Steamed cod with ginger

ONE SERVING

CALORIES 195

TOTAL FAT 7g

SATURATED FAT 1g

CARBOHYDRATES 4g

ADDED SUGAR 0

FIBRE 2g

SODIUM 130mg

SERVES 4
PREPARATION TIME: 10 minutes
COOKING TIME: 15 minutes

1 leek, trimmed, quartered lengthways, washed and thickly sliced
3 green sticks celery, trimmed and thinly sliced
1 medium red onion, peeled, thinly sliced and separated into rings

1 large carrot, peeled and thinly sliced
4 level teaspoons peeled and grated root ginger
4 cod steaks, each about 6oz (175g)
6 allspice berries, coarsely ground or crushed
2 spring onions, trimmed and thinly sliced
2 large sprigs parsley
Sprigs of fresh oregano or thyme
2 tablespoons lemon juice
2 tablespoons olive oil

1 Pour 1in (25mm) of water into the bottom of a fish-steamer or into a large saucepan with a bamboo steamer set on it. Bring the water to the boil. Mix the leek, celery, red onion, carrot and ginger and spread in an even layer on the steaming rack. Cover and steam for 5 minutes.

2 Arrange the cod steaks on the vegetables and sprinkle evenly with the allspice and spring onions. Lay the parsley and oregano or thyme on top, cover and steam for 5-6 minutes, or until the fish becomes opaque and the flesh flakes easily when tested with a fork.

3 Carefully lift the cod steaks onto a warmed serving dish and spoon the crisp vegetables round them, discarding the herbs. Cover the dish and keep hot.

4 Remove the rack or bamboo steamer from the pan. Pour the liquid into a small saucepan and boil it rapidly to reduce it to about half a cupful. Whisk in the lemon juice and oil and pour the sauce over the fish and vegetables.

Serve the cod steaks with new potatoes tossed in a little chopped parsley.

There is the simplicity and aroma of Chinese cuisine in these cod steaks steamed with vegetables and herbs and sharpened by the fire of ginger.

Haddock and goat's cheese soufflé

ONE SERVING	
CALORIES 235	
TOTAL FAT 12g	
SATURATED FAT 4g	
CARBOHYDRATES 13g	
ADDED SUGAR 0	
FIBRE 0	
SODIUM 715mg	

TIP
To give the soufflé a good rise, do not beat the egg whites to a dry foam. Slightly softer foam expands more during cooking.

SERVES 4
PREPARATION TIME: 30 minutes
COOKING TIME: 35 minutes
OVEN: Preheat to 190°C (375°F, gas mark 5)

8oz (225g) smoked haddock, skinned, boned, washed and cut into small pieces
8fl oz (225ml) skimmed milk
1oz (30g) polyunsaturated margarine
4 level tablespoons plain flour
2 eggs, separated, plus 2 egg whites, size 2
2oz (60g) medium-fat soft goat's cheese
Freshly ground black pepper

1 Simmer the haddock in 4 tablespoons of the milk in a covered saucepan for 2-3 minutes, until it will just flake. Drain the liquid into the rest of the milk.

2 Melt the margarine in a saucepan, stir in the flour and cook for 1-2 minutes. Gradually stir in the milk and bring the sauce to the boil, stirring continuously. Reduce the heat and simmer for 2-3 minutes, stirring frequently, until the sauce is thick. Remove from the heat and whisk in the egg yolks.

3 Mix the haddock and cheese in a large bowl and season lightly with pepper. Pour in the sauce and mix in gently.

4 Lightly grease a deep soufflé dish 7¼ in (19cm) in diameter. Whisk the egg whites until they will hold soft peaks. Fold one-quarter of the egg white into the fish sauce, using a metal spoon, to lighten the mixture. Then carefully fold in the remaining egg white. Pour into the prepared soufflé dish and cook in the heated oven for about 35 minutes, or until well risen and golden brown, but creamy in the centre.

Serve at once with bread and crunchy coleslaw (see p.315). You can add 1 level teaspoon of curry powder to the sauce for a spicy tang.

Robust as a mature hard cheese in its flavour, the soft goat's cheese marries well with the strong taste of the smoked fish in this soufflé.

Grilled halibut with red pepper sauce

ONE SERVING	
CALORIES 135	
TOTAL FAT 4g	
SATURATED FAT 1g	
CARBOHYDRATES 2g	
ADDED SUGAR 0	
FIBRE 1g	
SODIUM 105mg	

SERVES 4
PREPARATION TIME: 10 minutes
COOKING TIME: 15 minutes

2 medium red peppers
2 cloves garlic, unpeeled
2 teaspoons red wine vinegar
1 teaspoon olive oil
4 halibut steaks, each about 5oz (150g)
Freshly ground black pepper
Sprigs of flat-leaf parsley to garnish

Aubergine wedges, sautéed in a little olive oil, and french bread go well with the fish, while a crisp mixed salad adds a light touch. For a special occasion, you could serve asparagus baked in white wine (p.270), and new potatoes tossed in finely chopped chives.

1   Grill the peppers under a moderate heat for 5-8 minutes, turning occasionally until the skins turn brown and start to blister. Put the peppers in a small bowl and cover with a clean, damp cloth to keep in the steam and loosen the skins.

2   Meanwhile, wrap the cloves of garlic in a piece of foil, and grill for 5 minutes to soften. Leave to cool, then peel the cloves and set aside.

3   When the peppers are cool enough to handle, skin them and remove the seeds and stalks, working over a bowl to catch the juice. Blend the peppers, their juice, the garlic, vinegar and oil to a purée, using a food processor or a food mill.

4   Line the grill pan with foil. Lightly oil the grill rack, arrange the halibut steaks on it and season them lightly with black pepper. Cook under a moderately hot grill for 3-5 minutes each side, depending on thickness, until the flesh flakes easily and is opaque at the centre. Meanwhile, heat the pepper sauce gently in a small pan.

5   Lift the halibut onto individual warmed serving plates and spread a spoonful of the sauce alongside each steak; garnish with the sprigs of parsley.

Grilled steaks of this meaty, close-textured flatfish are low in calories but substantial. Here, a lively, easily made red-pepper sauce spiced with vinegar enhances the mild flavour of the halibut and moistens its firm flesh.

Baked monkfish

ONE SERVING

CALORIES 235

TOTAL FAT 5g

SATURATED FAT 1g

CARBOHYDRATES 20g

ADDED SUGAR 0

FIBRE 2g

SODIUM 270mg

SERVES 4
PREPARATION TIME: 15 minutes
COOKING TIME: 40 minutes
OVEN: Preheat to 220°C (425°F, gas mark 7)

½ level teaspoon black peppercorns
1½ lb (680g) monkfish tail, skinned
1lb (450g) potatoes, peeled and thinly sliced
1 large red onion, peeled and finely chopped
1 level teaspoon crumbled dried fennel

1 tablespoon olive oil
Juice of ½ lemon
1 bay leaf

1 Crush the peppercorns roughly in a mortar, or fold them in greaseproof paper and crush them with a rolling pin. Sprinkle the pepper over the monkfish and press it into the flesh.

2 Line an ovenproof dish with a large piece of nonstick baking paper. Arrange a thin layer of potato slices on it, cover them with half the onion, then sprinkle with half the fennel. Lay the monkfish on the vegetables, brush it with the oil and sprinkle on the lemon juice. Cover with the rest of the vegetables and fennel, and add the bay leaf. Fold the paper over closely and tuck under the ends to make a parcel.

3 Cook in the heated oven for 30 minutes, then open the parcel and cook for 5-10 minutes more, until lightly browned. Take out the bay leaf and lift the fish and vegetables onto a warmed serving plate.

A dish of hot ratatouille (see p.246) or a green salad contrasts with the firm fish. You can cook steaks of cod and haddock in the same way.

A favourite fish of Mediterranean Europe, monkfish has just a hint of sweetness, which is lightly echoed in this dish by the fennel.

Fish pie

ONE SERVING

CALORIES 260

TOTAL FAT 5g

SATURATED FAT 2g

CARBOHYDRATES 29g

ADDED SUGAR 0

FIBRE 4g

SODIUM 210mg

SERVES 4
PREPARATION TIME: 50 minutes
COOKING TIME: 30 minutes
OVEN: Preheat to 200°C (400°F, gas mark 6)

1lb (450g) potatoes, peeled and thickly sliced
8oz (225g) carrots, peeled and thickly sliced
Large pinch saffron threads
¾ pint (425ml) water
Freshly ground black pepper
2 level tablespoons low-fat natural yoghurt
2 level tablespoons chopped fresh parsley

For the filling:
24 fresh mussels, scrubbed and scraped
½ oz (15g) slightly salted butter
1 large leek, sliced thinly and washed
4 tablespoons water
1 level tablespoon cornflour mixed to a thin paste with 2 teaspoons water
12oz (340g) coley fillet, skinned and cubed
2 tomatoes, skinned, de-seeded and chopped

1 Put the potatoes and carrots in a large saucepan, with the saffron, and pour in the water. Bring to the boil then reduce the heat, cover and simmer for about 20 minutes, until tender. Drain and keep the cooking liquid.

2 Return the pan of vegetables to a gentle heat and stir constantly for 1-2 minutes until quite dry. Mash thoroughly, then beat in a little pepper and the yoghurt and parsley. Set aside.

3 Pour the reserved vegetable liquid into a saucepan with the mussels. Cover and cook over a high heat, shaking the pan frequently, for 3-4 minutes. Remove the mussels from their shells. Discard any that do not open. Strain the cooking liquid through a sieve lined with kitchen paper into a measuring jug and make it up to ½ pint (285ml) with water if necessary.

4 Melt the butter in a saucepan, toss the leek in it until coated, then add the tablespoons of water and cook, covered, over a gentle heat for 5 minutes until tender. Pour in the reserved cooking liquid and bring to simmering point. Mix in the cornflour paste and cook, stirring, for 2-3 minutes, until the sauce thickens, then take off the heat.

5 Stir the mussels, coley and tomatoes into the sauce and pour into a deep ovenproof dish. Spread the potato mixture evenly on top and crisscross with a fork. Bake the pie in the heated oven for 30 minutes, until golden brown.

Serve in shell dishes. Steamed curly kale or spinach goes well with the pie.

> **TIP**
> *After scrubbing and scraping the mussels, soak them for an hour in cold water sprinkled with a little flour; this helps to clear them of grit.*

Smooth potato, tinged golden with carrot and saffron, covers a blend of succulent white fish and mussels to make a crisply topped pie.

Stuffed plaice with nutmeg sauce

SERVES 4
PREPARATION TIME: 20 minutes
COOKING TIME: 25 minutes
OVEN: Preheat to 180°C (350°F, gas mark 4)

1 tablespoon olive oil
1 large spring onion, trimmed and chopped
1 small carrot, peeled and grated
3oz (85g) cooked brown rice (see p.17)
½ level teaspoon finely grated lemon rind
1 teaspoon lemon juice
¼ level teaspoon freshly grated nutmeg
Freshly ground black pepper
4 plaice double fillets, each about 6oz (175g), skinned
Wooden cocktail sticks to secure
Fine strips of lemon rind to garnish
8 cooked new carrots to garnish
4 spring onion curls (see p.256) to garnish

For the sauce:
1 tablespoon olive oil
4 level teaspoons plain flour
¼ pint (150ml) fish or vegetable stock (see p.19)
½ level teaspoon finely grated lemon rind
1 teaspoon lemon juice
¼ level teaspoon freshly grated nutmeg
Freshly ground white pepper
4 tablespoons dry white wine
1 level tablespoon chopped fresh parsley

ONE SERVING	
CALORIES	270
TOTAL FAT	10g
SATURATED FAT	1g
CARBOHYDRATES	14g
ADDED SUGAR	0
FIBRE	0
SODIUM	220mg

1 Heat the oil in a saucepan and cook the onion and carrot in it gently for 3-5 minutes, until just tender. Remove from the heat and stir in the rice, lemon rind and juice, and nutmeg. Season with pepper.

2 Lay the fish fillets skinned side up in a lightly oiled, lidded ovenproof dish and season with pepper. Press a quarter of the rice mixture onto the centre of the head end of each fillet, fold the tail end over the filling and secure with cocktail sticks.

3 Cover and cook the fish in the heated oven for 25 minutes, or until the flesh is opaque.

4 Meanwhile, prepare the sauce. Heat the oil in a saucepan over a moderate heat, stir in the flour and cook for 1-2 minutes, stirring continuously. Gradually blend in the stock, then add the grated lemon rind, lemon juice and nutmeg, and season with white pepper. Bring to the boil, stirring continuously, then simmer for 5 minutes before mixing in the wine and the parsley.

5 Lift the fish carefully onto a heated serving dish, remove the cocktail sticks and garnish with the strips of lemon rind, carrots and spring onion curls. Stir the juices from the fish into the sauce and reheat to serve.

Serve the plaice with fine green beans and steamed potatoes or hot crusty rolls (see p.366).

When freshly grated, nutmeg has no trace of bitterness. Here, it lends its distinctive flavour to both filling and sauce, but with a lightness to match that of the plaice.

Plaice and vegetable parcels

ONE SERVING

CALORIES 195

TOTAL FAT 9g

SATURATED FAT 2g

CARBOHYDRATES 2g

ADDED SUGAR 0

FIBRE 1g

SODIUM 230mg

SERVES 4
PREPARATION TIME: 15 minutes
COOKING TIME: 10 minutes
OVEN: Preheat to 200°C (400°F, gas mark 6)

1 rounded teaspoon finely snipped fresh chives
1 teaspoon lemon juice
½ level teaspoon paprika
1oz (30g) polyunsaturated margarine

1 small red pepper, de-seeded and thinly sliced
2 large spring onions, trimmed and sliced diagonally
4oz (115g) thin asparagus, trimmed and sliced diagonally
1 small courgette, trimmed and thinly sliced diagonally
4 plaice double fillets, each about 5oz (150g), skinned
4 thin slices lemon

Tender white plaice and crisp, colourful vegetables mingle their juices while cooking and release strong, fresh aromas as the steaming parcels are unwrapped.

1 Work the chives, lemon juice and paprika into the margarine with a knife and set aside.

2 Boil the vegetables for 1 minute in just enough water to cover. Drain and set aside.

3 Cut 4 pieces of nonstick baking paper, each large enough to enclose one plaice fillet. Lay a fillet on each sheet, skinned side down. Spoon a quarter of the vegetables onto each fillet and top the vegetables with a quarter of the chive mixture and a slice of lemon. Fold the edges of

the baking paper together over the fish and fold the ends over before tucking them beneath the fish to make secure parcels.

4 Lift the parcels carefully into a baking dish and cook in the heated oven for 10 minutes.

Serve the parcels for the diners to open. Crusty bread and a leafy salad go well with the plaice in summer, while baked garlic potatoes (see p.292) make a satisfying winter accompaniment. You can use sole or flounder instead of plaice.

Skate vinaigrette

SERVES 4
PREPARATION TIME: 25 minutes
COOKING TIME: 25 minutes

1¾ lb (800g) skate wings, rinsed and sticky film removed
8fl oz (225ml) vinegar
7oz (200g) onions, peeled and sliced
5 sprigs parsley
1 sprig thyme
1 bay leaf
8oz (225g) lamb's lettuce, washed and drained
1 level tablespoon chopped fresh parsley
1 level tablespoon chopped fresh chervil
2 shallots, peeled and chopped, or 2 spring onions, trimmed and chopped
1 level tablespoon capers, drained
1 tomato, skinned, de-seeded and diced
12 leaves flat-leaf parsley
4 tablespoons vinaigrette dressing (see p.17)

1 Place the skate wings, cut if necessary, in a large saucepan. Pour on 1¾ pints (1 litre) of water and the vinegar. Add the onions, sprigs of parsley and thyme, and the bay leaf. Bring to the boil, then reduce to a simmer and poach very gently, uncovered, for about 25 minutes or until the fish is tender.

2 Meanwhile, spread the lamb's lettuce on a serving dish and sprinkle with the chopped parsley, chervil and shallots or spring onions.

3 Drain the skate and remove the skin. Lift the flesh from the bones and arrange it on the salad. Scatter the capers, tomato and parsley leaves over the fish. Sprinkle on the vinaigrette dressing and serve immediately.

Warm wholemeal rolls and a dish of glazed carrots (see p.278) go well with this dish.

ONE SERVING
CALORIES 230
TOTAL FAT 9g
SATURATED FAT 1g
CARBOHYDRATES 7g
ADDED SUGAR 0
FIBRE 2g
SODIUM 255mg

Tenderised by the vinegar in the poaching liquid, but holding its firm shape, skate is ideal for salads. The capers and dressing give an extra piquancy in this dish.

TIP
To remove the sticky film from the skate wings, brush them gently with a clean, soft-bristled brush, rinsing frequently under cold running water.

Lemon sole with sesame seeds

ONE SERVING
CALORIES 285
TOTAL FAT 15g
SATURATED FAT 2g
CARBOHYDRATES 7g
ADDED SUGAR 0
FIBRE 2g
SODIUM 265mg

SERVES 4
PREPARATION TIME: 15 minutes, plus 30 minutes to set
COOKING TIME: 4 minutes

3 level tablespoons plain flour
6 level tablespoons sesame seeds

2 level teaspoons Dijon mustard
2 level teaspoons tomato purée (see p.16)
½ level teaspoon dried tarragon
2fl oz (60ml) semi-skimmed milk
4 lemon sole fillets, each about 5oz (150g), skinned
1 tablespoon olive oil
Lemon slices to garnish

Feather-light fillets of grilled sole are given more substance in this dish by their savoury, crunchy coating of mustard and sesame seeds. Two colourful vegetables complete a summer treat.

1 Mix the flour and sesame seeds together thoroughly and spread the mixture evenly on a dinner plate.

2 Combine the mustard with the tomato purée on a saucer, crumble on the tarragon and mix into the paste.

3 Pour the milk onto a wide dish or plate. Dip one fillet into the milk then turn it over. Spread half a teaspoon of the mustard mixture over the upper side of the fillet then lay the fillet, spread side down, on the sesame mixture. Spread the other side of the fillet with mustard mixture and turn it over into the sesame mixture. Lift the coated fillet onto a large dish.

4 Prepare the other fillets in the same way, then cover the dish and put in the refrigerator for 30 minutes for the coating to set.

5 Line the grill pan with foil and brush the rack with olive oil. Arrange the fillets on the rack, brush lightly with oil and cook under a hot grill for 2 minutes. Turn the fillets over carefully, brush lightly with oil and grill for a further 2 minutes. Lower the heat if the sesame seeds brown too quickly. Lift the fish carefully onto a heated serving dish and garnish with the lemon slices.

Serve the sole with tomatoes and mangetout for sweet and colourful accompaniments.

Stuffed whiting

....

ONE SERVING

....

CALORIES 240

....

TOTAL FAT 7g

....

SATURATED FAT 1g

....

CARBOHYDRATES 12g

....

ADDED SUGAR 0

....

FIBRE 1g

....

SODIUM 285mg

....

TIP
To scale a fish, put it inside a large polythene bag and hold it firmly by the tail. Scrape the back of a small knife from the tail down to the head until all the scales are off.

SERVES 4
PREPARATION TIME: 15 minutes
COOKING TIME: 30 minutes
OVEN: Preheat to 200°C (400°F, gas mark 6)

1 tablespoon olive oil
2 medium onions, peeled and finely chopped
1 clove garlic, peeled and finely chopped
1½ oz (45g) fresh white breadcrumbs
2 level tablespoons chopped fresh parsley
Finely grated rind of 1 lemon
Freshly ground black pepper
4 whole whiting, each about 8oz (225g), scaled and cleaned
Wooden cocktail sticks to secure
5 tablespoons dry white wine
Sprigs of flat-leaf parsley to garnish

1 Heat the oil in a frying pan and cook half the onion in it over a moderate heat for about 5 minutes, until soft. Remove from the heat, mix in the garlic, breadcrumbs, parsley and lemon rind and season with pepper.

2 Stuff each whiting with a quarter of the mixture and seal in the stuffing by threading wooden cocktail sticks through the belly flaps.

3 Scatter half the remaining onion in a large ovenproof dish. Arrange the fish in one layer on top and scatter on the rest of the onion. Pour in the wine, then cover the dish with a lid or foil. Cook in the heated oven for 30 minutes or until the fish flakes easily when tested with a fork. Remove the cocktail sticks and garnish with the sprigs of parsley.

Mashed potatoes, browned in the oven while the fish is cooking, and runner beans go well with the whiting. If you cannot buy whole fish, use fillets and secure them round the stuffing with cocktail sticks.

The delicate, small-flaked whiting flesh, so easy to digest, gives its juices to the filling and stays moist in the white wine that lends the dish a sharp edge.

Oatmeal herrings

SERVES 4
PREPARATION TIME: 15 minutes
COOKING TIME: 15 minutes
OVEN: Preheat to 180°C (350°F, gas mark 4)

2oz (60g) cooked brown rice (see p.17)
2oz (60g) medium oatmeal
1oz (30g) finely grated Cheddar cheese
2 level teaspoons chopped or snipped fresh chives
1 small tomato, finely chopped
2 level teaspoons whole-grain mustard
2 level teaspoons quark or low-fat natural yoghurt
Freshly ground black pepper
4 herrings, each about 8oz (225g), gutted and
cleaned, heads and bones removed
Wooden cocktail sticks for securing
Sprigs of flat-leaf parsley to garnish

1 Mix the rice with half the oatmeal, the
Cheddar, chives, tomato, mustard and quark
or yoghurt to make a well-blended stuffing.
Season with pepper.

2 Wash the herrings and pat dry with kitchen
paper. Fill each with a quarter of the stuffing
and pin the edges together securely with
cocktail sticks threaded along the belly flaps.

3 Sprinkle half the remaining oatmeal into a
shallow ovenproof dish and lay the herrings on
top in a single layer. Sprinkle with the rest of
the oatmeal.

4 Cook, uncovered, in the heated oven for
about 15 minutes, until the flesh flakes easily
when tested with a fork. Lift the herrings
carefully onto warmed dinner plates, remove
the cocktail sticks and garnish with the parsley.

*In the days when the fishing fleets of Scotland and
northern England spilled out copious catches of
silvery herring, the fish were everyday fare. Now
they are less common and paradoxically more
appreciated for their succulent flesh, which is kept
moist during cooking by its own oil.*

Swede, carrot and potato purée (see p.300)
makes a traditional north-country winter
accompaniment to the herrings, and a
watercress salad adds its own peppery quality to
the robust flavours of the dish. Coleslaw
(see p.315) and bread go equally well with it.

ONE SERVING	
CALORIES	400
TOTAL FAT	27g
SATURATED FAT	8g
CARBOHYDRATES	16g
ADDED SUGAR	0
FIBRE	2g
SODIUM	195mg

Soused herrings

SERVES 4
PREPARATION TIME: 20 minutes, plus 1-2 days
to marinate
COOKING TIME: 15 minutes
OVEN: Preheat to 180°C (350°F, gas mark 4)

½ pint (285ml) cider vinegar
½ pint (285ml) water
3 juniper berries
6 cloves
¼ level teaspoon ground allspice

6 black peppercorns, lightly crushed
1 bay leaf
4 herrings, each about 8oz (225g), scaled, heads
removed, gutted and boned
4 level teaspoons English mustard powder
2 teaspoons water
2 small red onions, peeled, thinly sliced and
separated into rings
1 level tablespoon pickled capers, drained
2 small dill-pickled cucumbers, halved lengthways
Wooden cocktail sticks

ONE SERVING	
CALORIES	340
TOTAL FAT	25g
SATURATED FAT	7g
CARBOHYDRATES	4g
ADDED SUGAR	0
FIBRE	1g
SODIUM	320mg

Richly spiced and sharpened by the mustard and capers, these plump, home-pickled herrings re-create a traditional Scandinavian delicacy.

1 Bring the vinegar, water, juniper berries, cloves, allspice, peppercorns and bay leaf to the boil in a stainless steel or enamel pan, then simmer, uncovered, for 10 minutes. Set aside.

2 Rinse the herrings, pat them dry with kitchen paper and lay them, skin side down, on a board covered with greaseproof paper. Mix the mustard with the water, spread a quarter of the mixture on each fish and arrange a few onion rings and capers on top. Lay a piece of pickled cucumber across the head end of each fillet, and roll up from head to tail. Secure each roll with a cocktail stick.

3 Pack the herrings snugly into an ovenproof glass or china dish and scatter the remaining onion rings on top. Pour the spiced vinegar over the fish. Cover the dish and bake in the heated oven for about 15 minutes, or until the flesh just begins to flake when tested with the tip of a knife. Leave to cool.

4 Remove the cocktail sticks and put the covered dish of herrings in the refrigerator for 1-2 days to 'souse'.

Potato salad, crisp lamb's lettuce and tomatoes are foils for the sharp taste of the herrings.

Fisherman's mackerel

SERVES 4
PREPARATION TIME: 5 minutes
COOKING TIME: 15 minutes

8 mackerel fillets, each about 4oz (115g)
Freshly ground black pepper
2 tablespoons lemon juice
Sprigs of fresh dill and lemon wedges to garnish

1 Rinse the mackerel and pat dry with kitchen paper. Season on both sides with pepper.

2 Line the grill pan with foil. Arrange the opened mackerel skin side down on the grill rack. Grill under a moderate heat without turning for 10-15 minutes, according to their thickness. The flesh should flake easily and be very slightly browned; do not overcook or the fish will be dry.

3 Turn the mackerel over one by one onto a warmed plate, peel off the skins, then arrange them, grilled side up, on a warmed serving dish and sprinkle with the lemon juice. Garnish with the sprigs of dill and lemon wedges.

Ratatouille (see p.246) and light rye bread go well with the full-flavoured fish.

ONE SERVING	
CALORIES	335
TOTAL FAT	27g
SATURATED FAT	5g
CARBOHYDRATES	0
ADDED SUGAR	0
FIBRE	0
SODIUM	215mg

Fresh mackerel fillets are often overlooked in favour of smoked – a pity, since they are quick to cook and satisfyingly rich to eat because of the oils they contain.

Mackerel with hot sour sauce

SERVES 4
PREPARATION TIME: 20 minutes
COOKING TIME: 15 minutes

1½ tablespoons olive oil
2 level teaspoons peeled and grated root ginger
1 clove garlic, peeled and crushed
1 shallot, peeled and finely chopped
1 medium carrot, peeled and cut into strips
4 miniature sweetcorn cobs, trimmed and sliced
1oz (30g) mangetout, trimmed and sliced diagonally
3 level tablespoons cornflour
7fl oz (200ml) red wine vinegar
2 tablespoons clear honey

1 tablespoon soy sauce
4 mackerel, each about 7oz (200g), gutted, cleaned and heads removed
Fresh dill fronds to garnish

ONE SERVING

CALORIES 455

TOTAL FAT 31g

SATURATED FAT 6g

CARBOHYDRATES 18g

ADDED SUGAR 8g

FIBRE 1g

SODIUM 440mg

1 Heat 1 tablespoon of the oil in a saucepan and cook the ginger, garlic and shallot in it gently for 1 minute, stirring occasionally. Mix in the carrot, sweetcorn and mangetout and cook for 2 minutes, then set aside.

2 Blend 1 tablespoon of the cornflour with the vinegar, then stir in the honey and soy sauce.

3 Wash and dry the mackerel. Brush them with the rest of the oil and dust with the remaining cornflour. Slash them in three or four places on both sides.

4 Line the grill pan with foil and place the mackerel on the rack. Cook for 5-6 minutes on each side under a hot grill, until the skin is crisp and brown and the flesh just firm. If the skin browns too quickly, lower the heat.

5 Meanwhile, stir the vinegar mixture into the vegetables in the saucepan and bring to the boil, stirring continuously. Reduce the heat and cook for 1 minute. Lift the mackerel onto heated individual serving plates, spoon the sauce round and garnish with dill. Leave the diners to remove the skin for themselves.

The sauce gives the mackerel the taste of the East, and Chinese noodles sprinkled with spring onion make an authentic accompaniment.

Red mullet with leeks and tomatoes

ONE SERVING

CALORIES 205

TOTAL FAT 6g

SATURATED FAT 1g

CARBOHYDRATES 3g

ADDED SUGAR 0

FIBRE 2g

SODIUM 220mg

SERVES 6
PREPARATION TIME: 25 minutes, plus 30 minutes to marinate
COOKING TIME: 15 minutes

2 tablespoons olive oil
1 level tablespoon finely chopped fresh rosemary

Freshly ground black pepper
6 large whole fresh red mullet (or frozen mullet, thawed), each about 10oz (275g), scaled and gutted
3 small leeks, trimmed, thinly sliced and washed
3 large tomatoes, skinned, de-seeded and chopped
Lemon wedges and fresh rosemary sprigs to garnish

1 Smear a large dish with 1 tablespoon of the oil, sprinkle in the chopped rosemary and season with pepper. Rinse the mullet, pat dry with kitchen paper and arrange them in the dish in one layer. Turn them until evenly coated with rosemary. Cover and leave to marinate at room temperature for 30 minutes.

2 Meanwhile, heat the remaining olive oil in a frying pan, and cook the leeks over a moderate heat for 6-8 minutes, stirring frequently, until softened. Stir in the tomatoes and bring to the boil. Boil rapidly for 2-3 minutes to evaporate the excess liquid. Leave to cool.

3 Spoon the leek and tomato mixture inside the mullet but do not overfill them. Oil the grill rack, lay the fish on it and cook under a moderate heat for 8-9 minutes. Turn them over carefully and cook for a further 5-6 minutes.

4 Lift the fish onto warmed plates and garnish with the lemon wedges and rosemary sprigs.

Warm french bread and lightly steamed mangetout go well with the fish. When the mullet are small, as they often are, allow two fish for each person.

Simply cooked with herbs and a moist filling, red mullet is a gourmet's delight. Beneath the vivid skin, the flesh is white and delicate in texture, but the flavour is surprisingly full. Choose large fish when you can, to get correspondingly bigger pieces of flesh among the plentiful bones.

Salmon with cucumber and dill sauce

ONE SERVING	
CALORIES	245
TOTAL FAT	15g
SATURATED FAT	3g
CARBOHYDRATES	3g
ADDED SUGAR	0
FIBRE	0
SODIUM	165mg

SERVES 6
PREPARATION TIME: 10 minutes
COOKING TIME: 25 minutes
OVEN: Preheat to 180°C (350°F, gas mark 4)

2lb (900g) middle-cut or tail-end salmon
in one piece
1 small cucumber, peeled, de-seeded and diced
4oz (115g) low-fat natural yoghurt

2 level teaspoons coarsely chopped fresh
dill, or ½ teaspoon dill seeds
1 teaspoon skimmed milk or water
½ level teaspoon made English mustard
Freshly ground white or black pepper
Thinly sliced cucumber and chopped fresh dill
to garnish

1 Lay the salmon in a baking dish lined with a large piece of foil. Pour in cold water to a depth of about ½ in (13mm), then bring all the sides of the foil together to enclose the salmon and water. Cook in the heated oven for about 25 minutes, or until the salmon is opaque and flakes easily.

2 Meanwhile, combine the diced cucumber, yoghurt, chopped dill or dill seeds, milk or water and mustard, and season with pepper. Cover the sauce and put in the refrigerator.

3 Unwrap the salmon, lift it carefully onto a serving plate and remove the skin. Cut into the fish horizontally along the sides as far as the spine, and lift off the upper part of the flesh. Remove the bones and replace the flesh.

Garnish the salmon with cucumber slices and dill, and serve it warm or cold with the sauce. New potatoes or wholemeal bread, and a leafy salad are simple foils for this summer treat.

Dill gives the sauce a warm, sweet taste similar to caraway. Combined with the freshness of cucumber, it makes a perfect complement to the rich salmon.

Salmon fish cakes

ONE SERVING	
CALORIES	360
TOTAL FAT	17g
SATURATED FAT	3g
CARBOHYDRATES	29g
ADDED SUGAR	0
FIBRE	3g
SODIUM	240mg

SERVES 4
PREPARATION TIME: 30 minutes
COOKING TIME: 10 minutes

11oz (300g) potatoes, peeled
12oz (340g) salmon steaks
2 level tablespoons low-fat natural yoghurt
1 beaten egg, size 2
1 medium carrot, peeled and finely grated

1 large onion, peeled and finely chopped
½ level teaspoon paprika
1 teaspoon lemon juice
2oz (60g) fine wholemeal breadcrumbs
1½ tablespoons corn oil
Lemon wedges and chervil sprigs to garnish

1 Put the potatoes in boiling water and cook for 8-10 minutes, until tender.

TIP
*To make
the salmon cakes
easier to shape
and coat, prepare
the mixture early
and put it in the
refrigerator for an
hour to chill.*

2 Meanwhile, line the grill pan with foil, lay the salmon steaks on the rack and grill for 2-3 minutes on each side, until opaque all through. Skin and bone the steaks and flake the flesh.

3 Mash the potatoes without milk or fat. Turn them into a bowl and mix in the salmon, yoghurt, egg, carrot, onion, paprika and lemon juice. Divide the mixture into eight and shape each piece into a flat cake.

4 Spread the crumbs on a plate and lay two or three cakes at a time on it. Use a spoon and palette knife to press crumbs gently onto the top and sides of the cakes.

5 Heat the oil in a large nonstick frying pan and fry the fish cakes in it over a moderate heat for 3 minutes on each side, until golden brown.

Serve the salmon fish cakes garnished with the lemon wedges and chervil. A mixed leafy salad makes a fittingly crisp accompaniment. Instead of making the cakes with salmon, you can use 7oz (200g) of tinned tuna, drained of oil.

Soft pink salmon inside a crust of crisp golden crumbs makes fish cakes that are the focus of a filling meal. Although substantial, the cakes are surprisingly light and go well with salads.

Grating horseradish for the sauce may bring tears to your eyes, but it gives an unmistakable piquancy to this simple dish of grilled salmon.

Grilled salmon with horseradish sauce

ONE SERVING

CALORIES 270

TOTAL FAT 18g

SATURATED FAT 4g

CARBOHYDRATES 4g

ADDED SUGAR 0

FIBRE 0

SODIUM 160mg

SERVES 4
PREPARATION TIME: 5 minutes
COOKING TIME: 5 minutes

5oz (150g) Greek yoghurt
5oz (150g) low-fat natural yoghurt
3 spring onions, trimmed and chopped
10 radishes, washed and chopped
3 level tablespoons freshly grated horseradish
½ level teaspoon ground cumin
Freshly ground black pepper
1 tablespoon olive oil
4 salmon steaks, each about 4oz (115g)
1 tablespoon lemon juice

1 To make the sauce, mix the yoghurts, onions, radishes, horseradish, cumin and pepper in a bowl. Cover and refrigerate.

2 Line the grill pan with foil, oil the rack and heat the grill. Rinse and dry the salmon and lay on the rack. Mix the remaining oil with the lemon juice, season with pepper and trickle half the mixture over the steaks. Cook under a medium grill for 2-3 minutes, until lightly browned. Turn the steaks over, trickle the remaining oil mixture over them and grill for a further 2-3 minutes, or until the steaks are opaque right through the centre.

Serve the salmon on warmed plates with a spoonful of the chilled sauce beside each steak. Saffron-tinted rice and steamed courgettes are perfect foils for the rich salmon. If you cannot find fresh horseradish, use 1 level tablespoon of Dijon mustard in the sauce instead, but it will have less character.

Lemon-marinated sardines

SERVES 4
PREPARATION TIME: 20 minutes,
plus 30 minutes to marinate
COOKING TIME: 8 minutes

1 tablespoon olive oil
Juice of 1 lemon
1 clove garlic, peeled and crushed
2 level tablespoons chopped fresh parsley
Freshly ground black pepper
2lb (900g) fresh sardines, scaled and gutted,
washed and dried with kitchen paper
Lemon wedges and parsley sprigs to garnish

1 Mix the oil, lemon juice, garlic and chopped parsley in a wide dish and season with pepper. Turn the fish in the mixture until coated, then cover and leave to marinate for 30 minutes.

2 Line the grill pan with foil and lay the fish on the rack. Cook under a hot grill for about 8 minutes, turning once. Baste frequently with the marinade. Lift the fish carefully onto a warmed serving dish, pour on the juices and garnish with lemon wedges and parsley sprigs.

Serve with spinach and rice cakes (see p.299).

ONE SERVING

CALORIES 220

TOTAL FAT 12g

SATURATED FAT 2g

CARBOHYDRATES 0

ADDED SUGAR 0

FIBRE 0

SODIUM 135mg

Fresh sardines are popular in many southern European countries, where they are usually grilled or barbecued. In this recipe, a marinade containing plenty of lemon juice balances the richness of the fish.

Gingered swordfish steaks

SERVES 4
PREPARATION TIME: 10 minutes, plus 2 hours
to marinate
COOKING TIME: 6 minutes

2½ tablespoons olive oil
1 level teaspoon grated lemon rind
2 tablespoons lemon juice
1 tablespoon dry sherry or water
2 teaspoons light soy sauce
2 cloves garlic, peeled and crushed
2 level teaspoons peeled and grated root ginger,
or ¼ level teaspoon ground ginger
Freshly ground black pepper
4 swordfish steaks, about 4oz (115g) each

ONE SERVING

CALORIES 190

TOTAL FAT 12g

SATURATED FAT 2g

CARBOHYDRATES 0

ADDED SUGAR 0

FIBRE 0

SODIUM 250mg

1 Make the marinade by mixing 2 tablespoons of the oil, the lemon rind and juice, sherry or water, soy sauce, garlic and ginger in a bowl. Season with pepper.

2 Lay the swordfish steaks in a dish in a single layer. Pour the marinade over the steaks and turn them to coat well. Cover and put in the refrigerator for 2 hours to marinate.

3 Heat the remaining oil in a frying pan. Lift the swordfish steaks out of the marinade and fry them over a moderate heat for 3 minutes on each side. Put the fish on a heated serving dish and pour on the cooking juices.

A salad of apple and lettuce balances the fish's fieriness, and warm rolls mop up the juices. You can cook tuna steaks in the same way.

The marinade tenderises the close-textured swordfish and gives its strong flavour a sharp, hot edge. Since the flesh is so firm, the marinated steaks are suitable for cooking on a barbecue.

TIP
Swordfish is a very firm, meaty fish that does not flake easily. It is cooked sufficiently when the flesh feels springy to the touch.

Trout in herb and wine jelly

SERVES 4
PREPARATION TIME: 45 minutes, plus
at least 4 hours to set and chill
COOKING TIME: 10 minutes

1 pint (570ml) fish stock (see p.19)
4fl oz (115ml) dry white wine
3 tablespoons white wine vinegar
1 large shallot, peeled and finely chopped
½ level teaspoon coarsely ground pink peppercorns
3 tablespoons cold water
1 level tablespoon powdered gelatine
2 rainbow trout, each about 8oz (225g), gutted and cleaned
1 smoked trout, about 9oz (250g), skin and all bones removed
2 level tablespoons each chopped fresh parsley, tarragon and chervil
Flat-leaf parsley sprigs to garnish

1 Pour the stock, wine and vinegar into a large stainless steel or enamel saucepan with the shallot and peppercorns, and bring to the boil. Boil rapidly for 10-15 minutes until the liquid is reduced to 8fl oz (225ml). Take off the heat.

2 Pour the water into a small saucepan and sprinkle on the gelatine. Leave for 5 minutes to swell, then heat very gently to dissolve. Pour a little of the fish-stock mixture onto the gelatine and mix well, then stir this liquid into the bulk of the stock. Leave to cool.

3 Line the grill pan with foil, lay the fresh trout on the rack and cook them under a high heat for about 4 minutes on each side, until the flesh turns opaque and flakes easily when tested with a fork. Leave to cool, then remove the skin and all bones.

4 Flake the fresh trout and the smoked trout into a bowl and gently fold in the parsley, tarragon and chervil. Stir in the cooled stock and pour the mixture into a nonstick loaf tin 7½ × 3½ in (19×9cm). Cover and chill for at least 4 hours until well set.

5 Dip the loaf tin into hot water for 10 seconds, or wrap it in a hot cloth, to loosen the jellied trout from the sides. Turn it out onto a serving dish, cut it into eight slices and garnish it with the parsley sprigs.

Serve new potatoes and asparagus with the trout, or have it with marinated carrots (see p.312) and thinly sliced wholemeal bread.

ONE SERVING	
CALORIES	180
TOTAL FAT	5g
SATURATED FAT	1g
CARBOHYDRATES	1g
ADDED SUGAR	0
FIBRE	0
SODIUM	140mg

A combination of wine and herbs complements the subtle flavour of the trout to create an elegantly marbled summer dish. Pink peppercorns and smoked trout give it extra colour and zest.

Trout with orange and mint stuffing

SERVES 4
PREPARATION TIME: 20 minutes
COOKING TIME: 30 minutes
OVEN: Preheat to 180°C (350°F, gas mark 4)

2oz (60g) wholemeal breadcrumbs
Finely grated rind of ½ orange
1 small stick celery, trimmed and finely chopped
½ small dessert apple, peeled, cored and diced
3 level teaspoons chopped fresh mint
About 1 tablespoon fromage frais
Freshly ground black pepper
4 rainbow trout, each about 8oz (225g), gutted,
cleaned, heads removed, washed and dried
Wooden cocktail sticks to secure
Juice of 1 lemon
Juice of 1 large orange
About ¼ pint (150ml) dry vermouth
1 clove garlic, peeled and crushed
1 shallot, peeled and finely chopped
1 tablespoon chopped fresh parsley
Orange slices and sprigs of fresh mint to garnish

1 Mix the breadcrumbs, orange rind, celery, apple and 1 teaspoon of the mint in a bowl. Stir in enough fromage frais to make a moist, crumbly stuffing. Season with pepper.

2 Fill the cavity in each trout with stuffing and secure with cocktail sticks. Lay the trout in a shallow ovenproof dish.

3 Strain the lemon and orange juice into a measuring jug and make up to ½ pint (285ml) with the vermouth. Stir in the garlic, shallot, chopped parsley and remaining mint.

4 Pour the mixture over the trout. Cover and cook in the heated oven for about 30 minutes, or until the flesh is opaque and flakes easily when tested with a fork.

5 Lift the fish onto a warm serving dish and remove the cocktail sticks. Pour the cooking liquid into a small pan and boil rapidly until reduced to a cupful. Pour it round the trout and garnish with orange slices and mint sprigs.

Serve new potatoes and a watercress salad with the fish. Leave the diners to remove the trout skin for themselves.

ONE SERVING	
CALORIES	240
TOTAL FAT	6g
SATURATED FAT	1g
CARBOHYDRATES	17g
ADDED SUGAR	0
FIBRE	2g
SODIUM	230mg

TIP
To remove the skin from cooked trout, make a cut right along the back of the fish, lift a corner of the skin at the head end and peel the skin back to the tail.

The tangy, crunchy stuffing and lively vermouth sauce make this colourful fish dish particularly suitable for serving at any special occasion.

Exploit the versatility of tinned tuna by combining it with Indian spices and a mixture of juicy fruits to create this refreshing summer dish.

Curried tuna and fruit

SERVES 4
PREPARATION TIME: 20 minutes, plus 1 hour to chill

4oz (115g) low-fat natural yoghurt
1 level tablespoon mild curry powder
¼ level teaspoon each ground cumin, ground
cardamom and coriander
14oz (400g) tinned tuna, drained of oil, flaked
1 large orange, peel and pith pared off, segments
cut free of membranes and each divided into three
5oz (150g) fresh pineapple, cut into chunks
3oz (85g) each red and green seedless grapes, halved
4oz (115g) water chestnuts, sliced
12 cos lettuce leaves, washed and dried

ONE SERVING

CALORIES 290

TOTAL FAT 10g

SATURATED FAT 2g

CARBOHYDRATES 22g

ADDED SUGAR 0

FIBRE 3g

SODIUM 340mg

1 Mix the yoghurt, curry powder, cumin, cardamom and coriander in a large bowl.

2 Gently mix in the tuna, orange, pineapple, grapes and water chestnuts until coated with dressing. Chill in the refrigerator for 1 hour.

3 Arrange the lettuce leaves on individual plates and spoon the tuna and fruit on top.

Serve with crusty rolls or brown rice dressed with lemon juice. You may prefer to peel the grapes and use well-drained unsweetened tinned pineapple in place of fresh.

Devilled crab

SERVES 4
PREPARATION TIME: 30 minutes
COOKING TIME: 15 minutes

1oz (30g) polyunsaturated margarine
3 medium spring onions, trimmed and
finely chopped
1 medium stick celery, trimmed and finely chopped
1 level tablespoon plain flour
¼ pint (150ml) skimmed milk
1 level teaspoon Dijon mustard
1 teaspoon lemon juice
¼ level teaspoon cayenne pepper
1lb (450g) cooked fresh crabmeat, white and
brown, roughly chopped
1 level tablespoon chopped fresh parsley
4 level tablespoons dry breadcrumbs

1 Melt half the margarine in a saucepan and
cook the spring onions and celery in it over a
moderate heat for about 5 minutes, until they
are just beginning to soften but not browned.
Blend in the flour and cook for 1 minute.
Gradually stir in the milk and bring to the boil,
stirring continuously, until the sauce is thick
and smooth. Simmer for 2 minutes.

2 Remove the sauce from the heat and
blend in the mustard, lemon juice and cayenne
pepper. Stir in the crabmeat and parsley, and
reheat the sauce to simmering point.

3 Melt the remaining margarine in a small
saucepan without letting it colour, and stir in
the breadcrumbs.

4 Divide the crab mixture between four
scallop shells or individual gratin dishes.
Sprinkle a quarter of the butter and crumb
mixture over the top of each.

5 Cook under a hot grill for 3-4 minutes,
until bubbling hot and golden brown on top,
and serve immediately.

The crunchy vegetables and breadcrumb topping
offer a contrast in texture to the soft crabmeat,
while the parsley and spices add a peppery spark.

A pasta salad or crusty bread and a leafy salad
will go well with this dish. In place of the fresh
crab you can use tinned crab, well drained, or
frozen crabmeat completely thawed.

ONE SERVING	
CALORIES	235
TOTAL FAT	8g
SATURATED FAT	1g
CARBOHYDRATES	10g
ADDED SUGAR	0
FIBRE	0
SODIUM	610mg

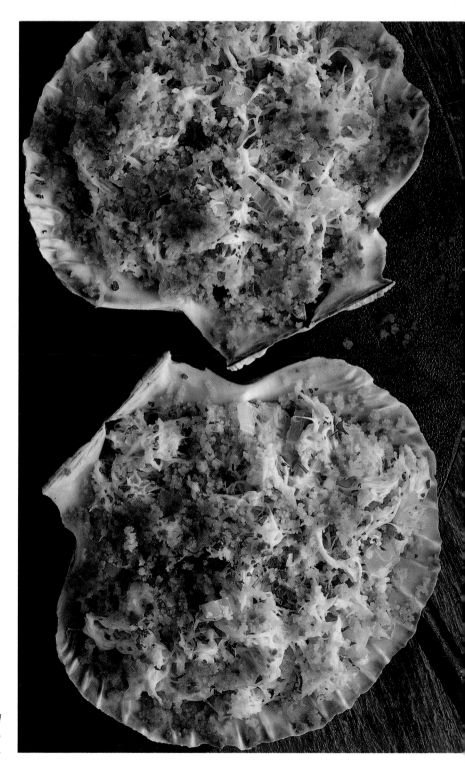

Souffléed Brixham crab

SERVES 4
PREPARATION TIME: 15 minutes
COOKING TIME: 20 minutes
OVEN: Preheat to 190°C (375°F, gas mark 5)

1oz (30g) slightly salted butter
4 level tablespoons dried breadcrumbs
1oz (30g) plain flour
¼ pint (150ml) skimmed milk
¼ pint (150ml) fish stock (see p.19)
Juice and finely grated rind of ½ small lemon
¼ teaspoon anchovy essence
1½ level teaspoons paprika
8oz (225g) fresh crabmeat, chopped
4 egg whites, size 2

1 Lightly butter four gratin dishes 6in (15cm) in diameter and sprinkle with the breadcrumbs.

2 Melt the remaining butter in a saucepan, stir in the flour and gradually blend in the milk and stock. Bring to the boil, stirring, then simmer for 2 minutes. Mix in the lemon juice and rind, anchovy essence, paprika and crabmeat.

3 Whisk the egg whites until they hold soft peaks. Using a metal spoon, fold the whites gently into the crab sauce and divide the mixture between the prepared dishes.

4 Bake in the heated oven for 20 minutes, until well risen but still creamy in the centre.

Warm rolls and a mixed bean salad (see p.309) make satisfying accompaniments. You can use frozen and thawed crab in place of fresh, and use one wide, shallow dish if you prefer.

ONE SERVING	
CALORIES	200
TOTAL FAT	7g
SATURATED FAT	4g
CARBOHYDRATES	14g
ADDED SUGAR	0
FIBRE	0
SODIUM	450mg

TIP
When preparing a fresh crab, use a long skewer or a clean knitting needle to get all the meat out of the claws and crevices.

The sea around Devon abounds with crabs, and some of the largest are landed at Brixham. In this dish, crabmeat sits in a buttery crumb coating and is swathed in a fluffy sauce.

Spiced prawns

SERVES 4
PREPARATION TIME: 20 minutes, plus 4 hours
to refrigerate
COOKING TIME: 10 minutes

2 tablespoons olive oil
1½ lb (680g) frozen, uncooked freshwater prawns,
thawed, peeled and de-veined
2 spring onions, trimmed, green part finely sliced,
white part chopped
2 level teaspoons peeled and grated root ginger,
or ¼ level teaspoon ground ginger
¼ pint (150ml) fish stock (see p.19)
2 tablespoons tomato purée (see p.16)
2 tablespoons dry sherry
2 tablespoons cider vinegar
¼ level teaspoon cayenne pepper
8 cos lettuce leaves, washed and patted dry

ONE SERVING

CALORIES 140

TOTAL FAT 8g

SATURATED FAT 1g

CARBOHYDRATES 1g

ADDED SUGAR 0

FIBRE 0

SODIUM 175mg

1 Heat half the oil in a frying pan and stir-fry the prawns in it over a moderate heat for 2 minutes. Spoon into a dish.

2 Heat the remaining oil in the pan, and stir-fry the white onion and ginger for 30 seconds. Stir in the stock, tomato purée, sherry, vinegar and cayenne pepper. Simmer for 3 minutes.

3 Return the prawns to the pan and cook for 3 minutes, stirring. Add half the green onion and pour the prawns and sauce into a bowl. Cool, then cover and refrigerate for 4 hours.

4 Arrange the lettuce on four plates, spoon in the prawns and scatter on the remaining onion.

Serve with brown rice and lamb's lettuce. You can use cooked and peeled North Atlantic prawns but their salt content is much higher.

Crisp lettuce leaves hold cool prawns, but in the sherry sauce there are sparks of fire, given by ginger and cayenne pepper.

Scallops with creamed celeriac

SERVES 4
PREPARATION TIME: 20 minutes
COOKING TIME: 25 minutes

1¹/₂ lb (680g) celeriac, peeled and grated
14oz (400g) potatoes, peeled and diced
Freshly ground black pepper
15 bay leaves
1 level tablespoon peeled and grated root ginger
16 fresh scallops, washed and wiped
¹/₂ oz (15g) slightly salted butter
1 tablespoon lemon juice
Fresh dill fronds and lemon rind to garnish

1 Cook the celeriac and potatoes in a steamer for about 15 minutes, or until they are tender, then pass them through a vegetable mill or sieve into a heatproof bowl. Thin the mixture with a little of the cooking water if necessary, and beat with a fork to make a fluffy purée.

Season well with pepper. Cover the bowl and stand it over a saucepan of hot water.

2 Line the steamer with the bay leaves, sprinkle on the grated ginger and lay the scallops on top. Cover and steam for 6-7 minutes, until the scallops turn opaque and are tender when pierced with a fork.

3 Melt the butter in a saucepan and stir in the lemon juice. Spoon the potato and celeriac purée neatly onto four warmed plates and arrange the scallops beside it. Pour the lemon butter over the scallops, sprinkle with pepper and garnish with the dill and lemon rind.

Serve immediately with lightly cooked fine green beans or a green salad. You can vary the dish by using large raw prawns or cubes of halibut in place of the scallops.

ONE SERVING	
CALORIES	245
TOTAL FAT	5g
SATURATED FAT	2g
CARBOHYDRATES	18g
ADDED SUGAR	0
FIBRE	6g
SODIUM	390mg

Lightly steamed scallops have a tender flesh, well matched by a light vegetable purée which is given a mildly peppery flavour here by the celeriac. The orange corals of the scallops add colour to the dish.

Stir-fried squid and vegetables

ONE SERVING	
CALORIES	195
TOTAL FAT	5g
SATURATED FAT	1g
CARBOHYDRATES	6g
ADDED SUGAR	0
FIBRE	2g
SODIUM	790mg

SERVES 4
PREPARATION TIME: 30 minutes
COOKING TIME: 5 minutes

3 medium squid, each about 6oz (175g), cleaned, tentacle cluster left whole, body cut into thin rings
1 egg white, size 4

2 level teaspoons cornflour
2 tablespoons olive oil
4fl oz (115ml) fish stock (see p.19) or water
6oz (175g) broccoli florets
1 clove garlic, peeled and finely chopped
2 level teaspoons peeled and grated root ginger,
or ¹/₄ teaspoon ground ginger

1 level teaspoon finely chopped clementine or orange rind
2 tablespoons dry sherry
1 level tablespoon black-bean sauce
1 level tablespoon oyster sauce
6oz (175g) mangetout, trimmed and sliced
4oz (115g) peeled prawns

1 Mix the squid with the egg white and half the cornflour.

2 Heat half the oil in a wok until very hot and stir-fry the squid in it for about 1 minute, until opaque. Spoon into a warmed dish.

3 Keep 1 teaspoon of the fish stock or water and bring the rest to the boil in a small saucepan. Cook the broccoli in it for 1 minute. Drain thoroughly, reserving the liquid.

4 Heat the remaining oil in the wok and stir-fry the garlic, ginger and clementine or orange rind for about 30 seconds. Stir in the reserved cooking liquid, the sherry, black-bean sauce and oyster sauce and bring to the boil. Mix the remaining cornflour with the reserved teaspoon of stock or water and blend it into the wok. Cook, stirring, until thickened.

5 Return the squid to the wok and add the broccoli, mangetout and prawns. Cook, stirring, for 1-2 minutes until all the ingredients are hot, and serve at once.

Steamed white rice is the best companion for the dish, and a light side salad of cucumber and tomatoes is refreshing. Instead of cleaning and preparing the squid, you can buy 12oz (340g) of prepared squid rings from a fishmonger.

Oriental-style batter makes the squid crisp but not heavy, and oyster sauce intensifies the seafood's flavour in this colourful dish.

115

Seafood gumbo

SERVES 6
PREPARATION TIME: 20 minutes
COOKING TIME: 1 hour 15 minutes

ONE SERVING

CALORIES 305

TOTAL FAT 7g

SATURATED FAT 1g

CARBOHYDRATES 35g

ADDED SUGAR 0

FIBRE 3g

SODIUM 490mg

2 tablespoons olive oil
2 medium onions, peeled and chopped
1 clove garlic, peeled and crushed
1 small green pepper, de-seeded and chopped
1 stick celery, trimmed and chopped
2 level tablespoons plain flour
1¼ pints (725ml) fish stock (see p.19)
14oz (400g) tinned chopped tomatoes

3oz (85g) cooked ham, chopped
1 bay leaf
¼ teaspoon Tabasco
8oz (225g) fresh okra, trimmed and sliced
6oz (175g) long-grain rice
8oz (225g) raw freshwater prawns, peeled
and de-veined
8oz (225g) fresh white crabmeat, chopped
12 fresh oysters, shelled

1 Heat the oil in a heavy, flameproof casserole
and cook the onions in it over a moderate heat
for 5 minutes. Mix in the garlic, pepper and
celery and cook, stirring often, for 5 minutes.

2 Sprinkle on the flour and cook, stirring, for
1 minute. Stir in the stock, tomatoes, ham, bay
leaf and Tabasco. Bring to the boil, partially
cover and simmer for 30 minutes. Add the okra
and cook, covered, for another 30 minutes.

3 Meanwhile, cook the rice (see p.17).

4 Stir the prawns and crabmeat into the
gumbo and cook for about 2 minutes until the
prawns are pink. Add the oysters and cook for
1 minute more. Remove the bay leaf.

Ladle the gumbo into bowls, and give each one
a serving of the rice. You can use frozen okra if
fresh okra is not available.

*Gumbo is another name for okra pods, whose sticky
juice thickens this Caribbean fish stew.*

Californian seafood stew

ONE SERVING

CALORIES 235

TOTAL FAT 6g

SATURATED FAT 1g

CARBOHYDRATES 8g

ADDED SUGAR 0

FIBRE 2g

SODIUM 320mg

SERVES 4
PREPARATION TIME: 15 minutes
COOKING TIME: 55 minutes

1 tablespoon olive oil
1 large onion, peeled and chopped
3 cloves garlic, peeled and crushed
1 green pepper, de-seeded and cut into strips
¼ pint (150ml) water
14oz (400g) tinned chopped tomatoes
½ pint (285ml) fish or vegetable stock (see p.19)
3½ fl oz (100ml) dry white wine

½ level teaspoon mild chilli powder
½ level teaspoon each dried oregano, thyme
and marjoram
1 bay leaf
16 fresh mussels, well scrubbed and scraped clean
8oz (225g) haddock, skinned, boned and
cut into cubes
5oz (150g) fresh scallops, cleaned
8oz (225g) raw freshwater prawns, peeled
and de-veined
8 large unpeeled cooked prawns to garnish
2 level tablespoons chopped fresh parsley to garnish

1   Heat the oil in a large, heavy-based saucepan. Stir in the onion, garlic, pepper and 2 tablespoons of the water and cook over a moderate heat for about 7 minutes, stirring frequently, until the onion begins to colour.

2   Add the tomatoes, remaining water, stock, wine, chilli powder, dried herbs and bay leaf. Cover and simmer for 45 minutes.

3   Put in the mussels and simmer for 1 minute. Mix in the haddock, scallops and raw prawns.

Cook over a low heat for 3-5 minutes, until the mussels have opened. Discard the bay leaf and garnish the stew with the unpeeled prawns and chopped parsley before taking to the table.

Serve this hearty stew in bowls with plenty of crusty bread to soak up the juices. A cucumber salad afterwards refreshes the palate. You can use cod or halibut in place of the haddock, and frozen rather than fresh peeled prawns; these need only be rinsed, not thawed, before being put in the stew.

TIP
When scrubbing mussels, tap the shells and discard any mussels that do not immediately close. After cooking, discard any that have not opened.

Tomatoes and wine, spiked with chilli powder and herbs, produce a rich broth in which fruits of the sea are poached to make a vivid, savoury stew.

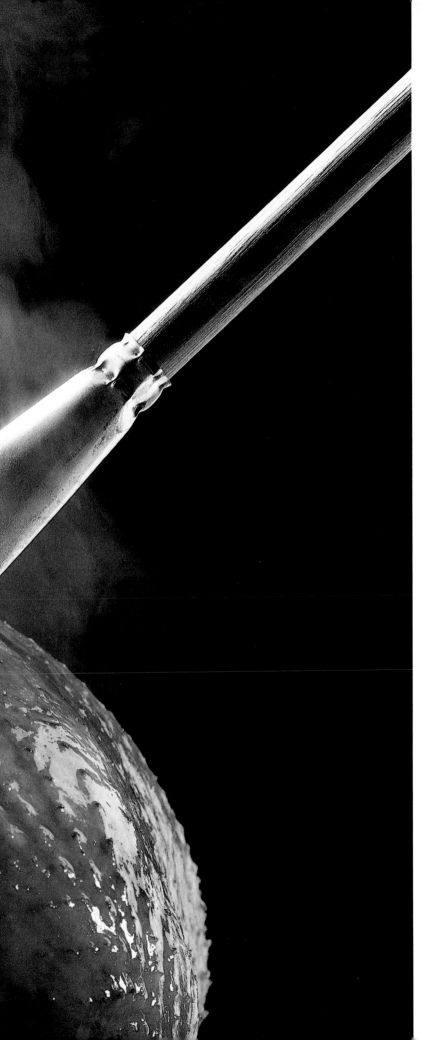

POULTRY AND GAME

Chicken and turkey are ever popular at the table and need never be predictable. Exploit their versatility and make simple burgers or sweet and sour apricot chicken, homely stews or exotic dishes from other continents. Poultry gives you meat as high in protein as red meat but lower in fat – if you remember to take off the skin. Game, too, can be low in fat, so there are tempting recipes for dainty quail, plump pigeons and full-flavoured venison.

American captain's chicken

SERVES 4
PREPARATION TIME: 15 minutes
COOKING TIME: 50 minutes

ONE SERVING	
CALORIES 305	
TOTAL FAT 14g	
SATURATED FAT 3g	
CARBOHYDRATES 10g	
ADDED SUGAR 0	
FIBRE 3g	
SODIUM 180mg	

1 tablespoon olive oil
3lb (1.4kg) chicken, cut into 8 pieces, 4 breast pieces, 2 thighs and 2 drumsticks
1 medium onion, peeled and chopped
1 medium green pepper, de-seeded and chopped
1 clove garlic, peeled and crushed
1 level tablespoon curry powder
14oz (400g) tinned chopped tomatoes
1 teaspoon lemon juice

½ level teaspoon dried thyme
Freshly ground black pepper
2 level tablespoons sultanas
1oz (30g) blanched almonds, cut into slivers

1 Heat the oil in a large frying pan and cook the chicken joints in it over a high heat for 5 minutes, turning them to brown all over. Lift the joints onto a plate lined with kitchen paper.

2 Gently fry the onion, green pepper, garlic and curry powder in the pan for 5 minutes, stirring often, until the onion softens. Stir in the tomatoes, lemon juice and thyme, season with pepper and simmer for 10 minutes.

3 Put the chicken pieces back in the pan and cook, covered, for 25 minutes, or until cooked all through and tender. Stir in the sultanas and cook for 5 minutes more, uncovered. Arrange the chicken on a warmed serving dish, pour the sauce round and scatter on the almonds.

Fluffy white rice is the right base for the sweet and spicy chicken. Give each diner a breast piece and a leg piece and leave them to remove the skin for themselves. Offer a refreshing spinach and orange salad (see p.330) separately.

This curried chicken sweetened with sultanas is reputed to have been the favourite dish of an American sea captain of long ago. He is credited with having introduced it to the southern states.

Chicken biriani

SERVES 4
PREPARATION TIME: 20 minutes
COOKING TIME: 55 minutes
OVEN: Preheat to 180°C (350°F, gas mark 4)

ONE SERVING	
CALORIES 520	
TOTAL FAT 16g	
SATURATED FAT 3g	
CARBOHYDRATES 54g	
ADDED SUGAR 0	
FIBRE 2g	
SODIUM 135mg	

6oz (175g) long-grain rice
5 cloves garlic, peeled, 3 of them crushed
1 cinnamon stick
1 bay leaf
1 small onion, peeled and chopped
1 tablespoon lemon juice

1 level tablespoon peeled and grated root ginger, or ½ level teaspoon ground ginger
½ level teaspoon each ground cumin, coriander and turmeric
¼ level teaspoon each ground cinnamon, cloves, cardamom and black pepper
8oz (225g) low-fat natural yoghurt
1lb (450g) skinned cooked chicken, cut into cubes
2oz (60g) sultanas
2oz (60g) blanched almonds, lightly toasted

1 Cook the rice in unsalted, simmering water with the whole garlic cloves, the cinnamon stick and the bay leaf for about 12 minutes, leaving the grains still slightly hard at the centre. Rinse with cold water, drain well and discard the garlic, cinnamon and bay leaf.

In India, biriani is an elaborate dish that is often served on grand occasions. The rice is an integral part, finishing its cooking on top of the meat, where it becomes fluffy and absorbs the perfumes of the spices.

2 Meanwhile, blend the onion, lemon juice, ginger, cumin, coriander, turmeric, ground cinnamon, cloves, cardamom, pepper and crushed garlic into the yoghurt. Use a food processor or beat with a wire whisk.

3 Put the chicken into a large bowl, pour on the yoghurt mixture and stir until all the meat is evenly coated.

4 Turn the chicken mixture into a shallow casserole, spoon the rice evenly on top, cover and bake in the heated oven for 35 minutes, or until the rice is completely cooked.

5 Meanwhile, cover the sultanas with cold water in a small saucepan and bring to the boil. Boil for 1 minute, then drain and keep warm.

6 When the rice is cooked, mix the rice and chicken and spoon onto a heated serving dish. Sprinkle with the sultanas and almonds.

Serve a salad of tomatoes and onion rings with the biriani. You can make the dish with turkey breast meat instead of chicken.

Caribbean lime chicken

SERVES 4
PREPARATION TIME: 10 minutes, plus 8 hours
to marinate
COOKING TIME: 40 minutes

TIP
*Never marinate food
in a metal dish. The
acidic ingredients
(lemon or lime
juice, or vinegar, for
example) will react
with the metal
and taint
the food.*

Grated rind and juice of 1 lime
2 tablespoons dark rum
3 cloves garlic, peeled and crushed
2 level teaspoons peeled and grated root ginger,
or ¼ level teaspoon ground ginger
1 tablespoon hot red pepper sauce, or ½ teaspoon
Tabasco sauce
4 boneless chicken breasts, each
about 6oz (175g), skinned
1 tablespoon olive oil
1 medium onion, peeled and chopped
14oz (400g) tinned chopped tomatoes
2 tablespoons molasses or black treacle
1 cinnamon stick
2 bananas and lime wedges to garnish

1 Mix together the lime rind and juice, rum, garlic, ginger and pepper sauce or Tabasco to make the marinade.

2 Lay the chicken breasts in one layer in a glass or china dish, coat with the marinade, cover and put in the refrigerator for about 8 hours. Turn the pieces over several times.

3 Remove the chicken from the marinade and pat dry with a paper towel, reserving the marinade. Heat the oil in a frying pan and brown the chicken in it over a high heat for about 2 minutes on each side. Remove from the pan and set aside.

It is the rich rum-based marinade, sharpened by the bite of fresh lime, that gives this spicy chicken dish its distinctly Caribbean flavour.

4 Cook the onion in the pan for 5 minutes over a moderate heat, until softened. Pour the marinade into the pan and stir in the tomatoes, molasses or treacle and cinnamon stick.

5 Return the chicken to the pan and bring to the boil, then reduce the heat and simmer gently, uncovered, for 20 minutes, until the chicken is cooked right through with no pink left in the middle.

6 Lift the chicken breasts onto a heated serving dish, cover and keep hot. Boil the sauce to thicken it. Remove the cinnamon stick, pour the sauce over the chicken and garnish with sliced banana and lime wedges.

Rice and a green salad are good foils for this sweet and spicy chicken. You can marinate the chicken overnight if more convenient, turning the pieces night and morning.

ONE SERVING	
CALORIES	335
TOTAL FAT	9g
SATURATED FAT	2g
CARBOHYDRATES	27g
ADDED SUGAR	9g
FIBRE	2g
SODIUM	180mg

Chicken and vegetable curry

SERVES 4
PREPARATION TIME: 25 minutes
COOKING TIME: 25 minutes

1 tablespoon vegetable oil
1 large onion, peeled and sliced
1 level tablespoon medium-hot curry powder
2 level teaspoons ground cumin
½ small cauliflower, divided into florets
1 small aubergine, trimmed and cut into cubes
1 bay leaf
¼ level teaspoon cayenne pepper
2 level tablespoons plain flour
¾ pint (425ml) chicken stock (see p.19)
8oz (225g) thinly sliced green cabbage
5oz (150g) fresh or frozen peas
3 cloves garlic, peeled and crushed
3 level tablespoons raisins
1lb (450g) boneless chicken breasts, skinned, beaten out thin and cut into strips
8oz (225g) low-fat natural yoghurt
2 tablespoons lemon juice
1 level tablespoon chopped fresh parsley

1 Heat the oil in a large, heavy-based saucepan and fry the onion in it gently for 5 minutes. Mix in the curry powder and cumin and cook, stirring, for 1 minute.

2 Stir in the cauliflower, aubergine, bay leaf and cayenne pepper, and cook for 1 minute. Sprinkle in the flour, then gradually mix in the stock and bring to the boil, stirring. Lower the heat, cover and simmer for 3 minutes.

3 Stir in the cabbage, peas, garlic and raisins, cover and simmer for 3 minutes. Add the chicken, bring to the boil and simmer for 5 minutes, stirring several times; discard the bay leaf. Stir in the yoghurt, lemon juice and

The combination of meat and vegetables in a rice ring makes a satisfying and balanced meal. Yoghurt gives the sauce a tartness and a creamy texture.

parsley, and heat for 1 minute without boiling or the sauce will curdle.

Spoon the curry into a ring of rice on a hot serving plate. You can garnish it with a few red pepper rings to add a touch of colour.

ONE SERVING	
CALORIES	325
TOTAL FAT	12g
SATURATED FAT	2g
CARBOHYDRATES	27g
ADDED SUGAR	0
FIBRE	7g
SODIUM	160mg

Roast chicken with a stuffing of figs, rice and thyme

SERVES 6
PREPARATION TIME: 50 minutes
COOKING TIME: 1 hour 30 minutes
OVEN: Preheat to 200°C (400°F, gas mark 6)

ONE SERVING	
CALORIES	330
TOTAL FAT	7g
SATURATED FAT	2g
CARBOHYDRATES	39g
ADDED SUGAR	0
FIBRE	4g
SODIUM	130mg

TIP
Use a potato peeler to pare off the lemon rind very thinly. It is easier to pare half the rind from a whole lemon than to grasp and pare a cut lemon.

For the stuffing:
1 large onion, peeled and finely chopped
1 clove garlic, peeled and crushed
1 carrot, peeled and finely diced
3 level teaspoons chopped fresh thyme leaves, or 1 level teaspoon dried thyme
4 level tablespoons chopped fresh parsley
Finely grated rind and juice of 1 lemon
5oz (150g) long-grain brown rice
6oz (175g) dried figs, roughly chopped
1½ pints (850ml) chicken stock (see p.19)
Freshly ground black pepper

4lb (1.8kg) oven-ready chicken, rinsed and well dried with kitchen paper
2 tablespoons water
Sprig of fresh thyme
Thinly pared rind of half a lemon
2 fresh figs, sprigs of thyme and parsley to garnish

1 To prepare the stuffing, put the onion, garlic, carrot, chopped or dried thyme, parsley, grated lemon rind, rice and figs into a large saucepan and pour in 1¼ pints (725ml) of the stock. Bring to the boil, then reduce the heat, cover and simmer for 35-40 minutes, or until the rice has absorbed all the stock. Remove from the heat, stir in the lemon juice and season with pepper.

2 Spoon about two-thirds of the rice mixture loosely inside the chicken. Do not overfill or the chicken will not cook thoroughly. Put the remainder of the stuffing into an ovenproof serving dish and stir in the remaining chicken stock. Put on the lid, or cover with foil, and set aside.

3 Place the chicken on a rack in a small roasting tin and tie its legs together with clean string. Put the water, the sprig of thyme and the thinly pared lemon rind into the tin. Roast the chicken in the heated oven for about 1 hour 30 minutes, until there is no trace of pink in the juice that seeps out when you push a fork into the thickest part of the thigh. During cooking, baste the chicken frequently with the juices that collect in the roasting tin. Put the reserved stuffing into the oven for the last 30 minutes of cooking to heat thoroughly.

4 Lift the cooked chicken onto a warmed serving plate. Cover it loosely with foil and leave to rest for 10 minutes. Skim all the fat from the roasting tin, then reheat the cooking juices and strain through a sieve into a warmed serving jug. Garnish the chicken with wedges of fresh fig and the sprigs of thyme and parsley just before serving.

Carve the chicken at the table, giving each diner some breast meat and leg meat and stuffing from inside the bird. Leave the diners to remove the chicken skin themselves. Hand round the sauce and extra stuffing separately and serve with a crisp green salad and some hot crusty rolls.

An unusual stuffing of sweet, moist figs, seasoned with aromatic thyme, makes traditional roast chicken a dish for a special occasion. The cooking juices are absorbed into the rice and dried fruit. Roasting with the skin on keeps the chicken moist and brings out its fullest flavour, but take off the skin as you eat or the dish's fat content will be much higher.

Fricasseed chicken with onions

ONE SERVING

CALORIES 225

TOTAL FAT 9g

SATURATED FAT 3g

CARBOHYDRATES 13g

ADDED SUGAR 0

FIBRE 3g

SODIUM 110mg

SERVES 4
PREPARATION TIME: 20 minutes
COOKING TIME: 50 minutes

2 tablespoons olive oil
4 chicken legs, each about 8oz (225g), skinned and
divided into thighs and drumsticks
8 small onions, peeled
4 cloves garlic, peeled and crushed

8fl oz (225ml) chicken stock (see p.19)
2 tablespoons whisky
½ level teaspoon dried tarragon
2 medium carrots, peeled and sliced diagonally
6oz (175g) button mushrooms, wiped
and quartered
2 teaspoons lemon juice
Freshly ground black pepper
4oz (115g) low-fat natural yoghurt

TIP
When skinning the chicken pieces, slit the skin with kitchen shears then grip one end of it with a piece of kitchen paper and pull firmly away from you.

This tender dish, using the darker meat from a chicken, has its creamy sauce laced with a dash of whisky.

1 Heat half the oil in a large frying pan and cook the chicken pieces in it over a moderate heat for 7-8 minutes, turning them to brown all over. Lift them from the pan and set aside.

2 Cook the onions and garlic gently in the pan for 8-10 minutes, until soft. Stir in the stock, whisky and tarragon. Return the chicken to the pan and bring the sauce to the boil. Lower the heat, cover and simmer for 25 minutes.

3 Heat the remaining oil in a heavy-based saucepan and cook the carrots and mushrooms

in it over a moderately high heat, uncovered, for 4-5 minutes, stirring frequently.

4 Add the carrots, mushrooms and lemon juice to the chicken, season with pepper, cover and cook gently for 5 minutes. Lift the chicken into a heated serving dish with a slotted spoon.

5 Stir the yoghurt into the sauce and heat without boiling, then pour over the chicken.

Serve with red cabbage, rice and parsley sprigs. Dry sherry or wine can replace the whisky.

Gardener's chicken

SERVES 4
PREPARATION TIME: 25 minutes
COOKING TIME: 1 hour 15 minutes
OVEN: Preheat to 200°C (400°F, gas mark 6)

....

ONE SERVING

CALORIES 290

TOTAL FAT 6g

SATURATED FAT 2g

CARBOHYDRATES 28g

ADDED SUGAR 0

FIBRE 7g

SODIUM 130mg

....

*Vegetables are the
main focus of this dish.
Cooked in the roasting
tin with the chicken,
they absorb the delicious
juices from the meat as
well as the flavours of
the stock and wine.*

16 small new potatoes, scrubbed
2 medium onions, peeled and quartered
4 medium carrots, peeled and cut into strips
*1 medium parsnip, peeled and cut into
finger-length strips*
*2 small leeks, trimmed, cut into rings and
well washed*
*4 chicken legs, each about 8oz (225g), divided
into thighs and drumsticks*
¾ pint (425ml) chicken stock (see p.19)
4fl oz (115ml) dry white wine
1 tablespoon lemon juice
3 cloves garlic, peeled and finely chopped
1 level teaspoon dried oregano
½ level teaspoon dried thyme
Freshly ground black pepper
4oz (115g) fresh or frozen peas
2 level tablespoons chopped fresh parsley

1 Mix the potatoes, onions, carrots,
parsnip and leeks in a small roasting tin and lay
the chicken pieces on top.

2 Pour the stock, wine and lemon juice over
the chicken. Sprinkle with the garlic, oregano
and thyme and season with pepper.

3 Cook, uncovered, for 1 hour 15 minutes,
or until no pink juices ooze from the chicken
thighs when pricked. During cooking, turn the
chicken and stir the vegetables occasionally, and
baste with the pan juices. Add the peas for the
last 10 minutes of cooking. If the juices
evaporate too quickly pour in a little water.

4 Put the chicken, vegetables and juices on a
warm serving dish and sprinkle with parsley.

Give each diner a thigh and a drumstick
and leave them to remove the skin themselves.
A fresh green salad contrasts well with the
succulent baked vegetables.

Poussins with garlic

ONE SERVING	
CALORIES	240
TOTAL FAT	9g
SATURATED FAT	2g
CARBOHYDRATES	13g
ADDED SUGAR	0
FIBRE	1g
SODIUM	110mg

TIP
If your grill has no alternative positions for the pan, halve the poussins just before cooking and grill breast side up, turning over after 10 minutes and again after 20 minutes.

SERVES 4
PREPARATION TIME: 40 minutes, plus 2-4 hours to marinate
COOKING TIME: 30 minutes
OVEN: Preheat to 200°C (400°F, gas mark 6)

2 oven-ready poussins, each about 1¼ lb (550g)
1 tablespoon olive oil
4 fl oz (115 ml) red wine vinegar
1 bay leaf
½ level teaspoon dried thyme
½ level teaspoon dried rosemary
Finely grated rind and strained juice of 2 oranges
Freshly ground black pepper
2 whole heads of garlic
1 large orange
Sprigs of fresh rosemary to garnish

1 Put the poussins in a deep glass or china dish. Mix the oil with the vinegar, bay leaf, thyme, rosemary and orange rind and season with pepper. Pour the mixture over the poussins, cover and place in the refrigerator to marinate for 2-4 hours. Turn the poussins several times to keep coated with marinade.

2 Wrap the garlic heads separately in foil, and cook them in the heated oven for 25 minutes, or until tender.

3 Meanwhile, pare the rind thinly from the whole orange and cut into fine shreds. Pare off the pith and outer membrane from the flesh with a sharp knife, then slice out the segments, cutting each free of the membrane on either side. Work over a bowl to catch the juice.

4 Unwrap the garlic to cool, then remove the skins and crush the cloves to a paste with a fork. Lift the poussins out of the marinade and pat dry with kitchen paper. Carefully loosen the skin from the breast of each poussin, working from the neck end and pushing your fingers first along one side of the breast, then along the other. Spread the garlic purée evenly under the skin with a round-ended knife.

5 Place the poussins breast down on the grill rack and place the grill pan on its lowest position so the poussins will not char. Grill under a high heat for 10-12 minutes. Turn the poussins over and cook for 10-12 minutes more, until golden brown and cooked through. When they are pierced at the thickest part of the thigh with the tip of a knife the juice should run clear, not pink.

6 When the poussins are almost ready, simmer the finely shredded orange rind in the orange juice for 3-4 minutes.

7 Arrange the poussins on a heated serving plate and garnish with the orange segments, shreds and juice, and rosemary sprigs.

Divide the poussins with a sharp knife and give each diner a breast and a leg with some of the garnishes. Leave the diners to remove the chicken skin for themselves. Simple accompaniments such as french bread and a green salad suit the savoury poussins.

The surprisingly mild, nutty flavour of a garlic purée combines with piquant herbs and orange, making this a delicious dish for a summer lunch or dinner celebration.

Skinning the chicken pieces lets them absorb the contrasting flavours of cool grapefruit and hot peppercorns, and it lowers the fat content.

Chicken with pink grapefruit

ONE SERVING	
CALORIES	195
TOTAL FAT	8g
SATURATED FAT	2g
CARBOHYDRATES	12g
ADDED SUGAR	0
FIBRE	2g
SODIUM	100mg

SERVES 4
PREPARATION TIME: 20 minutes
COOKING TIME: 50 minutes

1 tablespoon olive oil
1 clove garlic, peeled and halved
8 chicken thighs, each about 3oz (85g), skinned
¼ pint (150ml) chicken stock (see p.19)
1 whole pink grapefruit and juice of another
1 level teaspoon pink peppercorns
1 medium onion, peeled and cut into thin strips
2 medium carrots, peeled and cut into thin strips
1 level teaspoon arrowroot
1 tablespoon water
Flat-leaf parsley to garnish

1 Heat the oil and garlic in a frying pan and cook the chicken thighs in it over a moderate heat for 5-6 minutes, turning them until golden all over. Pour in the stock and bring to the boil, then cook over a high heat for about 3 minutes, until the liquid is reduced by half. Add the grapefruit juice, peppercorns, onion and carrots to the pan, cover and cook over a moderate heat for 40 minutes.

2 Meanwhile, cut the skin and pith off the remaining grapefruit, then cut across the segments into eight slices.

3 Blend the arrowroot and water and stir it into the pan juices, simmering until they thicken slightly. Add the grapefruit slices and heat for 1 minute. Arrange on a hot serving dish and garnish with the parsley.

Rice and green beans complement the subtle taste of the chicken. You can make the dish with ordinary grapefruit but pink ones are sweeter as well as more attractive.

Chicken and mushroom hotpot

SERVES 6
PREPARATION TIME: 30 minutes
COOKING TIME: 1hr 15 mins
OVEN: Preheat to 200°C (400°F, gas mark 6)

ONE SERVING	
CALORIES	225
TOTAL FAT	7g
SATURATED FAT	1g
CARBOHYDRATES	17g
ADDED SUGAR	0
FIBRE	2g
SODIUM	125mg

2 tablespoons olive oil
4 boneless chicken breasts, each about 5oz (150g), skinned and cut into cubes
1 medium onion, peeled and chopped
2 sticks celery, trimmed and chopped
2 cloves garlic, peeled and crushed
6oz (175g) button mushrooms, wiped and halved
2 level teaspoons peeled and grated root ginger, or ¼ level teaspoon ground ginger

2 sprigs fresh parsley or thyme
2 level tablespoons plain flour
¼ pint (150ml) dry white wine
½ pint (285ml) chicken stock (see p.19)
Freshly ground black pepper
1lb (450g) potatoes, peeled and thinly sliced

1 Heat the oil in a large, nonstick saucepan and fry the chicken in it over a high heat for 2-3 minutes, turning the cubes to brown all over. Put the chicken on a plate and set aside.

2 Brown the onion, celery and garlic in the pan over a moderate heat for 5 minutes. Stir in the mushrooms, ginger and one sprig of parsley or thyme, and cook for 3 minutes. Mix in the flour then, little by little, the wine and stock; bring to the boil, stirring. Season with pepper, add the chicken and cook for 5 minutes.

3 Pour the chicken into an ovenproof dish and cover with potato slices, seasoning with pepper.

4 Cover the dish with foil and cook in the heated oven for 1 hour. Take off the foil and cook for a further 15-20 minutes, until the potatoes are tender and golden brown on top.

Serve the hotpot right away, garnished with the remaining parsley or thyme and accompanied by strips of carrot and courgette, steamed but still slightly firm.

The crisp potato topping absorbs flavours from the aromatic sauce to create a warming winter dish.

Chicken with onion and herb stuffing

ONE SERVING	
CALORIES	235
TOTAL FAT	9g
SATURATED FAT	3g
CARBOHYDRATES	5g
ADDED SUGAR	0
FIBRE	1g
SODIUM	160mg

SERVES 6
PREPARATION TIME: 20 minutes
COOKING TIME: 1 hour 35 minutes
OVEN: Preheat to 230°C (450°F, gas mark 8)

4½ -5lb (2-2.3kg) oven-ready chicken
1 level tablespoon fresh thyme leaves, or 1 level teaspoon dried thyme

4 level tablespoons each chopped fresh basil and parsley, or 1 level tablespoon each dried basil and parsley
6 spring onions, trimmed and finely chopped
Freshly ground black pepper
1 tablespoon olive oil
1 large onion, peeled and finely chopped
1 stick celery, trimmed and finely chopped

3 cloves garlic, peeled and crushed
1lb (450g) ripe tomatoes, skinned, de-seeded
and chopped
¼ pint (150ml) dry white wine
1 bay leaf
½ level teaspoon fennel seeds, crushed
Thyme sprigs to garnish

1 Rinse the chicken under the cold tap and pat it dry with kitchen paper. Carefully loosen the skin from the breast on each side of the chicken by easing your fingertips under the skin from the neck end.

2 Mix half the thyme with the basil, parsley and spring onions, and season with pepper. Spread the stuffing evenly on the chicken breast under the skin, then tuck the neck flap under the chicken and secure it with a skewer.

3 Put the chicken in a roasting tin and cook for 20-30 minutes in the heated oven, until it is very lightly browned.

4 Meanwhile, heat the oil in a flameproof casserole and cook the onion, celery and garlic in it over a moderate heat, stirring frequently, for about 5 minutes. Stir in the tomatoes, bring to the boil then reduce to a simmer.

5 Lower the oven temperature to 200°C (400°F, gas mark 6). Lift the chicken into the casserole. Pour off the fat from the roasting tin, reserving the juices. Pour the wine into the roasting tin and set it over a direct heat, stirring with a wooden spoon to loosen the browned bits as it comes to the boil. Pour the juices over the chicken in the casserole.

6 Add the bay leaf, fennel seeds and the remaining half of the thyme and season with pepper. When the casserole returns to the boil, put on the lid and cook in the heated oven for about 1 hour.

7 Lift the chicken onto a warmed serving dish, garnish it with sprigs of thyme and keep hot. Remove the fat from the sauce, discard the bay

leaf and blend half the sauce in a food processor for 5-10 seconds. Stir this back into the casserole. Spoon some of the sauce over the chicken and serve the rest separately.

Carve the chicken at the table, leaving the diners to remove the skin for themselves. Lightly cooked cabbage and roast potatoes would complete a hearty dish.

> **TIP**
> *Draw pieces of kitchen paper across the sauce in the casserole to absorb the fat that has risen to the top.*

Cooking the chicken in a covered casserole keeps it beautifully moist and lets it take in the fragrance of the herbs and wine, and at the same time add its own rich taste to the tomato sauce.

Oven-fried chicken

SERVES 4
PREPARATION TIME: 15 minutes, plus 30 minutes
to refrigerate
COOKING TIME: 30 minutes
OVEN: Preheat to 190°C (375°F, gas mark 5)

3 cloves garlic, peeled and crushed
1 level teaspoon dried thyme
1 level teaspoon dried marjoram
4oz (115g) low-fat natural yoghurt
4 boneless chicken breasts, each
about 6oz (175g), skinned
2oz (60g) fresh wholemeal breadcrumbs
2 level tablespoons chopped fresh parsley
3 level tablespoons grated Parmesan cheese
Young sprigs of thyme to garnish

1   Mix the garlic, thyme and marjoram into the
yoghurt and coat the chicken breasts with it.

2   On a flat plate, mix the breadcrumbs,
parsley and Parmesan. Press both sides of the
chicken breasts into the breadcrumb mixture,
then put them on a plate, cover and refrigerate
for 30 minutes for the coating to firm up.

3   Lay the chicken breasts on a nonstick baking
tray and cook in the heated oven for about
30 minutes, or until cooked right through with
no pink juices oozing out when the thickest
part of each chicken breast is pricked with a
fork. Lift the chicken onto a serving dish and
garnish with the thyme sprigs.

Serve the chicken with wild rice and some
cooked cranberries, very lightly sweetened, to
enhance the tangy flavour of the chicken.
A crisp green salad and perhaps some herb
bread will complete a satisfying dish.

ONE SERVING	
CALORIES	295
TOTAL FAT	8g
SATURATED FAT	3g
CARBOHYDRATES	15g
ADDED SUGAR	0
FIBRE	2g
SODIUM	315mg

TIP
*To make
breadcrumbs
without a food
processor, keep the
bread, unsliced, for
three or four days,
until very dry, then
rub firmly down
a sharp metal
grater.*

*The delicious herb,
cheese and breadcrumb
coating makes an
unusual meal out of
tender chicken breasts,
and seals in their juices
while they cook.*

Pan-fried chicken with cucumber

SERVES 4
PREPARATION TIME: 15 minutes
COOKING TIME: 20 minutes

ONE SERVING	
CALORIES	245
TOTAL FAT	8g
SATURATED FAT	2g
CARBOHYDRATES	4g
ADDED SUGAR	0
FIBRE	1g
SODIUM	130mg

1 large cucumber, halved lengthways and de-seeded
1 tablespoon olive oil
4 tablespoons water
1 small onion, peeled and finely chopped
4 boneless chicken breasts, each about 6oz (175g), skinned and cut into thin strips
Strained juice of 2 lemons
Strained juice of 1 lime
Freshly ground black pepper
Shredded and whole basil leaves to garnish

1 Peel some strips of skin off the cucumber halves, leaving them striped. Cut them into chunks, put in a saucepan and barely cover with water. Bring to the boil, then lower the heat and simmer, uncovered, for 3 minutes. Drain, put aside the cucumber and discard the water.

2 Heat the oil and water in a frying pan and cook the onion in it over a moderate heat for about 4 minutes, until the liquid has almost evaporated. Stir in the strips of chicken and fry for about 5 minutes, stirring until cooked through and golden.

3 Pour on the lemon and lime juice, made up to 7fl oz (200ml) with water. Season with pepper, bring to the boil, add the cucumber and simmer for 5-6 minutes. Spoon the chicken and sauce onto a hot serving plate and sprinkle with the basil shreds and sprigs.

Saffron rice and crisp, grated carrots go well with this fresh-flavoured dish.

TIP
To de-seed a cucumber, cut it in half lengthways and draw the tip of a teaspoon along firmly from end to end of each half.

The bite-sized pieces of chicken and faintly bitter cucumber in a lime and lemon sauce make this a refreshing dish for an outdoor summer lunch.

Chicken breasts Provençal

ONE SERVING	
CALORIES 210	
TOTAL FAT 7g	
SATURATED FAT 2g	
CARBOHYDRATES 9g	
ADDED SUGAR 0	
FIBRE 3g	
SODIUM 185mg	

SERVES 4
PREPARATION TIME: 10-15 minutes
COOKING TIME: 45 minutes

1 tablespoon olive oil
2 boneless chicken breasts, each about 8oz (225g), skinned and cut in half
1 large onion, peeled and chopped
4 cloves garlic, peeled and chopped
1 medium red pepper, de-seeded and diced

1 medium courgette, trimmed and sliced
1 small aubergine, trimmed and cut into chunks
14oz (400g) tinned chopped tomatoes
2 small red chillies
½ level teaspoon each dried basil, dried oregano, and dried thyme
4 large green olives, stoned and quartered
2 level tablespoons chopped fresh parsley

1 Heat the oil in a large, nonstick frying pan, and brown the chicken breasts in it over a moderate heat for 5 minutes on each side. Put them on a plate and set aside.

2 In the same pan, fry the onion and garlic for 5-6 minutes, stirring occasionally. Add the red pepper and cook for another 5 minutes, then add the courgette and cook for 5 minutes more. Put the vegetables with the chicken.

3 Using the same pan, toss the aubergine for 5-7 minutes, until browned. Return the chicken and vegetables to the pan. Stir in the tomatoes, chillies, basil, oregano, thyme and olives. Bring to the boil and then simmer for 15 minutes, or until the chicken is tender.

Arrange the chicken on a heated serving dish and spoon the vegetables round, discarding the chillies. Sprinkle the chopped parsley on top. Serve with crusty rolls to mop up the piquant sauce and a light, leafy salad to make a contrast.

Olives and chillies add a rich, fiery element to the South-of-France combination of tomatoes, peppers, aubergines and courgettes enveloping the chicken.

Sweet and sour apricot chicken

ONE SERVING	
CALORIES 250	
TOTAL FAT 8g	
SATURATED FAT 2g	
CARBOHYDRATES 14g	
ADDED SUGAR 1g	
FIBRE 2g	
SODIUM 175mg	

SERVES 4
PREPARATION TIME: 20 minutes
COOKING TIME: 50 minutes, plus
at least 30 minutes to marinate
OVEN: Preheat to 200°C (400°F, gas mark 6)

2 tablespoons lemon juice
2 teaspoons olive oil
2 cloves garlic, peeled and crushed
Freshly ground black pepper

2½-3lb (1.1-1.4kg) chicken, divided
into 8 portions and skinned
3oz (85g) ready-to-use dried apricots
7fl oz (200ml) unsweetened orange juice
1 level teaspoon light brown sugar
1 tablespoon cider vinegar
2 level teaspoons peeled and grated root ginger, or ¼ level teaspoon ground ginger
1 level teaspoon Dijon mustard
Bay leaves to garnish

1 Mix the lemon juice with the oil and half the garlic, and season with pepper. Put the chicken in a dish, pour on the lemon marinade and turn the chicken pieces in it until thoroughly coated. Cover and leave in a cool place for at least 30 minutes or up to 2 hours, turning the chicken several times.

2 Meanwhile, simmer the apricots in the orange juice for 10 minutes, or until tender. Stir in the sugar, vinegar, ginger, mustard and remaining garlic. Simmer for another 2 minutes. Cool the mixture slightly, then liquidise it in a food processor for 15 seconds or pass it through a food mill.

3 Arrange the chicken portions in a single layer on a rack in a roasting tin and cook in the heated oven for 25 minutes.

The tartness of apricots, sharpened by the juice of citrus fruits, gives this dish its distinctive flavour. A trace of ginger in the attractive golden glaze reinforces the association with favourites from a Chinese cook's repertoire.

4 Brush over one side of the chicken pieces with half the apricot glaze and roast for 10 more minutes. Turn the pieces over, brush the other side with the remaining glaze and roast 10 minutes longer, or until the chicken is tender and the glaze lightly browned.

Serve the chicken with a garnish of bay leaves. Rice and mangetout go well with it. Give each diner a breast portion and a leg portion. You can use four chicken legs, divided into thighs and drumsticks, instead of a jointed chicken.

The spicy marinade permeating this chicken re-creates the authentic flavour of a classic Indian dish, which is traditionally cooked in a tandoor, a clay oven, over a charcoal fire.

Tandoori chicken

SERVES 4
PREPARATION TIME: 15 minutes, plus
at least 4 hours to marinate
COOKING TIME: 30 minutes
OVEN: Preheat to 180°C (350°F, gas mark 4)

4oz (115g) Greek yoghurt
1 small onion, peeled and very finely chopped
1 level tablespoon peeled and grated root ginger,
or ½ level teaspoon ground ginger
2 cloves garlic, peeled and crushed
1 tablespoon lime juice
1½ level teaspoons ground coriander
1 level teaspoon each ground cumin, ground
cardamom and turmeric
¼ level teaspoon cayenne pepper
1 level tablespoon paprika
4 chicken breast and wing portions, each
about 8oz (225g), skinned
Lime wedges and parsley to garnish

1 Blend the yoghurt, onion, ginger, garlic and
lime juice in a food processor for 30 seconds, or
combine them with a rotary hand whisk. Mix in
the coriander, cumin, cardamom, turmeric,
cayenne pepper and paprika. Pour into a large,
glass or china dish, put in the chicken pieces
and turn to coat with the yoghurt mixture.
Cover and refrigerate for at least 4 hours or up
to 24 hours, turning to recoat occasionally.

2 Heat the grill, arrange the chicken on the
grill rack and cook under a moderate heat for
8 minutes on each side, until browned.

3 Put the chicken pieces in a nonstick baking
tin and cook in the heated oven for about
15 minutes or until the juices run clear when
the chicken is pierced with a sharp knife.

4 Lift the chicken onto a warm serving plate
and garnish with the lime wedges and parsley.

The traditional accompaniment for the hot,
sharp taste of tandoori chicken cannot be
bettered so serve it with basmati rice (see p.17),
perhaps sprinkled with some chopped peppers.
A mixed salad makes a cooling side dish.

> **TIP**
> *For the fullest and freshest flavour from the spices, grind your own coriander, cumin and cardamom seeds as you need them, using a mortar and pestle.*

ONE SERVING

CALORIES 190

TOTAL FAT 7g

SATURATED FAT 3g

CARBOHYDRATES 2g

ADDED SUGAR 0

FIBRE 1g

SODIUM 110mg

Chicken and vegetable stew

SERVES 4
PREPARATION TIME: 30 minutes
COOKING TIME: 1 hour 35 minutes

3lb (1.4kg) oven-ready chicken
5 large sprigs of parsley
6 black peppercorns
1 bay leaf
1¼ pints (725ml) chicken stock (see p.19)
1½ level teaspoons each mixed dried herbs
and dried sage
4 small turnips, peeled and quartered
2 large sticks celery, trimmed and chopped
2 medium potatoes, peeled and thickly sliced
14oz (400g) tinned peeled tomatoes
1 medium onion, peeled and chopped
4oz (115g) fresh or frozen sweetcorn kernels
4oz (115g) runner beans, trimmed and sliced
Freshly ground black pepper

1 Rinse the chicken under the cold tap and
put it in a large saucepan. Tie the parsley,
peppercorns and bay leaf in a small square of
muslin or clean linen and put into the saucepan
with the stock and ½ teaspoon each
of the mixed herbs and sage.

2 Bring to the boil, then reduce the heat
and simmer, covered, for 1 hour or until the
chicken falls easily off the bone. Lift the
chicken onto a heated plate.

3 Skim all the fat off the stock and put in the
turnips, celery, potatoes, tomatoes, onion and
another ½ teaspoon of mixed herbs and sage.
Bring back to the boil, then cover and simmer
gently for 20 minutes.

4 Take the skin off the chicken and lift
the meat off the bones. Cut it into chunks
and return to the saucepan together with the
sweetcorn and runner beans. Continue to
simmer, covered, for 15 minutes, stirring
occasionally. Take out the wrapped herbs, and
season the stew with pepper and the
remaining mixed herbs and sage.

The original version of this dish, created by
American Indians, had rabbit and squirrel in it
instead of chicken. The stew develops a fuller flavour
if it is cooked the day before you need it.

Ladle the stew into warmed serving bowls and
have it piping hot with bread and a salad of
cauliflower and mushrooms (see p.312), or a
leafy green salad. If you make the stew in
advance and refrigerate it overnight, reheat it
thoroughly, bringing it to the boil and then
simmering it for 10 minutes before serving.

ONE SERVING	
CALORIES	280
TOTAL FAT	7g
SATURATED FAT	2g
CARBOHYDRATES	11g
ADDED SUGAR	0
FIBRE	4g
SODIUM	185mg

The thick skin keeps the duckling moist during cooking, but should not be eaten. It is high in fat and would increase the calorie count.

Roast duckling with lime sauce

ONE SERVING	
CALORIES	205
TOTAL FAT	7g
SATURATED FAT	2g
CARBOHYDRATES	6g
ADDED SUGAR	4g
FIBRE	0
SODIUM	165mg

SERVES 4
PREPARATION: 15 minutes
COOKING TIME: 1 hour 45 minutes
OVEN: Preheat to 230°C (450°F, gas mark 8)

4½ -5lb (2-2.3kg) oven-ready duckling
Freshly ground black pepper
1 small onion, peeled
1 small cooking apple, peeled and halved
2 limes, gently scrubbed, rind thinly peeled and
finely shredded, juice strained
1 level tablespoon granulated sugar
½ pint (285ml) chicken stock (see p.19)
Slices of lime to garnish

1 Rinse the duckling, wipe it inside and out with kitchen paper and season it with pepper. Push the onion and apple inside the duckling and prick its skin all over with a fork. Place the bird on a rack in a roasting tin and cook in the heated oven for 45 minutes. Turn down the heat to 200°C (400°F, gas mark 6) and cook for a further 45 minutes, basting the duckling from time to time with the cooking juices. Lift the duckling onto a heated plate lined with kitchen paper to drain, and keep hot.

2 Blanch the lime rind in boiling water for 2-3 minutes, then drain and put the shreds to one side.

3 Pour off and discard the fat from the roasting tin. Scrape the remaining cooking juices from the bottom of the tin into a small saucepan. Heat the juices gently with the lime juice and sugar for 1-2 minutes. Mix in the chicken stock, bring to the boil, and boil the sauce hard for 8-10 minutes, until reduced to about a cupful. Stir in the shreds of lime rind and keep hot.

4 Carve the duckling, placing some breast slices and a thigh or leg piece on each diner's heated plate. Leave the diners to remove the skin for themselves. Trickle 2 tablespoons of sauce round each serving and garnish with the lime slices.

When Seville oranges are in season you can use them instead of limes for an equally strong, sharp sauce. The duck is very rich, so serve steamed potatoes with it and have a fresh-tasting celeriac salad on the side.

Duck satay

ONE SERVING	
CALORIES 230	
TOTAL FAT 12g	
SATURATED FAT 3g	
CARBOHYDRATES 6g	
ADDED SUGAR 0	
FIBRE 0	
SODIUM 360mg	

TIP
If you are using wooden skewers, soak them in cold water for 15-20 minutes before threading the meat on them. This helps to prevent them from scorching.

SERVES 4
PREPARATION TIME: 10 minutes, plus 2 hours to marinate
COOKING TIME: 10 minutes
OVEN: Preheat to 200°C (400°F, gas mark 6)

½ level teaspoon ground ginger
1 tablespoon soy sauce
1 teaspoon Worcestershire sauce
Finely grated rind and juice of 2 oranges
Freshly ground black pepper
1lb (450g) duck breast, without skin or bone, cubed
4 long wooden or metal skewers
2oz (60g) unsalted cashew nuts
Orange wedges, strips of rind and parsley to garnish

1 Mix the ginger, soy sauce, Worcestershire sauce and orange rind and juice in a glass or china casserole, and season with pepper. Stir in the duck, cover and refrigerate for 2 hours.

2 Thread the duck onto the skewers. Put them in a roasting tin, spoon on the marinade and cook in the heated oven for about 10 minutes, or until the duck is cooked through and tender.

3 Meanwhile spread the cashew nuts on a baking tray and roast in the oven for 5 minutes, until golden brown. Set aside.

4 When the duck is cooked, lift the skewers onto a heated serving dish, cover and keep hot.

5 Put the cashew nuts into a food processor with the cooking juices from the duck and blend until smooth. Reheat, put into a warmed serving bowl and top with strips of orange rind.

Serve the duck satay with rice and garnish with orange wedges and parsley. Stir-fried mangetout make a crisp accompaniment.

In this adaptation of a traditional South-east Asian dish, the marinaded and skewered meat is roasted and its juices are added to the spicy nut sauce.

Stir-fried duck and vegetables

ONE SERVING	
CALORIES	255
TOTAL FAT	12g
SATURATED FAT	2g
CARBOHYDRATES	11g
ADDED SUGAR	0
FIBRE	4g
SODIUM	350mg

Stir-frying, in Chinese fashion, seals in natural juices and ensures that the food is crisp and keeps its fresh flavour.

SERVES 4
PREPARATION TIME: 20 minutes
COOKING TIME: 12 minutes

2 tablespoons sesame oil
1 large onion, peeled and thinly sliced
2 cloves garlic, peeled and crushed
2 level teaspoons peeled and grated root ginger,
or ¼ level teaspoon ground ginger
1lb (450g) boneless duck breasts, skinned, beaten
out thin and cut into strips
3 medium carrots, peeled and sliced diagonally
4 tablespoons water
12oz (340g) mangetout, trimmed
1 tablespoon soy sauce
Freshly ground black pepper

1 Heat the oil in a large, nonstick frying pan or wok over a moderately high heat, and stir-fry the onion in it for 1 minute. Mix in the garlic and ginger and stir-fry for 1 minute more.

2 Put in the duck and stir-fry for 2 minutes. Add the carrots and water, cover and cook for 5 minutes. Mix in the mangetout, cover and cook for about 3 minutes, until the mangetout begin to soften.

3 Remove the pan from the heat, stir in the soy sauce and season with pepper.

Serve the stir-fry on bowls of fresh noodles tossed with celery seeds and chopped mint.

This dish is named from the mellow Italian vinegar that gives the sauce a subtle edge. Turkey cooked so quickly stays beautifully moist.

Turkey balsamico

TIP
To beat out the escalopes, arrange them well apart between two wetted sheets of greaseproof paper on a sturdy chopping board and hit them with a rolling pin.

SERVES 4
PREPARATION TIME: 10 minutes
COOKING TIME: 15 minutes

2 level tablespoons plain flour
Freshly ground black pepper
4 turkey breast escalopes, each about 4oz (115g), beaten out very thin
3 tablespoons olive oil
2 large red peppers, de-seeded and cut into strips
3 cloves garlic, peeled and crushed
½ oz (15g) fresh basil, chopped, or 1 teaspoon dried basil, crumbled
2 tablespoons balsamic vinegar
Basil sprigs to garnish

1 Combine the flour and pepper on a plate and press the turkey escalopes into the mixture, turning to coat them evenly all over and shaking off any excess.

2 Heat 2 tablespoons of the oil in a large, heavy-based frying pan and fry the escalopes in it over a moderate heat for 2-3 minutes on each side. Lift them onto a heated dish and keep hot.

3 Add the remaining oil to the pan along with the red peppers and garlic. Reduce the heat and simmer for 5 minutes, stirring occasionally, until the peppers are tender.

4 Stir in the basil and vinegar and raise the heat to moderate. Put the turkey back in the pan and cook, stirring, for 2 minutes. Arrange the escalopes on a hot serving dish, pour on the sauce and garnish with the sprigs of basil.

Tagliatelle or spaghetti are unusual companions for turkey, but they go surprisingly well with these Mediterranean flavours. Serve a green-bean salad on separate plates.

Turkey burgers with soured cream

ONE SERVING
CALORIES 275
TOTAL FAT 10g
SATURATED FAT 3g
CARBOHYDRATES 19g
ADDED SUGAR 0
FIBRE 2g
SODIUM 320mg

SERVES 4
*PREPARATION TIME: 10 minutes, plus 20 minutes
to refrigerate*
COOKING TIME: 15 minutes

1lb (450g) minced, uncooked turkey meat
1 small onion, peeled and very finely chopped
3 tablespoons soured cream
1 egg, size 2, beaten

3oz (85g) wholemeal breadcrumbs
⅛ level teaspoon salt
Freshly ground black pepper
¼ level teaspoon freshly grated nutmeg
1 level teaspoon dried marjoram
½ level teaspoon dried thyme
1 tablespoon olive oil

1 Mix together the turkey, onion, soured
cream, egg and half the breadcrumbs. Work in
the salt, pepper, nutmeg, marjoram and thyme
until the ingredients are thoroughly combined.

2 Divide the mixture into four and shape into
neat round patties. Coat them with the
remaining breadcrumbs, lay them on a plate
and refrigerate for 20 minutes to firm up.

3 Heat the oil in a nonstick frying pan and
brown the burgers briskly on both sides,
turning very carefully with a fish slice. Then
cook over a moderate heat for a further
6-8 minutes on each side, or until cooked right
through, reducing the heat if they are browning
too much. Drain the turkey burgers on
kitchen paper before serving.

Serve the burgers piping hot with rolls, coleslaw
and an onion and tomato salad, or with new
potatoes, spring cabbage and grilled tomatoes.

*These light and crunchy burgers, fried to crisp
perfection, will be popular with all the family.
The cream helps to bind the turkey and herb mixture
and sharpens the flavour.*

Rolled turkey with mint

ONE SERVING
CALORIES 250
TOTAL FAT 7g
SATURATED FAT 2g
CARBOHYDRATES 2g
ADDED SUGAR 0
FIBRE 0
SODIUM 400mg

SERVES 4
PREPARATION TIME: 20 minutes
COOKING TIME: 1 hour
OVEN: Preheat to 190°C (375°F, gas mark 5)

*1¼ lb (550g) boneless turkey breast in one piece,
with skin and any fat removed*
4 cloves garlic, peeled and crushed
1 level teaspoon paprika

Freshly ground black pepper
*3 rashers unsmoked back bacon, with rind and
fat removed*
20 large mint leaves, finely chopped
String for securing
1 tablespoon olive oil
7fl oz (200ml) chicken stock (see p.19)
4 level tablespoons Greek yoghurt
Sprigs of fresh mint to garnish

1 Sandwich the turkey breast between two sheets of wetted greaseproof paper on a sturdy chopping board and beat out with a rolling pin until about ½ in (13mm) thick. Spread the garlic evenly over the turkey, then sprinkle with paprika and season with pepper. Lay the bacon rashers on top and sprinkle with the chopped mint. Roll the turkey breast up neatly and tie securely with clean, thin string.

2 Heat the oil in a flameproof casserole, and brown all parts of the turkey roll in it over a moderate heat. Pour in the stock and bring to the boil. Cover and cook in the heated oven for 50 minutes, or until the turkey feels tender and no pink juices ooze out when you push a fork right into the centre of the roll. During cooking, baste the turkey frequently with the stock to keep it moist.

3 Lift the turkey roll onto a heated serving dish, cover and leave to rest.

4 Stir the yoghurt into the cooking juices and reheat without boiling. Pour into a warmed serving jug.

5 Remove the string, cut the turkey roll into thick slices and garnish with mint sprigs.

Hand the sauce round for diners to help themselves. New potatoes and a crisp green salad are perfect accompaniments to this light, fresh-tasting turkey roll.

> **TIP**
> *To prevent the mint from blackening, put the whole leaves in a bowl and cover with boiling water. Turn into a sieve at once and rinse under cold water.*

The refreshing taste and aroma of mint give a summery feel to a bird so often associated with winter roasts; braising retains its moistness.

Turkey escalopes with sherry sauce

SERVES 4
PREPARATION TIME: 10 minutes
COOKING TIME: 10 minutes

ONE SERVING	
CALORIES 235	
TOTAL FAT 10g	
SATURATED FAT 3g	
CARBOHYDRATES 7g	
ADDED SUGAR 0	
FIBRE 0	
SODIUM 130mg	

3 level tablespoons plain flour
½ level teaspoon dried rosemary
½ level teaspoon dried thyme
Freshly ground black pepper
4 turkey breast escalopes, each about 4oz (115g),
beaten out thin
2 tablespoons olive oil

4 tablespoons dry sherry
6 tablespoons chicken stock (see p.19)
½ level teaspoon cornflour
4oz (115g) Greek yoghurt
1 level teaspoon Dijon mustard

1 Mix together the flour, rosemary, thyme and pepper. Coat each turkey escalope with the seasoned flour and shake off any excess.

2 Heat the oil in a nonstick frying pan and cook the escalopes in it over a moderate heat for 2-3 minutes on each side, until golden brown and cooked through. Lift them onto kitchen paper for a moment to drain, and then onto a heated serving dish. Keep hot.

3 Skim off any oil from the frying pan, stir the sherry into the browned juices in the pan and simmer for 30 seconds. Blend the stock with the cornflour and pour into the pan. Stir until it comes to the boil, then add the yoghurt and mustard. Stir over a low heat without boiling for 2-3 minutes, until the sauce is slightly thickened. Spoon the sauce over the turkey.

A mixture of white and wild rice is a good foil for the turkey in its rich sauce. Serve a leafy side-salad for a crisp and colourful contrast.

Quick and easy to prepare, the lavish sauce of sherry, Greek yoghurt and mustard transforms a simple dish into a succulent feast fit for any occasion.

Turkey with sweet potato stuffing

SERVES 8
PREPARATION TIME: 45 minutes
COOKING TIME: 1 hour 30 minutes
OVEN: Preheat to 230°C (450°F, gas mark 8)

ONE SERVING	
CALORIES 300	
TOTAL FAT 5g	
SATURATED FAT 1g	
CARBOHYDRATES 23g	
ADDED SUGAR 0	
FIBRE 3g	
SODIUM 110mg	

1½ lb (680g) orange-fleshed sweet potatoes,
peeled and cut into small pieces
2 tablespoons olive oil
1 medium carrot, peeled and chopped
1 medium onion, peeled and chopped

1 stick celery, trimmed and chopped
1 small leek, washed and chopped
8 leaves fresh sage, chopped
Grated rind and juice of 1 large orange
1 turkey crown (double breast), about 5lb (2.3kg),
in one piece on the bone and with skin on
Skewers or clean, thin string to secure
3 level tablespoons plain flour
1 pint (570ml) turkey or chicken stock (see p.19)
Orange wedges and sage sprigs to garnish

1 Cook the sweet potatoes in unsalted boiling water for about 15 minutes, until they feel tender when pierced with a knife.

2 Meanwhile heat half the oil in a heavy-based saucepan and cook the carrot, onion, celery and leek in it over a moderate heat for 10 minutes, stirring frequently. Mix in the sage and cook for 1 minute.

3 Drain and mash the sweet potato, beat in the orange rind and stir in the vegetable and sage mixture. Leave this stuffing to cool.

4 Loosen the skin round the neck end of the turkey by pushing your fingers between the flesh and the skin. Spoon the stuffing in under the skin and secure with skewers or by sewing with a large darning needle and string.

5 Rub the remaining oil round a roasting tin, lay the turkey in it and roast in the heated oven for 30 minutes. Lower the temperature to 190°C (375°F, gas mark 5), pour the orange juice over the turkey and cook for 45 minutes longer, basting occasionally. If the turkey skin browns too quickly, cover loosely with foil.

6 When the turkey feels tender and there is no trace of pink in the juice that oozes out when you push a fork into the thickest part of the meat, lift it onto a heated serving dish. Cover with foil and leave to rest.

7 Skim any fat from the juices remaining in the roasting tin. Blend the flour into the juices and gradually stir in the stock. Bring to the boil, stirring continuously, then simmer for 5 minutes. Pour into a warmed serving jug.

Remove the skewers or string from the turkey. Carve the meat and serve it with the stuffing and a garnish of orange wedges and sage sprigs. Hand round the gravy separately. Brussels sprouts offset the sweetness of the dish. If sweet potatoes are unobtainable you can use ordinary potatoes but the taste will be less rich.

The zest of fresh orange permeates the chestnut flavour of sweet potato in this stuffing. The combination is popular in the United States, where it is a traditional accompaniment to turkey and often forms part of November's annual Thanksgiving feast.

Pheasant casserole with apple and cabbage

SERVES 4
PREPARATION TIME: 35 minutes
COOKING TIME: 1 hour
OVEN: Preheat to 180°C (350°F, gas mark 4)

2 tablespoons olive oil
2 oven-ready pheasants, each about 1¼ lb (550g),
cut in half and any lead shot removed
4 shallots, or 1 medium onion, peeled and sliced

8oz (225g) white cabbage, finely sliced
8oz (225g) red cabbage, finely sliced
1lb (450g) potatoes, peeled and chopped
2 level teaspoons paprika
6 juniper berries, crushed
About ¼ pint (150ml) dry red wine
1lb (450g) cooking apples, peeled, cored and cut
into thick slices
Freshly ground black pepper

ONE SERVING	
CALORIES 510	
TOTAL FAT 20g	
SATURATED FAT 5g	
CARBOHYDRATES 34g	
ADDED SUGAR 0	
FIBRE 5g	
SODIUM 180mg	

Older pheasants can be used for this dish, since casseroling with wine and apple makes them meltingly tender.

1 Heat the oil in a large, flameproof casserole and brown the pheasants in it on all sides over a fairly high heat. Lift the pheasants onto a plate.

2 Cook the shallots or onion in the casserole for 1-2 minutes. Mix in all the cabbage, the potatoes, paprika and juniper berries and pour on the wine. Cover and cook for 5 minutes.

3 Add the apple slices and season with pepper. Lay the pheasant halves on top, pouring over any juices from the plate. Cover and cook in the

heated oven for about 1 hour, or until the meat feels tender and there is no pink in the juice that seeps out when you push a fork into the thickest part of the thigh. Check from time to time that there is some liquid in the casserole and add a little more wine if necessary.

Give each diner some vegetables, apple and sauce with their meat. Leave the diners to remove the skin from their pheasant. The dish is complete as it is but offer some rolls for mopping up the delicious sauce.

TIP
If the lid of your casserole does not fit very tightly, cover the dish with foil, crimped round the rim to fit snugly. The cabbage will burn on the base and spoil the flavour if all the liquid evaporates.

Roast pheasant with prunes

SERVES 4
PREPARATION TIME: 30 minutes
COOKING TIME: 1 hour
OVEN: Preheat to 220°C (425°F, gas mark 7)

2 oven-ready pheasants, each about 1 ½ lb (680g)
8-16 crushed juniper berries (to taste)
1 tablespoon fresh rosemary leaves,
or 1 level teaspoon dried rosemary, crumbled
1 tablespoon olive oil
4 bay leaves
16 ready-to-use stoned prunes
2 rashers unsmoked back bacon, fat removed
Wooden cocktail sticks
¼ pint (150ml) water
2 level teaspoons plain flour
¼ pint (150ml) chicken stock (see p.19)
1 level tablespoon redcurrant jelly
Sprigs of rosemary to garnish

1 Remove any feather tips and lead shot from
the birds, then rinse them out and wipe them
inside and out with kitchen paper.

2 Mix the juniper berries and rosemary leaves
with the oil and spread inside the pheasants.
Push a bay leaf and 8 prunes inside each bird.
Lay a bay leaf and a rasher of bacon across the
breast of each bird and fix with cocktail sticks.

3 Put the pheasants in a roasting tin and
add the water to keep them moist. Cook for
1 hour in the heated oven until browned and
tender, basting occasionally.

4 Lift the pheasants onto a warmed meat
plate, cover and leave to rest.

5 Stir the flour into the cooking juices and
gradually mix in the stock. Bring to the boil, to
work in the hardened juices from the bottom of
the tin. Stir in the redcurrant jelly and any
juices from the meat plate. Lower the heat and
simmer for 3-4 minutes until slightly
thickened. Strain into a warmed serving jug.

Rosemary and juniper berries inside the pheasants
give the meat a savoury bitterness with a hint of
gin, which is sweetened by the juicy prunes.

Remove the cocktail sticks, bacon and bay
leaves and give each diner some slices of breast
and a leg, some of the prunes and a spoonful or
two of sauce; hand round the rest of the sauce
separately. Garnish with the rosemary and leave
the diners to remove the pheasant skin for
themselves. A purée of root vegetables and
roast potatoes are well-flavoured enough to
match the robust taste of the pheasant.

ONE SERVING	
CALORIES 510	
TOTAL FAT 20g	
SATURATED FAT 6g	
CARBOHYDRATES 24g	
ADDED SUGAR 3g	
FIBRE 3g	
SODIUM 405mg	

Pigeons braised with orange and rice

SERVES 4
PREPARATION TIME: 20 minutes
COOKING TIME: 1 hour 30 minutes
OVEN: Preheat to 160°C (325°F, gas mark 3)

ONE SERVING	
CALORIES	630
TOTAL FAT	29g
SATURATED FAT	6g
CARBOHYDRATES	58g
ADDED SUGAR	0
FIBRE	4g
SODIUM	205mg

1 tablespoon olive oil
4 shallots, or 1 medium onion, peeled and chopped
1 clove garlic, peeled and crushed
4 oven-ready pigeons
About ½ pint (285ml) vegetable stock (see p.19)
¼ pint (150ml) fresh orange juice
6oz (175g) long-grain rice
2 large carrots, peeled and diced
8oz (225g) tinned peeled water chestnuts in water, drained and diced
1 level tablespoon coarsely chopped fresh parsley
⅛ level teaspoon salt
Freshly ground black pepper
1 large orange, peel and pith removed
2oz (60g) toasted pine nuts
Watercress sprigs to garnish

1 Heat the oil in a large, flameproof casserole and cook the shallots or onion and the garlic in it over a high heat for 1-2 minutes, stirring frequently, until lightly browned.

2 Put the pigeons in the casserole and brown them well on all sides. Lower the heat and pour in the stock and orange juice. Cover and cook in the heated oven for 45 minutes.

3 Stir the rice, carrots, water chestnuts and parsley into the casserole and season with the salt and pepper. Cover again and return to the oven for another 45 minutes. Stir the rice from time to time and add a little more stock or water if the casserole is becoming dry.

4 Using a small sharp knife, cut down the sides of the orange segments to free them from their membranes. When the rice is cooked all through and the pigeons are tender, spoon the rice mixture onto a warm serving dish and sprinkle with the pine nuts. Arrange the pigeons on top. Garnish with the orange segments and watercress.

The strong flavour and firm textures of the dish are complemented by a light salad of lamb's lettuce and beetroot (see p.320).

TIP
To toast the pine nuts, spread them on foil and grill under a medium heat for 1-2 minutes. Stir frequently to toast evenly as the nuts burn quickly.

Braising brings out the full flavour of the rich, dark pigeon meat, which is enhanced by the tartness of oranges and absorbed by the rice.

Braised quail make an attractive dish for a special occasion. These little game birds should not be hung, but enjoyed as fresh as possible.

Braised quail with mushrooms

ONE SERVING
....
CALORIES 295
....
TOTAL FAT 11g
....
SATURATED FAT 3g
....
CARBOHYDRATES 17g
....
ADDED SUGAR 0
....
FIBRE 2g
....
SODIUM 360mg
....

SERVES 4
PREPARATION TIME: 30 minutes
COOKING TIME: 40 minutes
OVEN: Preheat to 180°C (350°F, gas mark 4)

1 tablespoon olive oil
8 oven-ready quail
1 small onion, peeled and finely chopped
2 rashers unsmoked back bacon, trimmed of fat and finely chopped
1 level tablespoon plain flour
¾ pint (425ml) chicken stock (see p.19)

2oz (60g) pearl barley
1 large carrot, peeled and diced
4oz (115g) button mushrooms, wiped and finely chopped
1 teaspoon lemon juice
3 level tablespoons chopped fresh parsley
Freshly ground black pepper

1 Heat the oil in a large, flameproof casserole and cook the quail in it over a high heat for about 5 minutes, turning them to brown all over. Remove from casserole and set aside.

2 Fry the onion and bacon gently in the casserole for 2 minutes. Stir in the flour and then the stock, pearl barley and carrot. Bring to the boil, stirring continuously.

3 Add the mushrooms, lemon juice and 1 tablespoon of the parsley, and season with pepper. Return the quail to the casserole, bring to the boil, cover and cook in the heated oven for about 40 minutes, or until the quail are tender. Sprinkle with the remaining parsley.

Sautéed brussels sprouts and potato slices (see p.295) blend well with the quail. Leave the diners to remove the skin from their quail and remind them to watch out for the small bones.

Calabrian rabbit

ONE SERVING	
CALORIES 245	
TOTAL FAT 8g	
SATURATED FAT 2g	
CARBOHYDRATES 15g	
ADDED SUGAR 0	
FIBRE 2g	
SODIUM 90mg	

TIP
For meat similar to well-flavoured free-range chicken, choose farmed rabbit. For a fuller and more gamey flavour, try to get a wild rabbit.

SERVES 4
PREPARATION TIME: 20 minutes
COOKING TIME: 1 hour 15 minutes
OVEN: Preheat to 180°C (350°F, gas mark 4)

1 tablespoon olive oil
8 even-sized rabbit joints, about 1¾ lb (800g) together
1 level tablespoon plain flour
1 pint (570ml) chicken stock (see p.19)
12 small new potatoes, 8oz (225g) together, washed
12 small onions, about 6oz (175g) together, peeled
Thinly pared rind and juice of 1 lemon
½ oz (15g) fresh thyme sprigs
Freshly ground black pepper

1 Heat the oil in a large, flameproof casserole and brown the rabbit pieces in it over a high heat for about 5 minutes. Stir in the flour and then the stock. Add the potatoes, onions and lemon rind and juice. Set aside 4 thyme sprigs and put the rest in the casserole. Season with pepper and bring to the boil.

2 Cover and cook in the heated oven for 1 hour, or until the meat is ready to drop off the bones. Garnish with the reserved sprigs of fresh thyme.

Baked cabbage wedges (see p.277) go well with this simple and savoury casserole.

Cooking rabbit in this way keeps it succulent. Like all lean meats with no fat to moisten them, it is best cooked with plenty of liquid. The sweet thyme gives its aroma to the meat.

Grilled rabbit

ONE SERVING	
CALORIES	145
TOTAL FAT	6g
SATURATED FAT	3g
CARBOHYDRATES	0
ADDED SUGAR	0
FIBRE	0
SODIUM	75mg

SERVES 4
PREPARATION: 10 minutes, plus at least 6 hours to marinate
COOKING TIME: 15 minutes

1½ lb (680g) farmed rabbit, divided into even-sized joints
2 level tablespoons soured cream
Freshly ground black pepper

1 tablespoon lemon juice
Curly endive, lemon slices and flat-leaf parsley to garnish

1 Lay the rabbit joints in one layer in a dish. Season the cream well with pepper and coat the rabbit pieces evenly with it. Cover with a lid and refrigerate for at least 6 hours, and up to 24 hours if more convenient.

2 Thirty minutes before cooking, remove the rabbit from the refrigerator, uncover and leave at room temperature.

3 Arrange the rabbit joints on the grill rack and cook under a hot grill for about 7 minutes on each side, or until cooked through and golden brown.

4 Lift the rabbit joints onto a heated serving dish and sprinkle the lemon juice over them. Garnish with the endive, lemon slices and parsley, and serve immediately.

Steamed new carrots and warm herb rolls go well with this simple, quickly cooked dish.

The success of this dish depends on the tenderness of the meat, which is assured if you allow it ample time to marinate in the soured cream.

Rabbit pie

SERVES 4
PREPARATION TIME: 30 minutes
COOKING TIME: 1 hour 10 minutes
OVEN: Preheat to 200°C (400°F, gas mark 6)

ONE SERVING	
CALORIES	470
TOTAL FAT	15g
SATURATED FAT	4g
CARBOHYDRATES	40g
ADDED SUGAR	0
FIBRE	3g
SODIUM	525g

2 tablespoons olive oil
2 medium onions, peeled and sliced
1 clove garlic, peeled and crushed
2oz (60g) unsmoked back bacon with fat removed, chopped
1½ lb (680g) boneless rabbit portions cut into cubes
2 level tablespoons plain flour

1 pint (570ml) chicken stock (see p.19)
Sprig fresh thyme
Sprig fresh parsley
4oz (115g) ready-to-use stoned prunes
Freshly ground black pepper
3 filo pastry sheets, 20×12in (51×30cm)

1 Heat half the oil in a large frying pan and cook the onion, garlic and bacon in it over a moderate heat for 5 minutes, stirring frequently. Spoon into an ovenproof dish, using a slotted spoon.

2 Toss the rabbit in 1 tablespoon of the flour, shake off the excess and fry in the oil left in the pan until golden brown all over. Spoon the meat into the dish.

3 Stir the remaining flour into the pan juices and cook for 1 minute. Gradually stir in the stock and bring to the boil, stirring continuously, then add the thyme, parsley and prunes and season with pepper.

4 Pour the sauce over the rabbit and stir well. Cover with a lid or foil and cook in the heated oven for 1 hour.

5 When the rabbit is tender, quickly brush the filo pastry with the remaining oil and cut each sheet into 15 squares. Cut the squares in half diagonally to make triangles. Take the cover off the dish and arrange overlapping filo triangles over the pie filling.

6 Return the dish to the oven and cook for a further 5-10 minutes, until the pastry is crisp and golden brown.

Mashed swede or crisp curly kale, with their slightly peppery tastes, go well with the robust flavours of the pie.

The crisp filo pastry gives a light, elegant finish to an otherwise hearty pie that allies the savoury rabbit meat with dark, plump prunes.

These thick, pink slices of venison have been kept moist during cooking by the wrapping of cabbage leaves and a layer of redcurrant jelly.

Roast venison parcel

ONE SERVING	
CALORIES	190
TOTAL FAT	7g
SATURATED FAT	2g
CARBOHYDRATES	3g
ADDED SUGAR	1g
FIBRE	1g
SODIUM	115mg

SERVES 6
PREPARATION TIME: 20 minutes
COOKING TIME: 40 minutes, plus 15 minutes to rest
OVEN: Preheat to 200°C (400°F, gas mark 6)

1 tablespoon olive oil
1½ lb (680g) prime boneless venison joint
⅛ level teaspoon salt
Freshly ground black pepper
6-7 large green cabbage leaves
1 level tablespoon redcurrant jelly
2 level teaspoons fresh thyme leaves
Watercress to garnish

1 Rub the oil over the venison and season it with the salt and pepper.

2 Blanch the cabbage in unsalted boiling water for 2 minutes. Rinse with cold water, dry on kitchen paper and trim out the thick stalks.

3 Heat a nonstick frying pan over a high heat and dry-fry the meat in it quickly, turning until it is brown all over. Remove from the heat and leave until cooled enough to touch.

4 Snip off any string from the meat and trim off any fat. Spread the redcurrant jelly over the meat and sprinkle with thyme leaves. Cover the venison completely with the cabbage leaves, then wrap it in nonstick baking paper.

5 Put the parcel of venison in a roasting tin and cook in the heated oven for 40 minutes. Remove from the oven and leave to rest for 15 minutes before unwrapping.

Carve the meat into very thick slices; it will be cooked but still slightly pink. Garnish with the watercress and serve with braised leeks and sesame potatoes (see p.295).

Venison stew

ONE SERVING

CALORIES 320

TOTAL FAT 14g

SATURATED FAT 4g

CARBOHYDRATES 5g

ADDED SUGAR 0

FIBRE 1g

SODIUM 120mg

Lean, richly flavoured venison gives a luxury lift to this winter stew. Use saddle of venison when you can, to make the most tender dish.

SERVES 6
PREPARATION TIME: 20 minutes
COOKING TIME: 1 hour

2 tablespoons olive oil
1½ lb (680g) venison cubes, trimmed of fat
2 carrots, peeled and diced
2 sticks celery, trimmed and sliced
1 onion, peeled and cut into rings
1 level tablespoon plain flour
1 pint (570ml) veal stock (see p.19)
4 juniper berries
1 level tablespoon chopped fresh lovage or celery leaves
Freshly ground black pepper
Shredded lovage or celery leaves to garnish

1 Heat the oil in a large, heavy-based saucepan and toss the meat in it over a high heat to brown the cubes quickly. Lift out the meat into a heatproof dish, using a slotted spoon.

2 Fry the carrots, celery and onion in the same pan for 5 minutes. Stir in the flour and cook it for 2 minutes before gradually blending in the stock. Bring to the boil, stirring continuously.

3 Return the venison to the pan, stir in the juniper berries and chopped lovage or celery leaves and season with pepper. Bring back to the boil, then lower the heat, cover and simmer for 1 hour, or until the meat is very tender. Pour into a warmed serving dish and garnish with the shredded lovage or celery leaves.

Mashed potato and swede go well with the savoury broth of this dish.

BEEF, LAMB AND PORK

Red meat is invaluable for the complete protein, vitamins and minerals it contributes to the diet, but these go hand in hand with the saturated fats that should be avoided. The knack is to make a little meat go a long way, and these recipes show how to do it. They skilfully use prudent portions in delicious dishes, cooked by roasting and stewing and by quick grilling and stir-frying to cut down fat but keep flavour intact.

Beefburgers Scandinavian style

ONE SERVING

CALORIES 230

TOTAL FAT 13g

SATURATED FAT 5g

CARBOHYDRATES 8g

ADDED SUGAR 0

FIBRE 1g

SODIUM 190mg

SERVES 4
PREPARATION TIME: 10 minutes, plus 20 minutes
to chill
COOKING TIME: 15 minutes

12oz (340g) beef with fat removed, minced
3oz (85g) cooked beetroot, peeled and diced
2oz (60g) fresh wholemeal breadcrumbs

1 egg, size 3, beaten
2 teaspoons red wine vinegar
½ level teaspoon dried dill
Freshly ground black pepper
1 tablespoon olive oil
Shredded lettuce, onion rings and dill fronds
to garnish
Soured cream to garnish

1 Combine the beef, beetroot, breadcrumbs,
egg, vinegar and dried dill, and season with
pepper. Divide the mixture into four, shape
into flat cakes and refrigerate for 20 minutes.

2 Heat the oil in a frying pan and brown the
beefburgers over a high heat for 1-2 minutes on
each side. Lower the heat to moderate and cook
the burgers for 5 minutes more on each side.

3 Drain the beefburgers on kitchen paper
before arranging them on individual plates and
garnishing with the lettuce, onion and dill.
Hand the soured cream round for the diners to
put a teaspoonful on their burger; you can mix
a little chopped dill with the cream.

Serve the burgers with warm rolls (see p.366)
and side salads of cucumber, apple and lettuce.

*Beetroot gives the beefburgers a rich colour and a
hint of sweetness which is offset by soured cream in a
favourite Scandinavian combination.*

Beef wrapped in cabbage leaves

ONE SERVING

CALORIES 330

TOTAL FAT 11g

SATURATED FAT 4g

CARBOHYDRATES 24g

ADDED SUGAR 0

FIBRE 7g

SODIUM 400mg

SERVES 4
PREPARATION TIME: 40 minutes
COOKING TIME: 25 minutes
OVEN: Preheat to 200°C (400°F, gas mark 6)

1 tablespoon olive oil
1 large clove garlic, peeled and crushed
1 small red onion, peeled and finely chopped
2 rashers unsmoked back bacon, trimmed of fat
and chopped
1lb (450g) beef with fat removed, minced
Sprig fresh oregano

3 basil leaves, chopped, or ¼ level teaspoon
dried basil
¼ level teaspoon freshly grated nutmeg or
ground nutmeg
Freshly ground black pepper
1 level teaspoon arrowroot
1 tablespoon balsamic vinegar
3fl oz (85ml) unsweetened red grape juice
14oz (400g) tinned chopped tomatoes
8 large savoy cabbage leaves
8oz (225g) cooked borlotti or black-eyed
beans (see p.17)

1 Heat the oil in a large frying pan and toss the garlic and onion in it over a high heat for 1 minute. Add the bacon and cook for 1 minute. Stir in the beef and fry for about 10 minutes until brown, breaking up any lumps that form. Stir in the oregano, basil and nutmeg, and season with pepper.

2 Blend the arrowroot with the vinegar and grape juice and stir into the minced-beef mixture until the juices come to the boil and thicken. Pour in the tomatoes and simmer, covered, for 20 minutes.

3 Meanwhile bring a large saucepan of water to the boil and cook the cabbage for 2 minutes, then rinse with cold water and drain.

4 Mix the beans into the beef thoroughly, then turn the mixture into a sieve set over a bowl and discard the oregano. Let the juices drain out and keep them for the sauce.

5 Lay the cabbage leaves inside up on a board. Spoon the beef mixture onto the leaves, fold the sides in over the filling and roll the leaves up firmly. Arrange the rolls, seam side down, in one layer in a casserole. Add 2-3 tablespoons of water, put on the lid and bake in the heated oven for about 20 minutes, or until the leaf ribs are just tender.

6 Bring the reserved juices to the boil in a small saucepan while you lift the cabbage rolls onto a heated serving dish. Pour the sauce round them.

A tomato gratin and mashed potato with swede add colour and varied texture to the parcels of beef and beans.

Deep green, crinkly leaves of the savoy cabbage make attractive, crisp wrappings for a substantial, well-flavoured beef and bean filling.

Beef parcels with chestnuts and red wine

SERVES 4
PREPARATION TIME: 30 minutes
COOKING TIME: 1 hour
OVEN: Preheat to 160°C (325°F, gas mark 3)

4oz (115g) chestnuts, shell and inner skin removed, finely chopped
2oz (60g) mushrooms, wiped and finely chopped
1 small carrot, peeled and grated
1 clove garlic, peeled and crushed
1 level tablespoon whole-grain mustard
2 level teaspoons chopped fresh thyme
1/8 level teaspoon salt
Freshly ground black pepper
4 slices braising beef, each about 4oz (115g), fat removed, beaten out thin
Thin string to tie parcels
1 tablespoon olive oil
3 shallots or small onions, peeled and finely sliced
1 level tablespoon plain flour
1/4 pint (150ml) red wine
1/4 pint (150ml) vegetable or beef stock (see p.19)

1 Mix together thoroughly the chestnuts, mushrooms, carrot, garlic, mustard, thyme and salt, and season with pepper. Spread out the beef slices on a board and spoon a quarter of the chestnut mixture onto the centre of each. Wrap the meat round the stuffing to make four neat parcels and tie with clean, thin string.

2 Heat the oil in a flameproof casserole and brown the parcels in it over a high heat. Lift them out with a slotted spoon and set aside. Cook the shallots or onions in the casserole gently for 2-3 minutes. Stir in the flour and cook for 1 minute, then gradually stir in the wine and stock and continue stirring while the sauce comes to the boil and thickens.

3 Return the beef parcels to the casserole, cover and cook in the heated oven for 1 hour. Carefully snip and remove the string when you serve the parcels.

Cauliflower, baked tomatoes and jacket potatoes go well with the moist beef parcels. You can use ale in place of the wine and, when chestnuts are out of season, soaked and chopped dried chestnuts can replace them. If you gather your own chestnuts, be sure they are sweet chestnuts, not horse chestnuts.

ONE SERVING	
CALORIES	275
TOTAL FAT	10g
SATURATED FAT	3g
CARBOHYDRATES	16g
ADDED SUGAR	0
FIBRE	2g
SODIUM	140mg

TIP
Chestnuts peel easily if you cut a deep cross in the top of each, put them in a pan with cold water to cover, bring to the boil and simmer for 10 minutes. Spoon out one at a time to peel.

The sweet chestnut stuffing and the rich wine sauce are delicious accompaniments to the thinly beaten slices of beef. They combine to make an unusual autumn dish.

Beef kebabs with courgettes and tomatoes

SERVES 4
PREPARATION TIME: 20 minutes, plus 3 hours
to marinate
COOKING TIME: 15 minutes

4 level tablespoons low-fat natural yoghurt
2 tablespoons lemon juice
2 cloves garlic, peeled and finely chopped
2 level teaspoons peeled and grated root ginger,
or ½ level teaspoon ground ginger
2 level teaspoons paprika
½ level teaspoon each cayenne pepper, ground
nutmeg, cumin and coriander
1lb (450g) rump steak with fat removed,
cut into 12 cubes
1 medium courgette, trimmed and cut into 12 slices
1 large red pepper, de-seeded and cut
into 12 squares
4 long metal skewers
8 cherry tomatoes
2 small onions, peeled and cut into quarters
Fresh coriander leaves to garnish

1 Mix the yoghurt, lemon juice, garlic and
ginger with the paprika, cayenne pepper,
nutmeg, cumin and coriander. Whisk the
mixture well, or blend it in a food processor
for 10 seconds.

2 Pour the mixture into a glass or china bowl
and turn the beef cubes in it to coat well. Cover
and put in the refrigerator for 3 hours to
marinate. Turn the meat once during this time.

3 Blanch the courgette and pepper for one
minute in boiling water.

4 Lift the beef cubes out of the marinade and
thread onto four oiled skewers, with a share of
the courgette, red pepper, tomatoes and onion.
Lay the kebabs on the grill rack and cook under
a high heat for 15-20 minutes, frequently
brushing with the marinade and turning until
the meat and vegetables are tender. Reduce the
heat if the kebabs are browning too much.

Serve the kebabs very hot, still on their skewers,
on a bed of boiled green lentils and garnished
with fresh coriander. A dish of diced cucumber
mixed with low-fat natural yoghurt is a
welcome cool accompaniment to the spicy
kebabs. For a summer meal, you might prefer
rolls and a leafy salad with the kebabs.

ONE SERVING	
CALORIES	185
TOTAL FAT	6g
SATURATED FAT	3g
CARBOHYDRATES	8g
ADDED SUGAR	0
FIBRE	1g
SODIUM	90mg

*Marinating meat in yoghurt and lemon juice makes
it a fittingly tender partner for the vegetables in this
colourful dish. Here the yoghurt is warmly spiced.*

Spanish-style spiced beef

SERVES 4
PREPARATION TIME: 15 minutes
COOKING TIME: 45 minutes

12oz (340g) chuck steak with fat removed, minced
1 large Spanish onion, peeled and chopped
1 small green pepper, de-seeded and chopped
2 cloves garlic, peeled and crushed
1½ level teaspoons chilli powder
14oz (400g) tinned chopped tomatoes, drained
with 3fl oz (85ml) of their juice reserved
1oz (30g) raisins
2 tablespoons cider vinegar
2 teaspoons tomato purée (see p.16)
½ level teaspoon ground ginger
½ level teaspoon dried thyme
Freshly ground black pepper
1 small cos-type lettuce, cleaned and shredded
4 spring onions, trimmed
8-12 small radishes, trimmed and halved
3½ oz (100g) low-fat natural yoghurt

1 Cook the beef in a dry frying pan over a moderate heat for 3-5 minutes, stirring it to break up any lumps, until it is no longer pink.

2 Stir in the onion, green pepper, garlic and 1 teaspoon of the chilli powder, and continue cooking and stirring for 8 minutes.

3 Mix in the tomatoes and juice, the raisins, vinegar, tomato purée, ginger and thyme, and season with pepper. Simmer gently, uncovered, for 30 minutes, stirring occasionally.

4 Spread the lettuce on serving plates, pile a share of the beef on top and garnish with the spring onions and radishes. Stir the yoghurt until smooth, sprinkle the remaining chilli powder on it and hand round separately.

Wholemeal bread and a salad of green beans and courgettes are satisfying accompaniments.

ONE SERVING

CALORIES 195

TOTAL FAT 5g

SATURATED FAT 2g

CARBOHYDRATES 17g

ADDED SUGAR 0

FIBRE 3g

SODIUM 145mg

TIP
To minimise the fat, buy chuck steak, or if not available beef skirt, and mince it yourself after cutting off the fat. If you do not have a mincer, ask the butcher to trim and mince the meat.

The crunchy salad ingredients in this dish make a refreshing contrast to the spicy beef and a spoonful of yoghurt cools it.

Stir-frying seals in the beef's juices and keeps the vegetables crisp. You can serve the dish with egg noodles to complete the Chinese theme.

Beef stir-fry

ONE SERVING

CALORIES 235

TOTAL FAT 10g

SATURATED FAT 2g

CARBOHYDRATES 12g

ADDED SUGAR 0

FIBRE 3g

SODIUM 160mg

SERVES 4
PREPARATION TIME: 10 minutes
COOKING TIME: 15 minutes

1 tablespoon vegetable oil
12oz (340g) rump steak, cut into matchstick strips
1 large onion, peeled and sliced
1 green or red pepper, de-seeded and cut into strips
1 large carrot, peeled and cut into matchstick strips
8fl oz (225ml) beef stock (see p.19)
8oz (225g) button mushrooms, wiped and sliced
4fl oz (115ml) dry white wine
1 level tablespoon cornflour
2 tablespoons water
1 teaspoon soy sauce
1 teaspoon sesame oil
6oz (175g) bean sprouts

TIP
Chilling the beef in the freezer for 20-25 minutes makes it easier to cut into thin strips.

1 Heat the oil in a heavy-based frying pan and stir-fry the steak in it over a high heat for 1 minute. Use a slotted spoon to lift the steak onto a plate.

2 Stir-fry the onion, pepper and carrot in the pan with 2 tablespoons of stock for 1 minute.

3 Add the mushrooms, wine and remaining stock and simmer for 3 minutes. Blend the cornflour with the water and stir into the pan juices until the sauce thickens. Cook gently for 2 minutes.

4 Stir in the soy sauce, sesame oil and bean sprouts and return the meat to the pan. Cook for 1 minute. Serve at once while piping hot.

Sweet and sour braised beef

SERVES 6
PREPARATION TIME: 25 minutes, plus 24 hours
to marinate
COOKING TIME: 45 minutes
OVEN: Preheat to 160°C (325°F, gas mark 3)

2 tablespoons olive oil
4fl oz (115ml) white wine vinegar
6fl oz (175ml) dry white wine
Finely grated rind of 1 lemon
1/4 level teaspoon cayenne pepper

1 large onion, peeled, halved and thinly sliced
2 bay leaves
2lb (900g) rump steak with fat removed, cut
into six pieces
1 level tablespoon demerara sugar
2 level tablespoons plain flour
1 level tablespoon tomato purée (see p.16)
6fl oz (175ml) beef stock (see p.19)
1/8 level teaspoon salt
2 medium mangoes, peeled, stoned and sliced

ONE SERVING	
CALORIES	310
TOTAL FAT	12g
SATURATED FAT	4g
CARBOHYDRATES	15g
ADDED SUGAR	3g
FIBRE	2g
SODIUM	220mg

1 Mix half the oil with the vinegar, wine, lemon rind, cayenne pepper, onion and bay leaves in a shallow glass or china dish. Put in the steak and turn it over to coat it well with the marinade. Cover the dish and refrigerate for 24 hours, turning the meat from time to time. Lift the meat onto kitchen paper to drain. Take the onion and bay leaves out of the marinade and set aside. Strain and keep the liquid.

2 Heat the remaining oil over a gentle heat in a flameproof casserole. Sprinkle in the sugar, let it dissolve and as soon as it begins to brown, put in the pieces of steak and brown them all over. Lift the meat onto a plate and set aside.

3 Cook the onion in the casserole over a moderate heat for 1 minute, then stir in the flour and cook for 1 minute. Gradually mix in the marinade liquid, tomato purée and stock. Put back the bay leaves, add the salt and bring the sauce to the boil, stirring continuously.

4 Put the meat back in the casserole along with any juices from the plate. Stir in the mango, cover the casserole with a tightly fitting lid, or foil, and cook in the heated oven for about 45 minutes, or until the meat is tender.

Remove the bay leaves before serving. Serve the sweet and sour beef with broccoli and rice flavoured with thyme. You can use chuck steak instead of rump for a less expensive dish; increase the time in the oven to 2½ hours, adding the mango for the last hour.

Long marinating gives the beef a delicate fragrance; the marinade produces a rich, mellow sauce that is sweetened naturally with fresh mangoes.

Beef stew with tomatoes and basil

SERVES 4
PREPARATION TIME: 20 minutes
COOKING TIME: 2 hours 15 minutes

ONE SERVING	
CALORIES	320
TOTAL FAT	10g
SATURATED FAT	3g
CARBOHYDRATES	24g
ADDED SUGAR	0
FIBRE	7g
SODIUM	185mg

1lb (450g) chuck steak or beef skirt with
fat removed, cut into large cubes
Freshly ground black pepper
1 tablespoon olive oil
4fl oz (115ml) red wine
14fl oz (400ml) beef stock (see p.19)
14oz (400g) tinned peeled tomatoes

2 sticks celery, trimmed and sliced
4 cloves garlic, peeled and crushed
3 strips thinly pared orange rind
½ level teaspoon fennel seeds
½ level teaspoon dried thyme
1 bay leaf
2 medium onions, peeled and quartered
8 medium carrots, peeled and sliced
6oz (175g) shelled fresh (or frozen) peas
3 level tablespoons chopped fresh basil
2 tablespoons tomato purée (see p.16)

The classic combination of tomatoes and basil adds a distinctive undertone to this dish, giving a Mediterranean character to the traditional, full-bodied beef stew.

1 Season the beef with pepper. Heat the oil in a large, heavy-based saucepan and toss the meat in it over a high heat for 4-5 minutes. Spoon the beef onto a plate and set aside.

2 Pour the wine into the pan and boil for 2 minutes, stirring to mix in the browned juices. Stir in the stock, tomatoes, celery, half the garlic, the orange rind, fennel seeds, thyme and bay leaf, and bring to the boil. Put back the beef, cover and simmer for 1 hour 15 minutes.

3 Discard the bay leaf, stir in the onions and carrots, cover and simmer for 35 minutes. Test the beef with a fork and if not quite tender, cook for 15 minutes more. When it is tender, add the peas and cook for 10 minutes more.

4 Mix the basil, tomato purée and remaining garlic into the stew and reheat for 1 minute.

Pasta or chunks of crusty bread are the best companions for the savoury stew.

Roast beef with Yorkshire puddings and mushroom gravy

SERVES 6
PREPARATION TIME: 30 minutes
COOKING TIME: 1 hour 20 minutes
OVEN: Preheat to 230°C (450°F, gas mark 8)

ONE SERVING	
CALORIES	240
TOTAL FAT	8g
SATURATED FAT	3g
CARBOHYDRATES	15g
ADDED SUGAR	0
FIBRE	1g
SODIUM	115mg

1½ lb (680g) lean topside beef, wiped
½ level teaspoon each plain flour, mustard powder and ground allspice

For the Yorkshire puddings:
3oz (85g) plain flour
1 egg, size 2
¼ pint (150ml) skimmed milk
1 teaspoon vegetable oil

For the mushroom gravy:
½ pint (285ml) vegetable stock (see p.19)
8oz (225g) chestnut mushrooms, wiped and finely chopped
1 level tablespoon cornflour
1 teaspoon Worcestershire sauce
1 level teaspoon French or whole-grain mustard
Freshly ground black pepper

1 Put the beef in a small roasting tin. Mix the flour, mustard and allspice together and rub all over the beef. Cook in the heated oven for 20 minutes, then lower the temperature to 190°C (375°F, gas mark 5) and cook for a further 40 minutes for medium-rare beef or 50 minutes for well-done beef. Baste with the meat juices two or three times during cooking.

2 As soon as the meat goes in the oven, prepare the pudding batter. Whisk together the flour, egg and half the milk until smooth. Gradually whisk in the remaining milk. Cover and leave to stand.

3 To prepare the gravy, simmer the stock and mushrooms in a saucepan, uncovered, for 15 minutes. Take off the heat and set aside.

4 When the beef is cooked to taste, lift it onto a hot serving dish, cover and leave to rest.

5 Raise the oven temperature to 220°C (425°F, gas mark 7). Brush a 12-cup, nonstick bun tray very lightly with the vegetable oil and heat for 1 minute in the oven. Pour a little of the batter into each cup, dividing it as equally as possible, and cook for 10 minutes or until well risen and golden brown.

6 Meanwhile, blend a little of the mushroom stock with the cornflour and stir back into the pan with the Worcestershire sauce and mustard. Skim off the fat from the meat tin and discard. Pour the mushroom mixture into the meat tin and stir briskly over a direct heat to blend in the browned meat juices as the gravy comes to the boil. Cook for 1 minute, then season with pepper and pour into a warmed serving jug.

Trim the joint of any fat before carving it into thin slices and arranging it on a serving plate. A garnish of bay or basil leaves gives a touch of colour for an attractive presentation. Give each diner two of the Yorkshire puddings with the beef and hand round the gravy separately. Crunchy sesame potatoes (see p.295) and the flavour of broccoli or spring cabbage blend well with the spicy beef and gravy.

TIP
When mixing the Yorkshire pudding batter, use a balloon whisk. It produces a smooth batter quickly, and also incorporates tiny air bubbles in the mixture, which lighten the puddings.

Topside, one of the most popular cuts of beef, is an excellent source of lean meat and suitable for roasting or pot roasting. It is well-flavoured and, if properly kept by the butcher, makes a tender joint. In this recipe, a piquant mushroom gravy adds a new element to a traditional Sunday lunch.

Sirloin steak with basil sauce

SERVES 4
PREPARATION TIME: 15 minutes
COOKING TIME: 25 minutes

1lb (450g) sirloin steak, cut in one thick
piece, fat removed
Freshly ground black pepper
4oz (115g) shallots or onion, peeled and chopped
3 tablespoons water
12oz (340g) courgettes, trimmed and
coarsely grated
1 tablespoon olive oil
2 level teaspoons capers, drained and chopped
3 level tablespoons chopped fresh basil

1 Wipe the steak with kitchen paper, sprinkle it with pepper and set it aside.

2 Boil the shallots or onion in a medium saucepan with the water until they are transparent and the water is reduced by half. Stir in the courgettes and oil, cover and cook over a low heat for 8-10 minutes, stirring frequently, until the courgettes are soft.

3 Pass the vegetables through a food mill or blend in a food processor. Stir in the capers and basil, and season with pepper. Reheat the sauce, spoon into a serving dish, cover and keep hot.

4 Heat a heavy frying pan and sear the steak in it over a high heat for 30 seconds on each side. Turn down the heat and cook the meat for about 8 minutes for medium-rare, turning it once or twice. Cook for 1-2 minutes more on each side if you prefer steak well done.

5 Cut the steak downwards and slanting into thin slices and serve with the basil sauce.

This simply made but luxurious dish needs only a mixed leafy salad and french bread with it. You can garnish the meat and sauce with parsley sprigs and whole capers if you wish.

ONE SERVING

CALORIES 200

TOTAL FAT 9g

SATURATED FAT 3g

CARBOHYDRATES 4g

ADDED SUGAR 0

FIBRE 1g

SODIUM 90mg

The peppery clove flavour of basil and the pungency of capers are combined in the thick sauce that spices this plainly cooked steak.

Fillet steak with wild mushrooms

SERVES 4
PREPARATION TIME: 20 minutes
COOKING TIME: 15 minutes

1 teaspoon olive oil
1lb (450g) fillet steak, cut into 4 slices
Freshly ground black pepper

2 tablespoons whisky
7oz (200g) fresh wild mushrooms, cleaned and sliced, or dried porcini, soaked and sliced
1 bay leaf
1 clove garlic, peeled and crushed
1 level teaspoon plain flour
4oz (115g) low-fat natural yoghurt

ONE SERVING	
CALORIES	195
TOTAL FAT	7g
SATURATED FAT	3g
CARBOHYDRATES	3g
ADDED SUGAR	0
FIBRE	1g
SODIUM	95mg

Whisky and the rich juice of wild mushrooms give a warm, nutty flavour to the smooth and tart yoghurt sauce.

1 Heat the oil in a nonstick frying pan. Season the steaks with pepper and sear them on both sides over a high heat, then lower the heat to moderate and cook 2-3 minutes each side for rare meat, 3-4 for medium, 4-5 for well done.

2 Pour the whisky over the steaks and boil it for 1-2 minutes until reduced by half. Lift the steaks onto a heated plate, cover and keep hot.

3 Put the mushrooms in the pan with the bay leaf and garlic. Cover and cook quickly for 2-3 minutes, then uncover and boil until the juices have reduced by half. Blend the flour with the yoghurt until smooth. Stir the mixture into the mushrooms and heat without boiling until the sauce thickens. Season it with pepper and discard the bay leaf. Pour the mushroom sauce over the steaks and serve immediately.

Hot red cabbage and a wild rice mixture are perfect foils for the tender meat and rich sauce. You can add a sprig of bay, basil or sage for a touch of colour.

> **TIP**
> **Remove the stalks from the mushrooms and use in a soup or stew. They are tougher than the stalks of cultivated mushrooms and could spoil the succulent dish.**

Oriental steak

ONE SERVING	
CALORIES	200
TOTAL FAT	8g
SATURATED FAT	2g
CARBOHYDRATES	6g
ADDED SUGAR	5g
FIBRE	0g
SODIUM	70mg

SERVES 4
PREPARATION TIME: 5 minutes, plus 12 hours
to marinate
COOKING TIME: 10 minutes

1lb (450g) rump steak in one slice, fat removed
2 tablespoons soy sauce
1 level tablespoon soft brown sugar
1 tablespoon lemon juice

2 level teaspoons Dijon mustard
2 level teaspoons peeled and grated root ginger
2 cloves garlic, peeled and crushed
2 teaspoons sesame oil
3 tablespoons dry sherry or white wine
Freshly ground black pepper
2 tablespoons white vinegar
1 level teaspoon granulated sugar
2 tablespoons water

The steak absorbs the gingered sherry marinade which tenderises the meat and imparts a distinctly Eastern flavour, subtly enhanced by soy sauce and sesame oil.

1 Put the steak in a shallow glass or china dish that will just hold it and prick all over with a fork. Mix the soy sauce, brown sugar, lemon juice, mustard, ginger, garlic, sesame oil and half the sherry or wine, season with pepper and pour over the steak. Cover and refrigerate for about 12 hours, turning the meat a few times.

2 Take the steak out of the marinade and pat it dry with kitchen paper. Use a sharp knife to score it with crisscross cuts. Heat a frying pan and cook the steak over a moderately high heat, without fat or oil, for 3 minutes each side for rare, 4 for medium or 5 for well done. Lift the steak onto a heated serving dish.

3 Let the frying pan cool slightly before adding the remaining sherry or wine, the vinegar, granulated sugar and water. Boil, stirring all the time, until the mixture has reduced to about 2 tablespoons of concentrated glaze.

4 Cut downwards and slanting through the meat to carve it into thin slices. Spoon a little of the glaze onto each serving.

Serve the steak with a dish of lightly cooked Chinese noodles, tossed with a little sesame oil to continue the Oriental style of the dish. A raw vegetable salad and a parsley garnish add crispness and colour.

Peppered sirloin steak

SERVES 6
PREPARATION TIME: 10 minutes
COOKING TIME: 10 minutes
OVEN: Preheat to 240°C (475°F, gas mark 9)

ONE SERVING
CALORIES 170
TOTAL FAT 8g
SATURATED FAT 3g
CARBOHYDRATES 0
ADDED SUGAR 0
FIBRE 0
SODIUM 70mg

1½ lb (680g) sirloin steak, cut in one thick slice, fat removed
2 level tablespoons black peppercorns, crushed
1 tablespoon olive oil
3 spring onions, trimmed and finely chopped
2 tablespoons dry white wine
8fl oz (225ml) beef stock (see p.19)

1 Coat both sides of the steak with the crushed peppercorns.

2 Heat the oil in a heavy-based flameproof casserole over a very high heat and quickly sear the steak in it, for about 30 seconds on each side.

3 Put the casserole in the heated oven and roast the steak, uncovered, for 4-5 minutes for rare, 6-7 for medium, and 7-8 for well done. Lift the steak onto a heated serving dish and carve downwards and slanting into thin slices.

4 Stir the spring onions into the meat juices and cook over a direct heat for 30 seconds. Add the wine and cook, uncovered, for 1 minute before adding the beef stock and simmering for 2-3 minutes while scraping the hardened juices into the sauce. Boil to reduce to about half a cupful and pour round the steak.

Lightly steamed sugar snap peas and carrots provide a crisp, sweet contrast to the tender, peppery steak. Serve warm wholemeal rolls (see p.366) with the dish for mopping up the juices. If you like, you can garnish the dish with a few bay or sage leaves.

> **TIP**
> *To crush the peppercorns without a mortar and pestle, put them inside a double-thickness polythene bag and roll firmly on a sturdy board with a rolling pin.*

A crust of crunchy peppercorns seals in the juices of the lean sirloin, keeping beautifully moist a cut which can sometimes be dry. The meat's full flavour comes through the hot pungency of the crust.

Osso bucco

TIP
Make sure the veal is cut into four before you take it home. The butcher has the tools for sawing through the leg bone.

SERVES 4
PREPARATION TIME: 25 minutes
COOKING TIME: 2 hours

2 tablespoons olive oil
2lb (900g) veal shin or knuckle, cut into 4 rounds
1 onion, peeled and chopped
1 carrot, peeled and chopped
1 stick celery, trimmed and chopped
3 cloves garlic, peeled and finely chopped
6fl oz (175ml) dry white wine
1 large tomato, skinned, de-seeded and chopped
½ level teaspoon each dried thyme and dried sage
Freshly ground black pepper
1 bay leaf
¼ pint (150ml) beef or veal stock (see p.19)
2 level tablespoons chopped fresh parsley
1½ level teaspoons finely grated lemon rind
Sprigs of fresh bay or thyme to garnish

1 Heat 1 tablespoon of the oil in a large flameproof casserole and brown the veal in it over a high heat for 2 minutes on each side. Lift the veal onto a plate and set aside.

2 Reduce the heat, add the remaining oil to the casserole and cook the onion, carrot, celery and half the garlic in it for about 5 minutes, or until the onion is lightly coloured. Return the veal to the casserole, pour in the wine and cook over a moderate heat until the liquid is reduced by half.

3 Stir in the tomato, thyme and sage, season with pepper, put in the bay leaf and pour on the stock. Cover the casserole and simmer for 2 hours, or until the meat is almost falling off the bone. Pour in a little boiling water during cooking if the liquid evaporates too much.

4 Mix the parsley, lemon rind and remaining garlic. Discard the bay leaf, then sprinkle the mixture over the veal and garnish with the bay or thyme.

Serve the osso bucco with risotto rice, creamy in texture and perhaps tinted a pale gold with a few threads of saffron. A green salad makes a crisp, refreshing contrast.

The marrowbone in the veal makes a full-flavoured and slightly gelatinous broth for the meltingly tender meat in this hearty family dish.

Stuffed escalopes of veal with mushroom sauce

SERVES 4
PREPARATION TIME: 20 minutes, plus
15 minutes to soak
COOKING TIME: 20 minutes

2oz (60g) couscous
¼ pint (150ml) boiling water
4 spring onions, trimmed and finely sliced
4 ready-to-use dried apricots, finely chopped
2 tablespoons olive oil
8 small veal escalopes, each about 2oz (60g),
beaten out thin
Wooden cocktail sticks to secure
8 tablespoons veal or vegetable stock (see p.19)
1 clove garlic, peeled and crushed
4oz (115g) button mushrooms, wiped and sliced
1oz (30g) parsley, finely chopped
1 level tablespoon Dijon mustard
1 level tablespoon low-fat fromage frais
Freshly ground black pepper

1 Put the couscous into a bowl and cover with
the boiling water. Leave to stand for about
15 minutes, until the water has been absorbed.

2 Mix the onions, apricots and half the oil
with the couscous. Place 2 teaspoons of the
mixture on the broader end of each escalope,
roll up neatly and secure with cocktail sticks.

3 Heat the remaining oil in a frying pan and
fry the veal rolls over a moderate heat for
3 minutes, turning until the meat is opaque all
round. Pour in the stock, cover and simmer for
10 minutes or until the veal is cooked through
and the stuffing hot right to the centre.

4 Lift the veal rolls onto a warmed serving dish
and remove the cocktail sticks. Cover and keep
hot. Pour the juices into a bowl and set aside.

5 Toss the garlic and mushrooms in the frying
pan over a high heat for 1 minute, then scatter
in the parsley and cook for 1 minute more.

*Couscous, a coarsely milled wheat rather like
semolina, binds together the sweet stuffing in this
dish and absorbs the flavours of the veal, onions and
apricots. A creamy mushroom sauce spiked with
mustard and parsley gives the dish a luxury finish.*

6 Stir in the mustard, fromage frais and
reserved veal juices, and bring to the boil. Let
the sauce bubble for 1 minute, then season
with pepper and pour it over the veal rolls.

New carrots and broad beans are particularly
good with the veal, and you might like some
french bread so that none of the sauce is left
on the plate.

ONE SERVING	
CALORIES	290
TOTAL FAT	11g
SATURATED FAT	2g
CARBOHYDRATES	20g
ADDED SUGAR	0
FIBRE	3g
SODIUM	325mg

Lamb and asparagus stir-fry

SERVES 4
PREPARATION TIME: 20 minutes, plus 30 minutes
to marinate
COOKING TIME: 15 minutes

ONE SERVING	
CALORIES	330
TOTAL FAT	18g
SATURATED FAT	5g
CARBOHYDRATES	12g
ADDED SUGAR	0
FIBRE	3g
SODIUM	660mg

2 level tablespoons peeled and grated root ginger,
or 1 level teaspoon ground ginger
2 cloves garlic, peeled and crushed
2 tablespoons soy sauce
2 tablespoons dry sherry
2 tablespoons sesame oil
1lb (450g) lamb without bone or fat, cut into strips
1lb (450g) thin asparagus, trimmed and cut
diagonally into short lengths

1 Spanish onion, peeled, quartered and sliced
1 medium green pepper, de-seeded and sliced
1 level teaspoon cornflour
3fl oz (85ml) chicken or vegetable stock (see p.19)
3oz (85g) bamboo shoots
3oz (85g) water chestnuts, thinly sliced

1 Combine the ginger, garlic, soy sauce, sherry
and 1 teaspoon of the sesame oil in a glass or
china dish. Stir the lamb into this marinade,
cover and leave in a cool place for 30 minutes.

2 Heat 1 tablespoon of the sesame oil in
a large frying pan over a high heat and stir-fry
the asparagus in it for 3-5 minutes until just
becoming tender. Add the onion and green
pepper and stir-fry for 1 minute more, then
cover and cook for 1 minute. Using a slotted
spoon, lift all the vegetables onto a large plate.

3 Heat the remaining sesame oil in the pan
over a high heat and stir in the lamb. Pour on
the marinade and cook, stirring, for 5 minutes.
Blend the cornflour with the stock, stir into the
pan juices and boil until the liquid thickens.

4 Put the vegetables back in the pan, mix in
the bamboo shoots and water chestnuts
and toss over a moderate heat for 2 minutes.

Serve the stir-fry while piping hot with plenty
of fluffed-up rice.

*Young asparagus stalks are ideal for stir-frying and
their delicate flavour suits that of the lamb. Bamboo
shoots and water chestnuts add satisfying crunchiness.*

Lamb baked in aubergines

ONE SERVING	
CALORIES	195
TOTAL FAT	9g
SATURATED FAT	4g
CARBOHYDRATES	8g
ADDED SUGAR	0
FIBRE	3g
SODIUM	185mg

SERVES 4
PREPARATION TIME: 20 minutes, plus 30 minutes
to stand
COOKING TIME: 1 hour 5 minutes
OVEN: Preheat to 190°C (375°F, gas mark 5)

2 medium aubergines
¼ level teaspoon salt
1 teaspoon olive oil
1 onion, peeled and chopped

2 cloves garlic, peeled and chopped
12oz (340g) lamb without bone or fat, minced
1 level teaspoon each ground cumin and coriander
2 level teaspoons plain flour
7oz (200g) tinned chopped tomatoes
1oz (30g) pine nuts, lightly toasted
2 level tablespoons chopped fresh parsley
Freshly ground black pepper
2 level tablespoons fresh brown breadcrumbs
Lime wedges and coriander sprigs to garnish

TIP
For lean lamb, buy chump or gigot chops, bone and trim off all fat before mincing. Most butchers will do this for you.

Aubergines acting as edible gratin dishes provide a tinge of bitterness to offset the sweetness of the filling.

1 Halve the aubergines lengthways, score the cut surfaces crisscross fashion, sprinkle with the salt and leave to stand for 30 minutes.

2 Rinse the aubergines with plenty of cold water, pat them dry and put them cut side down on a sheet of nonstick baking paper on a baking sheet. Prick the skin all over and bake in the heated oven for 30 minutes.

3 Meanwhile, heat the oil in a heavy-based saucepan and toss the onion and garlic in it over a high heat until golden. Stir in the lamb and cook briskly until it begins to brown. Break up any lumps that form with a fork.

4 Sprinkle on the cumin, coriander and flour and cook, stirring, for 30 seconds. Pour in the tomatoes and bring to the boil, then stir, cover and simmer for about 10 minutes.

5 When the aubergines are tender, scoop out the flesh leaving shells about ¼ in (6mm) thick. Chop the flesh and stir it into the lamb along with the pine nuts and chopped parsley. Season the mixture with pepper.

6 Fill the aubergine shells with the lamb mixture, arrange them in an ovenproof dish and sprinkle on the breadcrumbs. Pour a thin covering of water into the bottom of the dish. Bake the filled aubergines in the heated oven for about 50 minutes, or until they are crisp and golden brown on top.

Garnish the aubergines with the lime wedges and coriander and serve with bulgur wheat simmered with a few sultanas to emphasise the Balkan flavour of the dish. Side salads of tomato and onion sprinkled with snipped dill fronds or parsley will provide a sharp contrast.

Lamb and barley stew

SERVES 4
PREPARATION TIME: 15 minutes
COOKING TIME: 1 hour 45 minutes

2 teaspoons olive oil
1lb (450g) meat from boned leg of lamb
or neck fillet with fat removed, cut into cubes
1 onion, peeled and sliced
1 clove garlic, peeled and chopped
1½ pints (850ml) chicken or vegetable
stock (see p.19)
2oz (60g) pearl barley
Freshly ground black pepper
1 turnip, peeled and cut into wedges
2 large carrots, peeled and sliced
2 medium leeks, sliced and washed
2 sticks celery, trimmed and sliced
2 level tablespoons chopped fresh parsley

1 Heat the oil in a heavy-based saucepan and toss the lamb, onion and garlic in it over a moderate heat for 5 minutes, until browning.

2 Pour in the stock, stir in the barley, season with pepper and bring to the boil. Reduce the heat, cover the saucepan and simmer for 1 hour, stirring from time to time.

3 Mix in the turnip, carrots, leeks and celery, cover and cook for 40 minutes, or until the vegetables are tender. Scatter on the parsley just before serving in warmed individual bowls.

Steamed potatoes and savoy cabbage go well with the stew. You can steam the potatoes on top of the stew, sitting the steamer on top of the pan for the last 30 minutes of cooking.

ONE SERVING	
CALORIES 295	
TOTAL FAT 13g	
SATURATED FAT 5g	
CARBOHYDRATES 20g	
ADDED SUGAR 0	
FIBRE 3g	
SODIUM 120mg	

TIP
Buy 1½ lb (680g)
of meat to give the
right amount after
boning and
trimming.

There is a north-country character about this hearty stew, which is flavoured with winter vegetables and thickened with pearl barley.

Lamb stew with carrots and runner beans

SERVES 4
PREPARATION TIME: 30 minutes
COOKING TIME: 1 hour 10 minutes

2 tablespoons olive oil
*1lb (450g) meat from chump ends or lean shoulder
of lamb with bone and fat removed, cut into cubes*
12-16 small shallots or pickling onions, peeled
1 clove garlic, peeled and crushed

2 level tablespoons plain flour
¾ pint (425ml) vegetable or beef stock (see p.19)
*1 level tablespoon chopped fresh marjoram,
or 1 level teaspoon dried marjoram*
Freshly ground black pepper
2 medium carrots, peeled and diced
4 medium potatoes, peeled and cut into chunks
*6oz (175g) runner beans, trimmed and
sliced diagonally*

ONE SERVING	
CALORIES	385
TOTAL FAT	18g
SATURATED FAT	6g
CARBOHYDRATES	30g
ADDED SUGAR	0
FIBRE	4g
SODIUM	115mg

1 Heat the oil in a large, heavy-based saucepan and toss the lamb cubes in it over a high heat for about 5 minutes, until browned all over. Lift out the lamb with a slotted spoon and put it to drain on kitchen paper.

2 Cook the shallots or onions in the saucepan over a high heat, stirring, for about 4 minutes until browned, then mix in the garlic and cook for about 30 seconds.

3 Pour off the fat from the saucepan and discard. Stir the flour into the browned vegetables and cook over a moderate heat for 1 minute before gradually blending in the

stock. Stir to loosen the browned cooking juices from the base of the pan while the sauce comes to the boil and thickens.

4 Put the lamb back in the pan, sprinkle on the marjoram and season with pepper. Bring to the boil, stirring, then turn down the heat, cover the saucepan and simmer for 30 minutes.

5 Mix in the carrots and potatoes and cook for 15 minutes, then stir in the green beans and simmer for a further 10 minutes.

Serve the stew in individual heated bowls with warm, crusty french bread.

*Browning the meat
before stewing improves
both the colour and
taste of this stew. It is
worth spending time
trimming chump ends
or shoulder because of
their sweet meat.*

177

Lamb curry

ONE SERVING

CALORIES 325

TOTAL FAT 15g

SATURATED FAT 6g

CARBOHYDRATES 21g

ADDED SUGAR 0

FIBRE 5g

SODIUM 160mg

TIP
You will find it quicker to brown the cubes of lamb a few at a time so the heat in the pan remains high.

SERVES 4
PREPARATION TIME: 25 minutes
COOKING TIME: 55 minutes

1 tablespoon corn oil
1lb (450g) meat from boned chump ends or neck fillet of lamb, fat removed, cut into small cubes
1 medium onion, peeled and thinly sliced
½ small stick celery, trimmed and thinly sliced
1 clove garlic, peeled and crushed
1-2 level tablespoons curry powder
½ level teaspoon each ground cumin, ground cardamom and ground coriander
1 small carrot, peeled and grated
4fl oz (115ml) beef stock (see p.19) or water
¼ level teaspoon cayenne pepper
1 cooking apple, unpeeled, cored and cut into cubes
8oz (225g) small okra or fine green beans, trimmed
2oz (60g) raisins
4oz (115g) low-fat natural yoghurt

1 Heat the oil in a large, heavy-based frying pan and brown the lamb cubes in it on all sides over a high heat. Use a slotted spoon to lift the meat out and put it to drain on kitchen paper.

2 Cook the onion, celery and garlic gently in the frying pan for 5 minutes, stirring frequently. Add the curry powder, cumin, cardamom and coriander and stir for 1 minute. Stir in the lamb, carrot, stock or water and cayenne pepper. Cover and simmer for 40 minutes, or until the lamb is tender.

3 Mix in the apple, okra or beans, and raisins, and a little water if necessary. Cover and cook for 5 minutes, or until the okra is tender.

4 Blend in the yoghurt and heat, taking care not to boil or it will curdle.

Brown or basmati rice and a side dish of thinly sliced tomatoes and onion rings, or coarsely grated carrots would go well with the curry. You can add a garnish of parsley or coriander sprigs for a fresh touch of colour.

Raisins accentuate the tender sweetness of the lamb, striking a perfect balance with the hot, savoury curry spices and sharp, crisp apple.

In common with all pulses, flageolet beans are a good source of fibre; their delicate flavour and tender skin make them a subtle and satisfying partner for the lamb in this colourful dish.

Braised lamb chops with flageolet beans

SERVES 4
PREPARATION TIME: 25 minutes
COOKING TIME: 40 minutes
OVEN: Preheat to 180°C (350°F, gas mark 4)

1 tablespoon olive oil
4 lamb chump chops, each about 6oz (175g), fat removed
2 cloves garlic, peeled and chopped
2 onions, peeled and chopped
3 sticks celery, trimmed and sliced
2 carrots, peeled and sliced
14oz (400g) tinned chopped tomatoes
2 tablespoons tomato purée (see p.16)
2 level teaspoons dried rosemary, finely crumbled
2 level teaspoons paprika
1 level teaspoon Dijon mustard or made English mustard
12oz (340g) cooked flageolet beans (see p.17)
Freshly ground black pepper
Flat-leaf parsley to garnish

1 Heat the oil in a flameproof casserole and brown the chops in it over a high heat for 2-3 minutes on each side. Lift the chops onto kitchen paper to drain.

2 Brown the garlic, onions, celery and carrots in the casserole over a moderate heat for about 5 minutes, stirring occasionally. Mix in the tomatoes and their juice, the tomato purée, rosemary, paprika and mustard. Gently mix in the flageolet beans, season with pepper and bring the casserole to the boil.

3 Arrange the chops on top of the vegetables, put the lid on the casserole and cook in the heated oven for about 40 minutes, or until the lamb is tender.

Serve crusty bread with the dish. A garnish of parsley and a side dish of peppery kale or savoy cabbage give a contrast in flavour and colour.

Herbed lamb cutlets

SERVES 4
PREPARATION TIME: 5 minutes
COOKING TIME: 8 minutes

ONE SERVING	
CALORIES	218
TOTAL FAT	14g
SATURATED FAT	5g
CARBOHYDRATES	0
ADDED SUGAR	0
FIBRE	0
SODIUM	100mg

8 lamb cutlets, each about 4oz (115g), fat trimmed
2 cloves garlic, peeled and halved
1 tablespoon olive oil
1 level tablespoon chopped mixed fresh thyme,
marjoram and rosemary, or 1 level teaspoon dried
mixed herbs
Freshly ground black pepper
Fresh mint and lemon wedges to garnish

1 Lay the cutlets in a shallow dish and rub all over with the cut side of the garlic cloves. Brush both sides of the cutlets with the oil, coat with the herbs and season with pepper.

2 Place the cutlets on the grill rack and cook under a high heat for 4 minutes on each side. Arrange them on warmed serving plates and garnish with the mint and lemon.

Serve with new potatoes and a green salad, and let the diners remove any remaining fat.

> **TIP**
> *To enhance the herb flavour of the cutlets, coat them 4-5 hours before cooking, cover the dish and put in the refrigerator to marinate.*

For ease of preparation and freshness of taste, nothing beats young and tender lamb cutlets briefly grilled in a coating of lively herbs.

Lancashire hotpot

ONE SERVING

CALORIES 360

TOTAL FAT 12g

SATURATED FAT 5g

CARBOHYDRATES 39g

ADDED SUGAR 0

FIBRE 4g

SODIUM 120mg

Long, slow cooking lets the vegetables absorb the flavour of the meltingly tender lamb, and creates a warmly satisfying winter dish.

SERVES 4
PREPARATION TIME: 20 minutes
COOKING TIME: 2 hours 15 minutes
OVEN: Preheat to 180°C (350°F, gas mark 4)

8 middle or best end of neck lamb chops,
about 2lb (900g) together, fat removed
2 bay leaves
1 level tablespoon chopped fresh mixed herbs,
or 1 level teaspoon dried mixed herbs
Freshly ground black pepper
1 pint (570ml) beef or vegetable stock (see p.19)
1 large onion, peeled and sliced
2 medium carrots, peeled and sliced
1 large leek, trimmed, sliced and washed
1½ lb (680g) potatoes, peeled and thickly sliced
1 teaspoon olive oil

1 Arrange the lamb chops in a casserole. Tuck 1 bay leaf underneath and 1 on top, sprinkle on the herbs and season with pepper. Pour in just enough of the stock to cover the meat.

2 Spread the onion, carrots and leek over the chops and season with pepper. Lay overlapping slices of potato on top of the vegetables and brush sparingly with the olive oil.

3 Cover the casserole and cook in the heated oven for 1 hour 30 minutes, then uncover and cook for 45 minutes more to brown the top. Remove the bay leaves as you serve the hotpot.

Lightly cooked cabbage or sautéed brussels sprouts make a crisp contrast to the hotpot.

Kidneys Creole

TIP
To remove the white core easily from a kidney, snip it out with kitchen scissors.

SERVES 4
PREPARATION TIME: 10 minutes
COOKING TIME: 20 minutes

1 tablespoon olive oil
2 level teaspoons peeled and grated root ginger, or ¼ level teaspoon ground ginger
1 clove garlic, peeled and crushed
1 small onion, peeled and finely chopped
2oz (60g) button mushrooms, wiped and sliced
1¼ lb (550g) lambs' kidneys, skinned, halved and cored
1lb (450g) tomatoes, skinned and chopped
½ medium green pepper, de-seeded and diced
½ medium red pepper, de-seeded and diced
2 teaspoons tomato purée (see p.16)
2 level teaspoons muscavado or soft brown sugar
1 tablespoon raspberry vinegar
1 tablespoon lime juice
½ teaspoon hot pepper sauce
Freshly ground black pepper

1 Heat the oil in a frying pan and cook the ginger, garlic and onion in it over a moderate heat for 2-3 minutes. Stir in the mushrooms and cook for 1 minute. Add the kidneys and brown over a high heat, stirring, for 5 minutes.

2 Stir in the tomatoes, green and red peppers, tomato purée, sugar, raspberry vinegar, lime juice and hot pepper sauce. When the mixture comes to the boil, season with pepper, lower the heat and simmer, uncovered, for 10 minutes or until the kidneys are just cooked through.

Serve the kidneys with fluffy rice; you can give a touch of colour with fresh parsley sprigs.

Delicate kidneys are enlivened by a hot sauce with the tomatoes, onions and peppers of Creole cooking sharpened by raspberry vinegar and lime juice.

Lamb's liver with orange and onion

SERVES 4
PREPARATION TIME: 15 minutes
COOKING TIME: 30 minutes
OVEN: Preheat to 180°C (350°F, gas mark 4)

1 tablespoon olive oil
1¼ lb (550g) lamb's liver, very thinly sliced
1 large onion, peeled, sliced and separated into rings

1 level tablespoon plain flour
½ pint (285ml) chicken stock (see p.19)
Grated rind and juice of half a small orange
1 level tablespoon chopped fresh thyme or marjoram, or 1 level teaspoon dried thyme or marjoram
Freshly ground black pepper
Orange rind and thyme sprigs to garnish

Braised lamb's liver produces a rich gravy, which is given an edge here with orange and sweetened with thyme.

TIP
To prevent liver from curling during cooking, remove its fine outer membrane. Ease away a corner with the tip of a knife then gently pull the membrane off.

1 Heat the oil in a frying pan and brown the liver in it quickly on each side over a fairly high heat. Remove the liver from the pan and set aside on kitchen paper to drain. Cook the onion gently in the frying pan, stirring occasionally, until lightly browned.

2 Stir in the flour and cook for 1 minute before gradually stirring in the stock. Bring to the boil, stirring continuously, then add the orange rind, orange juice and herbs, season with pepper, and simmer for 1 minute.

3 Pour two-thirds of the onion sauce into a shallow ovenproof serving dish. Arrange the slices of liver on top in one layer and spoon the rest of the sauce over them.

4 Cover the dish with a lid or foil and bake in the heated oven for 30 minutes, until the liver is just cooked through. Garnish with the orange rind and thyme sprigs.

Serve rice with the liver and give colour and bite with lightly cooked carrots and broccoli.

Stuffed leg of lamb with orange sauce

SERVES 8
PREPARATION TIME: 25 minutes
COOKING TIME: 2 hours 30 minutes–3 hours
OVEN: Preheat to 230°C (450°F, gas mark 8)

ONE SERVING	
CALORIES	335
TOTAL FAT	18g
SATURATED FAT	7g
CARBOHYDRATES	7g
ADDED SUGAR	0
FIBRE	2g
SODIUM	285mg

TIP
Push the stuffing into the leg cavity with a wooden spoon, using the handle end if necessary to reach the centre.

1 tablespoon olive oil
1 large onion, peeled and finely chopped
4 cloves garlic, peeled and crushed
1lb (450g) button mushrooms, wiped and chopped
2oz (60g) wholemeal bread with crusts cut off, diced
1oz (30g) fresh parsley, finely chopped
1 level teaspoon dried marjoram
½ level teaspoon dried basil
1 medium orange
Freshly ground black pepper
6lb (2.7kg) leg of lamb, bone and fat removed
1 level tablespoon plain flour
½ pint (285ml) vegetable or beef stock (see p.19)
Orange wedges and sprigs of marjoram to garnish

1 Heat the oil in a large frying pan and cook the onion and garlic in it gently for 5 minutes, until lightly coloured. Add the mushrooms and cook for a further 8 minutes, or until the mushroom juices have evaporated.

2 Take the pan off the heat and mix in the bread, parsley, marjoram and basil. Grate in about 1 teaspoon of rind from the orange, season with pepper and stir well.

3 Stuff the lamb with the mushroom mixture, packing the stuffing, not too tightly, along the cavity left by removing the bone. Secure with skewers or thin, clean string if necessary to hold the meat in shape.

4 Put the lamb on a rack in a shallow roasting tin and roast in the heated oven, uncovered, for 15 minutes. Reduce the oven temperature to 180°C (350°F, gas mark 4), and continue cooking for another 2 hours for meat that is slightly pink and 2 hours 20 minutes for well-done meat.

5 Pare off the skin and outer membrane of the orange with a very sharp knife. Free the segments by cutting down each side of them to remove the membranes.

6 When the lamb is cooked, lift it onto a warmed serving dish, cover with foil and leave to rest for 10 minutes. Skim off and discard the fat from the juices in the roasting tin. Mix the flour into the remaining juices and gradually stir in the stock. Bring to the boil over a low heat, stirring to incorporate the browned juices from the bottom of the tin. Reduce the heat and simmer for 5 minutes, stirring frequently. Add the orange segments and heat through for 1 minute, then pour into a heated sauceboat.

7 Uncover the lamb and remove any skewers and string. Slice the meat, not too thinly, leaving the diners to remove any remaining fat. Garnish with the orange wedges and marjoram. Serve with the sauce.

The traditional accompaniments of new potatoes and peas cannot be bettered, but you can offer a different look with mangetout or sugar snap peas.

A mushroom stuffing, seasoned with onion, garlic and herbs, and a sauce infused with orange juice and zest, moisten the meat and sharpen the mild flavour of the roast lamb. The leg, a popular cut, provides plenty of tender, lean meat, delicious hot or cold.

Lamb and lentil shepherd's pie

SERVES 4
PREPARATION TIME: 35 minutes
COOKING TIME: 20 minutes
OVEN: Preheat to 200°C (400°F, gas mark 6)

3oz (85g) green lentils
1 tablespoon olive oil
1 medium onion, peeled and chopped
1 clove garlic, peeled and crushed
12oz (340g) boned leg of lamb, trimmed of fat and minced
2 small carrots, peeled and diced
2oz (60g) mushrooms, wiped and chopped
2oz (60g) frozen sweetcorn kernels
1 level teaspoon chopped fresh rosemary, or ½ level teaspoon dried rosemary

1 level teaspoon chopped fresh mint, or ½ level teaspoon dried mint
1 tablespoon tomato purée (see p.16)
14oz (400g) tinned chopped tomatoes
1½ lb (680g) potatoes, peeled and cut up
4 tablespoons skimmed milk
⅛ level teaspoon salt
Freshly ground black pepper

ONE SERVING	
CALORIES	425
TOTAL FAT	13g
SATURATED FAT	4g
CARBOHYDRATES	52g
ADDED SUGAR	0
FIBRE	6g
SODIUM	215mg

1 Cook the lentils (see p.17) and drain them thoroughly.

2 Meanwhile, heat the oil in a large saucepan and toss the onion and garlic in it over a high heat for 2 minutes, until lightly browned. Stir in the lamb and cook for about 5 minutes, until the meat is no longer pink, breaking up any lumps with a fork.

3 Mix in the carrots, mushrooms, sweetcorn, rosemary and mint and cook for 2 minutes, then add the tomato purée and the tomatoes with their juice. Cover the saucepan and simmer for 20 minutes.

4 Boil or steam the potatoes until soft. Drain and mash them, then add the milk and beat until smooth. Cover and set aside.

5 Uncover the pan of lamb and vegetables and cook more briskly for 5 minutes to evaporate some of the liquid. Stir in the cooked lentils and salt, and season with pepper.

6 Turn the lamb mixture into an ovenproof dish, spread the potato over the top and mark with a fork. Cook in the heated oven for about 20 minutes, until golden brown.

Peas and carrots go particularly well with the sweet flavour of the lamb. Instead of lamb you can use lean minced beef, seasoned with 1 teaspoon of prepared mustard and ½ teaspoon dried thyme, or lean minced pork seasoned with 1 teaspoon dried sage and ½ teaspoon dried marjoram.

This variation of the traditional recipe is packed with colourful lentils, tomatoes and sweetcorn, making it a good source of fibre and a substantial, warming dish.

Pork and chickpea stew

TIP
Dried mushrooms may be gritty, so lift them out of the soaking liquid with a slotted spoon and strain the liquid through a sieve lined with a piece of kitchen paper.

SERVES 4
PREPARATION TIME: 35 minutes, plus 30 minutes to soak
COOKING TIME: 1 hour 20 minutes

6fl oz (175ml) boiling water
½ oz (15g) dried porcini mushrooms, well rinsed
12oz (340g) cubes of pork shoulder, fat removed
2 level tablespoons plain flour
2 tablespoons olive oil
1 medium onion, peeled and chopped
2 cloves garlic, peeled and crushed
3 tablespoons port
6fl oz (175ml) chicken stock (see p.19)
1 bay leaf
1 level teaspoon finely chopped fresh rosemary leaves
Freshly ground black pepper
8oz (225g) cooked chickpeas (see p.17)
8oz (225g) button mushrooms, wiped and quartered
1 tablespoon lemon juice

1 Pour the boiling water on the dried mushrooms and leave to stand for 30 minutes. Drain the mushrooms and keep the liquid.

2 Meanwhile, roll the pork cubes in the flour on a plate and shake off any excess. Heat the oil in a large, heavy-based saucepan and brown the pork cubes in it on all sides over a moderate heat. Lift the meat out of the pan with a slotted spoon and put to drain on a plate covered with kitchen paper.

3 In the same pan, fry the onion and garlic gently for about 5 minutes, until lightly browned. Put the pork back in the pan and stir in the port, stock, bay leaf, rosemary, soaked mushrooms and 4 tablespoons of their soaking liquid. Season with pepper, cover and simmer for 20 minutes.

4 Stir the chickpeas into the stew and simmer, covered, for 30 minutes. Add the button mushrooms and cook for a further 10 minutes. Take out the bay leaf and stir in the lemon juice just before serving.

Green beans or cabbage and some crusty rolls will complete a satisfying meal.

Chickpeas add a nutty taste and smooth texture to this hearty, port-flavoured stew of pork and juicy mushrooms.

Indonesian-style pork kebabs

ONE SERVING

CALORIES 205

TOTAL FAT 11g

SATURATED FAT 2g

CARBOHYDRATES 5g

ADDED SUGAR 3g

FIBRE 1g

SODIUM 160mg

SERVES 4
PREPARATION TIME: 20 minutes, plus 1 hour to marinate
COOKING TIME: 20 minutes

½ level teaspoon ground ginger
2 cloves garlic, peeled
1 small onion, peeled and chopped
1 teaspoon soy sauce
2 level tablespoons unsalted peanuts, toasted
1 teaspoon olive oil
2 level teaspoons soft brown sugar

2 teaspoons lemon juice
½ level teaspoon each ground coriander, cumin and cinnamon
2 tablespoons water
12oz (340g) pork tenderloin, trimmed of fat and cut into cubes
4 metal or wooden skewers
Finely shredded lemon rind, spring onion and parsley leaves to garnish

1 Put the ginger, garlic, onion, soy sauce, peanuts, oil, sugar, lemon juice, coriander, cumin and cinnamon in a food processor with the water. Blend for 8-10 seconds, until smooth, then pour into a glass or china dish. Stir the pork cubes into the mixture, cover and put in the refrigerator to marinate for 1 hour.

2 Thread the meat onto the skewers, ensuring that the cubes do not touch one another.

3 Lay the kebabs on a grill rack and brush them with the marinade. Grill for about 20 minutes under a high heat, turning and brushing with the marinade several times, until the pork is cooked through. Arrange the kebabs on a heated serving dish and garnish with the lemon rind, spring onion and parsley.

Boiled rice provides a simple base for the richly flavoured meat, and a crunchy bean sprout and pepper salad refreshes the palate.

The spicy peanut marinade gives an exotic taste of the East to beautifully tender morsels of pork grilled on skewers to brown every side to perfection.

Stuffed loin of pork

ONE SERVING

CALORIES 345

TOTAL FAT 14g

SATURATED FAT 4g

CARBOHYDRATES 12g

ADDED SUGAR 0

FIBRE 2g

SODIUM 185mg

SERVES 4
PREPARATION TIME: 25 minutes
COOKING TIME: 45 minutes
OVEN: Preheat to 200°C (400°F, gas mark 6)

2 tablespoons olive oil
2 tablespoons water
1 large onion, peeled and chopped
1 large carrot, peeled and finely chopped

1 medium red pepper, de-seeded and finely chopped
Freshly ground black pepper
1oz (30g) wholemeal breadcrumbs
1 level teaspoon ground ginger
⅛ level teaspoon ground cloves
1½ lb (680g) rolled loin of pork, trimmed of fat
2 tablespoons lemon juice
7fl oz (200ml) vegetable or chicken stock (see p.19)

The pork is trimmed of fat but, moistened from within by a savoury stuffing and from outside by stock, it cooks to tempting succulence.

1 Heat one tablespoon of the oil in a frying pan with the water and cook the onion, carrot and red pepper in it over a low heat for 6-8 minutes, until the vegetables are soft. Season with black pepper and stir in the breadcrumbs, ginger and cloves to make a well-blended stuffing.

2 Cut a pocket in the centre of the pork for the filling. Push in the stuffing, but not too tightly or it will be squeezed out as the meat shrinks during cooking. Sprinkle the lemon juice over the meat and rub it in well.

3 Heat the remaining oil in a small roasting tin over a moderately high direct heat and quickly brown the stuffed pork all over. Pour the stock in with the meat and bring it to the boil, then put the tin in the heated oven and cook the pork for 20 minutes. Lower the heat to 180°C (350°F, gas mark 4) and cook for another 20 minutes, basting from time to time with the stock, until the pork is cooked through.

4 Lift the pork onto a hot serving plate, cover it loosely with foil and leave it to rest for 10 minutes. Skim off and discard the fat from the juices in the roasting tin.

5 Reheat the roasting juices while you cut the meat into slices. Spoon the juices round the meat before serving.

New potatoes, mangetout and tiny sweetcorn cobs add bite and extra colour to the tender slices of pork.

> **TIP**
> *To make the pocket for the stuffing, push a very sharp long-bladed knife through the centre of the meat from end to end. Move the knife gently from side to side until the slit is large enough to hold the stuffing.*

Apple and cider, popular ingredients in the cooking of Normandy, mellow the lively herb flavouring in the sauce as well as the meatballs.

Normandy meatballs and cider sauce

ONE SERVING

CALORIES 340

TOTAL FAT 14g

SATURATED FAT 5g

CARBOHYDRATES 21g

ADDED SUGAR 0

FIBRE 3g

SODIUM 295mg

SERVES 4
PREPARATION TIME: 15 minutes
COOKING TIME: 25 minutes
OVEN: Preheat to 200°C (400°F, gas mark 6)

1lb (450g) boneless pork with fat removed, minced
3oz (85g) wholemeal breadcrumbs
2oz (60g) ready-to-use stoned prunes,
finely chopped
1 dessert apple, about 4oz (115g), peeled, cored
and finely chopped
1oz (30g) walnuts, chopped
1 level tablespoon coarsely chopped fresh sage,
or 1 level teaspoon dried sage
1/8 level teaspoon salt
Freshly ground black pepper
1 egg, size 2, lightly beaten
1/2 oz (15g) slightly salted butter
1 small onion, peeled and finely chopped
1 level tablespoon plain flour
1/4 pint (150ml) vegetable or chicken stock
(see p.19)
1/4 pint (150ml) medium sweet cider
1 level tablespoon chopped fresh parsley
2 level tablespoons low-fat natural yoghurt
Sage leaves to garnish

1 Mix the pork, breadcrumbs, prunes, apple, walnuts and sage, season with salt and pepper and work in the egg to bind the mixture. Divide it into 20 pieces and roll each into a ball.

2 Put the pork balls into a nonstick roasting tin and cook in the heated oven for about 25 minutes, or until golden brown.

3 Meanwhile, melt the butter in a saucepan, and cook the onion in it gently for about 5 minutes, or until soft. Stir in the flour and cook for 30 seconds. Gradually stir in the stock and cider and bring to the boil, stirring continuously. Mix in the parsley, season with pepper and set the sauce aside.

4 When the meatballs are cooked, stir the yoghurt into the sauce and reheat, but do not boil or it will curdle. Pour into a warmed jug for serving. Turn the meatballs into a serving dish and garnish with sage leaves.

Mashed potato goes well with the meatballs, while crisp spring greens or broccoli will make a pleasing contrast with their tenderness.

Pork with roasted peppers

SERVES 4
PREPARATION TIME: 30 minutes
COOKING TIME: 25 minutes

ONE SERVING	
CALORIES	300
TOTAL FAT	9g
SATURATED FAT	2g
CARBOHYDRATES	27g
ADDED SUGAR	0
FIBRE	4g
SODIUM	185mg

Roasting the sweet red peppers enhances their characteristically smoky flavour. Partnered by tomatoes and sharpened by a little vinegar and cayenne, they give a vivid touch of the hot south to the pork.

2 large red peppers
1lb (450g) boned shoulder of pork with fat removed, cut into 4 slices
1 level tablespoon plain flour
1 tablespoon olive oil
1 medium onion, peeled and chopped
2 cloves garlic, peeled and crushed
2lb (900g) tinned tomatoes, drained and chopped
2oz (60g) sultanas
1 tablespoon red wine vinegar
¼ level teaspoon cayenne pepper
1 level teaspoon dried oregano

1 Grill the peppers under a moderate heat for 10-12 minutes, turning often, until they are browned all over. Put them in a bowl, cover with a clean damp cloth and set aside. When they are cool enough to handle, pull off their skins, working over a bowl to catch any juice. Remove the seeds and cut the flesh into strips.

2 Meanwhile, put the pork slices between sheets of greaseproof paper and beat them with a rolling pin until they are very thin. Coat the slices lightly with the flour.

3 Heat the oil in a frying pan, and cook the pork slices in it over a moderate heat for 4 minutes on each side. Lay the slices on a plate covered with kitchen paper and set aside.

4 Fry the onion and garlic gently in the same pan for 5 minutes, until softened. Stir in the tomatoes, sultanas, vinegar, cayenne pepper, oregano and any juice from the grilled peppers. Bring to the boil, reduce the heat, cover and cook for 5 minutes, stirring occasionally.

5 Put the pork slices in the sauce, scatter in the pepper strips, cover and heat through for about 5 minutes.

Fresh pasta and a mixed green salad make simple accompaniments for the subtly flavoured pork and its sauce.

Pork and red-cabbage casserole

SERVES 4
PREPARATION TIME: 35 minutes
COOKING TIME: 1 hour
OVEN: Preheat to 180°C (350°F, gas mark 4)

ONE SERVING	
CALORIES 230	
TOTAL FAT 11g	
SATURATED FAT 2g	
CARBOHYDRATES 13g	
ADDED SUGAR 0	
FIBRE 3g	
SODIUM 75mg	

12oz (340g) boned pork shoulder with
fat removed, cut into cubes
2 level tablespoons plain flour
2 tablespoons olive oil
1 medium onion, peeled and thinly sliced
1 medium carrot, peeled and sliced
3 cloves garlic, peeled and crushed
1 large dessert apple, peeled, cored and sliced
6oz (175g) red cabbage, coarsely shredded
3 tablespoons red wine vinegar

4fl oz (115ml) chicken stock (see p.19)
7 allspice berries
6 black peppercorns
¼ level teaspoon dried sage, crumbled
2 bay leaves

1 Roll the pork cubes in the flour until coated. Heat the oil in a flameproof casserole and cook the pork in it, uncovered, over a moderate heat for about 10 minutes, turning to brown all over. Lift out the meat with a slotted spoon and put it on kitchen paper to drain.

2 Cook the onion, carrot and garlic in the uncovered casserole for about 5 minutes until

TIP
This casserole develops a richer flavour if cooked a day before you need it and kept in the refrigerator once cooled. Before serving, lift off any fat from the surface, bring the casserole to the boil on a direct heat and simmer for 10-15 minutes.

The sweet and sour combination of apple, vinegar and spices not only makes a perfect sauce for the lean pork, but also helps to tenderise the meat and keep the warm ruby colour of the cabbage.

lightly coloured. Mix in the apple and cabbage, cover and cook for about 15 minutes. Stir in the vinegar, stock, allspice, peppercorns, sage, pork cubes and bay leaves. Cover the casserole and cook in the heated oven for 1 hour.

Take out the bay leaves before serving, but you can add a garnish of fresh bay leaves for a touch of rich green. Serve mashed potatoes and french beans with the casserole and offer a little pot of English mustard.

Spicy pork loin

SERVES 4
PREPARATION TIME: 5 minutes, plus 1 hour to marinate
COOKING TIME: 10 minutes

2 dried bay leaves, finely ground
1 level teaspoon ground cumin
½ level teaspoon each ground coriander and ginger
¼ level teaspoon ground turmeric
1lb (450g) boneless pork loin with fat removed, cut into 8 thin slices
Lime wedges and coriander leaves to garnish

1 Mix the ground bay, cumin, coriander, ginger and turmeric and rub into both sides of the pork slices. Cover and leave to marinate at room temperature for 1 hour.

2 Lay the pork on the grill rack and cook under a hot grill for about 10 minutes, turning 3 or 4 times, until cooked through and golden brown. Garnish with the lime and coriander.

Braised fennel or celery hearts and fresh noodles go well with this aromatic dish.

ONE SERVING	
CALORIES	145
TOTAL FAT	4g
SATURATED FAT	2g
CARBOHYDRATES	0
ADDED SUGAR	0
FIBRE	0
SODIUM	85mg

TIP
Grind the bay leaves thoroughly in a mortar with a pestle, or in an electric coffee grinder. Fragments of bay are very sharp; they can stick in the throat and cause choking.

The dry Indian-style marinade creates a mouthwatering aroma whose promise is amply fulfilled in the eating.

Pork and vegetable stir-fry

SERVES 4
PREPARATION TIME: 15 minutes
COOKING TIME: 10 minutes

ONE SERVING

CALORIES 195

TOTAL FAT 7g

SATURATED FAT 1g

CARBOHYDRATES 7g

ADDED SUGAR 0

FIBRE 1g

SODIUM 75mg

Mild rice vinegar, soy sauce and amber Chinese sesame oil, together with crunchy fresh bean sprouts, add to the authenticity of this quickly made dish of crisp vegetables and tender strips of pork.

1 level tablespoon cornflour
4fl oz (115ml) chicken stock (see p.19)
½ teaspoon soy sauce
1 teaspoon rice vinegar or white wine vinegar
1 tablespoon sesame oil
4 tablespoons dry sherry
1 level teaspoon peeled and grated root ginger
1 clove garlic, peeled and chopped
1 medium carrot, peeled and sliced
½ red pepper, de-seeded and chopped
½ medium cucumber, peeled and sliced
4oz (115g) fresh bean sprouts, rinsed and drained
1 spring onion, trimmed and sliced
12oz (340g) pork tenderloin with fat removed, thinly sliced and cut into strips

1 Mix the cornflour to a smooth paste with 2 tablespoons of the stock. Stir in the rest of the stock, the soy sauce, the vinegar, half the oil and half the sherry.

2 Heat the remaining oil in a nonstick frying pan and toss the ginger and garlic in it over a high heat for 30 seconds. Mix in the carrot and red pepper and cook for 2 minutes, stirring.

3 Add the cucumber and cook for 1 minute, then the bean sprouts, onion and remaining sherry and cook for 1 minute more, stirring. Spoon the vegetables onto a plate and set aside.

4 Toss the pork in the pan over a high heat for about 4 minutes, until the meat starts to lose its pinkness. Return the vegetables to the pan, add the stock mixture and cook for about 1 minute, stirring, until the sauce thickens.

Serve the stir-fry piping hot with white rice to give a final Oriental touch. You can slice and fan out the cucumber tip as a garnish.

Black-eyed beans are also known as southern peas in the United States, where cooks in the south often use them to absorb bacon's flavour.

Southern bacon and beans

ONE SERVING

CALORIES 365

TOTAL FAT 10g

SATURATED FAT 3g

CARBOHYDRATES 37g

ADDED SUGAR 0

FIBRE 4g

SODIUM 950mg

SERVES 4
PREPARATION TIME: 10 minutes
COOKING TIME: 30 minutes

1 teaspoon olive oil
12oz (340g) unsmoked bacon chops or back
rashers, rind and fat removed, cut into small pieces
2 large leeks, sliced and washed
2oz (60g) chestnut mushrooms, wiped and sliced
1 level teaspoon dried marjoram
3oz (85g) long-grain rice
12oz (340g) cooked black-eyed beans (see p.17)
½ pint (285ml) chicken or vegetable
stock (see p.19)
Freshly ground black pepper

1 Heat the oil in a large, heavy-based saucepan and cook the bacon in it for 2-3 minutes. Mix in the leeks and mushrooms and cook for 5 minutes, stirring from time to time.

2 Sprinkle on the marjoram and stir in the rice for 1 minute. Mix in the cooked beans, then pour in the stock and season with pepper. Cover and simmer for about 20 minutes, or until the rice is cooked. Fluff up with a fork from time to time and pour in a little water if the mixture becomes too dry.

Garnish this hearty dish with crisp lettuce leaves and serve with a colourful tomato salad.

Gammon and lentil loaf

SERVES 8
PREPARATION TIME: 30 minutes
COOKING TIME: 1 hour 15 minutes
OVEN: Preheat to 190°C (375°F, gas mark 5)

ONE SERVING	
CALORIES	285
TOTAL FAT	12g
SATURATED FAT	5g
CARBOHYDRATES	16g
ADDED SUGAR	0
FIBRE	2g
SODIUM	790mg

6oz (175g) red lentils, washed and drained
1 pint (570ml) vegetable stock (see p.19)
1 tablespoon olive oil
1 medium onion, peeled and chopped
2oz (60g) mushrooms, wiped and finely chopped
2 level tablespoons chopped fresh parsley
2oz (60g) wholemeal breadcrumbs
4oz (115g) Red Leicester cheese, finely grated

1lb (450g) unsmoked raw gammon, trimmed
of fat and minced
2 eggs, size 2, lightly beaten
Freshly ground black pepper

1 Bring the lentils and stock to the boil in a large, uncovered saucepan. Lower the heat, cover the pan and simmer for 25 minutes, or until the lentils are soft. Drain and set aside.

2 Heat the oil in a frying pan and cook the onion in it over a moderate heat for 3 minutes to soften. Stir in the mushrooms and cook for a further 2 minutes, shaking from time to time.

3 Mix the onion and mushrooms into the lentils, work in the parsley, breadcrumbs, cheese, gammon and eggs, and season the mixture with pepper.

4 Line a loaf tin about 5×9in (12×23cm) with nonstick baking paper. Spoon the gammon mixture into the tin and level the top. Bake in the heated oven for 1 hour 15 minutes, until firm to the touch.

5 Leave to cool slightly before turning out onto a serving plate and removing the paper. Cut into thick slices to serve.

Serve a leafy green salad with cherry tomatoes and parsley as colourful accompaniments. Cold slices of the loaf, with cucumber and chutney, are very good on open sandwiches.

This well-flavoured meatloaf is easy to make and can be enjoyed with jacket potatoes for a substantial meal, or with salads for a lighter lunch.

Gammon in plum sauce

ONE SERVING	
CALORIES	265
TOTAL FAT	6g
SATURATED FAT	3g
CARBOHYDRATES	18g
ADDED SUGAR	4g
FIBRE	2g
SODIUM	1280mg

SERVES 4
PREPARATION TIME: 10 minutes
COOKING TIME: 20 minutes

1lb (450g) red dessert plums, halved and stoned
¼ pint (150ml) fresh orange juice
4 unsmoked gammon steaks, about ¼ in (6mm)
thick, each about 3oz (85g)

1 level tablespoon soft brown sugar or
demerara sugar
2 tablespoons raspberry vinegar
1 level teaspoon made English mustard
¼ level teaspoon ground cinnamon
¼ level teaspoon ground ginger
Freshly ground black pepper
Fresh dill fronds to garnish

1 Simmer the plums in the orange juice in a covered saucepan for 5-10 minutes, until the plums are soft but retain their shape.

2 Using a slotted spoon, lift 8 plum halves onto a plate and set them aside. Continue cooking the remaining plums until they are very soft. Let them cool slightly, then pour the plums and juice into a food processor and blend to a smooth purée.

3 Meanwhile, arrange the gammon steaks on the grill rack and cook them under a high heat for 6-8 minutes, turning two or three times.

4 When the gammon is almost cooked, pour the plum purée into a saucepan with the sugar and raspberry vinegar. Stir in the mustard, cinnamon and ginger, and season with pepper. Heat gently for 1-2 minutes, stirring. Put the reserved plum halves gently into the sauce and heat through for 1 minute.

5 Serve the gammon steaks garnished with the reserved plum halves, a little of the sauce and the dill fronds. Hand round the rest of the sauce separately.

Leave the diners to trim off any fat from the gammon. Cauliflower and new potatoes steamed in their skins make a pleasing contrast to the full flavours of the gammon and sauce. You can make the sauce with fresh apricots when plums are not available.

> **TIP**
> *To keep the gammon steaks flat during grilling, snip them first with kitchen scissors at ½in (13mm) intervals all round the edge.*

A sharp and rosy plum sauce made with fresh fruit purée is a delicious partner for mild, pink gammon steaks.

PASTA AND GRAINS

Substantial helpings of starchy food teamed with quite small amounts of protein are a winning combination with nutritionists as well as with families. Here are your favourite pasta recipes and risottos, carefully pruned of fat, and some more unusual dishes that will soon become favourites. Often quick to make and inexpensive, many of these recipes originated in countries fringing the Mediterranean, where the diets are among the healthiest in the world.

Cannelloni with chicken and walnuts

ONE SERVING

CALORIES	465
TOTAL FAT	23g
SATURATED FAT	5g
CARBOHYDRATES	39g
ADDED SUGAR	0
FIBRE	2g
SODIUM	410mg

TIP
*An easy way
to put the chicken
filling into the
cannelloni tubes is
to use a piping bag
fitted with a large
plain nozzle.*

SERVES 4
PREPARATION TIME: 20 minutes
COOKING TIME: 35 minutes
OVEN: Preheat to 180°C (350°F, gas mark 4)

2oz (60g) shelled walnuts, finely chopped
*6oz (175g) cooked chicken without skin or bone,
minced or finely chopped*
¼ level teaspoon ground mace
4oz (115g) ricotta cheese
4oz (115g) cottage cheese
12 tubes ready-to-use cannelloni
1oz (30g) polyunsaturated margarine
1oz (30g) plain flour
Freshly ground black pepper
¾ pint (425ml) skimmed milk
Bay leaf
14oz (400g) tinned chopped tomatoes
1oz (30g) grated reduced-fat Cheddar cheese

1 Reserve 1 tablespoon of the walnuts. Mix the rest, and the chicken and mace into the ricotta. Fill the cannelloni with the mixture.

2 Melt the margarine in a saucepan, stir in the flour, season with pepper, and cook gently for 1 minute. Gradually mix in the milk, put in the bay leaf and bring to the boil, stirring until the sauce thickens. Discard the bay leaf.

3 Spread the tomatoes in a large gratin dish and lay the cannelloni in one layer on top. Cover with the sauce and scatter on the Parmesan and reserved walnuts. Cook in the heated oven, covered, for 15 minutes, then uncover and cook for 20 minutes more, or until browned on top.

Garnish the cannelloni with parsley, and serve with colourful side salads or steamed broccoli.

*A delicately flavoured
mixture of chicken and
soft cheese fills the
pasta tubes, which cook
in béchamel sauce and
juicy tomatoes.*

Cannelloni with ricotta and spinach

ONE SERVING

CALORIES	470
TOTAL FAT	18g
SATURATED FAT	6g
CARBOHYDRATES	57g
ADDED SUGAR	0
FIBRE	5g
SODIUM	455mg

SERVES 4
PREPARATION TIME: 35 minutes
COOKING TIME: 30 minutes
OVEN: Preheat to 180°C (350°F, gas mark 4)

1 tablespoon olive oil
1 large onion, peeled and chopped

2 cloves garlic, peeled and chopped
1 level tablespoon chopped fresh basil
½ level teaspoon dried marjoram
Freshly ground black pepper
14oz (400g) tinned peeled tomatoes
1 tablespoon tomato purée (see p.16)
9oz (250g) fresh spinach, washed and trimmed

3oz (85g) ricotta or curd cheese
4oz (115g) cottage cheese
½ level teaspoon freshly grated nutmeg
8 large sheets fresh homemade lasagne (see p.18)
1oz (30g) grated Parmesan cheese

1 Heat the oil in a frying pan and cook the onion and half the garlic in it over a moderate heat for about 5 minutes. Stir in the basil and marjoram and season with pepper. Take out and set aside 2 tablespoons of the mixture.

2 Stir the tomatoes, their juice and the tomato purée into the pan of onion mixture and cook over a moderate heat for 20 minutes, stirring occasionally to break down the tomatoes.

3 In the meantime, prepare the filling. Blanch the spinach in unsalted boiling water for 30 seconds, pour it into a colander and rinse it with cold water. Squeeze the spinach hard, then turn it into a bowl, chop it roughly and work in the ricotta or curd cheese, cottage cheese, remaining garlic, reserved onion mixture and nutmeg, and season with pepper.

4 Cook the lasagne (see p.18) for 2-3 minutes, then rinse it with cold water and drain well. Lay the sheets on a board and spread some filling across a narrow end of each sheet, dividing the mixture equally between them. Roll the sheets up to form cannelloni.

5 Pour half the tomato sauce into a baking dish and lay the cannelloni on top, seam side down. Pour the remaining sauce over them.

6 Cover the dish and cook in the heated oven for 25 minutes, then uncover, sprinkle with the Parmesan and cook for 5 minutes more to brown lightly before serving.

You can use dried pasta instead of fresh. Cook the sheets (see p.18) before filling to make them pliable. They will absorb more liquid, so use an extra 7oz (200g) of tomatoes in the sauce. Serve a crisp cauliflower and mushroom salad (see p.312) with the cannelloni.

The astringent flavour of spinach combines well with mild soft cheese to make a creamy filling for rolls of fresh pasta. A tomato sauce tangy with herbs makes a pleasingly sharp contrast in taste and colour.

Farfalle with broccoli and nuts

SERVES 4
PREPARATION TIME: 15 minutes
COOKING TIME: 30 minutes

*14oz (400g) broccoli, trimmed and divided
into florets*
1 tablespoon olive oil
2 cloves garlic, peeled and finely chopped
*2lb (900g) ripe tomatoes, peeled, de-seeded
and chopped*
2 level tablespoons seedless sultanas, chopped
¼ level teaspoon cayenne pepper
2oz (60g) pine nuts or chopped blanched almonds
3 level tablespoons chopped fresh parsley
10oz (275g) farfalle
1oz (30g) grated Parmesan cheese

ONE SERVING	
CALORIES	505
TOTAL FAT	18g
SATURATED FAT	3g
CARBOHYDRATES	70g
ADDED SUGAR	0
FIBRE	8g
SODIUM	185mg

1 Simmer the broccoli in a little unsalted water in a covered saucepan for 4-5 minutes, until just beginning to soften. Rinse with cold water and drain.

2 Heat the oil in a large frying pan and cook the garlic in it over a moderate heat for about 2 minutes, or until golden. Stir in the tomatoes, sultanas and cayenne pepper and cook, uncovered, for 15 minutes. Add the nuts and parsley and cook for a further 5 minutes.

3 Meanwhile, cook the farfalle (see p.18), drain and spread in a warmed serving dish.

4 Stir the broccoli into the tomato sauce and heat through for 2-3 minutes. Pour the sauce over the farfalle and sprinkle with the Parmesan just before serving.

A crunchy side salad of celeriac in a lemon dressing balances the sweet tomato sauce.

This attractive dish with its tightly budded broccoli florets and butterfly pasta is a rich source of fibre.

Fusilli with bacon and mushrooms

SERVES 4
PREPARATION TIME: 10 minutes
COOKING TIME: 15 minutes

ONE SERVING

CALORIES 450

TOTAL FAT 15g

SATURATED FAT 6g

CARBOHYDRATES 58g

ADDED SUGAR 0

FIBRE 3g

SODIUM 810mg

TIP
It is quicker to snip parsley than to chop it. Bunch the parsley sprigs together, hold them near the tips and snip them finely with kitchen scissors, gradually moving your grip down the stems as you snip.

The creamy bacon and mushroom sauce with its added tang of wine is easy to make, and turns the pasta spirals called fusilli into a satisfyingly savoury dish.

2oz (60g) grated Parmesan cheese
2 tablespoons freshly chopped parsley
6oz (175g) Greek yoghurt
Freshly ground black pepper
1 tablespoon olive oil
4oz (115g) unsmoked back bacon with fat removed, cut into thin strips
6oz (175g) mushrooms, wiped and thinly sliced
1 medium onion, peeled and chopped
2 cloves garlic, peeled and finely chopped
10oz (275g) fusilli
4 tablespoons dry white wine
Chopped fresh parsley or basil to garnish

1 Mix the Parmesan and parsley into the yoghurt and season with pepper. Cover and put in the refrigerator.

2 Heat the oil in a small saucepan and toss the bacon in it over a moderate heat for 2-3 minutes until lightly browned. Add the mushrooms, onion and garlic and cook, stirring occasionally, for about 5 minutes, or until the onion softens.

3 Meanwhile, cook the fusilli (see p.18).

4 Pour the wine onto the bacon and mushrooms and cook for 2-3 minutes, or until it has almost evaporated. Stir in the yoghurt mixture and reheat the sauce without boiling.

5 When the fusilli are cooked 'al dente', drain and spread on a warmed serving dish. Pour on the sauce and garnish with the parsley or basil.

A dish of sweet fresh garden peas or a crisp fennel and cabbage salad would give a pleasing contrast to the flavours of the pasta sauce.

Vegetable lasagne

SERVES 4
PREPARATION TIME: 45 minutes
COOKING TIME: 35 minutes
OVEN: Preheat to 200°C (400°F, gas mark 6)

2 bulbs garlic
2 tablespoons olive oil
1 small onion, peeled and chopped
9oz (250g) courgettes, trimmed and diced
9oz (250g) mushrooms, wiped and finely sliced
5oz (150g) shelled fresh peas or frozen peas
2 teaspoons lemon juice
¼ level teaspoon cayenne pepper
Freshly ground black pepper
2½ level tablespoons plain flour
½ pint (285ml) skimmed milk
½ level teaspoon dried oregano
2oz (60g) grated Parmesan cheese
16 small sheets homemade green lasagne (see p.18)

ONE SERVING

CALORIES 545

TOTAL FAT 22g

SATURATED FAT 6g

CARBOHYDRATES 71g

ADDED SUGAR 0

FIBRE 6g

SODIUM 315mg

1 Wrap the two whole unpeeled garlic bulbs separately in foil and cook them in the heated oven for 20 minutes. Remove and leave to cool, then separate the cloves and peel them. Mash them in a bowl with a fork and set aside.

2 Heat half the oil in a saucepan and cook the onion and courgettes in it over a moderate heat for about 5 minutes. Stir in the mushrooms and cook for 3 minutes, then the peas and cook for 1 more minute. Sprinkle in the lemon juice and cayenne pepper, and season lightly with black pepper. Remove from the heat.

3 Heat the remaining oil in a small saucepan, stir in the flour and cook gently for 1 minute. Gradually stir in the milk, bring to the boil, stirring, then simmer for 3 minutes. Mix in the oregano, Parmesan and garlic. Mix all but about 6 tablespoons of the sauce into the vegetables.

4 Cook the lasagne (see p.18) for 2-3 minutes and drain. Cover the bottom of a lightly oiled ovenproof dish with a third of the lasagne. Spread on half the vegetable mixture. Repeat with another layer of lasagne and vegetables, then top with the remaining lasagne. Spread the reserved sauce on top.

5 Cover the dish and cook in the heated oven for 20 minutes. Uncover and cook for a further 15 minutes, until browned on top.

Serve a salad of radicchio and red onion with the dish. You can use dried lasagne instead of fresh but it will need a third more sauce.

The generous amount of garlic used in the sauce does not give an extravagantly garlicky flavour, but serves to intensify the taste of the vegetables in this variation on a filling pasta favourite.

Linguine with peas and tuna

SERVES 4
PREPARATION TIME: 5 minutes
COOKING TIME: 20 minutes

10oz (275g) fresh homemade linguine (see p.18)
1 tablespoon olive oil

1 level tablespoon plain flour
¹/₂ pint (285ml) skimmed milk
7oz (200g) frozen peas
7oz (200g) tinned tuna in oil, drained and flaked
2oz (60g) grated Parmesan cheese
Freshly ground black pepper

Sweet green peas and meaty tuna in a light sauce mingle with thin strips of pasta, which have the best texture when they are newly made.

ONE SERVING	
CALORIES	560
TOTAL FAT	23g
SATURATED FAT	6g
CARBOHYDRATES	58g
ADDED SUGAR	0
FIBRE	5g
SODIUM	455mg

1 Heat the oil in a large saucepan, mix in the flour and gradually stir in the milk. Bring to the boil over a moderate heat, stirring all the time, then reduce the heat and continue cooking for 2 minutes, until the sauce thickens slightly.

2 Add the peas to the sauce and cook for 4 minutes. Mix in the tuna and Parmesan and season with pepper. Heat through gently, without boiling, for about 5 minutes.

3 Meanwhile, cook the linguine (see p.18) for 2-3 minutes and drain well.

Serve the linguine in heated bowls. Side salads of grated carrots give a crisp finishing touch.

Linguine and tomato pie

ONE SERVING	
CALORIES	385
TOTAL FAT	13g
SATURATED FAT	5g
CARBOHYDRATES	50g
ADDED SUGAR	0
FIBRE	4g
SODIUM	300mg

SERVES 4
PREPARATION TIME: 20 minutes
COOKING TIME: 35 minutes
OVEN: Preheat to 190°C (375°F, gas mark 5)

1 tablespoon olive oil
8oz (225g) linguine
1 medium onion, peeled and finely chopped
3 cloves garlic, peeled and finely chopped

2 level tablespoons chopped fresh parsley
1½ level teaspoons dried oregano
1 level teaspoon dried basil
1 tablespoon lemon juice
Freshly ground black pepper
3oz (85g) ricotta or curd cheese
1 egg, size 2, beaten
1lb (450g) tomatoes, skinned and sliced
3oz (85g) grated low-fat Cheddar cheese
½ oz (15g) grated Parmesan cheese

1 Grease a loose-bottomed or hinged-side cake tin 8in (20cm) in diameter with a little oil.

2 Cook the linguine (see p.18) and drain well.

3 Meanwhile, heat the rest of the oil in a heavy-based saucepan and fry the onion and garlic in it over a moderate heat for about 5 minutes. Mix in the linguine, scatter on the parsley, oregano and basil, sprinkle with the lemon juice, season with pepper and toss well.

4 Combine the ricotta or curd cheese and the egg with the linguine. Spoon half the mixture into the prepared tin and press it down lightly.

5 Arrange half the tomato slices on top and scatter half the Cheddar over them. Spoon the remaining pasta mixture on top and press down lightly. Cover with the rest of the tomatoes and Cheddar and sprinkle with the Parmesan.

6 Cover and bake in the heated oven for 30 minutes, then uncover and bake for a further 5 minutes, or until browned on top.

7 Leave the pie to cool for 10 minutes, then run a knife round the edge to loosen it from the tin. Remove the side of the tin and slide the pie onto a warmed serving plate.

Cut the pie into wedges and serve with tomato sauce (see p.16) and a crisp green salad. You can vary the pie by grating two courgettes into the linguine mixture.

Tomato layers and herbs moisten and flavour an original treat – narrow ribbons of tender pasta bound with egg to make an unusual cheese-topped pie.

Macaroni with leeks and tarragon

ONE SERVING	
CALORIES	475
TOTAL FAT	17g
SATURATED FAT	9g
CARBOHYDRATES	60g
ADDED SUGAR	0
FIBRE	5g
SODIUM	385mg

TIP
Always add mustard as near as possible to the end of cooking, because its flavour is lessened by cooking.

SERVES 4
PREPARATION TIME: 25 minutes
COOKING TIME: 25 minutes
OVEN: Preheat to 200°C (400°F, gas mark 6)

7oz (200g) macaroni or macaroni spirals
½ oz (15g) slightly salted butter
3 medium leeks, trimmed, finely sliced and washed
3 level tablespoons plain flour
1¼ pints (725ml) skimmed milk
Freshly ground black pepper
2 level tablespoons chopped fresh tarragon
1 level teaspoon English mustard powder
4oz (115g) grated mature Cheddar cheese
1 level tablespoon wholemeal breadcrumbs
1½ level tablespoons sesame seeds
Tomato slices and sprigs of fresh tarragon to garnish

1   Cook the macaroni (see p.18) and drain it thoroughly.

2   Meanwhile, melt the butter in a saucepan and gently cook the leeks in it, covered, for 3 minutes. Mix in the flour, cook for 1 minute, then gradually stir in the milk. Bring the sauce slowly to the boil, stirring continuously.

3   Season with pepper, mix in the tarragon and simmer for about 5 minutes. Mix the mustard with a little of the sauce, then stir it back into the pan. Fold in the Cheddar and macaroni.

4   Pour the mixture into a deep ovenproof dish. Mix the breadcrumbs and sesame seeds and scatter them over the macaroni. Bake in the heated oven for about 25 minutes, until bubbling and lightly browned on top. Garnish with the tomato slices and tarragon sprigs.

A crisp salad of frisée and lamb's lettuce makes a refreshing accompaniment.

Traditional macaroni cheese is given an appetising new edge with leeks, tarragon and a crisp sesame topping.

Ham, pea and noodle gratin

SERVES 4
PREPARATION TIME: 10 minutes
COOKING TIME: 20 minutes

ONE SERVING	
CALORIES 465	
TOTAL FAT 7g	
SATURATED FAT 3g	
CARBOHYDRATES 80g	
ADDED SUGAR 0	
FIBRE 6g	
SODIUM 795mg	

10oz (275g) Italian noodles or tagliatelle
½ oz (15g) slightly salted butter
2 level tablespoons plain flour
¼ level teaspoon dried sage
¼ level teaspoon dried marjoram
½ level teaspoon dried thyme
⅛ level teaspoon ground mace

¾ pint (425ml) skimmed milk
Freshly ground black pepper
6oz (175g) cooked ham with fat removed, diced
8oz (225g) cooked peas
3 tomatoes, sliced
1½ oz (45g) fresh fine white breadcrumbs

1 Cook the noodles (see p.18) and drain.

2 Meanwhile, melt the butter in a saucepan and stir in the flour, sage, marjoram, thyme and mace. Cook over a gentle heat for 1 minute, then gradually stir in the milk. Bring to the boil, stirring continuously, until the sauce thickens slightly. Season with pepper, then mix in the ham and peas, and simmer for 2 minutes to heat thoroughly.

3 Mix the pasta in until it is coated with the sauce, then turn everything into a heatproof serving dish. Arrange the sliced tomatoes on top and sprinkle with the breadcrumbs.

4 Put the gratin under a hot grill for about 3 minutes, until browned on top.

A green salad or a cucumber and fruit salad goes well with this dish. For a change of flavour you can use cooked prawns or smoked haddock in place of the ham.

Savoury ham and sweet green peas are combined with a herb sauce in this simple dish of Italian noodles which is finished with a crisp, bright topping.

Chinese noodles with nuts and apricots

SERVES 4
PREPARATION TIME: 15 minutes
COOKING TIME: 20 minutes

ONE SERVING	
CALORIES 640	
TOTAL FAT 27g	
SATURATED FAT 6g	
CARBOHYDRATES 92g	
ADDED SUGAR 0	
FIBRE 7g	
SODIUM 435mg	

12oz (340g) Chinese medium egg noodles
2 tablespoons sesame oil
2 level teaspoons peeled and chopped root ginger
1 clove garlic, peeled and finely chopped
1 small onion, peeled and finely chopped
1 medium carrot, peeled and cut into fine strips

1 stick celery, trimmed and cut into fine strips
4oz (115g) ready-to-use dried apricots, chopped
2oz (60g) unsalted shelled peanuts, lightly toasted and skinned
2oz (60g) unsalted cashew nuts
4oz (115g) silken tofu, diced
1 tablespoon soy sauce
1 tablespoon hoisin sauce
1 tablespoon dry sherry
4oz (115g) fresh bean sprouts

The crunchy texture of this unmistakably Chinese dish is elegantly balanced by the soft, tangy apricots. Rich brown hoisin sauce adds its spicy sweetness, while the dry sherry is a substitute for the authentic rice wine.

1 Cook the noodles in unsalted water (see p.18) and drain.

2 Heat the oil in a large wok or frying pan and toss the ginger, garlic and onion in it over a high heat for 2-3 minutes. Stir in the carrot and celery and toss for 2 minutes more.

3 Mix in the apricots, peanuts, cashew nuts and tofu and cook gently for 2 minutes, stirring frequently, before pouring in the soy sauce, hoisin sauce and sherry.

4 Add the noodles and bean sprouts and toss together until the ingredients are well mixed. Cook over a moderate heat for 2-3 minutes, until everything is piping hot.

Serve the noodles at once in warmed individual bowls with side salads of cos-type lettuce.

TIP
When the peanuts are toasted, fold them a few at a time in kitchen paper and rub briskly between your palms to take off the brown skins, which tend to stick in the throat if left in the dish.

Penne with spinach and cheese

SERVES 4
PREPARATION TIME: 20 minutes
COOKING TIME: 15 minutes

9oz (250g) penne
1 tablespoon olive oil
1 small onion, peeled and chopped
2 cloves garlic, peeled and finely chopped

1lb (450g) fresh spinach, trimmed, well washed
and torn into shreds
4fl oz (115ml) skimmed milk
4fl oz (115ml) vegetable or chicken stock
(see p.19)
1½ oz (45g) grated Parmesan cheese
4oz (115g) cottage cheese
Freshly ground black pepper

The astringent spinach harmonises well with the slightly smoky Parmesan in creating a delicious light sauce to coat the quill-shaped pasta.

ONE SERVING
CALORIES 365
TOTAL FAT 9g
SATURATED FAT 3g
CARBOHYDRATES 55g
ADDED SUGAR 0
FIBRE 5g
SODIUM 480mg

1 Cook the penne (see p.18) and drain.

2 Meanwhile, heat the oil in a large saucepan and cook the onion and garlic in it over a moderate heat for 5 minutes, until the onion softens. Stir in the spinach, milk, stock, Parmesan and cottage cheese, and season with pepper. Bring to the boil, stirring, and simmer for about 3 minutes, until the sauce thickens.

3 Turn the penne into the spinach sauce and mix well until the pasta is coated before serving onto warmed plates.

A tomato salad sprinkled with chives makes a colourful side dish. When fresh spinach is not available, you can use 8oz (225g) frozen leaf spinach, completely thawed and drained well before being added to the sauce.

Pasta shells with chickpeas

ONE SERVING	
CALORIES	335
TOTAL FAT	7g
SATURATED FAT	1g
CARBOHYDRATES	61g
ADDED SUGAR	0
FIBRE	10g
SODIUM	195mg

Leek, olives and a generous amount of herbs enliven this simple dish, which combines wholemeal pasta and chickpeas, providing an excellent source of fibre.

SERVES 4
PREPARATION TIME: 10 minutes
COOKING TIME: 15 minutes

10oz (275g) wholemeal pasta shells
1 tablespoon olive oil
1 small leek, trimmed, thinly sliced and washed
1 small onion, peeled and finely chopped
4 fresh sage leaves, chopped, or ½ level teaspoon dried sage
1 small sprig fresh rosemary, or ½ level teaspoon dried rosemary
2 large ripe tomatoes, chopped
8oz (225g) cooked chickpeas (see p.17) with 3 tablespoons of their cooking liquid
1 level tablespoon dried oregano
Freshly ground black pepper
6 green olives, stoned and chopped
Shredded fresh lovage or celery leaves

1 Cook the pasta shells (see p.18) and drain.

2 Meanwhile, heat the oil in a saucepan and cook the leek and onion in it over a high heat for 2 minutes. Add the sage, rosemary and tomatoes, cover and simmer for 5 minutes.

3 Rub the chickpeas and the reserved cooking liquid through a sieve, or reduce them to a purée in a blender. Stir in the oregano, season with pepper and heat to boiling point.

4 Turn the pasta into a heated serving dish and spoon the vegetables on top, discarding the rosemary sprig. Top with the chickpea purée and garnish with the olives and lovage or celery.

A crisp green salad and some bread are the best accompaniments for this savoury pasta dish.

Stuffed pasta shells and watercress sauce

SERVES 4
PREPARATION TIME: 40 minutes
COOKING TIME: 15 minutes
OVEN: Preheat to 220°C (425°F, gas mark 7)

ONE SERVING

CALORIES 210

TOTAL FAT 8g

SATURATED FAT 2g

CARBOHYDRATES 22g

ADDED SUGAR 0

FIBRE 4g

SODIUM 105mg

1 tablespoon olive oil
8oz (225g) button mushrooms, wiped and chopped
1 medium onion, peeled and finely chopped
6oz (175g) courgettes, trimmed and chopped
6oz (175g) red pepper, de-seeded and chopped
4oz (115g) chicken breast without skin or bone, finely chopped
¹/₂ oz (15g) wholemeal breadcrumbs
2 level teaspoons dried mixed herbs
Freshly ground black pepper
3 tablespoons chicken stock (see p.19)
16 large pasta shells, about 2¹/₄ in (55mm) long

For the watercress sauce:
6fl oz (175ml) chicken stock (see p.19)
6oz (175g) watercress, trimmed and washed
5oz (150g) fromage frais

1 Heat the oil in a frying pan and cook the mushrooms, onion, courgettes and red pepper in it over a moderate heat for 10 minutes, until softened, stirring from time to time.

2 Mix in the chicken and stir over a moderate heat for 5 minutes or until cooked through. Sprinkle in the breadcrumbs and herbs, season with black pepper and moisten with the stock. Bring to the boil, then set aside.

3 Cook the pasta shells (see p.18) and drain.

4 Meanwhile, to prepare the watercress sauce, boil the stock rapidly in a saucepan until reduced by half, then stir in the watercress and boil for 1 minute. Cool slightly before blending with the fromage frais in a food processor.

5 Fill the pasta shells with the mushroom mixture and arrange them in one layer in a baking dish. Pour the watercress sauce round them, cover the dish and cook in the heated oven for 15 minutes or until bubbling hot.

A tomato salad and lightly toasted bread with a little olive oil and basil to sprinkle on add extra Italian touches to the pasta.

Pasta shells come in several sizes; these giant ones are packed with mushroom and chicken stuffing to make an attractive, substantial dish.

Pasta shells with sardines and pesto

SERVES 4
PREPARATION TIME: 20 minutes
COOKING TIME: 25 minutes

2 large red peppers, halved and de-seeded
2 beef tomatoes, peeled and chopped
1 tablespoon tomato purée (see p.16)
1 clove garlic, peeled and crushed
4 level tablespoons pesto sauce
12oz (340g) pasta shells
4 fresh sardines, each about 4oz (115g), with
heads removed, scaled, cleaned, gutted and boned
8 black olives, stoned and quartered
1oz (30g) pine nuts
1 level tablespoon chopped fresh oregano leaves

ONE SERVING	
CALORIES	545
TOTAL FAT	19g
SATURATED FAT	2g
CARBOHYDRATES	72g
ADDED SUGAR	0
FIBRE	5g
SODIUM	555mg

1   Grill the red peppers, skin side up, until the skin blisters. Leave to cool in a covered bowl, then peel off the skin and chop the flesh.

2   Use a food mill or food processor to blend the pepper, tomatoes, tomato purée, garlic and pesto. Pour the sauce into a frying pan and simmer, uncovered, for 10 minutes or until slightly reduced and thickened.

3   Meanwhile, cook the pasta shells (see p.18).

4   Lay the sardines in the sauce and cook over a gentle heat for 10 minutes.

5   Turn the drained pasta shells onto warmed plates and arrange the sardines on top. Stir the olives into the sauce, then pour it over the fish. Scatter with the pine nuts and oregano immediately before serving.

A salad of lamb's lettuce gives a touch of sharpness to contrast with the rich fish sauce.

TIP
When you cannot get fresh sardines, you can use sardines tinned in oil, but drain them well and press them lightly with kitchen paper to absorb as much oil as you can.

Pesto, a classic Italian partner for pasta, lends some of its peppery taste to the sauce, and penetrates the delicate sardines. Pine nuts and olives reinforce the Mediterranean flavours.

Spaghetti with prawns and capers

SERVES 4
PREPARATION TIME: 5 minutes
COOKING TIME: 20 minutes

1 tablespoon olive oil
1 clove garlic, peeled and finely chopped

14oz (400g) tinned peeled tomatoes
1 level teaspoon dried basil
9oz (250g) spaghetti
5oz (150g) frozen peeled prawns
2 level tablespoons capers, rinsed, dried and chopped
2 level tablespoons chopped fresh marjoram

Capers add their sharp tang to the sweetness of the tomato sauce, giving it a flavour strong enough to complement the savoury prawns.

ONE SERVING	
CALORIES 305	
TOTAL FAT 5g	
SATURATED FAT 1g	
CARBOHYDRATES 50g	
ADDED SUGAR 0	
FIBRE 3g	
SODIUM 765mg	

1 Heat the oil in a frying pan and toss the garlic in it over a high heat for 30 seconds to flavour the oil. Pour in the tomatoes, stir in the basil and bring to the boil. Reduce the heat and simmer, uncovered, for about 15 minutes to reduce and thicken the sauce. Stir from time to time to break down the tomatoes.

2 Meanwhile, cook the spaghetti (see p.18) and drain well.

3 Stir the prawns and capers into the sauce and heat through for 5 minutes.

4 Turn the spaghetti onto warmed plates. Pour on the sauce and sprinkle with the marjoram just before serving.

Serve the pasta with a side salad of spicy cucumber and red peppers. You can use tinned tuna, drained and flaked, instead of the prawns.

Tagliatelle bolognese

ONE SERVING	
CALORIES	480
TOTAL FAT	10g
SATURATED FAT	3g
CARBOHYDRATES	70g
ADDED SUGAR	0
FIBRE	4g
SODIUM	450mg

SERVES 4
PREPARATION TIME: 15 minutes
COOKING TIME: 40 minutes

1 tablespoon olive oil
1 small onion, peeled and finely chopped
1 clove garlic, peeled and finely chopped
1 medium carrot, peeled and coarsely grated
2oz (60g) mushrooms, wiped and finely chopped

8oz (225g) lean beef, minced
2oz (60g) chicken livers, finely chopped
2oz (60g) Parma ham with fat removed, chopped
1 level teaspoon dried oregano
14oz (400g) tinned tomatoes rubbed through a sieve
Freshly ground black pepper
12oz (340g) tagliatelle
2 level tablespoons fromage frais
Fresh oregano leaves to garnish

1 Heat the oil in a saucepan and cook the onion and garlic in it over a moderate heat for 5 minutes, until soft. Mix in the carrot and mushrooms and cook for 1 minute.

2 Stir in the beef and chicken livers and cook briskly until they lose all traces of pink, breaking up any lumps that form. Mix in the ham, oregano and tomatoes, and season with pepper. Cover and simmer for 25 minutes.

3 Cook the tagliatelle (see p.18) and drain.

4 Turn the tagliatelle into a warmed serving dish and pour the bolognese sauce over it. Top with the fromage frais and oregano leaves.

Serve green beans or a leafy salad with the tagliatelle for a crisp and colourful contrast.

Parma ham and chicken livers give extra flavour to the beef and tomato sauce that is one of Italy's most appreciated exports — and used here on ribbons of pasta.

Armenian bulgur pilau

ONE SERVING	
CALORIES	595
TOTAL FAT	29g
SATURATED FAT	7g
CARBOHYDRATES	55g
ADDED SUGAR	0
FIBRE	6g
SODIUM	165mg

SERVES 4
PREPARATION TIME: 20 minutes
COOKING TIME: 35 minutes

1 tablespoon olive oil
12oz (340g) neck of lamb fillet with fat removed, thinly sliced
1 medium onion, peeled and chopped
1 small green pepper, de-seeded, and cut into small pieces
6oz (175g) medium-ground bulgur wheat
1¼ pints (725ml) vegetable stock (see p.19)

1 large carrot, peeled and finely chopped
2 sticks celery, trimmed and finely chopped
6oz (175g) ready-to-use dried apricots, chopped
1 level teaspoon dried thyme
⅛ level teaspoon salt
Freshly ground black pepper
2 cloves garlic, peeled and crushed
4oz (115g) tahina paste
3fl oz (85ml) water
Strained juice of 1 lemon
Mint sprigs or 2 tablespoons chopped fresh chives to garnish

TIP
After the bulgur wheat has absorbed the stock and become plump, take the pilau off the heat and let it stand in the covered pan for 10 minutes to make the bulgur tender and fluffy.

1 Heat the olive oil in a large saucepan and cook the lamb in it over a moderate heat for about 5 minutes, until lightly browned all over. Lift the meat out of the pan with a slotted spoon and set aside.

2 Cook the onion in the pan over a moderate heat for 5 minutes, until lightly browned. Stir in the green pepper and bulgur wheat and cook for 1 minute. Return the lamb to the pan.

3 Pour in the stock, add the carrot, celery, apricots, thyme and salt, and season with black pepper. Bring to the boil, then turn down the

heat, cover and simmer for about 15 minutes, or until the stock is absorbed.

4 Meanwhile, put the garlic and tahina paste in a medium bowl and gradually whisk in the water and the lemon juice, until the mixture has the consistency of whipped cream.

5 Turn the pilau into a warmed serving dish and scatter on the mint sprigs or chives. Serve the tahina sauce separately.

A colourful roasted pepper salad makes a moist, sweet contrast to the pilau.

In some parts of Turkey bulgur wheat, a cracked wheat, replaces rice in the national dish, pilau. This usually contains nuts and fruits and may accompany meat, most often lamb, but here the lamb is cooked in the dish.

Bulgur and lentils with pepper sauce

SERVES 4
PREPARATION TIME: 15 minutes
COOKING TIME: 40 minutes

1 tablespoon olive oil
1 medium onion, peeled and finely chopped
14oz (400g) tinned chopped tomatoes
¼ level teaspoon cayenne pepper
5oz (150g) medium-ground bulgur wheat
½ pint (285ml) beef or chicken stock (see p.19)
2 medium onions, peeled, each studded with a clove
1 bay leaf
5oz (150g) brown lentils, cleaned of grit and rinsed
1 carrot, peeled and thickly sliced
1 garlic clove, unpeeled
Fresh bouquet garni
¾ pint (425ml) water
Freshly ground black pepper
1 level tablespoon chopped fresh coriander

1 Heat the oil in a saucepan and fry the chopped onion in it over a low heat for 5 minutes, until golden. Stir in the tomatoes and cayenne pepper. Bring to the boil, then lower the heat, cover and leave to simmer for about 25 minutes, until thickened.

2 Meanwhile, bring the bulgur to the boil in the stock. Put in one of the studded onions and the bay leaf, then simmer, covered, for 25 minutes, until the bulgur is tender and all the stock absorbed. Take off the heat and leave in the covered pan for 10 minutes.

3 While the bulgur is cooking, bring the lentils to the boil in a large saucepan with the carrot, garlic, the remaining onion, the bouquet garni and the water. Once boiling, turn down the heat, cover the pan and simmer for about 25 minutes, or until the lentils are softened.

4 Drain the lentils and season with black pepper. Turn into a warmed serving dish, discarding the bouquet garni, and sprinkle with the coriander. Spoon the bulgur into a warmed serving dish and garnish with the onion and bay leaf. Pour the sauce into a third warmed dish.

Put the separate dishes of lentils, bulgur wheat and tomato sauce on the table for the diners to help themselves. A side salad of celery and apple adds bite, and you can use some of the celery leaves to garnish the three dishes.

ONE SERVING	
CALORIES	310
TOTAL FAT	4g
SATURATED FAT	1g
CARBOHYDRATES	55g
ADDED SUGAR	0
FIBRE	6g
SODIUM	50mg

> **TIP**
> *You can make a bouquet garni from 1 sprig each of fresh thyme, parsley and rosemary, 1 bay leaf and a small stick of celery. Simply gather the herbs into a small posy and tie securely with fine string.*

The protein in the lentils is enhanced by that in the bulgur wheat. Here this robust pairing has its mild, nutty flavours sharpened by the peppery tomato sauce.

Rabbit couscous

SERVES 4
PREPARATION TIME: 35 minutes
COOKING TIME: 1 hour
OVEN: Preheat to 190°C (375°F, gas mark 5)

1 pint (570ml) chicken stock (see p.19)
12oz (340g) couscous
1 tablespoon olive oil
1 medium onion, peeled and chopped
1 clove garlic, peeled and chopped
1 level teaspoon peeled and grated root ginger
1 level teaspoon coriander seeds, crushed
½ level teaspoon fennel seeds, crushed
1lb (450g) fresh rabbit portions, wiped
1lb (450g) tomatoes, skinned and chopped
4oz (15g) okra, trimmed
3 level tablespoons chopped fresh coriander leaves
Fresh coriander leaves to garnish

1 Bring the stock to the boil, pour it over the couscous in a heatproof dish, cover and leave to stand for about 15 minutes, until all the stock has been absorbed.

2 Meanwhile, heat the olive oil in a large frying pan and cook the onion and garlic in it over a moderate heat for 5 minutes to brown lightly. Scatter in the ginger, coriander seeds and fennel seeds and stir over a moderate heat for 2-3 minutes.

3 Arrange the rabbit portions in the pan and mix in the tomatoes and okra. Simmer for about 10 minutes, turning the rabbit portions over two or three times.

4 Mix the chopped coriander leaves into the couscous, then spread half the mixture in a casserole. Cover with the rabbit and vegetables and spoon the rest of the couscous over the top. Put on the lid and cook in the heated oven for about 45 minutes, then uncover and cook for a further 15 minutes.

Fluffy, versatile couscous – granules made from wheat and similar to semolina – provides a satisfying accompaniment to this aromatic rabbit casserole. Okra thickens the spicy cooking juices which are flavoured with fennel seeds, ginger and coriander.

Serve the dish on individual warmed plates. Give each diner a share of the rabbit joints placed on a pile of couscous with sauce spooned round them and a garnish of coriander. Lightly steamed green beans or leafy salads make crisp accompaniments to this dish.

ONE SERVING	
CALORIES	425
TOTAL FAT	8g
SATURATED FAT	2g
CARBOHYDRATES	68g
ADDED SUGAR	0
FIBRE	4g
SODIUM	80mg

Polenta with tomatoes and artichokes

SERVES 4
PREPARATION TIME: 30 minutes
COOKING TIME: 35 minutes

ONE SERVING

CALORIES 395

TOTAL FAT 12g

SATURATED FAT 4g

CARBOHYDRATES 57g

ADDED SUGAR 0

FIBRE 5g

SODIUM 455mg

Artichokes and the maize porridge called polenta are both widely used in Italian cooking. Sun-dried tomatoes and goat's cheese provide further echoes of the Mediterranean in this filling country fare.

1 tablespoon oil from a jar of sun-dried tomatoes
1 large onion, peeled and chopped
2 cloves garlic, peeled and chopped
3oz (85g) sun-dried tomatoes, well drained on kitchen paper and finely chopped
1lb (450g) tomatoes, skinned and chopped
2 courgettes, trimmed and sliced
1 green pepper, de-seeded and chopped
14oz (400g) tinned artichoke hearts, well rinsed, drained and halved
2 pints (1.1 litres) water
8oz (225g) polenta
3½ oz (100g) goat's cheese, crumbled or sliced
Fresh basil leaves to garnish

1 Heat the oil in a large saucepan and fry the onion and garlic in it over a moderate heat for about 5 minutes, until softened.

2 Add the sun-dried tomatoes, fresh tomatoes, courgettes, green pepper and artichoke hearts. Bring the mixture to the boil, then reduce the heat and cover. Simmer for about 30 minutes, stirring from time to time, until the vegetables are tender and the sauce has thickened slightly.

3 Meanwhile, bring the water to the boil in a large saucepan and pour in the polenta in a thin, steady stream, stirring all the time. Keep stirring the polenta over a low heat and, as it thickens, beat it. When the mixture becomes very stiff and begins to pull away from the sides of the pan, spoon it onto a lightly oiled, warmed serving plate. Make a well in the centre and pour in the tomato sauce.

4 Scatter the cheese over the sauce and cook under a hot grill for 4-5 minutes, until the cheese browns lightly. Garnish with the basil.

You can use cornmeal in place of polenta.

Chicken liver risotto

SERVES 4
PREPARATION TIME: 10 minutes, plus 30 minutes to soak
COOKING TIME: 45 minutes

2 tablespoons olive oil
1 red onion, peeled and thinly sliced
1 clove garlic, peeled and finely chopped
8oz (225g) button mushrooms, wiped and sliced
8oz (225g) fresh chicken livers, rinsed and dried
8oz (225g) arborio or risotto rice
1oz (30g) wild rice, parboiled for 5 minutes
1oz (30g) dried ceps, soaked in hot water
for 30 minutes, drained and roughly chopped
1¾ pints (1 litre) chicken stock (see p.19)
3 level tablespoons chopped fresh parsley
1½ oz (45g) grated Parmesan cheese

1 Heat the oil in a large, heavy-based saucepan and gently fry the onion, garlic and button mushrooms in it for about 5 minutes, until browned. Stir in the chicken livers and cook over a moderate heat, turning to brown both sides.

2 Pour the arborio or risotto rice and the wild rice in with the livers and stir in the ceps. Cook over a low heat, stirring frequently, for about 5 minutes, until the rice is shiny.

3 Pour ¼ pint (150ml) of the stock into the rice and stir over a low heat until the liquid is absorbed. Continue to stir in these small amounts of stock, letting the rice absorb each addition before adding the next. It will take about 35 minutes to use all the stock.

4 Stir in the parsley, turn the risotto into a warm serving dish and top with the Parmesan.

An oakleaf lettuce salad makes a crisp, sharp contrast to the succulent risotto. If you cannot find dried ceps, or porcini as they are called in Italian delicatessen, use an extra 2oz (60g) of button mushrooms.

ONE SERVING	
CALORIES	450
TOTAL FAT	16g
SATURATED FAT	5g
CARBOHYDRATES	59g
ADDED SUGAR	0
FIBRE	2g
SODIUM	175mg

Wild rice and mushrooms give extra taste and texture to a delicious risotto, whose flavour is dominated by the light and crumbly chicken livers.

Paella

SERVES 6
PREPARATION TIME: 35 minutes
COOKING TIME: 1 hour

ONE SERVING	
CALORIES 425	
TOTAL FAT 10g	
SATURATED FAT 2g	
CARBOHYDRATES 52g	
ADDED SUGAR 0	
FIBRE 3g	
SODIUM 460mg	

1 pint (570ml) fresh mussels
2 tablespoons olive oil
2 boneless chicken breasts, each about 8oz (225g), skinned and cut into 3 equal pieces
1 medium onion, peeled and finely chopped
1 medium fennel bulb, trimmed and finely chopped
1 clove garlic, peeled and finely chopped
1 small red pepper, de-seeded and chopped
12oz (340g) Valencia or long-grain white rice
½ level teaspoon saffron strands
1¼ pints (725ml) chicken stock (see p.19)
1 bay leaf
8oz (225g) cleaned fresh squid, cut into rings
4oz (115g) unpeeled prawns
2oz (60g) peeled prawns
4oz (115g) frozen petits pois
Freshly ground black pepper
Chopped fennel fronds to garnish

TIP
To ensure that the whole dish is enhanced by the subtle saffron, steep the strands in a cupful of heated stock for 10 minutes. Add to the dish with the rest of the stock.

1 Scrub the mussels well, remove the beards and put the mussels in cold water until needed.

2 Heat the oil in a paella pan or large, flameproof casserole. Fry the chicken pieces in it for 15 minutes, turning frequently. Drain the chicken on kitchen paper and keep hot.

3 Put the onion, fennel, garlic and red pepper in the pan and cook over a moderate heat for 5 minutes, until softening. Mix in the rice and cook over a low heat for 5 minutes, stirring. Add the saffron and stock, and stir until it boils. Put in the chicken pieces and bay leaf, and simmer, uncovered, for 15 minutes.

4 Mix in the squid and drained mussels, cover and simmer for about 8 minutes, until the squid is tender and the mussels are open. Discard any mussels that remain closed.

5 Stir in the prawns and peas and cook gently for 5 minutes more, stirring occasionally. Remove the bay leaf, season with pepper and garnish with fennel fronds.

Serve a light, leafy salad as a foil for the varied flavours of the paella.

The ingredients in this Spanish dish vary with the seasons, but the hearty blend always includes a variety of seafoods in plump golden rice.

Rice with egg and prawns

ONE SERVING	
CALORIES	405
TOTAL FAT	13g
SATURATED FAT	3g
CARBOHYDRATES	54g
ADDED SUGAR	0
FIBRE	1g
SODIUM	770mg

SERVES 4
PREPARATION TIME: 15 minutes
COOKING TIME: 15 minutes

2 spring onions, trimmed and chopped
3 eggs, size 2, beaten
2 teaspoons and 1 tablespoon olive oil
1 shallot or small onion, peeled and finely chopped

1 clove garlic, peeled and finely chopped
2oz (60g) frozen petits pois
2oz (60g) frozen sweetcorn kernels
2oz (60g) cooked ham, chopped
4oz (115g) cooked shelled prawns
1 level teaspoon paprika
8oz (225g) cooked long-grain rice (see p.19)
1 teaspoon soy sauce

This adaptation of a Chinese fried rice recipe makes an attractive and well-flavoured dish which is given extra crunch and colour by adding the sweetcorn.

1 Set aside the green part of the spring onions. Mix the white part with the eggs. Heat the 2 teaspoons of oil in an omelette pan and cook the mixture in it, stirring until just set. Turn it onto a plate and break it up with a fork.

2 Heat the tablespoon of oil in a wok or large frying pan and cook the shallot or onion and garlic in it over a moderate heat for about 5 minutes, until soft. Mix in the petits pois and sweetcorn and cook for 3-4 minutes more.

Stir in the ham and prawns, sprinkle with the paprika and cook for 2-3 minutes more.

3 Spoon in the rice, stirring to keep the grains separate. Stir in the soy sauce and egg mixture, and heat through for 1-2 minutes. Turn into a warmed serving dish and garnish with the reserved spring onion.

This dish goes well with a mangetout and mushroom salad.

Jambalaya

ONE SERVING	
CALORIES	340
TOTAL FAT	9g
SATURATED FAT	2g
CARBOHYDRATES	47g
ADDED SUGAR	0
FIBRE	3g
SODIUM	60mg

Jambalaya, now a dish associated with the southern United States, is a tribute to the French settlers there, for its name comes from a Provençal word for a chicken and rice stew.

SERVES 4
PREPARATION TIME: 20 minutes
COOKING TIME: 30 minutes

1 tablespoon olive oil
1 small red pepper, de-seeded and chopped
1 small green pepper, de-seeded and chopped
1 stick celery, trimmed and thinly sliced
1 small onion, peeled and chopped
1 clove garlic, peeled and finely chopped
5oz (150g) long-grain rice
1lb (450g) ripe tomatoes, skinned and chopped
½ pint (285ml) chicken or vegetable stock (see p.19)
½ level teaspoon dried thyme
⅛ level teaspoon each ground allspice, ground cloves and cayenne pepper
7oz (200g) cooked chicken or turkey, without skin or bone, diced
6oz (175g) frozen sweetcorn kernels
2 level tablespoons chopped fresh parsley

1 Heat the oil in a large, heavy-based saucepan and cook the peppers, celery, onion and garlic in it over a moderate heat for about 5 minutes, stirring frequently, until the onion is browned.

2 Stir in the rice and cook for another 3 minutes, until the rice is lightly coloured.

3 Mix in the tomatoes, stock, thyme, allspice, cloves and cayenne pepper. Bring to the boil, reduce the heat, cover and cook gently for 20 minutes.

4 Stir in the chicken or turkey and the sweetcorn and simmer for a further 5 minutes, until the rice is tender and the chicken and sweetcorn cooked through. Sprinkle with the parsley and serve immediately.

Steamed broccoli or a mixed salad would provide a contrast in texture to the jambalaya.

Lamb and courgette risotto

SERVES 4
PREPARATION TIME: 30 minutes
COOKING TIME: 45 minutes

12oz (340g) lamb neck fillets with fat removed,
cut into thin strips
1 tablespoon olive oil
1 clove garlic, peeled and crushed
1 large onion, peeled and finely chopped

9oz (250g) courgettes, trimmed and cut into
small cubes
8oz (225g) risotto or long-grain rice
1 pint (570ml) vegetable stock (see p.19)
6oz (175g) asparagus tips, cut in half lengthways
2 level tablespoons grated Parmesan cheese
1 level tablespoon low-fat natural yoghurt
Freshly ground black pepper
1 level tablespoon finely shredded basil leaves

ONE SERVING	
CALORIES	440
TOTAL FAT	14g
SATURATED FAT	5g
CARBOHYDRATES	55g
ADDED SUGAR	0
FIBRE	2g
SODIUM	120mg

Lean and tender strips of lamb and lightly cooked asparagus tips create a delicately flavoured partnership with creamy rice and courgettes.

1 Heat a heavy-based nonstick saucepan and dry-fry the lamb in it for 5-6 minutes, tossing it frequently until lightly browned all over. Turn the meat onto a plate and set aside.

2 Heat the oil in the same pan and cook the garlic and onion in it over a low heat for 5 minutes. Add the courgettes and cook for a further 5 minutes, stirring frequently.

3 Stir the rice into the pan and cook for 3 minutes over a moderate heat. Pour in the stock and bring to the boil, stirring. Reduce the

heat, cover and simmer for about 10 minutes, or until most of the liquid has been absorbed. Stir in the lamb and asparagus and continue cooking for about 10 minutes more.

4 When the rice is tender, turn off the heat, mix in the Parmesan and yoghurt, and season with pepper. Cover and leave the risotto to rest for 5-10 minutes. Spoon it onto warmed plates for serving and sprinkle with the basil.

A tomato salad makes a simple and juicy contrast to the risotto.

TIP
For the creamiest risotto, use arborio rice, but have an extra ½ pint (285ml) of stock ready to add during cooking. Arborio absorbs more liquid than other rice and develops a distinctive tender texture.

Kidney bean risotto

SERVES 4
PREPARATION TIME: 20 minutes
COOKING TIME: 30 minutes

ONE SERVING	
CALORIES 330	
TOTAL FAT 7g	
SATURATED FAT 2g	
CARBOHYDRATES 52g	
ADDED SUGAR 0	
FIBRE 11g	
SODIUM 105mg	

4oz (115g) long-grain brown rice
1 tablespoon olive oil
1 large onion, peeled and chopped
2 cloves garlic, peeled and chopped
1lb (450g) tomatoes, skinned and chopped
2 medium carrots, peeled and chopped
1 large stick celery, trimmed and chopped
1 level tablespoon chopped fresh basil,
or 1 level teaspoon dried basil, crumbled
1 level teaspoon dried oregano, crumbled
Freshly ground black pepper
1lb (450g) cooked red kidney beans (see p.17)
1oz (30g) finely shaved or grated Parmesan cheese
2 level tablespoons chopped fresh parsley

TIP
**Use a very sharp
knife for chopping
fresh herbs such as
basil. This will cut
cleanly and avoid
the bruising that
makes tender leaves
blacken.**

*Brown rice and
burgundy-red kidney
beans, bursting with
fibre, form the basis
of this substantial,
herb-flavoured risotto,
which will appeal
strongly to vegetarians.*

1 Cook the rice (see p.17).

2 Meanwhile, heat the oil in a large, heavy-based saucepan and fry the onion and garlic in it over a moderate heat for about 5 minutes, until the onion is browned. Add the tomatoes, carrots, celery, basil and oregano, season with pepper and bring to the boil. Cover, reduce the heat and simmer for 15 minutes.

3 Mix in the kidney beans, cover and cook for a further 5 minutes.

4 Stir in the cooked rice, spoon the risotto into a warmed serving dish and scatter on the Parmesan and parsley.

A mixed salad makes a refreshing side dish.

Nutty brown rice with eggs

SERVES 4
PREPARATION TIME: 10 minutes
COOKING TIME: 35 minutes

1¼ pints (725ml) chicken stock (see p.19)
Freshly ground black pepper
8oz (225g) brown rice
4 eggs, size 2

2 sticks celery, trimmed and finely chopped
4 spring onions, trimmed and finely chopped
2 teaspoons olive oil
2oz (60g) shelled, unsalted pistachios
1 level tablespoon chopped fresh parsley
1 level tablespoon snipped fresh chives
Mustard and cress to garnish

1 Bring the chicken stock to the boil in a large, heavy-based saucepan. Season it with pepper and stir in the rice. Reduce the heat, cover and simmer for about 35 minutes, stirring occasionally, until the rice is tender and the stock has been absorbed.

2 Meanwhile, boil the eggs for 10 minutes until hard, then cool them under the cold tap and shell. Halve the eggs and cut each half into three wedges.

3 Use a fork to mix the celery, onions and oil into the rice, and heat through. Stir in the pistachios, parsley and chives, then spoon into a serving dish. Arrange the eggs round the rice and garnish with the mustard and cress.

A spicy cucumber and red pepper salad makes a sharp and colourful accompaniment to this dish. You can use prawns or chopped cooked turkey or ham in place of the eggs.

As well as containing more fibre than white rice, brown rice has a deliciously nutty taste and a firm, satisfying texture. Combining it with mild, unsalted pistachios and fresh boiled eggs produces a harmony of subtle flavours.

Spiced seafood and coconut pilau

SERVES 4
PREPARATION TIME: 20 minutes,
plus 30 minutes to soak
COOKING TIME: 35 minutes

8oz (225g) basmati rice
1 tablespoon vegetable oil
1 medium onion, peeled and chopped

2 level teaspoons peeled and grated root ginger
1 clove garlic, peeled and finely chopped
1 level teaspoon each ground cumin, ground coriander, ground turmeric and paprika
6 cardamom pods, crushed
4oz (115g) fine green beans, trimmed and cut into short lengths
2oz (60g) blanched almonds

½ pint (285ml) fish or vegetable stock (see p.19)
½ pint (285ml) tinned coconut milk
Meat of 1 small fresh lobster, about 6oz (175g),
cut into pieces
2oz (60g) queen scallops, cut into small pieces
4oz (115g) uncooked tiger prawns, shelled
Freshly ground black pepper
Juice of 1 small lime or lemon
Lime or lemon slices to garnish

1 Cover the rice with cold water and leave it to soak for 30 minutes.

2 Heat the oil in a large frying pan and toss the onion, ginger and garlic in it over a moderately high heat for 5 minutes, or until lightly coloured. Stir in the cumin, coriander, turmeric, paprika and cardamom.

3 Drain the rice and stir it into the pan along with the beans and almonds. Pour in the stock and coconut milk and bring to the boil, then mix in the lobster, scallops and prawns. Turn down the heat, cover the pan and simmer the pilau for about 20 minutes, stirring occasionally with a fork to make sure that the rice grains remain separate.

4 When the rice is tender and fluffy and all the liquid has been absorbed, season with pepper and stir in the lime or lemon juice. Turn the pilau into a warmed serving dish, garnish it with the lime or lemon slices and serve at once while piping hot.

A cucumber and fruit salad is a refreshing side dish to have with the spicy pilau.

Coconut milk, widely used in the cuisines of South-east Asia, gives its distinctive flavour to this dish of rice and seafood, which has a sprinkling of nuts for texture and spices to prickle the palate.

VEGETARIAN MAIN DISHES

Growing numbers of people are narrowing down the types of protein they eat, but these recipes show that the range of dishes without meat or fish is far from narrow. By combining peas, beans or lentils with nuts or grain and varying them with dairy foods, you will get plenty of protein. Add a dash of adventure and the range of mouthwatering possibilities widens — pies and hotpots, paella and pancakes, curries and quiches — and there is a whole new repertoire of meals not just for vegetarian visitors but for the family as well.

Aubergine and cheese gratin

SERVES 4
PREPARATION TIME: 25 minutes
COOKING TIME: 45 minutes
OVEN: Preheat to 180°C (350°F, gas mark 4)

ONE SERVING	
CALORIES	210
TOTAL FAT	14g
SATURATED FAT	4g
CARBOHYDRATES	10g
ADDED SUGAR	0
FIBRE	3g
SODIUM	305mg

1 tablespoon olive oil
2 tablespoons lemon juice
1lb (450g) aubergines, trimmed and thickly sliced
14oz (400g) tinned tomatoes, sieved
14oz (400g) tinned chopped tomatoes
2 cloves garlic, peeled and crushed
1 level teaspoon dried oregano
1 level tablespoon chopped fresh basil
2oz (60g) grated Parmesan cheese
1oz (30g) wholemeal breadcrumbs
4oz (115g) ricotta cheese
1oz (30g) mozzarella cheese, grated or thinly sliced

1 Mix the oil and lemon juice together and brush both sides of the aubergine slices with the mixture. Grill them for 2 minutes on each side under a high heat until golden brown.

2 Bring the sieved tomatoes and chopped tomatoes to the boil in a saucepan and stir in the garlic and oregano. Boil briskly for about 5 minutes until reduced by a third. Remove from the heat and stir in the basil.

3 Mix the Parmesan with the breadcrumbs in a small bowl. Spread a third of the tomato mixture over the bottom of an ovenproof dish and sprinkle on half the breadcrumb mixture. Arrange half the aubergine slices over the top and crumble half the ricotta over them. Repeat these layers and spread the remaining tomato mixture on top. Cover with the mozzarella.

4 Cook in the heated oven for 45 minutes, or until bubbling hot and browned on top.

Serve the gratin piping hot with granary bread.

Grilling the aubergine slices before they go in the gratin gives them extra flavour to add to the layers of basil and tomato sauce and three Italian cheeses.

Stuffed aubergines

ONE SERVING	
CALORIES	280
TOTAL FAT	18g
SATURATED FAT	4g
CARBOHYDRATES	21g
ADDED SUGAR	0
FIBRE	6g
SODIUM	270mg

SERVES 4
PREPARATION TIME: 30 minutes
COOKING TIME: 20 minutes
OVEN: Preheat to 200°C (400°F, gas mark 6)

2 aubergines, each about 8oz (225g), trimmed
1 tablespoon olive oil
1 medium onion, peeled and finely chopped
2 cloves garlic, peeled and crushed
4oz (115g) mushrooms, wiped and finely chopped
1 large carrot, peeled and coarsely grated
2 level teaspoons dried basil
1 level teaspoon dried marjoram
4oz (115g) fresh wholemeal breadcrumbs
1oz (30g) macadamia or brazil nuts, roughly chopped
1 level tablespoon sunflower seeds
1 level tablespoon pumpkin seeds
Freshly ground black pepper
3oz (85g) soft goat's cheese, thinly sliced
1 level tablespoon pine nuts
Sprigs of fresh marjoram to garnish

1 Halve the aubergines lengthways and scoop out the flesh with a teaspoon, leaving the shells about ¼ in (6mm) thick. Blanch the shells in boiling water for 2 minutes, then drain.

2 Heat the oil in a saucepan and cook the onion and garlic in it over a moderate heat for 5 minutes until lightly browned. Stir in the mushrooms, carrot, basil and marjoram. Chop the aubergine flesh and mix it in with the vegetables. Cook gently for about 10 minutes, uncovered, stirring frequently. Mix in the breadcrumbs, chopped nuts and sunflower and pumpkin seeds, and season with pepper.

3 Arrange the aubergine shells in a lightly oiled baking dish and fill with the stuffing. Top each with cheese slices and sprinkle with pine nuts. Bake in the heated oven for 20 minutes, or until the cheese has melted and the stuffing is hot all through. Garnish with the marjoram sprigs before serving.

Serve warm rolls (see p.366) with the aubergines. A side dish of braised fennel and tomatoes will complement the subtle flavours. Instead of using the stuffing in aubergines, you can fill mushrooms or large, scooped-out tomatoes or courgettes with it.

Large, boat-shaped aubergine shells are delicious containers for a savoury vegetable, nut and herb stuffing. Pine nuts and sunflower and pumpkin seeds add a crunchy element to this moist Mediterranean-style dish, and the goat's-cheese topping gives a tart finish.

Bean and aubergine moussaka

SERVES 4
PREPARATION TIME: 30 minutes
COOKING TIME: 40 minutes
OVEN: Preheat to 180°C (350°F, gas mark 4)

ONE SERVING	
CALORIES 370	
TOTAL FAT 16g	
SATURATED FAT 4g	
CARBOHYDRATES 36g	
ADDED SUGAR 0	
FIBRE 9g	
SODIUM 240mg	

3oz (85g) split red lentils, cleaned of grit, rinsed and drained
2 tablespoons olive oil
1 tablespoon lemon juice
1lb (450g) aubergines, trimmed and thickly sliced
1 medium onion, peeled and chopped

1 clove garlic, peeled and crushed
2oz (60g) mushrooms, wiped and finely chopped
1 level teaspoon dried thyme
¼ level teaspoon ground cinnamon
14oz (400g) tinned chopped tomatoes
2 tablespoons tomato purée (see p.16)
Freshly ground black pepper
8oz (225g) cooked red kidney beans (see p.17)
3 eggs, size 2, beaten
10oz (275g) low-fat natural yoghurt
½ oz (15g) grated Parmesan cheese

Kidney beans, lentils and mushrooms replace the lamb of a Greek moussaka, but the melting aubergines are kept.

TIP
For a fluffy topping, separate one of the eggs, whisk the white and fold it into the egg and yoghurt mixture just before pouring it onto the aubergines.

1 Simmer the lentils for 20 minutes in unsalted water. Meanwhile, mix half the oil with the lemon juice. Lay the aubergines on a grill rack and brush both sides with the oil and lemon. Cook under a medium grill for about 2 minutes each side, until golden, and set aside.

2 Heat the remaining oil in a saucepan and cook the onion and garlic in it over a moderate heat for 5 minutes, until softened. Stir in the

mushrooms, thyme, cinnamon, tomatoes and tomato purée and simmer for 5 minutes.

3 When the lentils are tender, drain them, season with pepper and mix into the tomatoes.

4 Lay half the aubergine slices in an ovenproof dish. Spread half the beans on top and cover with the tomato mixture. Top with the rest of the beans, then the rest of the aubergine slices.

5 Mix the eggs into the yoghurt and season with pepper. Pour the mixture over the aubergine slices. Sprinkle with the Parmesan and bake in the heated oven for about 40 minutes, until bubbling and browned.

A salad of finely sliced onion and white cabbage, tossed in a lemon vinaigrette dressing (see p.17), provides a sharp, crisp contrast to the soft, moist moussaka. Serve warm crusty bread for mopping up the sauce.

Broccoli and Cheddar soufflé

ONE SERVING	
CALORIES	225
TOTAL FAT	15g
SATURATED FAT	8g
CARBOHYDRATES	10g
ADDED SUGAR	0
FIBRE	2g
SODIUM	255mg

TIP
Be sure to steam the broccoli only lightly so that it does not become soggy. Waterlogged broccoli will spoil the soufflé's rise.

Firm morsels of steamed broccoli make a well-flavoured addition in this fluffy soufflé. Their slightly peppery taste is intensified by mustard and cayenne pepper.

SERVES 4
PREPARATION TIME: 30 minutes
COOKING TIME: 35 minutes
OVEN: Preheat to 200°C (400°F, gas mark 6)

½ oz (15g) slightly salted butter
3 level tablespoons plain flour
8fl oz (225ml) skimmed milk
1 bay leaf
2 whole eggs, separated, plus 3 egg whites, size 2
1 level teaspoon made English mustard
3oz (85g) finely grated mature Cheddar cheese
7oz (200g) broccoli, very lightly steamed and finely chopped
¼ level teaspoon cayenne pepper

1 Melt the butter in a saucepan, stir in the flour, cook gently for 1 minute and take off the heat. Gradually stir in the milk, put in the bay leaf and then bring to the boil over a moderate heat, stirring continuously. Simmer for about 2 minutes, until the sauce thickens.

2 Remove from the heat, discard the bay leaf and beat in the egg yolks. Stir in the mustard, Cheddar, broccoli and cayenne pepper.

3 Lightly grease a deep soufflé dish 7in (18cm) in diameter. Whisk the egg whites until they stay in soft peaks when you pull up the whisk. Using a metal spoon, fold 2 tablespoons of the egg whites into the cheese sauce, then fold in the rest. Spoon into the soufflé dish and cook in the heated oven for about 35 minutes, or until risen and golden brown. Serve at once.

Poppy-seed rolls (see p.366) and a crisp mixed salad go well with this light soufflé.

Butter-bean hotpot

ONE SERVING	
CALORIES 290	
TOTAL FAT 8g	
SATURATED FAT 2g	
CARBOHYDRATES 42g	
ADDED SUGAR 0	
FIBRE 16g	
SODIUM 115mg	

SERVES 4
PREPARATION TIME: 15 minutes
COOKING TIME: 1 hour 40 minutes

4oz (115g) butter beans, soaked in cold water
overnight (see p.17)
1¼ pints (725ml) vegetable stock (see p.19)
8 button onions, peeled, or 2 medium onions, peeled
and thickly sliced

8oz (225g) swede, peeled and cut into cubes
8oz (225g) parsnips, peeled, quartered lengthways
and thickly sliced
8oz (225g) carrots, peeled and cut into chunks
2 sprigs thyme
2 bay leaves
4 level tablespoons chopped fresh parsley
2 sprigs tarragon
3oz (85g) shelled broad beans, or frozen broad
beans, rinsed
1 tablespoon corn oil
1 level tablespoon plain wholemeal flour
4oz (115g) medium-fat soft cheese
Freshly ground black pepper
Parsley sprigs to garnish

1 Rinse and drain the butter beans and put
them into a large saucepan with the stock.
Bring to the boil and skim off any scum that
rises. Put on the lid and simmer for about
1 hour, until the beans begin to soften.

2 Stir in the onions, swede, parsnips, carrots,
thyme, bay leaves, parsley and tarragon, and
simmer, covered, for 20 minutes. Mix in the
broad beans and cook for a further 10 minutes,
until all the vegetables are tender. Remove
from the heat and pour off the stock into a
measuring jug. Remove the thyme, bay leaves
and tarragon from the pan. Leave the pan off
the heat with the lid on.

3 Keep ½ pint (285ml) of the stock, topping
up with water if necessary. Heat the oil in a
small saucepan, mix in the flour, then gradually
stir in the stock. Bring to the boil, stirring, then
reduce the heat and simmer for 2-3 minutes.
Remove from the heat, whisk in the cheese and
season with the pepper. Pour the sauce over the
vegetables and reheat gently, stirring carefully,
then turn into a warm serving dish and garnish
with the parsley sprigs.

Serve the hotpot with crusty wholemeal bread.
You can vary the fresh herbs according to what
is available. Shallots or leeks and celeriac can
replace the onions and parsnips, and you can
add mushrooms to vary the dish.

*This comforting winter hotpot brims with vegetables,
including fibre-rich broad beans and butter beans,
and will satisfy the healthiest of appetites.*

Cabbage noodle casserole

SERVES 4
PREPARATION TIME: 10 minutes
COOKING TIME: 25 minutes

1 tablespoon olive oil
1 medium onion, peeled and chopped
1lb (450g) savoy cabbage, trimmed and shredded
½ level teaspoon caraway seeds
½ level teaspoon celery seeds
4fl oz (115ml) dry white wine
Freshly ground black pepper
4oz (115g) Chinese egg noodles
2 level tablespoons cornflour
¾ pint (425ml) vegetable stock (see p.19)
4oz (115g) Greek yoghurt
2oz (60g) flaked almonds
1oz (30g) wholemeal breadcrumbs
1oz (30g) grated Parmesan cheese
Marjoram sprigs to garnish

ONE SERVING	
CALORIES	380
TOTAL FAT	20g
SATURATED FAT	4g
CARBOHYDRATES	36g
ADDED SUGAR	0
FIBRE	6g
SODIUM	200mg

Crinkly, crisp shreds of savoy cabbage give a lively flavour, colour and texture to this casserole, which is moistened by a smooth yoghurt sauce flavoured with white wine and caraway and celery seeds.

1 Heat the oil in a heavy-based saucepan and cook the onion in it over a moderate heat for 5 minutes to brown. Stir in the cabbage, caraway and celery seeds, and wine, and season with pepper. Cover and simmer for 10 minutes.

2 Cook the noodles in unsalted water (see p.18).

3 Blend the cornflour with 2 tablespoons of stock. Mix with the rest of the stock, pour onto the cabbage and stir over a low heat until it thickens. Mix in the yoghurt and noodles, turn into a wide heatproof dish and top with almonds, breadcrumbs and Parmesan. Brown under a moderate grill and garnish with the marjoram.

Serve crusty bread (see p.366) with the dish.

Carrot and rice terrine

SERVES 6
PREPARATION TIME: 35 minutes
COOKING TIME: 50 minutes
OVEN: Preheat to 180°C (350°F, gas mark 4)

....
ONE SERVING
....
CALORIES 360
....
TOTAL FAT 20g
....
  SATURATED FAT 6g
....
CARBOHYDRATES 35g
....
  ADDED SUGAR 0
....
FIBRE 2g
....
SODIUM 175mg
....

Plump, firm brown rice, chewy, aromatic wild rice and tender, sweet carrots combine in a terrine enriched with walnuts and the savour of mature cheese.

1 pint (570ml) vegetable stock (see p.19)
4oz (115g) brown rice
4oz (115g) wild rice mixture
2 tablespoons olive oil
1 large onion, peeled and finely chopped
2 sticks celery, trimmed and finely chopped
4 medium carrots, peeled and grated
3 level tablespoons chopped fresh parsley
2 eggs, size 2, lightly beaten
2oz (60g) chopped walnuts
2 level teaspoons ground cumin
4oz (115g) grated mature Cheddar cheese
Freshly ground black pepper

1 Bring the stock to the boil in a large saucepan, stir in all the rice and simmer, covered, for about 15 minutes, until the rice has absorbed most of the liquid. Turn the heat very low and continue cooking, covered, for 5 minutes, stirring occasionally.

2 Meanwhile, heat the oil in a frying pan and cook the onion and celery in it over a moderate heat for about 5 minutes. Mix in the carrots and cook for 3 minutes. Leave to cool slightly.

3 Stir the vegetables into the rice and mix in the parsley, eggs, walnuts, cumin and 3oz (85g) of the Cheddar. Season with pepper.

4 Turn the mixture into a lightly oiled loaf tin about 10×5in (25×13cm) and sprinkle with the remaining Cheddar. Cook in the heated oven for about 50 minutes, until golden and firm to the touch. Let the terrine cool for 10 minutes before turning it out of the tin.

Slice the terrine to serve hot with a green vegetable or cold with a leafy salad.

The concentrated flavours of Gruyère and spring onions make a piquant contrast to the gentle taste of fresh ricotta in this warming pie.

Cheese and potato pie

ONE SERVING

CALORIES 350

TOTAL FAT 18g

SATURATED FAT 10g

CARBOHYDRATES 32g

ADDED SUGAR 0

FIBRE 3g

SODIUM 290mg

SERVES 4
PREPARATION TIME: 15 minutes
COOKING TIME: 30 minutes
OVEN: Preheat to 200°C (400°F, gas mark 6)

1½ lb (680g) potatoes, peeled
6oz (175g) ricotta cheese
1 egg, size 2
Freshly ground black pepper
1 teaspoon olive oil
4 spring onions, trimmed and chopped
2oz (60g) finely grated Gruyère cheese

1 Boil the potatoes in unsalted water until cooked but still firm. Drain and slice thinly.

2 Blend the ricotta with the egg and season with pepper.

3 Brush an ovenproof dish with the oil. Layer a third of the sliced potatoes over the bottom of the dish, spread on half the ricotta mixture and sprinkle a third of the spring onion and Gruyère on top. Repeat the layers, then cover with the rest of the potato and sprinkle the remaining spring onions and Gruyère on top. Cook in the heated oven for about 30 minutes, until golden brown on top.

Serve the pie with a mixed salad or brussels sprouts with garlic crumbs (see p.276).

Cheese and vegetable pudding

ONE SERVING

CALORIES 365

TOTAL FAT 15g

SATURATED FAT 5g

CARBOHYDRATES 40g

ADDED SUGAR 0

FIBRE 5g

SODIUM 630mg

SERVES 4
PREPARATION TIME: 15 minutes, plus 1 hour
to stand
COOKING TIME: 40 minutes
OVEN: Preheat to 160°C (325°F, gas mark 3)

1 tablespoon olive oil
1 small onion, peeled and chopped
1 small stick celery, trimmed and chopped
½ small green or red pepper, de-seeded and
finely chopped

2 tomatoes, skinned, de-seeded and chopped
3oz (85g) frozen sweetcorn kernels, rinsed
8 slices wholemeal bread, about ¼ in (6mm) thick,
cut into quarters
1oz (30g) grated Gruyère cheese
2 eggs, plus 1 egg white, size 2
12fl oz (340ml) skimmed milk
¾ level teaspoon mustard powder
¾ level teaspoon paprika
⅛ level teaspoon cayenne pepper
1oz (30g) grated Parmesan cheese

Layers of wholemeal bread triangles and a brilliantly coloured medley of crunchy chopped vegetables give body to this savoury cheese custard.

1 Heat the oil in a frying pan and cook the onion, celery and green or red pepper in it over a moderate heat for 5 minutes until they are beginning to soften. Take off the heat and stir in the tomatoes and sweetcorn.

2 Lightly grease a shallow ovenproof dish and arrange the bread in it in overlapping layers. Spoon the vegetable mixture evenly over the bread and sprinkle the Gruyère on top.

3 Whisk the eggs and egg white with the milk, mustard, paprika and cayenne. Slowly pour into the dish without moving the bread. Put in the refrigerator for 1 hour for the bread to soak.

4 Sprinkle the Parmesan on the top and cook in the heated oven for 40 minutes, or until set.

A salad of lamb's lettuce, beetroot and celery makes a contrast with the dish.

Chilli with rice

SERVES 4
PREPARATION TIME: 10 minutes
COOKING TIME: 1 hour 10 minutes

1½ tablespoons olive oil
1 large onion, peeled and chopped
1 large carrot, peeled and chopped
3 cloves garlic, peeled and finely chopped
1 green pepper, de-seeded and chopped
1 red pepper, de-seeded and chopped
4oz (115g) green lentils, cleaned of grit, washed and drained
½ level teaspoon chilli powder
1 level teaspoon ground cumin
1 bay leaf
⅛ level teaspoon cayenne pepper
14oz (400g) tinned chopped tomatoes
¾ pint (425ml) vegetable stock (see p.19)
6oz (175g) long-grain rice
8oz (225g) cooked red kidney beans (see p.17)
8oz (225g) cooked chickpeas (see p.17)
Coriander or parsley sprigs to garnish

ONE SERVING	
CALORIES	565
TOTAL FAT	11g
SATURATED FAT	1g
CARBOHYDRATES	94g
ADDED SUGAR	0
FIBRE	16g
SODIUM	60mg

1 Heat the oil in a heavy-based saucepan and cook the onion, carrot, garlic and green and red peppers in it over a moderate heat for 10 minutes, until the vegetables are softened.

2 Add the lentils, chilli powder, cumin, bay leaf, cayenne pepper, tomatoes and stock. Cover and simmer for 50 minutes.

3 Meanwhile, cook the rice (see p.17).

4 Stir the kidney beans and chickpeas into the lentil mixture, cover and simmer for a further 10 minutes, until the lentils are tender but not mushy. Remove the bay leaf.

5 Spoon the rice into individual serving bowls with a helping of the chilli on top. Garnish with the coriander or parsley.

A salad of cucumber with yoghurt and mint makes a cooling side dish for the spicy chilli.

This substantial dish combines sweet peppers and tomatoes with fiery chilli and cayenne pepper to make a sauce for fibre-rich lentils, beans and chickpeas.

Cottage cheese and basil quiche

ONE SERVING	
CALORIES	325
TOTAL FAT	18g
SATURATED FAT	5g
CARBOHYDRATES	25g
ADDED SUGAR	0
FIBRE	3g
SODIUM	380mg

TIP
If the top of the quiche is browning too quickly, lay a piece of greaseproof paper loosely on top. Do not lower the temperature or the pastry under the quiche will not be cooked crisp.

SERVES 4
PREPARATION TIME: *25 minutes*
COOKING TIME: *25 minutes*
OVEN: *Preheat to 200°C (400°F, gas mark 6)*

1 medium courgette, trimmed and thinly sliced
3 tablespoons water
2oz (60g) plain white flour
2oz (60g) wholemeal flour
2oz (60g) polyunsaturated margarine
2 eggs, size 2, separated
8oz (225g) cottage cheese, well drained
3 level tablespoons chopped fresh basil
4 spring onions, trimmed and chopped
2oz (60g) frozen sweetcorn kernels, rinsed
Freshly ground black pepper
Basil leaves to garnish

1 Simmer the courgette with 2 tablespoons of the water in a small, covered saucepan for 5 minutes until softening. Drain and set aside.

2 Mix the flours in a bowl and rub in the margarine with your fingertips until the mixture resembles fine breadcrumbs. Use a round-ended knife to work in 1 egg yolk and just enough of the remaining water to form a dough.

3 Knead the dough on a lightly floured surface, then roll it out to fit a fluted flan tin 8½ in (21.5cm) in diameter. Line the tin with the pastry, smoothing it out from the centre and pressing it well into the flutes to make sure no air is trapped underneath. Trim the excess pastry from the edge.

4 Mix the cottage cheese, basil, courgette, onions, sweetcorn and the remaining egg yolk, and season with pepper. Whisk the egg whites until they hold soft peaks, then carefully fold them into the cheese mixture.

5 Place the pastry-lined flan tin on a baking sheet and pour in the filling. Cook in the heated oven for about 25 minutes, or until the pastry is golden brown and the filling set. Garnish with basil before serving hot or cold.

A crisp green salad goes well with the delicately flavoured quiche.

Cottage cheese gives a beautifully light texture to this quiche, while pungent fresh basil creates an irresistible aroma. You can prepare the pastry case one day in advance and put it, uncooked, in a polythene bag in the refrigerator until needed.

Courgette and carrot quiche

SERVES 4
PREPARATION TIME: 45 minutes
COOKING TIME: 20 minutes, plus 15 minutes to rest
OVEN: Preheat to 180° (350°F, gas mark 4)

1 medium onion, peeled and finely chopped
1 medium carrot, peeled and grated
1 medium courgette, trimmed and grated
½ level teaspoon dried marjoram
7fl oz (200ml) vegetable stock (see p.19)
6oz (175g) arborio or long-grain rice
3oz (85g) grated Gruyère cheese
3 egg whites, plus 1 whole egg, size 2
2 level teaspoons cornflour
¼ pint (150ml) skimmed milk
Freshly ground black pepper
Marjoram sprigs to garnish

1 Simmer the onion, carrot, courgette and marjoram in the stock, uncovered, for 15 minutes. Raise the heat and boil briskly for about 10 minutes, stirring frequently, until the liquid has evaporated and the vegetables are almost glazed.

2 Meanwhile, cook the rice (see p.17), and line a straight-sided, spring-clip tin 8½ in (21.5cm) in diameter with nonstick baking paper.

3 Mix the rice thoroughly with 2 tablespoons of the Gruyère and 1 egg white. Spread the mixture over the base and up the sides of the flan tin, pressing it well with the back of a spoon. Bake in the heated oven for 5 minutes, then lift out and leave to cool slightly, still in the tin.

4 Mix the cornflour to a smooth, thin cream with a little of the milk, then stir in the remaining milk and whisk in the whole egg and remaining egg whites. Add the remaining Gruyère, season with pepper and cook over a very low heat, stirring continuously, until the custard thickens.

5 Spread the vegetables in the flan case, pour on the custard and cook in the heated oven for 20 minutes, until the filling is set. Leave to rest for 15 minutes before removing very carefully from the tin and garnishing with marjoram.

Sliced tomatoes and cucumber sprinkled with lemon juice and mixed fresh herbs add sharpness and colour to the quiche.

The extra care needed to make the case and filling are amply rewarded by this quiche with its delicately flavoured filling set in a crisp, light crust of rice.

Curried vegetables with cucumber sauce

ONE SERVING

CALORIES 325

TOTAL FAT 6g

SATURATED FAT 1g

CARBOHYDRATES 59g

ADDED SUGAR 0

FIBRE 7g

SODIUM 85mg

SERVES 4
PREPARATION TIME: 15 minutes
COOKING TIME: 40 minutes

4oz (115g) cauliflower florets
1 tablespoon olive oil
1 onion, peeled and chopped
2 cloves garlic, peeled and crushed

1 level tablespoon medium or hot curry powder
½ level teaspoon ground cinnamon
1 pint (570ml) vegetable stock (see p.19)
4oz (115g) long-grain rice
2 medium tomatoes, skinned and chopped
2 carrots, peeled and chopped
8oz (225g) cooked black-eyed or butter beans
(see p.17)
2oz (60g) raisins
4oz (115g) frozen peas
2 teaspoons lemon juice
2 level tablespoons chopped fresh coriander leaves

For the sauce:
8oz (225g) low-fat natural yoghurt
2oz (60g) grated cucumber
Freshly ground black pepper
¼ level teaspoon paprika
Fresh mint to garnish

1 Blanch the cauliflower in boiling water for
2 minutes, then drain and set aside.

2 Heat the oil in a large, heavy-based saucepan
and cook the onion in it for 5 minutes over a
moderate heat, until golden. Stir in the garlic,
curry powder and cinnamon and cook for
30 seconds, stirring.

3 Add the stock, rice, tomatoes and carrots to
the pan and bring to the boil. Cover and
simmer for 20 minutes. Stir in the beans,
raisins, peas and cauliflower, cover and cook
for 8 minutes more.

4 Meanwhile, mix the yoghurt and cucumber
and season with pepper to make the sauce.
Turn it into a small serving bowl, dust with the
paprika and garnish with mint.

5 Stir the lemon juice and coriander into the
curry and spoon it into a heated serving dish.

Individual side dishes of skinned tomato
wedges and grated celeriac sprinkled with
lemon juice make cooling accompaniments
to offer with the curry.

*Yoghurt is often served plain as a foil to searing
curries in the Middle East and Asia. It is especially
refreshing when, as in this dish, it is combined
with cucumber to make an Indian-style 'raita'.*

A speciality of Middle Eastern cookery, spicy chickpea patties served with crisp salad in pockets of pitta bread are filling and easy to make.

Falafel in pitta bread

ONE SERVING

CALORIES 460

TOTAL FAT 12g

SATURATED FAT 1g

CARBOHYDRATES 75g

ADDED SUGAR 0

FIBRE 9g

SODIUM 540mg

TIP
Wash and dry the lettuce 30 minutes before it is needed and refrigerate it in an airtight plastic box to make it especially crisp.

SERVES 4
PREPARATION TIME: 25 minutes
COOKING TIME: 10 minutes

10oz (275g) cooked chickpeas (see p.17)
1 level teaspoon ground cumin
1 level teaspoon ground coriander
2 cloves garlic, peeled and chopped
¼ level teaspoon cayenne pepper
2 teaspoons groundnut oil
3 tablespoons lemon juice
⅛ level teaspoon salt
6oz (175g) low-fat natural yoghurt
1 tablespoon olive oil
8-10 leaves of cos-type lettuce, washed and torn into pieces
8oz (225g) ripe tomatoes, skinned, de-seeded and diced
4 wholemeal oval pitta breads
1 level tablespoon sesame seeds, lightly toasted

1 Using a food processor or food mill, blend the chickpeas, cumin, coriander, garlic, cayenne pepper, groundnut oil, 2 tablespoons of the lemon juice and the salt to a smooth purée. If the mixture is too dry to hold together, mix in 2-3 teaspoons cold water.

2 Divide the mixture into eight and shape the pieces into flat, round patties, or falafel. Lightly grease a nonstick frying pan with groundnut oil and cook the falafel in it over a moderate heat for 4 minutes on each side, until golden brown and crisp.

3 Meanwhile, whisk together the yoghurt and olive oil with the remaining lemon juice. Set aside 4 tablespoons of this dressing. Pour the rest over the lettuce and tomatoes, and toss to coat well.

4 Slit each pitta bread open along one side only, and fill with 2 falafel and a quarter of the salad mixture. Trickle 1 tablespoon of the reserved dressing into each pitta, sprinkle with the sesame seeds and serve at once.

Diced pickled beetroot, perhaps mixed with cucumber, makes a sharp and refreshing side dish for the falafel.

Fennel and potato hotpot

ONE SERVING	
CALORIES	235
TOTAL FAT	8g
SATURATED FAT	3g
CARBOHYDRATES	22g
ADDED SUGAR	0
FIBRE	4g
SODIUM	195mg

SERVES 4
PREPARATION TIME: 20 minutes
COOKING TIME: 40 minutes
OVEN: Preheat to 200°C (400°F, gas mark 6)

*1lb (450g) fennel bulbs, trimmed and
thickly sliced*
2 cloves garlic, peeled and finely chopped
2 level tablespoons chopped fresh parsley

1 level teaspoon crushed fennel seeds
1lb (450g) potatoes, peeled and thinly sliced
1 tablespoon olive oil
3oz (85g) grated reduced-fat Cheddar cheese
Freshly ground black pepper
7fl oz (200ml) dry white wine
2 level tablespoons grated Parmesan cheese
Fennel fronds to garnish

1 Cook the fennel in boiling, unsalted water
for 10 minutes, then drain thoroughly and mix
in the garlic, parsley, fennel seeds and potatoes.

2 Grease an ovenproof dish with half the olive
oil and spread half the vegetables in the dish.
Sprinkle on the Cheddar and spread the rest of
the vegetables over the top. Season with
pepper, pour in the wine and remaining olive
oil and scatter the Parmesan over the top.

3 Bake in the heated oven for 40 minutes,
or until the top is crisp and golden brown and
the vegetables are tender. Garnish with the
fennel fronds just before serving.

A tomato and cucumber salad dressed with
lemon juice makes a sharp contrast to the mild
aniseed flavour of the fennel.

*Fennel bulbs are often eaten crisp and raw in salads,
but they are particularly satisfying when cooked until
tender and lending their flavour to other vegetables.*

Gougère ring filled with ratatouille

SERVES 4
PREPARATION TIME: 30 minutes
COOKING TIME: 40 minutes
OVEN: Preheat to 220°C (425°F gas mark 7)

ONE SERVING	
CALORIES	360
TOTAL FAT	26g
SATURATED FAT	8g
CARBOHYDRATES	21g
ADDED SUGAR	0
FIBRE	4g
SODIUM	290mg

For the gougère:
¼ pint (150ml) water
2oz (60g) polyunsaturated margarine
*2½ oz (70g) mixed plain white and wholemeal
flour, or all wholemeal flour*
2 eggs, size 3, beaten
2oz (60g) finely grated Gruyère cheese

For the ratatouille:
1 tablespoon olive oil
1 medium onion, peeled and sliced
1 medium aubergine, trimmed and chopped
2 courgettes, trimmed and sliced
½ green pepper, de-seeded and chopped
½ red pepper, de-seeded and chopped
1lb (450g) firm red tomatoes, chopped
1 tablespoon tomato purée (see p.16)
1 level teaspoon dried basil
Freshly ground black pepper
Basil or oregano sprigs to garnish

1 Put the water and margarine into a saucepan and bring to the boil slowly, so that the margarine melts before the water boils. Take the pan off the heat and quickly tip in all the flour. Beat well with a wooden spoon until the paste forms a ball that rolls cleanly round the pan. Leave for 5 minutes.

2 Gradually beat the eggs into the cooled paste, using a hand-held electric mixer or a wooden spoon, then beat in three-quarters of the Gruyère. Place spoonfuls of the mixture touching one another in a ring inside the rim of an ovenproof dish 9in (23cm) in diameter. Sprinkle with the remaining Gruyère. Bake in the heated oven for 20 minutes, then reduce the heat to 190°C (375°F, gas mark 5) and cook for a further 10 minutes.

3 Meanwhile, prepare the ratatouille. Heat the oil in a large saucepan and cook the onion in it over a moderate heat for 5 minutes. Mix in the aubergine, courgettes, green and red peppers, tomatoes, tomato purée and dried basil, and season with pepper. Cover and cook, stirring occasionally, for 20 minutes or until tender.

4 Fill the centre of the ring with ratatouille and garnish with basil or oregano sprigs.

A simple leafy salad is all that is needed with the puffy ring and moist filling.

Airy choux pastry flavoured with cheese is used for gougères. Here this French delicacy from Burgundy is made into a ring to hold a colourful ratatouille.

Potato and parsnip mashed with garlic and cheese give a deliciously savoury topping to these simple, satisfying lentil and vegetable pies.

Lentil cottage pie

ONE SERVING	
CALORIES 475	
TOTAL FAT 9g	
SATURATED FAT 3g	
CARBOHYDRATES 77g	
ADDED SUGAR 0	
FIBRE 10g	
SODIUM 200mg	

TIP
Always pick over lentils carefully before cooking them, to remove any discoloured ones and any grit. It is easiest to check the lentils if you spread them on a large white plate.

SERVES 4
PREPARATION TIME: 45 minutes
COOKING TIME: 30 minutes
OVEN: Preheat to 200°C (400°F, gas mark 6)

8oz (225g) split red lentils, cleaned and well rinsed
1 pint (570ml) vegetable stock (see p.19)
1 tablespoon olive oil
1 medium onion, peeled and finely chopped
2 carrots, peeled and diced
7oz (200g) tinned tomatoes
2oz (60g) frozen petits pois
1½ lb (680g) potatoes, peeled and diced
8oz (225g) parsnips, peeled and diced
1 clove garlic, peeled and finely chopped
¼ pint (150ml) semi-skimmed milk
2oz (60g) grated low-fat Cheddar cheese
Freshly ground black pepper
1 level teaspoon sesame seeds
Parsley sprigs to garnish

1 Put the lentils into a saucepan with the stock, bring to the boil and skim off any scum that rises. Cover and simmer for 25 minutes, stirring occasionally until the lentils are tender, all the liquid has been absorbed and the mixture has thickened to a rough purée.

2 Meanwhile, heat the olive oil in a heavy-based saucepan and cook the onion in it over a moderate heat for about 5 minutes, until golden. Mix in the carrots and cook for 5 minutes. Stir in the tomatoes, cover and simmer for 25 minutes. Remove the pan from the heat and mix in the peas.

3 While the tomato mixture is cooking, steam the potatoes, parsnips and garlic for about 15 minutes, or until tender. Mash until smooth, stir in the milk and Cheddar, and season with pepper.

4 Stir the lentil purée into the tomato mixture, then spoon into four individual ovenproof dishes. Top with the mashed-potato mixture, fluffing it up with a fork. Sprinkle a share of the sesame seeds over each dish. Cook for 30 minutes in the heated oven, until the tops are golden. Garnish with the parsley just before serving.

Cabbage steamed with fennel seeds makes a crunchy contrast to the pies. You can make one large pie instead of individual ones. A large pie will need 10-15 minutes longer in the oven.

Lentil dhal and spiced cabbage

SERVES 4
PREPARATION TIME: 15 minutes
COOKING TIME: 25 minutes

10oz (275g) split red lentils, cleaned of grit,
rinsed and drained
2 shallots, peeled
1 bay leaf
1¼ pints (725ml) water
1 tablespoon olive oil
2 level teaspoons peeled and chopped root ginger
2 small onions, peeled and chopped
1 level teaspoon medium curry powder
1 large cooking apple, peeled, cored and chopped
2 tablespoons corn oil
1 clove garlic, peeled and crushed
1 level teaspoon cumin seeds
½ level teaspoon coriander seeds
1½ lb (680g) cabbage, trimmed and shredded
1 tablespoon lemon juice
Freshly ground black pepper
Coriander sprigs to garnish

1 Put the lentils, shallots, bay leaf and water into a saucepan and bring to the boil. Skim off any scum that rises, then reduce the heat and simmer, uncovered, for about 25 minutes, or until the lentils are tender and the water has been absorbed. Add a little more boiling water during cooking if the lentils become dry.

2 Meanwhile, heat the olive oil in a small saucepan and cook the ginger and half the chopped onions in it over a moderate heat for about 5 minutes, until tender. Stir in the curry powder and apple. Cover and cook gently for 5 minutes, stirring occasionally, until the apple is tender. Take off the heat and set aside.

3 Heat the corn oil in a saucepan and cook the remaining onion and the garlic in it over a moderate heat for 2-3 minutes. Sprinkle in the cumin and coriander seeds and cook for 30 seconds. Mix in the cabbage and stir-fry for 2-3 minutes, until wilted. Cover and cook slowly for 5 minutes, until just softened.

In India and Southeast Asia dhal, a spiced purée of
lentils or beans may be an accompaniment
or, as here, the focus of a meal. Serve it with rice to
improve the quality of protein in the lentils.

4 When the lentils are cooked, remove the shallot and bay leaf. Beat the lentils with a wooden spoon to form a purée. Mix in the onion and apple mixture and the lemon juice, and season with pepper. Turn the cabbage onto a warm serving plate, make a well in the centre, spoon in the dhal and garnish with coriander.

Boiled basmati rice flavoured with cloves is the best accompaniment to this spicy Indian dish.

ONE SERVING	
CALORIES	405
TOTAL FAT	13g
SATURATED FAT	2g
CARBOHYDRATES	54g
ADDED SUGAR	0
FIBRE	9g
SODIUM	40mg

Lentil, split pea and nut rissoles

ONE SERVING	
CALORIES	285
TOTAL FAT	14g
SATURATED FAT	2g
CARBOHYDRATES	30g
ADDED SUGAR	0
FIBRE	4g
SODIUM	35mg

SERVES 4
PREPARATION TIME: 20 minutes, plus 8 hours
to soak
COOKING TIME: 25 minutes

2oz (60g) split red lentils, cleaned, soaked in
cold water for 8 hours and drained
4oz (115g) yellow split peas, soaked in cold
water for 8 hours and drained

2oz (60g) skinned hazelnuts, toasted
¼ level teaspoon ground coriander
2 level tablespoons chopped fresh coriander
Finely grated rind of 1 small lemon
1 clove garlic, peeled and crushed
¼ level teaspoon bicarbonate of soda
2 level tablespoons plain wholemeal flour
2 tablespoons groundnut oil
Lemon wedges and coriander sprigs to garnish

Coriander, garlic and toasted hazelnuts give a tempting aroma to this version of a vegetarian favourite. Crisp and brown outside, chewy within, these rissoles make a satisfying dish.

1 Grind the lentils and peas in a food processor for about 25 seconds, until finely ground. Add the hazelnuts and blend again for about 10 seconds.

2 Turn the mixture into a bowl and work in the ground and chopped coriander, lemon rind, garlic, bicarbonate of soda and flour.

3 Divide the mixture into 12 equal portions. Roll each portion between wetted palms into a ball, then flatten slightly.

4 Heat the oil in a large, nonstick frying pan and fry the rissoles in it over a moderate heat for 5 minutes, turning two or three times, until well browned. Drain on kitchen paper. If the frying pan will not hold the rissoles easily, cook them in two batches and keep the first batch hot while you fry the second.

Serve the rissoles garnished with the lemon wedges and coriander leaves. A salad of chicory, watercress and rocket leaves will add a peppery touch to the mild flavours of the rissoles.

Lentil and potato stew

SERVES 6
PREPARATION TIME: 30 minutes
COOKING TIME: 1 hour

1½ pints (850ml) vegetable stock (see p.19)
8oz (225g) red lentils, cleaned of grit and rinsed
1 medium onion, peeled and chopped
2 cloves garlic, peeled and finely chopped
2 sticks celery, trimmed and sliced
4 carrots, peeled and cut into fingers
1¾ lb (800g) tinned chopped tomatoes
1 level teaspoon chopped fresh rosemary,
or ½ level teaspoon dried rosemary
1 tablespoon olive oil
16 button onions, peeled
1lb (450g) potatoes, peeled and cut into cubes
Freshly ground black pepper
4oz (115g) button mushrooms, wiped and halved
1 level tablespoon chopped fresh parsley

1 Put the stock, lentils, chopped onion, garlic, celery, carrots, tomatoes and rosemary into a large saucepan, bring to the boil and skim off any scum. Cover and simmer for 35 minutes.

2 Meanwhile, heat the oil in a frying pan and brown the button onions in it over a moderate heat for 5 minutes, shaking the pan frequently.

3 Mix the button onions and the potatoes into the lentils and vegetables, cover and simmer for a further 15-20 minutes, until the lentils and potatoes are tender. Season with pepper and stir in the mushrooms for the last 5 minutes of cooking. Sprinkle with the parsley and serve.

Serve wholemeal rolls and a crisp salad of grated celeriac (see p.314) or of lettuce and cucumber with this savoury stew.

ONE SERVING
CALORIES 250
TOTAL FAT 4g
SATURATED FAT 1g
CARBOHYDRATES 44g
ADDED SUGAR 0
FIBRE 5g
SODIUM 90mg

TIP
To peel the button onions, blanch them in a pan of boiling water for 3 minutes, then cool slightly. Gently remove the skins, leaving the root end intact so that the onions remain whole.

Whole button onions add a hint of sweetness to this warming winter stew, thickened and coloured by the lentils which absorb its hearty flavour as they swell.

Noodle and tofu stir-fry

SERVES 4
PREPARATION TIME: 15 minutes, plus 20 minutes
to marinate
COOKING TIME: 20 minutes

1 tablespoon each soy sauce, dry sherry
and sesame oil
8oz (225g) firm tofu, cut into cubes
4oz (115g) Chinese egg noodles
1 tablespoon olive oil
2 cloves garlic, peeled and chopped
1 level teaspoon peeled and grated root ginger
8 medium spring onions, trimmed and cut
into short lengths
2 carrots, peeled and thinly sliced
2 sticks celery, trimmed and thinly sliced
8oz (225g) broccoli, trimmed and divided
into florets
4oz (115g) mushrooms, wiped and sliced
8fl oz (225ml) vegetable stock (see p.19)
1 level tablespoon cornflour

ONE SERVING	
CALORIES	280
TOTAL FAT	13g
SATURATED FAT	1g
CARBOHYDRATES	29g
ADDED SUGAR	0
FIBRE	4g
SODIUM	355mg

1 Mix the soy sauce, sherry and sesame oil in a shallow dish. Put in the tofu and turn it gently to coat the cubes, then cover and leave to marinate for 20 minutes.

2 Cook the noodles in unsalted water (see p.18), drain and set aside.

3 Heat the olive oil in a wok or a large, heavy-based saucepan and stir-fry the garlic, ginger, onions, carrots and celery in it over a high heat for 2 minutes. Stir in the broccoli, mushrooms and half the stock, then lower the heat, cover and simmer for 3 minutes.

4 Drain the marinade off the tofu into a small bowl and blend in the cornflour. Stir in the remaining stock, pour onto the vegetables and cook, stirring constantly, until thickened.

5 Mix in the noodles and tofu, cover and simmer for 3-4 minutes, until heated through.

Serve a sweet-and-sour salad of marinated carrots (see p.312) with this Chinese-style dish.

Tofu, a mild, cheese-like curd made from soya beans, soaks up the flavours of the Orient in this medley of crisp vegetables, soft noodles and sharp sauce.

Sunflower seeds give a crunchy topping to this moist and chewy roast of mixed nuts and vegetables, which is bound with eggs and easy to make.

Nut roast

ONE SERVING

CALORIES 270

TOTAL FAT 16g

SATURATED FAT 2g

CARBOHYDRATES 21g

ADDED SUGAR 0

FIBRE 4g

SODIUM 230mg

SERVES 4
PREPARATION TIME: 20 minutes
COOKING TIME: 1 hour 15 minutes
OVEN: Preheat to 180°C (350°F, gas mark 4)

2 medium onions, peeled and finely chopped
1 small green pepper, de-seeded and finely chopped
3 sticks celery, trimmed and finely chopped
1 carrot, peeled and grated
3oz (85g) unsalted mixed nuts (cashews, hazelnuts, peanuts, almonds), finely chopped
4oz (115g) wholemeal breadcrumbs
1 level teaspoon dried mixed herbs
Freshly ground black pepper
2 eggs, size 2, lightly beaten
1 tablespoon tomato purée (see p.16)
1 level tablespoon sunflower seeds

1 Mix the onions, green pepper, celery, carrot, nuts, breadcrumbs and mixed herbs in a bowl.

Season with black pepper, then work in the eggs and tomato purée to bind the mixture.

2 Spoon the mixture into a lightly oiled nonstick loaf tin about 8×4in (20×10cm) and press it down firmly with the back of the spoon. Sprinkle the sunflower seeds evenly over the mixture.

3 Cook the roast in the heated oven for about 1 hour 15 minutes, or until the top is crisp and a skewer inserted into the centre comes out clean. Ease the sides of the roast gently away from the tin with a round-ended knife. Turn the loaf out carefully onto a board, and then turn again onto a warmed serving plate with the sunflower seeds uppermost.

Serve thick slices of the roast with tomato sauce (see p.16), a green salad and baked garlic potatoes.

Vegetable paella with eggs

ONE SERVING	
CALORIES 370	
TOTAL FAT 11g	
SATURATED FAT 2g	
CARBOHYDRATES 57g	
ADDED SUGAR 0	
FIBRE 6g	
SODIUM 120mg	

Eggs replace the traditional seafood and chicken in this version of the Spanish paella. The result is a colourful dish built round the creamy-textured rice.

SERVES 4
PREPARATION TIME: 20 minutes
COOKING TIME: 35 minutes

1 tablespoon olive oil
1 medium onion, peeled and chopped
1 clove garlic, peeled and finely chopped
1 level teaspoon paprika
¼ level teaspoon cayenne pepper
1 small red pepper, de-seeded and cut into strips
1 medium yellow pepper, de-seeded and cut into strips
4 medium tomatoes, skinned and chopped
2 small potatoes, peeled and diced
2 medium carrots, peeled and cut into strips
7oz (200g) Valencia or long-grain rice
⅛ level teaspoon salt
1 pint (570ml) vegetable stock (see p.19)
2 medium courgettes, quartered and thickly sliced
8oz (225g) frozen peas

3 eggs, size 2, hard-boiled, shelled and quartered
1 level tablespoon chopped fresh parsley

1 Heat the oil in a large, heavy-based saucepan and gently fry the onion and garlic in it for 5 minutes. Add the paprika, cayenne, peppers and tomatoes, and cook for 2 minutes, stirring.

2 Mix in the potatoes, carrots, rice and salt, pour in the stock and bring to the boil. Cover and simmer for 15 minutes, until most of the liquid is absorbed.

3 Stir in the courgettes and peas, and simmer for a further 10 minutes, then turn out onto a heated serving dish. Arrange the eggs round the paella and sprinkle the parsley over the top.

Serve a mixed leafy salad to add crispness and fresh colour to the tender paella.

TIP
Use Valencia rice, when you can get it, for the authentic texture of paella. The rice is short-grained and readily absorbs the cooking liquid to become plump and moist, but not sticky.

Pancakes with Mexican stuffing

ONE SERVING	
CALORIES 545	
TOTAL FAT 15g	
SATURATED FAT 5g	
CARBOHYDRATES 75g	
ADDED SUGAR 0	
FIBRE 10g	
SODIUM 320mg	

SERVES 4
PREPARATION TIME: 1 hour 30 minutes
COOKING TIME: 30 minutes
OVEN: Preheat to 190°C (375°F, gas mark 5)

8oz (225g) plain flour
2 eggs, size 2, lightly beaten

¾ pint (425ml) skimmed milk
1 medium onion, peeled and finely chopped
1 clove garlic, peeled and crushed
1lb (450g) tomatoes, skinned and chopped
1 level teaspoon cumin seeds
2 teaspoons tomato purée (see p.16)
12oz (340g) cooked red kidney beans (see p.17)

4oz (115g) cooked black-eyed beans (see p.17)
4 teaspoons corn oil
Greaseproof paper squares for layering pancakes
4oz (115g) grated reduced-fat Cheddar cheese
Flat-leaf parsley sprigs to garnish

1 Sift the flour into a bowl, make a well in the centre and pour in the eggs. Whisk the eggs into the flour, adding milk little by little to form a thick, smooth batter. Stir in the rest of the milk, pour the batter into a large measuring jug, cover and leave to stand for 30 minutes.

2 Simmer the onion, garlic, tomatoes, cumin seeds and tomato purée in an uncovered saucepan for about 15 minutes, until the onion is tender and the mixture slightly thickened.

3 Mash all the beans roughly in a large bowl, then stir in the tomato mixture.

4 Heat ½ teaspoon of the oil over a moderate heat in a nonstick frying pan 8in (20cm) in diameter. Pour in an eighth of the batter and run it round the pan to coat the base. Cook for 2-3 minutes and when it is opaque on the surface and lightly browned underneath, flip it over with a fish slice. Cook the other side for 2 minutes until golden. Tip the pancake onto a lightly oiled plate, with the side cooked first underneath. Put a piece of greaseproof paper on top. Make 7 more pancakes in the same way.

5 Spoon a share of the filling onto the top pancake in the pile, roll it up and put it seam down in a greased shallow ovenproof dish. Fill the other pancakes and put them in the dish.

6 Sprinkle the Cheddar over the pancakes. Cover the dish and cook in the heated oven for 10 minutes, then uncover and cook for another 20 minutes, until browned on top.

Serve the pancakes garnished with parsley sprigs and accompanied by a light, leafy salad. You can make the pancakes a day in advance and instead of filling them, wait until they are cold, wrap them in a polythene bag and store them in the refrigerator.

A tomato and bean filling, well flavoured with garlic, onion and cumin seeds, gives these cheese-topped pancakes their spicy Mexican character.

Pancakes oriental style

SERVES 4
PREPARATION TIME: 1 hour
COOKING TIME: 1 hour 5 minutes

ONE SERVING	
CALORIES 485	
TOTAL FAT 21g	
SATURATED FAT 3g	
CARBOHYDRATES 58g	
ADDED SUGAR 0	
FIBRE 3g	
SODIUM 385mg	

TIP
To make a spring onion curl, trim off the base and all but 2in (50mm) of the green leaves. Make several cuts down the leaves and just into the white part. Put into ice-cold water, refrigerate for 30 minutes and the leaves will curl back.

2 level tablespoons chopped fresh coriander leaves
8oz (225g) plain flour
1 egg, size 2, beaten
1 pint (570ml) skimmed milk
1 tablespoon soy sauce
1 teaspoon sesame oil
1 level tablespoon peeled and grated root ginger
1 clove garlic, peeled and crushed
8oz (225g) firm tofu, cut into small cubes
½ oz (15g) dried shiitake mushrooms
2 tablespoons corn oil
Greaseproof paper squares for layering pancakes
1 red pepper, de-seeded and finely diced
4 spring onions, trimmed and finely sliced
2oz (60g) sugar snap peas or mangetout, trimmed and halved
1oz (30g) blanched almonds, cut into thin slivers
1 large spring onion, trimmed, quartered lengthways and separated into strands
Spring onion curls to garnish

1 Put the coriander and flour into a large bowl, make a well in the centre and pour the egg into it. Whisk vigorously, adding milk a little at a time to form a thick, smooth batter. Stir in the rest of the milk, pour the batter into a large measuring jug, cover and leave to stand for 30 minutes.

2 Meanwhile, mix the soy sauce, sesame oil, ginger and garlic in a shallow dish. Put the tofu in the dish, spoon the mixture over the cubes to coat them, then cover and leave to marinate for 1 hour.

3 Rinse the mushrooms well, put them in a bowl and pour on ¼ pint (150ml) of water, just off the boil. Leave to stand for 30 minutes.

4 Heat a scant ½ teaspoon of the corn oil over a moderate heat in a nonstick frying pan 8in (20cm) in diameter. Pour in a twelfth of the batter, tilting the pan until the base is coated with a very thin layer. Cook for 2-3 minutes, or until the pancake is opaque on the surface and lightly browned underneath. Flip it over with a fish slice and cook the other side for 1-2 minutes until lightly browned. Tip the pancake out of the pan onto an oiled plate, with the side that was cooked first underneath. Put a piece of greaseproof paper on top. Make 11 more pancakes in the same way.

5 Drain the mushrooms and chop them finely. Drain the tofu, reserving the marinade. Heat the remaining drops of corn oil in a wok or large frying pan. Stir-fry the red pepper, sliced spring onions and mushrooms in it over a high heat for 2 minutes. Stir in the peas and almonds and cook for 2 minutes. Reduce the heat, spoon in the tofu carefully and heat through gently for 2-3 minutes. Pour in the reserved marinade and bring to the boil.

6 Spoon equal amounts of the filling onto each pancake. Carefully bring the edges together above the filling to form a small 'purse' and tie with a strand of spring onion.

7 Put the pancakes onto two lightly greased plates, cover with upturned heatproof dishes and steam over pans of simmering water for 5 minutes, to heat through. If you have a bamboo or tiered steamer, line it with nonstick baking paper and heat the pancakes in it.

Lift the pancakes carefully onto heated plates and garnish with spring onion curls. Serve with a salad of bean sprouts and lamb's lettuce, and side dishes of spring onion slivers. It is often more convenient to make the pancakes a day in advance. Stack with greaseproof paper between them, and instead of filling them, wait until they are cold, put them in a polythene bag and store in the refrigerator.

Pancake purses are plump with an assortment of crisp, colourful stir-fried vegetables and tofu flavoured with soy sauce, sesame oil and ginger. The purses, speckled with aromatic coriander, are steamed at the end of cooking, keeping them moist and the fillings warm and tender.

Layered pease pudding

ONE SERVING

CALORIES 360

TOTAL FAT 5g

SATURATED FAT 2g

CARBOHYDRATES 57g

ADDED SUGAR 0

FIBRE 6g

SODIUM 135mg

SERVES 4
PREPARATION TIME: 50 minutes
COOKING TIME: 1 hour, plus 10 minutes to stand

6oz (175g) yellow split peas, rinsed and drained
6oz (175g) green split peas, rinsed and drained
1 large onion, peeled and finely chopped
1 large stick celery, trimmed and finely chopped
1½ pints (850ml) vegetable stock (see p.19)

8oz (225g) low-fat natural yoghurt
Handful of coriander leaves, finely chopped
Small fresh red chilli, de-seeded and finely chopped
2 level tablespoons grated Parmesan cheese
1 level tablespoon Dijon mustard
1 egg, size 3, beaten
Freshly ground black pepper

1 Put the yellow and green peas into two separate large saucepans. Put half the onion, half the celery and half the stock into each pan and bring them to the boil, stirring frequently with a wooden spoon.

2 Lower the heat under both pans and simmer gently, uncovered and stirring occasionally, for about 35 minutes, or until the peas are very soft and all the liquid has been absorbed. If the liquid evaporates before the peas are tender, add a little boiling water.

3 Meanwhile, mix the yoghurt, coriander and chilli in a small bowl, cover and chill.

4 Remove the pans of peas from the heat and leave to cool for about 10 minutes. Use a fork to beat the Parmesan into the yellow peas and the mustard into the green peas, then beat half the egg into each and season with pepper.

5 Spoon one-third of the yellow purée into a lightly oiled 2 pint (1.15 litres) pudding basin, and cover it with a third of the green purée. Spread the remaining yellow purée on top and finish with the remaining green purée.

6 Cover tightly with greaseproof paper tied with string under the rim of the dish and steam for 1 hour. Remove from the heat and leave to stand for 10 minutes before uncovering. Run a round-ended knife round the pudding and turn it out carefully onto a warmed serving plate.

Serve the pudding at once, cut into wedges. Hand round the yoghurt sauce separately. Serve rolls and a crisp salad with the pudding.

Green split dried peas and the milder yellow variety make up the contrasting layers in this adaptation of a traditional warming winter dish.

Peppers with artichoke stuffing

SERVES 4
PREPARATION TIME: 35 minutes
COOKING TIME: 40 minutes
OVEN: 190°C (375°F, gas mark 5)

ONE SERVING	
CALORIES	235
TOTAL FAT	9g
SATURATED FAT	5g
CARBOHYDRATES	29g
ADDED SUGAR	0
FIBRE	4g
SODIUM	455mg

4 red or green peppers, each about 7oz (200g),
tops trimmed and sliced off, de-seeded
4oz (115g) macaroni
6oz (175g) tinned or bottled artichoke hearts,
rinsed, drained and roughly chopped
2 spring onions, trimmed and chopped
2 level tablespoons chopped fresh basil or dill
4oz (115g) fetta cheese, diced
¼ pint (150ml) vegetable stock (see p.19)
1 egg, size 2
2 tablespoons lemon juice
Freshly ground black pepper

1 Blanch the peppers and their tops in unsalted boiling water for 4 minutes. Drain and put them open end down on kitchen paper so that any remaining water is absorbed.

2 Meanwhile, cook the macaroni (see p.18) and drain it thoroughly. Mix it with the artichoke hearts, onions, basil or dill and half the fetta cheese to make the stuffing.

3 Heat the stock without boiling in a small saucepan. Whisk together the egg and lemon juice, then whisk in half the stock. Season with pepper and stir into the stuffing.

4 Stand the peppers in an ovenproof dish that holds them snugly, and spoon in the stuffing. Scatter on the remaining fetta and replace the tops on the peppers. Pour the remaining stock into the dish.

5 Cover with a lid or foil and cook in the heated oven for about 40 minutes, until tender, basting occasionally with the stock.

Serve the peppers garnished with basil or dill, with a crisp green salad and wholemeal bread.

TIP
Cut a very thin sliver from the base of the peppers to make them stand upright.

Stuffed smoky-flavoured peppers make perfect lidded pots to fill with a mouth-watering artichoke, onion and macaroni stuffing. The addition of Greek fetta cheese continues the Mediterranean theme.

Peppers with bean and mushroom filling

SERVES 4
PREPARATION TIME: 55 minutes
COOKING TIME: 25 minutes
OVEN: Preheat to 190°C (375°F, gas mark 5)

ONE SERVING	
CALORIES 345	
TOTAL FAT 16g	
SATURATED FAT 3g	
CARBOHYDRATES 41g	
ADDED SUGAR 0	
FIBRE 8g	
SODIUM 125mg	

TIP
When fresh broad beans are reaching the end of their season, their grey-green skin may be tough and slightly bitter. Pull the skin off the beans so that it does not spoil the filling.

2 medium onions, peeled and finely chopped
1 pint (570ml) vegetable stock (see p.19)
4oz (115g) mushrooms, wiped and chopped
1 clove garlic, peeled and finely chopped
4oz (115g) brown rice
1lb (450g) tomatoes, skinned and chopped
2 level tablespoons chopped fresh parsley
1 tablespoon olive oil
1 level teaspoon each ground cumin and ground coriander
1 red pepper, de-seeded and cut into strips
4 green peppers, each about 7oz (200g), halved lengthways and de-seeded
2oz (60g) shelled and chopped walnuts
2oz (60g) shelled fresh broad beans or frozen broad beans
Freshly ground black pepper
2oz (60g) grated mature Cheddar cheese

1   Put half the onion into a saucepan with 2 tablespoons of the stock, the mushrooms and garlic, and cook for 3-4 minutes over a moderate heat, stirring occasionally. Pour in the rice and cook for 2-3 minutes.

2   Stir about one-third of the tomatoes, all the parsley and ¾ pint (425ml) of the stock into the pan. Bring to the boil, cover and simmer for about 30 minutes, until the rice is tender and the liquid has been absorbed.

3   Meanwhile, heat the oil in a frying pan and fry the remaining onion in it for about 5 minutes, until golden. Sprinkle in the cumin and coriander, and cook for 1 minute.

4   Stir the remaining tomatoes and stock and the red pepper into the frying pan. Bring to the boil, then simmer for about 15 minutes, until the liquid is reduced and the mixture slightly thickened. Pass the mixture through a food mill or sieve, or cool it slightly and blend in a food processor to make a smooth sauce.

5   Blanch the green pepper halves in boiling water for 4 minutes and drain. Arrange the peppers, cut side up, in a single layer in a baking dish.

Broad beans, chewy brown rice and walnuts are moistened by mushrooms and packed into sweet peppers, which are served in a spiced tomato sauce.

6 Stir the walnuts and beans into the rice mixture, season it with pepper and pack it into the peppers. Cover and cook in the heated oven for about 15 minutes, then uncover, sprinkle with the Cheddar and cook for 10 minutes more, until the peppers are tender but not collapsing, and the cheese has melted.

7 Reheat the sauce and pour it round the peppers before taking them to the table.

Serve wholemeal rolls (see p.366) with the peppers for mopping up all the juices. You can replace half or all the green peppers with yellow ones for a more colourful dish.

Pizza with three-pepper topping

SERVES 4
PREPARATION TIME: 30 minutes,
plus 45 minutes to rise
COOKING TIME: 25 minutes
OVEN: Preheat to 220°C (425°F, gas mark 7)

ONE SERVING	
CALORIES	440
TOTAL FAT	20g
SATURATED FAT	5g
CARBOHYDRATES	51g
ADDED SUGAR	0
FIBRE	6g
SODIUM	375mg

TIP
You can save time by using quick-acting yeast to make the pizza base. Or you can plan ahead and prepare a larger batch of dough, making enough for three pizza bases and freezing two after they are rolled out.

¼ pint (150ml) lukewarm water
½ level teaspoon caster sugar
1 level teaspoon dried yeast
4oz (115g) plain flour
4oz (115g) wholemeal flour
3½ tablespoons olive oil
3 small peppers, green, red and yellow, de-seeded and sliced into rings
1 medium onion, peeled and chopped
14oz (400g) tinned tomatoes, drained and chopped
2 cloves garlic, peeled and crushed
2 level teaspoons dried oregano
1 level tablespoon chopped fresh basil
Freshly ground black pepper
4oz (115g) mozzarella or low-fat Cheddar cheese, grated
8 black olives, stoned and quartered
Fresh basil leaves to garnish

1 Pour the water into a small bowl, stir in the sugar until dissolved, then whisk in the yeast. Cover and leave to stand in a warm place for 10 minutes, until frothy.

2 Mix the plain and wholemeal flour in a bowl, make a well in the centre and pour in 2 tablespoons of the oil and all the yeast liquid. Mix to form a dough, then knead on a floured surface for about 5 minutes, until even-textured, springy and no longer sticky. Put the dough in a clean bowl, cover and set in a warm place – for example, in an airing cupboard or near a hot radiator. Leave to rise for 45 minutes, or until the dough has doubled in size.

3 Meanwhile, heat 1 tablespoon of the remaining oil in a frying pan and cook the peppers in it for 5 minutes over a moderate heat, until they start to soften. Spoon out the peppers and set them aside.

4 Stir the onion, tomatoes, garlic, oregano and basil into the pan and season with black pepper. Bring to the boil, reduce the heat and simmer for 10 minutes, stirring frequently, until the sauce has thickened slightly. Remove from the heat and leave to cool.

5 Knead the risen dough for 2-3 minutes, then roll it into a circle 10in (25cm) in diameter and lay it in a pizza tin or on a baking sheet greased with a little of the remaining oil. Brush the rest of the oil over the dough.

6 Spread the tomato sauce over the dough, leaving ½ in (13mm) clear round the rim. Spoon the green, red and yellow peppers over the sauce, then sprinkle with the mozzarella or Cheddar. Arrange the olives on top and cook the pizza in the heated oven for 20-25 minutes, until the base is crisp and the cheese melted and beginning to brown. Scatter on the garnish of basil leaves.

Serve a crisp, leafy salad with the pizza to make a sharp contrast with the colour and texture of the soft, sweet-pepper topping.

A combination of brown and white flours produces a plump, puffy pizza base with a nutty, wholesome flavour. Red, yellow and green pepper rings make a colourful and intricate topping to stud with savoury pieces of olive. A thick, spicy tomato sauce and melted strands of cheese complete the Italian mood.

Spinach ring with white-bean sauce

SERVES 4
PREPARATION TIME: 20 minutes
COOKING TIME: 45 minutes
OVEN: Preheat to 180°C (350°F, gas mark 4)

1lb (450g) fresh spinach, trimmed, washed and shredded
½ oz (15g) polyunsaturated margarine
2 level tablespoons plain flour
¼ pint (150ml) skimmed milk
1oz (30g) grated Parmesan cheese
1 egg, separated, plus 1 egg white, size 2
11oz (300g) cooked butter beans, or haricot or lima beans (see p.17)
2 tablespoons olive oil
2 level tablespoons low-fat natural yoghurt
1 tablespoon lemon juice
⅛ level teaspoon salt
⅛ level teaspoon cayenne pepper
¼ pint (150ml) vegetable stock (see p. 19)
Watercress to garnish

ONE SERVING	
CALORIES 440	
TOTAL FAT 17g	
SATURATED FAT 4g	
CARBOHYDRATES 47g	
ADDED SUGAR 0	
FIBRE 16g	
SODIUM 612mg	

1 Put the spinach in a large saucepan without any water, cover and cook it for 2 minutes over a moderate heat in the juice that runs from it. Take off the lid and continue cooking, stirring often, for about 4 minutes, until the spinach is just tender. Drain off any remaining juice.

2 Melt the butter in a medium saucepan over a low heat, stir in the flour and gradually mix in the milk. Bring to the boil, stirring, then simmer for 2 minutes until the sauce thickens. Remove the pan from the heat and stir in the Parmesan, the egg yolk and the spinach.

3 Grease a 1 pint (570ml) ring mould and toss a little flour round in it to coat it; shake out the excess. Whisk the egg whites until they will hold soft peaks and use a metal spoon to fold them gently into the spinach mixture. Pour into the mould and spread evenly. Cook in the heated oven for about 40 minutes, until the spinach ring is well risen and feels firm when pressed lightly with a fingertip.

4 Meanwhile, blend the beans, oil, yoghurt, lemon juice, salt, cayenne pepper and vegetable stock in a food processor until smooth. Pour into a saucepan.

5 When the spinach ring is ready, take it out of the oven and let it cool in the tin for 5 minutes. Meanwhile, stir the bean sauce over a moderate heat until hot, but do not let it boil. Pour the sauce into a heated serving jug.

6 Run a knife round the inner and outer rim of the spinach ring and turn it out onto a warmed serving plate. Garnish it with the watercress and serve at once, handing round the sauce separately.

The dish is a substantial one, but you may like some wholemeal or herb-flavoured rolls and a tomato salad with it.

A creamy sauce combined with dark green spinach creates this attractive ring. Egg whites fluff it into a light and airy partner for a rich white-bean purée.

This highly spiced dish, reminiscent of traditional North African dishes, is served on a fluffy bed of couscous, granules made from wheat.

Spiced vegetable stew with couscous

ONE SERVING	
CALORIES	360
TOTAL FAT	7g
SATURATED FAT	1g
CARBOHYDRATES	62g
ADDED SUGAR	0
FIBRE	7g
SODIUM	160mg

SERVES 4
PREPARATION TIME: 15 minutes
COOKING TIME: 25 minutes

1 small cauliflower, trimmed and divided into florets
1 tablespoon olive oil
1 medium onion, peeled and chopped
3 cloves garlic, peeled and crushed
1 level teaspoon each turmeric, ground ginger, paprika
½ level teaspoon chilli powder
1¾ lb (800g) tinned chopped tomatoes
1 red pepper, de-seeded and thickly sliced
1 carrot, peeled and thinly sliced
2oz (60g) stoned prunes, halved
¼ pint (150ml) vegetable stock (see p.19)
1 cinnamon stick
6oz (175g) runner beans, strings removed, sliced
8oz (225g) cooked chickpeas (see p.17)
8oz (225g) couscous
16fl oz (485ml) boiling water
⅛ level teaspoon salt
Freshly ground black pepper

1 Blanch the cauliflower in boiling unsalted water for 2 minutes, drain and set aside.

2 Heat the oil in a large, heavy-based frying pan and cook the onion and garlic in it over a moderate heat for 5 minutes, until the onion colours. Add the turmeric, ginger, paprika and chilli powder, and fry for 30 seconds more.

3 Stir in the tomatoes, red pepper, carrot, prunes and stock, and put in the cinnamon stick. Cover and cook for 15 minutes. Mix in the cauliflower, beans and chickpeas, and cook for a further 5 minutes.

4 Meanwhile, put the couscous into a bowl with the boiling water. Stir, cover the bowl and leave to stand for about 15 minutes, or until the water has been absorbed. Season the couscous with the salt and black pepper and fluff it up with a fork.

5 Pile the couscous onto a warmed serving dish. Remove the cinnamon stick from the stew and spoon the stew over the couscous.

You can garnish the stew with mint sprigs or pale celery leaves, and serve warm rolls with it.

Tofu and vegetable stir-fry with rice

ONE SERVING	
CALORIES	455
TOTAL FAT	17g
SATURATED FAT	1g
CARBOHYDRATES	61g
ADDED SUGAR	0
FIBRE	3g
SODIUM	315mg

SERVES 4
PREPARATION TIME: 15 minutes, plus 1 hour
to marinate
COOKING TIME: 20 minutes

1 level tablespoon peeled and grated root ginger
2½ tablespoons sesame oil
2 cloves garlic, peeled and crushed
1 tablespoon soy sauce

1lb (450g) firm tofu, cut into cubes
8oz (225g) long-grain rice
6 spring onions, trimmed and sliced diagonally
1 small onion, peeled and finely chopped
4oz (115g) mangetout, trimmed
3 sticks celery, trimmed and thinly sliced
Small red pepper, de-seeded and thinly sliced
Small yellow pepper, de-seeded and thinly sliced
Small fresh green chilli, de-seeded and finely chopped
2 small carrots, peeled and cut into matchstick strips
6fl oz (175ml) vegetable stock (see p.19)
2 level teaspoons cornflour
2 tablespoons dry white wine or dry sherry
1 level tablespoon sesame seeds, lightly toasted

1 Mix half the ginger, 1 tablespoon of the oil, half the garlic and the soy sauce in a shallow dish. Put in the tofu and turn gently to coat the cubes. Cover and put in the refrigerator to marinate for 1 hour. Fifteen minutes before the hour is up, start cooking the rice (see p.17).

2 While the rice is cooking, heat 1 tablespoon of the remaining oil in a wok or large frying pan. Stir-fry the spring onions and the rest of the ginger and garlic in it over a high heat for 30 seconds, then mix in the chopped onion, mangetout, celery, peppers and chilli, and stir-fry for 2-3 minutes.

3 Stir in the carrots and half the stock, then add the tofu and its marinade. Lower the heat, cover and simmer for 3-4 minutes, until the vegetables are just cooked but firm.

4 Meanwhile, blend the cornflour with the remaining sesame oil and mix with the wine or sherry and the rest of the stock. Pour into the wok or pan and stir carefully over a moderate heat for 2-3 minutes, until the sauce thickens. Take care not to break up the tofu.

5 Pile the rice onto a heated serving dish, spoon the tofu and vegetable mixture on top and sprinkle with the sesame seeds.

Serve a salad of lamb's lettuce and watercress to provide a sharp contrast to the stir-fry.

Mild tofu readily soaks up the strong flavours of a ginger, sesame oil and soy sauce marinade, making it a welcome addition to this vegetable stir-fry.

Two-layer tortilla

SERVES 4
PREPARATION TIME: 20 minutes
COOKING TIME: 10 minutes
OVEN: Preheat to 120°C (250°F, gas mark ½)

ONE SERVING	
CALORIES	425
TOTAL FAT	22g
SATURATED FAT	4g
CARBOHYDRATES	20g
ADDED SUGAR	0
FIBRE	4g
SODIUM	300mg

1 tablespoon olive oil
1 medium onion, peeled and chopped
¾ pint (425ml) tomato sauce (see p.16)
6 eggs, size 2
4oz (115g) frozen leaf spinach, thawed
12oz (340g) potatoes, boiled but firm, diced
Freshly ground black pepper
1 level tablespoon chopped fresh parsley

1   Heat the oil in a frying pan and gently cook the onion in it for 10 minutes, until softened. Put the tomato sauce to simmer in a small pan.

2   Break 3 eggs into each of two bowls and beat lightly. Mix the spinach into one bowl and the potato into the other. Mix half the onion into each bowl and season with pepper.

3   Heat the grill to high. Heat a nonstick omelette pan 8in (20cm) in diameter. Pour in the spinach mixture and spread it evenly in the pan. Cook gently for about 4 minutes, until the mixture comes away easily from the sides. Put under the grill for 1-2 minutes to set the top. Slide from the pan onto a warm serving plate and spoon on half the tomato sauce. Cover and put in the heated oven.

4   Cook the potato mixture in the same way. Slide it on top of the spinach tortilla, and spoon the remaining tomato sauce on top. Sprinkle with the parsley.

Serve the tortilla with sprigs of parsley to garnish, if you like, and with plenty of bread.

TIP
If you have no grill to cook the top of each tortilla, put a large plate over the pan and turn pan and plate over together so that the tortilla is on the plate. Carefully slide it back into the pan to cook the other side.

The name 'tortilla' shows that Spain is the source of this layered omelette. You can vary the vegetable additions, but potato is one of the best as it makes the dish more filling.

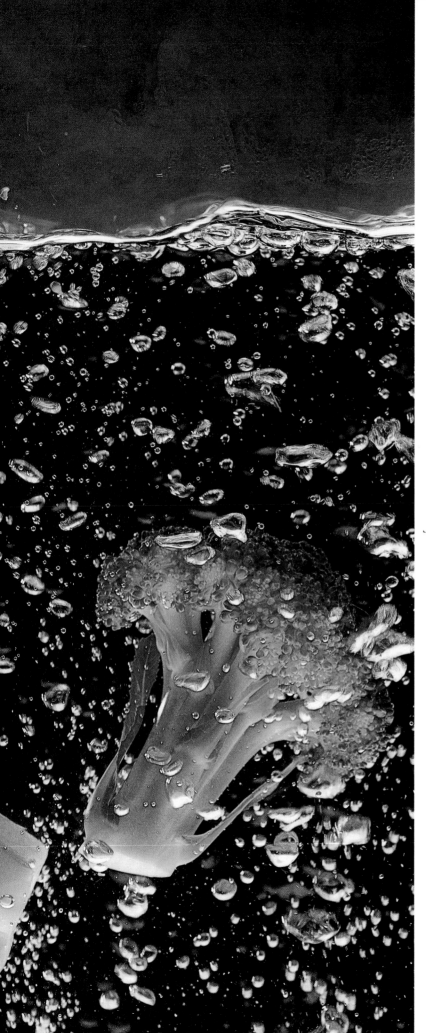

VEGETABLE SIDE DISHES

Whether blanched or steamed for crispness, or baked or roasted to intensify the taste, vegetables are one of nature's most bountiful sources of nourishment, offering fibre, vital minerals and vitamins, and some protein as well. Here are dozens of ideas for presenting them – some in novel combinations, others using healthy ways of creating traditional rich flavours.

Asparagus baked in white wine

SERVES 4
PREPARATION TIME: 5 minutes
COOKING TIME: 20 minutes
OVEN: Preheat to 180°C (350°F, gas mark 4)

ONE SERVING	
CALORIES 70	
TOTAL FAT 5g	
SATURATED FAT 3g	
CARBOHYDRATES 2g	
ADDED SUGAR 0	
FIBRE 2g	
SODIUM 6mg	

1lb (450g) fresh asparagus, trimmed and stalks peeled
5fl oz (150ml) dry white wine
3 tablespoons double cream
⅛ level teaspoon paprika

1 Put the asparagus in a shallow casserole dish with all the tips pointing the same way.

2 Pour in the wine, cover with a tightly fitting lid or foil, and bake in the heated oven for 15 minutes. Carefully turn the asparagus once during cooking.

3 When the asparagus is just tender, stir in the cream until well blended, taking care not to damage the delicate tips. Return to the oven and bake for 5 minutes.

4 Stir the sauce again just before serving and sprinkle the stalk ends of the asparagus with a dusting of paprika.

TIP
Use a potato peeler to pare off the outermost skin of the bottom half of the asparagus stalks. This ensures that the stalks cook as fast as the tips.

Bathed in a creamy wine sauce, delicate young asparagus makes a simple, delicious treat for family or guests.

Aubergine and pumpkin gratin

SERVES 4
PREPARATION TIME: 15 minutes
COOKING TIME: 25 minutes

ONE SERVING	
CALORIES 75	
TOTAL FAT 4g	
SATURATED FAT 1g	
CARBOHYDRATES 6g	
ADDED SUGAR 0	
FIBRE 4g	
SODIUM 8mg	

1 tablespoon olive oil
1 clove garlic, peeled and crushed
1 small onion, peeled and finely chopped
2 tablespoons water
1 bay leaf
2 level teaspoons chopped fresh rosemary, or 1 level teaspoon dried rosemary
4 chopped fresh sage leaves

1lb (450g) pumpkin, peeled, de-seeded and cubed
1lb (450g) aubergine, cut into cubes
2 level tablespoons Greek yoghurt
2 teaspoons lemon juice
1 level tablespoon chopped fresh parsley
Freshly ground black pepper
Sage sprig to garnish

1 Heat the oil in a large, nonstick frying pan and put in the garlic, onion and water. Cook over a moderate heat for 2 minutes, or until the water has evaporated.

2 Add the bay leaf, rosemary and sage, and cook for 1 minute, then stir in the pumpkin and aubergine. Cover and cook over a low heat, stirring occasionally, for about 15 minutes, or until the vegetables are tender.

3 Take the pan off the heat, discard the bay leaf, stir in the yoghurt, lemon juice and parsley, and season with pepper. Turn into a heatproof dish and brown under a hot grill for 5 minutes. Garnish with the sage sprig.

Aubergine and tomato slices

SERVES 4
PREPARATION TIME: 10 minutes
COOKING TIME: 20 minutes
OVEN: Preheat to 190°C (375°F, gas mark 5)

ONE SERVING

CALORIES 60

TOTAL FAT 5g

SATURATED FAT 1g

CARBOHYDRATES 3g

ADDED SUGAR 0

FIBRE 2g

SODIUM 5mg

1 medium aubergine, trimmed and cut into 8 thick slices
1½ tablespoons olive oil
2 small ripe tomatoes, each cut into 4 slices
2 level tablespoons chopped fresh basil, or 1 level teaspoon dried basil
Freshly ground black pepper
8 fresh basil leaves to garnish

1 Arrange the aubergine slices in a single layer on a nonstick baking sheet and bake in the heated oven for 15 minutes, or until tender.

2 Brush the aubergine slices with half the oil and lay a slice of tomato on top of each one. Trickle on the remaining oil, sprinkle the chopped basil on top and season with pepper.

3 Put the baking sheet under the grill, and cook under a medium heat for 6 minutes, or until the tomatoes are soft. Garnish each aubergine slice with a basil leaf for serving.

Colourful, adaptable aubergines can be gently softened with golden pumpkin cubes and flavoured with herbs before being browned under the grill. They are equally good when sliced and baked in olive oil before being topped with tomato rounds and spicy basil.

Broad beans in parsley sauce

ONE SERVING

CALORIES 115

TOTAL FAT 2g

SATURATED FAT 1g

CARBOHYDRATES 14g

ADDED SUGAR 0

FIBRE 8g

SODIUM 20mg

SERVES 4
PREPARATION TIME: 20 minutes
COOKING TIME: 8 minutes

3lb (1.4kg) fresh broad beans in their pods, to give 1lb (450g) shelled beans
Freshly ground black pepper
4 level tablespoons Greek yoghurt
2 level tablespoons chopped fresh parsley
1 level teaspoon paprika

1 Bring 1¾ pints (1 litre) of unsalted water to the boil in a large saucepan and cook the beans in it, covered, for 8 minutes, or until tender.

2 Drain the beans well, season with pepper and stir in the yoghurt, parsley and paprika. Turn into a warmed dish and serve.

When broad beans are out of season, you can use 1lb (450g) of frozen broad beans.

Green beans with dill dressing

ONE SERVING

CALORIES 50

TOTAL FAT 3g

SATURATED FAT 2g

CARBOHYDRATES 3g

ADDED SUGAR 0

FIBRE 2g

SODIUM 15mg

SERVES 4
PREPARATION TIME: 10 minutes
COOKING TIME: 6 minutes

1lb (450g) fine green beans, tops and tails removed
½ oz (15g) slightly salted butter
2 teaspoons lemon juice
Freshly ground mixed peppercorns
2 level tablespoons chopped fresh dill, or ½ level teaspoon dried dill

1 Cook the beans in unsalted boiling water for 3-4 minutes, until almost tender. Turn into a colander, rinse under a cold tap and drain.

2 Melt the butter in a large, nonstick frying pan over a moderate heat until it sizzles. Cook the beans in it, tossing and stirring, for 2-3 minutes. Season with the lemon juice and pepper, mix in the dill and turn into a warmed serving dish.

> **TIP**
> *To top and tail beans quickly, hold a bunch loosely, tap down on a board to align the tips, then cut off the tips with scissors or a sharp knife. Tap to align the stem ends and cut them off.*

Runner beans with cherry tomatoes

ONE SERVING

CALORIES 55

TOTAL FAT 3g

SATURATED FAT 0

CARBOHYDRATES 6g

ADDED SUGAR 0

FIBRE 3g

SODIUM 9mg

SERVES 4
PREPARATION TIME: 10 minutes
COOKING TIME: 7 minutes

1lb (450g) runner beans with tops, tails and strings removed, thinly sliced
2 teaspoons olive oil
12oz (340g) cherry tomatoes
2 level tablespoons chopped fresh basil, or 1 level teaspoon dried basil
1 tablespoon red wine vinegar
Shredded basil to garnish

1 Bring 1in (25mm) of unsalted water to the boil in a saucepan and cook the beans in it, covered, for 3-4 minutes, until softening but still slightly firm. Keep 2 tablespoons of the cooking water, drain off the remainder and set the beans aside.

2 Heat the oil in a frying pan and fry the tomatoes in it over a moderately high heat, shaking the pan frequently, for about 2 minutes, until the skins begin to split.

3 Stir in the basil, beans, reserved cooking water and vinegar. Heat through for 3 minutes, uncovered, tossing occasionally. Turn into a warmed dish and garnish with the basil.

Three contrasting dishes show the versatility of beans: broad beans in a satisfyingly creamy yoghurt and parsley sauce, fine green beans flavoured with butter and dill, and crisp runner beans paired with jewel-bright and juicy cherry tomatoes.

Beetroots with horseradish sauce

SERVES 4
PREPARATION TIME: 15 minutes
COOKING TIME: 1 hour 30 minutes

1lb (450g) beetroots, with skin undamaged, washed
4oz (115g) low-fat natural yoghurt
2 level tablespoons freshly grated horseradish
3 level tablespoons chopped fresh dill
Freshly ground black pepper

1 Cook the beetroots in a large, covered pan of unsalted boiling water for 1 hour 30 minutes,

until tender when pierced with a knife tip. Drain, peel off the skin and dice the flesh.

2 Mix the yoghurt, horseradish and half the dill in a dish, and season with pepper. Turn the beetroot in the sauce and sprinkle with the remaining dill.

You can cook the beetroots a day in advance, cool, cover and keep in the refrigerator. Before serving, peel and dice the beetroots and heat through in the sauce without boiling.

ONE SERVING
CALORIES 50
TOTAL FAT 0
SATURATED FAT 0
CARBOHYDRATES 10g
ADDED SUGAR 0
FIBRE 2g
SODIUM 85mg

Simple steamed broccoli is dressed up with a rich and exuberant basil sauce and scattered with crunchy nuts, while the fire of horseradish and tartness of yoghurt blend with the mild sweetness of beetroots to create a piquant pink sauce.

Broccoli with basil sauce

ONE SERVING
CALORIES 135
TOTAL FAT 10g
SATURATED FAT 2g
CARBOHYDRATES 3g
ADDED SUGAR 0
FIBRE 4g
SODIUM 50mg

SERVES 4
PREPARATION TIME: 10 minutes
COOKING TIME: 8 minutes

1¼ lb (550g) broccoli, trimmed and divided into florets
10 basil leaves, stems trimmed off

1 clove garlic, peeled
1½ oz (45g) pine nuts or shelled walnuts
½ oz (15g) grated Parmesan cheese
4 tablespoons vegetable stock (see p.19)
1 teaspoon lemon juice
Freshly ground black pepper
Basil leaves to garnish

1 Steam the broccoli for 6-8 minutes, until cooked but still slightly firm.

2 Meanwhile, prepare the sauce. Blend the trimmed basil leaves, garlic, two-thirds of the nuts and the Parmesan with the stock and

lemon juice in a food processor for about 30 seconds, or until smooth.

3 Turn the broccoli into a warmed dish. Season with pepper, pour on the sauce and garnish with the basil and remaining nuts.

ONE SERVING

CALORIES 100

TOTAL FAT 5g

SATURATED FAT 1g

CARBOHYDRATES 6g

ADDED SUGAR 0

FIBRE 4g

SODIUM 15mg

Broccoli with sweet pepper

SERVES 4
PREPARATION TIME: 15 minutes
COOKING TIME: 10 minutes

4 teaspoons olive oil
1 small onion, peeled and chopped
2 cloves garlic, peeled and crushed
1 tablespoon water
1¼ lb (550g) broccoli, trimmed and divided into florets
1 small red pepper, de-seeded and cut into thick strips
1 level teaspoon dried oregano, crumbled

1 Heat the oil in a heavy-based saucepan and put in the onion, garlic, water, broccoli, red pepper and oregano. Cook, stirring, over a moderately high heat for 2 minutes.

2 Reduce the heat and simmer, covered, for about 6 minutes more, stirring frequently, until the broccoli is tender but still crisp. Turn into a warmed dish and serve at once.

The bright, contrasting colours and crisp textures are preserved by part stir-frying, part steaming.

Brussels sprouts with garlic crumbs

SERVES 4
PREPARATION TIME: 10 minutes
COOKING TIME: 10 minutes

1lb (450g) fresh button sprouts, trimmed
1 tablespoon olive oil
2 cloves garlic, peeled and crushed
1½ oz (45g) coarse crumbs of wholemeal bread

ONE SERVING

CALORIES 85

TOTAL FAT 4g

SATURATED FAT 1g

CARBOHYDRATES 8g

ADDED SUGAR 0

FIBRE 4g

SODIUM 65mg

1 Blanch the sprouts in boiling, unsalted water for 2 minutes, then drain.

2 Gently heat the oil and garlic in a frying pan for 2 minutes; do not let the garlic brown. Add the sprouts, cover and cook over a moderate heat, tossing the sprouts once or twice, for 4 minutes, or until just tender.

3 Using a slotted spoon, lift the sprouts into a warmed serving dish, shaking off any excess juices into the frying pan. Cover the dish to keep the sprouts hot.

4 Stir the breadcrumbs into the juices in the frying pan and cook over a moderate heat, stirring constantly, for about 2 minutes, until crisp and golden brown. Sprinkle the crumbs over the sprouts and serve at once.

If button sprouts are unavailable, use larger sprouts cut in half.

Crunchy breadcrumbs and a generous flavouring of garlic make a delectable dish out of button sprouts.

This is a fresh and appetising way to serve cabbage, which blends particularly well with the full, savoury taste of Cheddar. The cabbage remains crunchy but soaks up the stock, which is enriched by wine.

Baked cabbage wedges with cheese

ONE SERVING	
CALORIES 80	
TOTAL FAT 5g	
SATURATED FAT 3g	
CARBOHYDRATES 3g	
ADDED SUGAR 0	
FIBRE 2g	
SODIUM 85mg	

SERVES 6
PREPARATION TIME: 20 minutes
COOKING TIME: 45 minutes
OVEN: Preheat to 200°C (400°F, gas mark 6)

1 savoy or other firm green cabbage, about 1½ lb
(680g), trimmed, cored and cut into 6 wedges
6fl oz (175ml) chicken stock (see p.19)
4 tablespoons dry white wine
Freshly ground black pepper
½ oz (15g) slightly salted butter
3 level tablespoons white or wholemeal breadcrumbs
1½ oz (45g) grated mature Cheddar cheese
2 level tablespoons chopped fresh parsley

1 Arrange the cabbage wedges in a single layer
in a shallow, flameproof casserole. Pour in the
stock and wine, and season with pepper. Bring
to the boil over a direct heat, then put the
casserole in the heated oven, and cook for
about 40 minutes, or until the cabbage is
cooked but still crisp.

2 Meanwhile, melt the butter in a small,
heavy-based saucepan and cook the
breadcrumbs in it over a moderate heat for
about 2 minutes, stirring, until they are lightly
browned. Remove from the heat and set aside.

3 When the cabbage is cooked, sprinkle the
breadcrumbs and the Cheddar over the top
and put the casserole under a hot grill for
2-3 minutes, or until the cheese is golden
brown. Sprinkle with the parsley before serving.

Braised red cabbage with cranberries

SERVES 4
PREPARATION TIME: 10 minutes
COOKING TIME: 35 minutes

2 teaspoons corn oil
1 medium onion, peeled and chopped
2 cloves garlic, peeled and crushed
1lb (450g) red cabbage, trimmed, cored
and thinly sliced
4oz (115g) cranberries, stalks removed
1 tablespoon red wine vinegar
1 teaspoon honey
Juice of 1 orange
¼ level teaspoon ground ginger
¼ level teaspoon ground cloves
1 bay leaf

ONE SERVING	
CALORIES	65
TOTAL FAT	2g
SATURATED FAT	0
CARBOHYDRATES	9g
ADDED SUGAR	2g
FIBRE	4g
SODIUM	30mg

1 Heat the oil in a heavy-based saucepan and cook the onion and garlic in it, uncovered, over a moderate heat for 5 minutes. Stir in the cabbage, cover and cook for another 5 minutes.

2 Mix in the cranberries, vinegar, honey, orange juice, ginger and cloves, and put in the bay leaf. Cover and cook for 25 minutes, or until almost all the liquid has evaporated and the cabbage is tender. If there is still considerable liquid left, take off the lid and bring to a rapid boil for 1-2 minutes to reduce it. Remove the bay leaf before serving.

If you cannot find cranberries, replace them with a diced, sharp-flavoured dessert apple.

Carrots and peppers in onion sauce

SERVES 4
PREPARATION TIME: 15 minutes
COOKING TIME: 20 minutes

1 tablespoon olive oil
3 spring onions, trimmed and white and green parts
chopped separately
1 level tablespoon plain flour
½ pint (285ml) vegetable stock (see p.19)
1lb (450g) carrots, peeled and sliced diagonally
Freshly ground black pepper
1 medium green pepper, de-seeded and cut
into short strips
2 level tablespoons Greek yoghurt
1 teaspoon lemon juice

ONE SERVING	
CALORIES	80
TOTAL FAT	4g
SATURATED FAT	1g
CARBOHYDRATES	9g
ADDED SUGAR	0
FIBRE	3g
SODIUM	30mg

1 Heat the oil in a large frying pan and fry the white part of the spring onions in it over a moderate heat for 3 minutes. Stir in the flour

and cook for 1 minute, then mix in the stock a little at a time and bring to the boil, stirring continuously. Reduce the heat and simmer for 3 minutes, stirring frequently, until the sauce has thickened.

2 Stir the carrots into the sauce and season with pepper. Cook, uncovered, for 8 minutes, stirring occasionally. Add the green pepper, cover and cook for a further 3-4 minutes, until the vegetables are tender.

3 Mix the yoghurt and lemon juice into the sauce and heat gently for 1 minute, but do not boil or the sauce may curdle.

4 Pour the vegetables and sauce into a warmed serving dish. Sprinkle with the green part of the spring onions before serving.

> **TIP**
> Watch the orange glaze carefully once you turn up the heat. It can quickly burn and make the carrots bitter.

Carrots glazed with orange and ginger

SERVES 4
PREPARATION TIME: 10 minutes
COOKING TIME: 15 minutes

½ oz (15g) slightly salted butter
6fl oz (175ml) orange juice

2 teaspoons peeled and grated root ginger,
or ¼ level teaspoon ground ginger
Thinly pared rind of ¼ of an orange
1lb (450g) carrots, peeled and cut into
long fingers
1 level tablespoon chopped fresh parsley

ONE SERVING	
CALORIES	70
TOTAL FAT	3g
SATURATED FAT	2g
CARBOHYDRATES	10g
ADDED SUGAR	0
FIBRE	2g
SODIUM	40mg

1 Melt the butter in a saucepan, stir in the orange juice, ginger, orange rind and carrots, and bring to the boil.

2 Reduce the heat, cover and simmer for 10 minutes, or until the carrots are cooked but still slightly firm. Take out the orange rind, turn up the heat and boil, uncovered, until the liquid has reduced to a syrupy glaze.

3 Turn the carrots into a heated serving dish and sprinkle with the parsley.

Refreshingly acid cranberries make an excellent partner for red cabbage in a rich ruby side dish that goes particularly well with pork or ham. Carrots may be served crisp with crunchy strips of pepper in a sharp onion and yoghurt sauce, or slightly softer with a luscious spicy glaze.

Red peppers blended to a smooth sauce tinge lightly steamed cauliflower a deep amber and flavour the crisp florets with smoky sweetness.

Cauliflower in red pepper sauce

SERVES 4
PREPARATION TIME: 15 minutes
COOKING TIME: 25 minutes

2 teaspoons olive oil
1 medium onion, peeled and thinly sliced
2 cloves garlic, peeled and crushed
2 medium red peppers, de-seeded and sliced
into thick strips
6fl oz (175ml) chicken or vegetable stock
(see p.19)
1lb (450g) cauliflower florets
1 level tablespoon chopped fresh parsley

1 Heat the oil in a heavy-based saucepan
and cook the onion, garlic and peppers in it
over a moderately high heat, stirring frequently
for 10 minutes, or until the peppers become
tender and the onion golden brown. Pour in
the stock, bring the mixture to the boil and
cook for 2 minutes more.

2 Let the pepper mixture cool slightly,
then pour it into a food processor and blend for
15-20 seconds to make a smooth purée. Return
it to the pan and leave to simmer.

3 Steam the cauliflower for about 6 minutes,
until just becoming tender, then mix it gently
into the red pepper sauce. Turn the cauliflower
and sauce into a warmed serving dish, sprinkle
with the parsley and serve.

ONE SERVING	
CALORIES 95	
TOTAL FAT 3g	
SATURATED FAT 1g	
CARBOHYDRATES 9g	
ADDED SUGAR 0	
FIBRE 4g	
SODIUM 15mg	

Cauliflower in spicy tomato sauce

ONE SERVING	
CALORIES 75	
TOTAL FAT 2g	
SATURATED FAT 0	
CARBOHYDRATES 9g	
ADDED SUGAR 0	
FIBRE 4g	
SODIUM 20mg	

SERVES 4
PREPARATION TIME: 20 minutes
COOKING TIME: 25 minutes

1 small onion, peeled and chopped
2 cloves garlic, peeled
4 teaspoons peeled and grated root ginger
1lb (450g) tomatoes, skinned, de-seeded
and chopped

1 level teaspoon each ground cumin and
ground coriander
1/2 level teaspoon ground turmeric
1/8 level teaspoon cayenne pepper
4fl oz (115ml) water
Freshly ground black pepper
1 medium cauliflower, about 1 1/2 lb (680g),
trimmed, with a deep cross cut in the base
2 teaspoons lemon juice

1 Blend the onion, garlic and ginger with the tomatoes for about 30 seconds in a food processor, to make a smooth purée.

2 Pour the purée into a saucepan, stir in the cumin, coriander, turmeric, cayenne pepper and water, and season with black pepper. Bring to the boil, then turn down the heat and leave

to simmer and thicken, uncovered, while you cook the cauliflower.

3 Steam the cauliflower for 20 minutes, until tender, then lift it into a heated serving dish.

4 Stir the lemon juice into the sauce and pour it over the cauliflower to serve.

Tomatoes and hot spices make a pungent sauce for mild cauliflower, while vivid cherry tomatoes add fruitiness to melting courgette slices.

Courgettes and cherry tomatoes

ONE SERVING

CALORIES 55

TOTAL FAT 4g

SATURATED FAT 1g

CARBOHYDRATES 4g

ADDED SUGAR 0

FIBRE 2g

SODIUM 5mg

SERVES 4
PREPARATION TIME: 10 minutes
COOKING TIME: 10 minutes

1 tablespoon olive oil
1 clove garlic, peeled and crushed
1lb (450g) courgettes, trimmed and thinly sliced
8oz (225g) cherry tomatoes, halved
1 tablespoon cider vinegar
½ level teaspoon dried basil
Freshly ground black pepper

1 Heat the oil in a large frying pan and soften the garlic and courgettes in it over a moderate heat for 5 minutes, stirring them frequently to prevent colouring.

2 Mix in the tomatoes, vinegar and basil, and season with pepper. Cook for 2 minutes, or until the tomatoes are hot but not collapsed. Stir constantly to keep the courgettes moving; they taste bitter if browned. Turn the vegetables into a warmed serving dish.

Braised fennel and potatoes

ONE SERVING

CALORIES 100

TOTAL FAT 3g

SATURATED FAT 0

CARBOHYDRATES 15g

ADDED SUGAR 0

FIBRE 6g

SODIUM 60mg

SERVES 4
PREPARATION TIME: 15 minutes
COOKING TIME: 1 hour
OVEN: Preheat to 200°C (400°F, gas mark 6)

1 teaspoon olive oil
8oz (225g) potatoes, peeled and thinly sliced
4 medium fennel bulbs, trimmed and chopped into small pieces

Freshly ground black pepper
14oz (400g) tinned chopped tomatoes
1 clove garlic, peeled and finely chopped
½ level teaspoon crushed fennel seeds
1 level teaspoon oregano, crumbled
4fl oz (115ml) vegetable or chicken stock (see p.19)
1 tablespoon sunflower seeds
Fennel fronds to garnish

The light aniseed flavour of fennel spreads through the potato in this moist side dish, which goes well with roast chicken and other plain roast meats.

1 Grease a shallow, ovenproof dish with the oil. Arrange half the potato slices over the bottom of the dish, spread the fennel on top and season with pepper.

2 Combine the tomatoes, garlic, fennel seeds, oregano and stock, and pour the mixture over the fennel. Arrange the remaining potato slices on top, overlapping them to cover the fennel.

3 Cover the dish and cook in the heated oven for 30 minutes. Uncover and cook for a further 30 minutes, or until the vegetables feel tender when tested with a fork, and the top is golden brown.

4 Sprinkle the sunflower seeds over the vegetables and garnish with the fronds of fennel to serve.

Jerusalem artichokes braised in wine

SERVES 4
PREPARATION TIME: 15 minutes
COOKING TIME: 45 minutes

1 tablespoon olive oil
2 cloves garlic, peeled and finely chopped
1 small onion, peeled and chopped
1½ lb (680g) Jerusalem artichokes, peeled and sliced
4fl oz (115ml) dry white wine
4fl oz (115ml) vegetable stock (see p.19)
1 fresh bouquet garni (see p.218)
½ level teaspoon freshly grated nutmeg
Freshly ground black pepper
1 level tablespoon chopped fresh parsley
Sprigs of fresh herbs to garnish

1   Heat the oil in a large frying pan and cook the garlic and onion in it gently for 5 minutes.

2   Stir in the Jerusalem artichokes and cook for 5 minutes, turning the slices over several times to colour lightly. Pour on the wine and stock and put in the bouquet garni. Bring to the boil, then reduce the heat, partially cover the pan and simmer for about 35 minutes, or until the artichokes are tender and most of the liquid has evaporated. Stir gently from time to time to make sure that the artichokes are not sticking at the bottom of the pan.

3   Remove the bouquet garni, sprinkle in the nutmeg and season with pepper. Turn the artichokes into a warmed serving dish and scatter the parsley over them. Garnish with the herb sprigs before serving.

If you cannot find herbs for a fresh bouquet garni, you can use a made-up sachet.

TIP
To prevent the artichoke slices from going brown, drop them as fast as you cut them into a large bowl of cold water with a few drops of lemon juice added. Blot the slices quickly with kitchen paper just before they go in the pan.

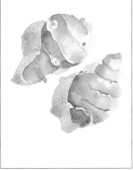

A light seasoning of nutmeg and pepper highlights the delicate flavour absorbed by the artichokes during gentle braising in white wine, herbs and stock.

Leek stir-fry with herb croutons

ONE SERVING	
CALORIES 70	
TOTAL FAT 4g	
SATURATED FAT 1g	
CARBOHYDRATES 6g	
ADDED SUGAR 0	
FIBRE 3g	
SODIUM 45mg	

The croutons absorb the strong flavours of the garlic and parsley, and their crispness makes a pleasing contrast to the smooth vegetables.

SERVES 4
PREPARATION TIME: 10 minutes
COOKING TIME: 12 minutes

1 clove garlic, peeled and crushed
1 level tablespoon chopped fresh parsley
1 slice of wholemeal bread with crusts removed, cut into cubes
1 tablespoon olive oil
1lb (450g) leeks, trimmed, cut into thick slices and washed
4oz (115g) button mushrooms, wiped, trimmed and halved
1 tablespoon vegetable stock (see p.19) or water
Freshly ground black pepper

1 Blend the garlic and parsley with a fork. Mix in the bread cubes until coated, and set aside.

2 Heat the oil in a large frying pan, and stir-fry the leeks and mushrooms in it over a moderate heat for 2 minutes, until beginning to soften but not to colour.

3 Mix in the stock or water and cook, uncovered, for about 6 minutes, until the vegetables are just tender and very lightly coloured, and the liquid has evaporated. Stir frequently during the cooking. Spoon the leeks and mushrooms into a warmed serving dish, cover, and keep hot.

4 Cook the bread cubes in the same pan, stirring and tossing frequently, until they are crisp and browned all over. Sprinkle the herb croutons over the leeks and mushrooms and serve at once.

Mangetout, French for 'eat everything', are so named because the tiny immature peas are eaten complete with their sweet, crisp pods; they go particularly well with other crunchy vegetables such as the lightly cooked carrots and pepper in this dish.

ONE SERVING

CALORIES 75

TOTAL FAT 3g

SATURATED FAT 0

CARBOHYDRATES 8g

ADDED SUGAR 0

FIBRE 3g

SODIUM 10mg

Mangetout with carrots and red pepper

SERVES 4
PREPARATION TIME: 15 minutes
COOKING TIME: 10 minutes

1 tablespoon olive oil
2 medium carrots, peeled and thinly sliced
1 red pepper, de-seeded and cut into thin strips
12oz (340g) mangetout, trimmed
Finely shredded rind of ½ lemon
1 teaspoon lemon juice
Freshly ground black pepper

1 Heat the oil in a frying pan and cook the carrots and red pepper in it over a moderate heat, covered, for 3 minutes.

2 Mix in the mangetout, cover again, and cook for 3 minutes or until the vegetables are softening but still slightly firm.

3 Stir in the lemon rind and juice, season the vegetables with pepper and stir again. Turn into a warmed dish and serve.

Marrow with ginger and almonds

SERVES 4
PREPARATION TIME: 10 minutes
COOKING TIME: 15 minutes

1 tablespoon olive oil
2oz (60g) whole blanched almonds
2 small red onions, peeled and sliced
2 level teaspoons peeled and grated root ginger
1½ lb (680g) marrow, quartered lengthways,
peeled, de-seeded and cut into thick slices
2 tablespoons orange juice
1 level tablespoon chopped fresh parsley

ONE SERVING

CALORIES 135

TOTAL FAT 11g

SATURATED FAT 1g

CARBOHYDRATES 5g

ADDED SUGAR 0

FIBRE 2g

SODIUM 5mg

1 Heat the oil in a large frying pan and stir the almonds in it over a moderate heat for 2 minutes, until golden. Lift the almonds out of the pan with a slotted spoon and set aside.

2 Cook the onion and ginger in the same pan for about 2 minutes, or until the onion just begins to soften.

3 Stir in the marrow and orange juice, and cook over a moderate heat for about 8 minutes, stirring frequently but gently, until the marrow becomes just tender without losing its shape.

4 Mix in the parsley and almonds. Turn into a warmed serving dish and serve at once, perhaps with a sprig of parsley for extra colour.

The delicate flavour of firm young marrow is enlivened by fresh ginger, orange juice and onion, while the golden fried almonds provide a deliciously crunchy contrast in texture.

TIP
To blanch almonds, put them in a heatproof dish, pour on boiling water to cover and leave to stand for 3 minutes. Drain, then slip off the swollen skins.

Mushrooms in red wine

SERVES 4
PREPARATION TIME: 15 minutes
COOKING TIME: 20 minutes

1 tablespoon olive oil
3 tablespoons water
1 small red onion, peeled and finely chopped
1lb (450g) button mushrooms, wiped and trimmed

1 bay leaf
1½ level teaspoons whole-grain mustard
1½ level teaspoons Dijon mustard
1 level tablespoon cornflour
4fl oz (115ml) dry red wine
Freshly ground black pepper
1 level tablespoon snipped chives
Parsley or marjoram sprigs to garnish

*This is a sumptuous
and satisfying dish that
marries the subtle
flavour and melting
texture of bite-sized
button mushrooms with
a sparky mustard and
wine sauce.*

1 Heat the oil and 2 tablespoons of the water in a frying pan and cook the onion in it over a moderate heat for 3 minutes. Mix in the mushrooms, add the bay leaf and cook gently for a further 5 minutes, stirring frequently, until the mushrooms just begin to soften.

2 Mix the whole-grain and Dijon mustard with the remaining water and stir into the mushrooms. Blend the cornflour with the wine, pour it into the pan and stir until

the liquid comes to the boil. Simmer for 10 minutes more, stirring frequently as the sauce thickens.

3 Remove the bay leaf, season the mushrooms with pepper and stir in the chives. Pour into a heated serving dish and garnish with the parsley or marjoram.

This rich dish goes particularly well with roast pheasant, other game or turkey.

Mushrooms with yoghurt and dill sauce

ONE SERVING

CALORIES 60

TOTAL FAT 3g

SATURATED FAT 1g

CARBOHYDRATES 4g

ADDED SUGAR 0

FIBRE 2g

SODIUM 15mg

The earthy, nutty taste of mushrooms pervades a creamy yoghurt and dill sauce. The dish will vary slightly according to the combination of mushrooms you use.

SERVES 4
PREPARATION TIME: 15 minutes
COOKING TIME: 12 minutes

2 teaspoons olive oil
1 medium onion, peeled and finely chopped
1lb (450g) mixed mushrooms, wiped and trimmed
2fl oz (60ml) dry white wine
2 level teaspoons cornflour
½ level teaspoon paprika
4fl oz (115ml) chicken stock (see p.19)
2 level tablespoons Greek yoghurt
2 level tablespoons chopped fresh dill
Dill fronds to garnish

1 Heat the oil in a heavy-based saucepan and fry the onion in it over a moderate heat for 5 minutes, or until lightly coloured. Stir in the mushrooms and wine, cover the pan, and cook for 4 minutes.

2 Blend the cornflour and paprika into the stock, and stir the mixture into the pan. Bring to the boil, stirring all the time, then simmer for 2-3 minutes until the sauce is thickened and smooth.

3 Mix the yoghurt and chopped dill into the sauce and heat through gently for 30 seconds without boiling or the sauce may curdle. Turn the mushrooms and sauce into a warmed serving dish, and garnish with the dill fronds.

For a full flavour use a mixture of button, oyster and chestnut mushrooms in the dish. It is particularly good with a plain roast chicken.

The creamy-textured but light sauce, with its enticing fragrance of mixed herbs, creates a special dish out of tiny sweet-flavoured onions.

Onions in herb sauce

ONE SERVING

CALORIES 90

TOTAL FAT 3g

SATURATED FAT 0

CARBOHYDRATES 13g

ADDED SUGAR 0

FIBRE 2g

SODIUM 20mg

SERVES 4
PREPARATION TIME: 15 minutes
COOKING TIME: 25 minutes

1 tablespoon corn oil
1lb (450g) button onions, peeled
2 level tablespoons plain flour
7fl oz (200ml) vegetable stock (see p.19)
4fl oz (115ml) skimmed milk
1 level teaspoon dried mixed herbs
Freshly ground black pepper
1 level tablespoon chopped fresh parsley

1 Heat the oil in a frying pan or heavy-based saucepan and cook the onions in it over a moderate heat for 5 minutes, stirring and shaking frequently, until they are lightly browned all over.

2 Mix in the flour and cook it gently for 1 minute, stirring, then gradually stir in the stock and milk. Scatter on the herbs, season with pepper and cook over a moderate heat, stirring continuously, for about 5 minutes or until the sauce is smooth and thickened.

3. Lower the heat and simmer, covered, for about 15 minutes, stirring occasionally, until the onions are tender. Pour into a warmed serving dish and sprinkle with the parsley.

Red onions in raisin sauce

SERVES 4
PREPARATION TIME: 15 minutes
COOKING TIME: 30 minutes

1 tablespoon olive oil
1lb (450g) red onions, peeled and quartered
1 clove garlic, peeled and finely chopped
4 tablespoons dry white wine
7fl oz (200ml) beef stock (see p.19)
2 tablespoons tomato purée (see p.16)
2 level tablespoons seedless raisins
Finely grated rind of 1 small orange
½ level teaspoon dried thyme
1 level teaspoon dried marjoram
Freshly ground black pepper

ONE SERVING	
CALORIES	85
TOTAL FAT	3g
SATURATED FAT	0
CARBOHYDRATES	13g
ADDED SUGAR	0
FIBRE	2g
SODIUM	10mg

1 Heat the oil in a large, heavy-based saucepan and cook the onions in it over a moderate heat, stirring frequently, for about 5 minutes.

2 Stir in the garlic, wine, stock, tomato purée, raisins and orange rind. Sprinkle in the thyme and marjoram, and season with pepper. Bring to the boil, then reduce the heat and simmer, uncovered, stirring frequently for 20 minutes, or until the onions are tender.

3 Increase the heat and boil gently for about 3 minutes, until the sauce is reduced by a third and slightly thickened. Turn into a warmed dish for serving.

French-style peas

SERVES 4
PREPARATION TIME: 5 minutes
COOKING TIME: 15 minutes

1 teaspoon olive oil
2 spring onions, trimmed and thinly sliced
2 small cos-type lettuce hearts, trimmed, quartered and washed
12oz (340g) frozen peas
½ level teaspoon dried marjoram
3 teaspoons lemon juice

ONE SERVING	
CALORIES	80
TOTAL FAT	2g
SATURATED FAT	0
CARBOHYDRATES	10g
ADDED SUGAR	0
FIBRE	5g
SODIUM	5mg

1 Heat the oil in a large, heavy-based saucepan and fry the spring onions in it over a moderate heat, stirring, for about 2 minutes, or until they start to soften.

2 Put the lettuce in the pan, cover and cook for about 4 minutes, until tender, shaking the pan frequently during cooking. Stir in the peas, marjoram and lemon juice, cover and cook for a further 5 minutes before serving. A few mint leaves add a lively finish.

Green pea purée

SERVES 4
PREPARATION TIME: 5 minutes
COOKING TIME: 45 minutes

1 tablespoon olive oil
2 spring onions, trimmed and sliced
1 small onion, peeled and chopped
1½ oz (45g) dried split green peas, rinsed
1 small potato, peeled and sliced
4 fresh mint leaves
8fl oz (225ml) vegetable stock (see p.19)
8oz (225g) frozen peas
Sprigs of fresh mint to garnish

ONE SERVING	
CALORIES	120
TOTAL FAT	4g
SATURATED FAT	1g
CARBOHYDRATES	16g
ADDED SUGAR	0
FIBRE	6g
SODIUM	6mg

1 Heat the oil in a saucepan and fry all the onions in it over a moderate heat for 5 minutes. Stir in the dried peas, potato, mint leaves and stock. Bring to the boil, cover and simmer, stirring occasionally, for 30 minutes.

2 Stir in the frozen peas. If the vegetables look dry, add a little water. Cook, covered, for 5 minutes, then take off the heat. Leave to cool for 5 minutes before blending in a food processor for 30 seconds to make a smooth purée. Serve the purée garnished with the sprigs of mint.

Simple ingredients are transformed into dishes with a continental feel and sufficient elegance to set before guests. Dried and frozen peas combine to make a fluffy purée, mild red onions are bathed in a rich sauce, and French-style peas with lettuce are gently sautéed to make a bitter-sweet blend.

Even a small amount of flavoured olive oil can penetrate the flesh of a straightforward baked potato and transform it into a golden treat.

Baked garlic potatoes

ONE SERVING

CALORIES 140

TOTAL FAT 1g

SATURATED FAT 0

CARBOHYDRATES 30g

ADDED SUGAR 0

FIBRE 3g

SODIUM 75mg

SERVES 4
PREPARATION TIME: 5 minutes
COOKING TIME: 1 hour
OVEN: Preheat to 220°C (425°F, gas mark 7)

2 large baking potatoes, well scrubbed
1 teaspoon olive oil
⅛ level teaspoon salt
1 clove garlic, peeled and crushed
¼ level teaspoon paprika

1 Cut the potatoes in half lengthways and use a small sharp knife to score the cut surface deeply with a crisscross pattern. Arrange the potatoes on a baking sheet.

2 Mix the oil, salt and garlic, and brush the scored surfaces with the mixture. Sprinkle the paprika evenly over them, then bake in the heated oven for 1 hour, or until the potatoes are tender and their tops golden brown.

For a more strongly spiced flavour, add ¼ level teaspoon each of ground cumin, ground coriander and cayenne pepper to the oil mixture before brushing it on the potatoes.

Curried potatoes

ONE SERVING

CALORIES 150

TOTAL FAT 4g

SATURATED FAT 1g

CARBOHYDRATES 28g

ADDED SUGAR 0

FIBRE 3g

SODIUM 15mg

Traditional Indian herbs and spices are combined with stock to create a curry coating for the potato slices. This dish is delicious with cold meats.

SERVES 4
PREPARATION TIME: 15 minutes
COOKING TIME: 30 minutes

1 tablespoon olive oil
½ level teaspoon fennel seeds
1 level teaspoon cumin seeds
1 clove garlic, peeled and crushed
2 level teaspoons peeled and grated root ginger
2 level teaspoons ground cumin
2 level teaspoons ground coriander
½ level teaspoon ground turmeric
¼ level teaspoon cayenne pepper
1 level teaspoon paprika
1½ lb (680g) small potatoes, peeled and cut into thick slices
¾ pint (425ml) vegetable or chicken stock (see p.19)
2 level tablespoons chopped fresh coriander or parsley

1 Heat the oil in a large frying pan and stir the fennel and cumin seeds, garlic and ginger in it over a high heat for 30 seconds. Stir in the ground cumin, coriander, turmeric, cayenne and paprika and cook for a further 30 seconds.

2 Add the potato slices and stir until they are evenly coated with the spice mixture. Pour in the stock and bring to the boil, then lower the heat, cover and simmer for about 30 minutes, occasionally stirring gently, until the potatoes are tender and most of the stock has been absorbed, leaving just a coating of sauce.

3 Sprinkle the potatoes with the chopped coriander or parsley before serving.

You can use ready-mixed curry powder instead of ground cumin, coriander and turmeric.

New potatoes with creamy mint sauce

SERVES 4
PREPARATION TIME: 10 minutes
COOKING TIME: 15 minutes

1½ lb (680g) small new potatoes with skins on,
well washed
10 fresh mint leaves
1 level tablespoon snipped fresh chives
6oz (175g) Greek yoghurt
¼ level teaspoon cayenne pepper or freshly
ground black pepper
¼ level teaspoon paprika
Chives or mint sprigs to garnish

1 Steam the potatoes for about 15 minutes, or until they are just tender.

2 Meanwhile, put the mint leaves in boiling water for 10 seconds, then drain and immediately plunge them into cold water. Pat the leaves dry with kitchen paper and roughly snip them with scissors. Mix the mint and snipped chives into the yoghurt, and season with the cayenne or black pepper.

3 As soon as the potatoes are cooked, turn them into a warmed serving dish, spoon the sauce on them and dust with paprika. Garnish with the chives or mint sprigs before serving.

Minted new potatoes, a symbol of summer days, are made even more tempting by adding creamy yoghurt.

ONE SERVING	
CALORIES	170
TOTAL FAT	4g
SATURATED FAT	2g
CARBOHYDRATES	28g
ADDED SUGAR	0
FIBRE	3g
SODIUM	50mg

Sesame potatoes

ONE SERVING	
CALORIES	165
TOTAL FAT	6g
SATURATED FAT	1g
CARBOHYDRATES	25g
ADDED SUGAR	0
FIBRE	2g
SODIUM	10mg

SERVES 4
PREPARATION TIME: 10 minutes
COOKING TIME: 1 hour
OVEN: Preheat to 200°C (400°F, gas mark 6)

1½ lb (680g) equal-sized potatoes, peeled
1 tablespoon sesame oil
2 level tablespoons sesame seeds

1 Make vertical parallel cuts in each potato, about ¼ inch (6mm) apart and almost down to the base. Pat the potatoes with kitchen paper to dry them well.

2 Brush the potatoes sparingly with the oil and press the top of each firmly into the sesame seeds.

3 Put the potatoes in a lightly oiled baking tin, coated side up. Bake in the heated oven for about 1 hour, or until they are tender inside and crisply browned outside.

You can give potatoes the full and satisfying taste of orthodox roast potatoes, but use only a tiny amount of oil, or none at all. The puffy slices and the crunchy sesame-coated potatoes are perfect partners for a Sunday roast.

Potato slices

ONE SERVING	
CALORIES	110
TOTAL FAT	0
SATURATED FAT	0
CARBOHYDRATES	25g
ADDED SUGAR	0
FIBRE	2g
SODIUM	10mg

SERVES 4
PREPARATION TIME: 10 minutes
COOKING TIME: 40 minutes
OVEN: Preheat to 220°C (425°F, gas mark 7)

1½ lb (680g) baking potatoes, peeled and washed

1 Cut the potatoes into ½ in (13mm) slices with a crinkle potato cutter or a sharp knife. Dry the slices thoroughly on both sides with kitchen paper.

2 Spread the potato slices out in a single layer on a nonstick baking tray and bake in the heated oven for 20 minutes. Turn the potatoes over and cook for about 20 minutes more, or until golden brown, tender in the centre and slightly puffed.

Two-potato cake

SERVES 4
PREPARATION TIME: 15 minutes
COOKING TIME: 30 minutes

8fl oz (225ml) dry cider
⅛ level teaspoon salt
⅛ level teaspoon ground cloves
Freshly ground black pepper

1oz (30g) polyunsaturated margarine, melted
1lb (450g) baking potatoes, peeled and thinly sliced
12oz (340g) sweet potatoes, peeled and thinly sliced
2 level tablespoons snipped fresh chives

1 Pour the cider into a saucepan, sprinkle in the salt and cloves, and season with pepper. Boil gently for about 5 minutes, until the cider is reduced by half, then set aside.

2 Brush a deep nonstick frying pan about 8in (20cm) in diameter with melted margarine. Cover the bottom of the pan with a third of the potatoes, then trickle over them 1 teaspoon of the margarine and 1½ tablespoons of the cider. Cover the potatoes with half the sweet potatoes and trickle on 1 teaspoon of the margarine and 1½ tablespoons of the cider. Repeat the layers, then finish with the remaining potatoes and trickle on the rest of the margarine and cider.

3 Cook the potato cake for about 5 minutes over a moderate heat, until it starts to sizzle, then turn down the heat, cover and simmer for a further 20 minutes.

4 Take the lid off the pan, increase the heat and cook for about 5 minutes, until the potatoes are tender and all the liquid has been absorbed. Shake the pan frequently to prevent the potatoes from sticking.

5 Cover the pan with a large, warmed heatproof plate. Protecting your hands with oven gloves, turn pan and plate over together to turn out the cake. If one or two potato slices stick to the pan, lift them out carefully and put them in place on the cake. Put the cake under a hot grill to give it a crisp finish. Sprinkle on the chives just before serving.

Layers of sweet potato add a musky scent and contrasting texture to this potato cake. A basting of cider flavoured with cloves, melds the layers and brings out the subtle fruity flavour.

Grated lemon rind gives these spinach balls a delicate citrus flavour, while basil-flavoured tomato sauce completes an attractive side dish.

Spinach balls in tomato sauce

ONE SERVING	
CALORIES 205	
TOTAL FAT 9g	
SATURATED FAT 2g	
CARBOHYDRATES 17g	
ADDED SUGAR 0	
FIBRE 7g	
SODIUM 450mg	

TIP
To cool the spinach quickly, spread it in a shallow heatproof dish and stand it in a baking tin of cold water. Change the water after 2 minutes.

SERVES 4
PREPARATION TIME: 20 minutes, plus 20 minutes to cool and refrigerate
COOKING TIME: 30 minutes
OVEN: Preheat to 180°C (350°F, gas mark 4)

1 ½ tablespoons olive oil
2 medium onions, peeled and finely chopped
2lb (900g) fresh spinach, trimmed, washed and chopped, or 1lb (450g) frozen spinach, thawed
4 cloves garlic, peeled and crushed
2oz (60g) wholemeal breadcrumbs
Finely grated rind of 1 lemon
½ oz (15g) grated Parmesan cheese
1 egg, size 2, beaten
Freshly ground black pepper
14oz (400g) tinned tomatoes, rubbed through a sieve
2 level tablespoons chopped fresh basil

1 Heat 1 tablespoon of the oil in a wide saucepan and cook half the onion in it over a moderate heat for 5 minutes. Add the spinach and half the garlic, and cook for 2-3 minutes,

covered. Uncover, raise the heat and stir for 2 minutes, or until the liquid has evaporated.

2 Cool for 5 minutes, then mix in the breadcrumbs, lemon rind, Parmesan and egg. Season with pepper and divide into 16 portions. Shape into balls and put in an oiled ovenproof dish. Cover and refrigerate for 15 minutes.

3 Meanwhile, heat the remaining oil in a medium saucepan and cook the rest of the onion in it over a moderate heat for 5 minutes. Stir in the remaining garlic, the tomatoes and half the basil. Season with pepper, cover and simmer for 30 minutes, stirring occasionally.

4 Cook the spinach balls, covered, in the heated oven for 30 minutes. Pour the tomato sauce over them and sprinkle with the remaining basil before serving.

This dish goes well with baked fish or roast turkey breast.

Sharp lemon juice and savoury garlic are suitably robust partners for the assertive flavour of spinach, and the combination makes a lively side dish for a light summer meal.

TIP
Blanching the spinach rids it of excess bitterness and helps it to keep its rich green colour during cooking.

Sautéed spinach with lemon and garlic

SERVES 4
PREPARATION TIME: 20 minutes
COOKING TIME: 10 minutes

1½ lb (680g) fresh spinach, trimmed and washed
1½ teaspoons olive oil
1 medium onion, peeled and finely chopped
1 large clove garlic, thinly sliced lengthways
Freshly ground mixed peppercorns
2 teaspoons lemon juice

1 Blanch the spinach in a pan of boiling unsalted water for 1 minute, then rinse with cold water and drain, pressing with a wooden spoon to remove as much liquid as possible.

2 Heat the oil in a nonstick saucepan and cook the onion and garlic in it, uncovered, over a moderate heat for about 5 minutes. Add the spinach, cover and cook for about 4 minutes, stirring frequently.

3 Season the spinach with pepper and the lemon juice, and toss well. Turn it into a warm dish and serve at once.

For a richer dish, you can leave out the lemon juice, season the spinach with freshly grated nutmeg and stir in 2 level tablespoons of Greek yoghurt just before serving. This goes particularly well with steamed or grilled fish.

ONE SERVING
CALORIES 60
TOTAL FAT 3g
SATURATED FAT 0
CARBOHYDRATES 5g
ADDED SUGAR 0
FIBRE 4g
SODIUM 205mg

Spinach and rice cakes

ONE SERVING	
CALORIES 245	
TOTAL FAT 5g	
SATURATED FAT 2g	
CARBOHYDRATES 46g	
ADDED SUGAR 0	
FIBRE 3g	
SODIUM 150mg	

Sweet-tasting water chestnuts give these upturned speckled cups of astringent spinach and plump rice a slight crunch and a touch of the exotic.

SERVES 4
PREPARATION TIME: 10 minutes
COOKING TIME: 20 minutes

7oz (200g) long grain rice
1lb (450g) fresh spinach, trimmed and washed
½ oz (15g) slightly salted butter
2oz (60g) water chestnuts, finely chopped
2 tablespoons lemon juice
Freshly ground black pepper

1 Cook the rice (see p.17).

2 Meanwhile, put the spinach in a saucepan without water. Cover and cook over a low heat for about 5 minutes, until softened.

3 Pour the spinach into a colander, press out as much liquid as possible with a wooden spoon, then chop the spinach finely. Melt the butter in the same saucepan and reheat the cooked spinach in the butter over a gentle heat for 1-2 minutes, stirring continuously.

4 Mix the spinach with the rice, water chestnuts and lemon juice, and season with pepper. Divide the mixture between four lightly oiled dariole moulds and press it down, or press all the mixture into an oiled shallow dish. Leave to stand for 1 minute, then turn out upside-down onto a warmed serving dish.

You can use 10oz (275g) of frozen leaf spinach instead of fresh spinach. Cook it gently without any water until it is completely thawed, and break it up in the pan with a wooden spoon before turning it into a sieve or colander to press out the liquid.

Swede, carrot and potato purée

SERVES 4
PREPARATION TIME: 15 minutes
COOKING TIME: 35 minutes

2 teaspoons olive oil
1 small onion, peeled and thinly sliced
2 cloves garlic, peeled and crushed
2 medium carrots, peeled and thinly sliced
1lb (450g) swede, peeled, quartered
and thinly sliced
1 bay leaf
8oz (225g) potatoes, peeled and thinly sliced
½ pint (285ml) vegetable or chicken stock
(see p.19)
1 level tablespoon chopped fresh parsley

1 Heat the oil in a large, heavy-based saucepan and put in the onion, garlic, carrots, swede and bay leaf. Cover and cook over a low heat for about 8 minutes, or until the vegetables just begin to soften.

2 Mix in the potatoes, pour in the stock and cook, covered, over a moderate heat for about 20 minutes, until the vegetables are tender and almost all the stock has been absorbed. Discard the bay leaf.

3 Blend the vegetables in a food processor for 10-15 seconds, or pass through a food mill or sieve, to make a smooth purée.

4 Return the purée to the pan and heat gently for 2-3 minutes, stirring all the time. Turn it into a heated serving dish and scatter the parsley over the top.

ONE SERVING	
CALORIES	90
TOTAL FAT	2g
SATURATED FAT	0
CARBOHYDRATES	16g
ADDED SUGAR	0
FIBRE	3g
SODIUM	25mg

Peppery swede gives this smooth warming winter combination its distinctive character and, along with the carrot, creates its glowing colour.

The sharpness of the apples makes a mouthwatering contrast to the sweetness of the potatoes in this stylish, unusual dish which is an ideal accompaniment to serve with pork.

TIP
Use Cox-type or Granny Smith apples. Their strong, sharp flavour and crisp flesh give the best taste and texture in this dish.

ONE SERVING
....
CALORIES 130
....
TOTAL FAT 3g
....
SATURATED FAT 1g
....
CARBOHYDRATES 26g
....
ADDED SUGAR 0
....
FIBRE 3g
....
SODIUM 70mg

Sweet potatoes with apples

SERVES 4
PREPARATION TIME: 10 minutes
COOKING TIME: 40 minutes
OVEN: Preheat to 190°C (375°F, gas mark 5)

½ oz (15g) polyunsaturated margarine
1lb (450g) sweet potatoes, peeled and cut diagonally into thin slices
8oz (225g) dessert apples, peeled, cored and thinly sliced into rings
¼ level teaspoon freshly grated nutmeg

1 Grease a shallow, ovenproof dish with a little of the margarine. Arrange half the potatoes overlapping in the dish and cover with the apple rings. Arrange the remaining potato slices on top, dot with the remaining margarine and sprinkle with the nutmeg.

2 Cover and bake in the heated oven for 30 minutes. Uncover and bake for 10 minutes more, or until the potatoes are tender and golden brown on top.

A scattering of crisp breadcrumbs covers the juicy layers of tomato slices, which are sandwiched with a lively mixture of onion and herbs.

Tomato gratin

ONE SERVING

CALORIES 70

TOTAL FAT 3g

SATURATED FAT 0

CARBOHYDRATES 9g

ADDED SUGAR 0

FIBRE 2g

SODIUM 75mg

SERVES 4
PREPARATION TIME: 5 minutes
COOKING TIME: 35 minutes
OVEN: Preheat to 190°C (375°F, gas mark 5)

½ level teaspoon each dried basil and dried thyme
Freshly ground black pepper
1lb (450g) ripe tomatoes, sliced
1 small onion, peeled and finely chopped
1oz (30g) wholemeal breadcrumbs
2 teaspoons olive oil
1 level tablespoon chopped fresh basil or chives
to garnish

1 Mix the dried basil and thyme together and season with pepper.

2 Cover the base of a shallow, ovenproof dish with a third of the tomatoes. Sprinkle a third of the herb mixture and half the onion on top. Repeat, then lay the remaining tomatoes on top. Scatter with the breadcrumbs and the rest of the herbs, and trickle the oil over the top.

3 Bake in the heated oven for 30 minutes, or until the tomatoes are tender and the crumbs browned. Sprinkle with basil or chives to serve.

Mustard-glazed turnips

SERVES 4
PREPARATION TIME: 5 minutes
COOKING TIME: 15 minutes

1lb (450g) small turnips, peeled and trimmed
Sprig of fresh rosemary
7fl oz (200ml) vegetable stock (see p.19)
2 level teaspoons whole-grain mustard
½ level teaspoon soft brown sugar
Sprigs of fresh thyme or rosemary to garnish

1 Put the turnips, rosemary and stock in a heavy-based saucepan and bring to the boil. Turn down the heat and simmer, covered, for about 10 minutes, or until just tender.

2 Stir in the mustard and sugar, and increase the heat. Boil gently for about 5 minutes, stirring frequently, until the liquid has reduced and the turnips are evenly coated with the mustard glaze. Take care not to let the glaze burn or it will taste bitter.

3 Turn into a warmed serving dish and garnish with the sprigs of thyme or rosemary.

Use turnips about the size of golf balls, or less, if possible. If they are larger, cut them into halves or quarters. You can prepare carrots and parsnips in the same way, cutting them into large chunks to cook.

ONE SERVING	
CALORIES	25
TOTAL FAT	1g
SATURATED FAT	0
CARBOHYDRATES	5g
ADDED SUGAR	1g
FIBRE	2g
SODIUM	55mg

The subtly peppery taste of turnips is matched by the mustard glaze in a dish that makes a fine complement for roasts of red meat or game.

SIDE SALADS

Salad days can fall on any day of the year now that most fresh vegetables are in the shops all the year round. Forget about limp lettuce and insipid tomatoes; salads can be much more interesting. Light and crunchy green salads, crisped in the refrigerator and tossed in a little low-fat dressing make the perfect accompaniment to main dishes, while a variety of raw and cooked vegetables can become almost an appetising meal on their own, especially when they include some meat, fish, pasta or cheese.

Artichoke, broccoli and cheese salad

ONE SERVING	
CALORIES	95
TOTAL FAT	6g
SATURATED FAT	2g
CARBOHYDRATES	6g
ADDED SUGAR	0
FIBRE	3g
SODIUM	55mg

SERVES 4
PREPARATION TIME: 20 minutes
COOKING TIME: 5 minutes

4oz (115g) Jerusalem artichokes, peeled and thinly sliced
1 teaspoon lemon juice
8oz (225g) broccoli, trimmed and divided into florets

1 tablespoon virgin olive oil
1½ teaspoons balsamic vinegar or red wine vinegar
1 level tablespoon fresh tarragon leaves, or 1 level teaspoon dried tarragon
Freshly ground black pepper
6 cherry tomatoes, cut in half
6oz (175g) tinned artichoke hearts, well rinsed, drained and cut in half
1oz (30g) mozzarella cheese, cut into small cubes

Jerusalem and globe artichokes, different in texture but similar in taste, blend with sweet tomatoes and gentle mozzarella to mellow the broccoli.

1 Cook the Jerusalem artichoke slices in unsalted boiling water, with the lemon juice added, for 2-3 minutes, until just becoming tender. Rinse in a colander under cold water and drain well.

2 Meanwhile, steam the broccoli for about 4 minutes, until slightly softened but still crisp. Rinse in a colander under cold running water and drain well.

3 Combine the oil with the vinegar and tarragon, and season with pepper. Gently stir in the broccoli, tomatoes, artichoke hearts, Jerusalem artichokes and mozzarella, taking care not to break the broccoli florets.

Serve the salad at once, or cover it and refrigerate for up to 1 hour if more convenient; turn the salad again just before serving. It goes particularly well with grilled fish.

Aubergine salad

SERVES 4
PREPARATION TIME: 15 minutes, plus 1 hour to stand and 5 hours to cool and refrigerate
COOKING TIME: 30 minutes
OVEN: Preheat to 200°C (400°F, gas mark 6)

ONE SERVING

CALORIES 100

TOTAL FAT 8g

SATURATED FAT 1g

CARBOHYDRATES 5g

ADDED SUGAR 0

FIBRE 3g

SODIUM 250mg

Baking gives aubergines a melting texture and full, nutty flavour. This is enhanced by the oil and herb dressing which penetrates the aubergine fans.

8 small aubergines, about 1¼ lb (550g) together
½ level teaspoon salt
8oz (225g) ripe tomatoes, skinned, de-seeded and diced
3 cloves garlic, peeled and crushed
1 level tablespoon chopped fresh parsley
1 level tablespoon chopped fresh coriander
6 tablespoons water
Freshly ground black pepper
2 tablespoons virgin olive oil
Sprigs of fresh coriander to garnish

1 Slice the aubergines thinly from the tip towards the stalk, leaving the slices joined at the stalk end. Leave the stalk in place but trim it of any prickly bristles.

2 Put the aubergines in a wide dish, sprinkle with the salt and leave for 1 hour for the bitter juices to be drawn out. Meanwhile, mix the tomatoes with the garlic, parsley and coriander.

3 Rinse the aubergines well with cold water and pat dry with kitchen paper. Arrange them close together in an ovenproof dish and spread a little of the tomato mixture between the slices. Pour in the water and season with pepper. Trickle the oil over the aubergines. Cover and cook in the heated oven for 30 minutes or until soft, basting occasionally.

4 Remove from the oven, leave to cool, then refrigerate for 4 hours while the flavour develops. Serve garnished with the coriander.

When small aubergines are unavailable, use four medium ones. Halve them lengthways, then place cut side down and slice thinly as for small aubergines.

Avocado, bean and cucumber salad

ONE SERVING

CALORIES 155

TOTAL FAT 13g

SATURATED FAT 2g

CARBOHYDRATES 6g

ADDED SUGAR 0

FIBRE 5g

SODIUM 65mg

The creamy texture and subtle taste of avocado contrast with crisp cucumber and beans in a salad that is an ideal partner for prawns.

SERVES 4
PREPARATION TIME: 20 minutes
COOKING TIME: 5 minutes

6oz (175g) shelled or frozen broad beans
6oz (175g) bobby or pencil beans, trimmed and cut into short lengths
¼ cucumber, peeled, halved lengthways and sliced
1 tablespoon lemon juice
1 level teaspoon Dijon mustard
1 tablespoon virgin olive oil
1 level tablespoon chopped fresh parsley
1 level tablespoon chopped fresh chervil
Freshly ground black pepper
1 ripe avocado halved, stoned, peeled and quartered
Parsley sprigs to garnish

1 Cook the broad beans and bobby or pencil beans in unsalted boiling water for 4 minutes, until just tender. Rinse, drain and cool slightly.

2 Pop the inner part of the broad beans from the outer skins by gently squeezing each bean between a thumb and forefinger. Put all the beans into a bowl with the cucumber.

3 Whisk the lemon juice, mustard, oil and herbs together, and season with pepper. Pour over the vegetables and toss well.

4 Cut the avocado quarters across into slices and stir into the salad. Garnish with parsley sprigs and serve at once.

TIP
Prepare the avocado and mix it into the salad just before serving. If it is prepared too soon, it will discolour.

Green bean and courgette salad

ONE SERVING

CALORIES 55

TOTAL FAT 4g

SATURATED FAT 1g

CARBOHYDRATES 3g

ADDED SUGAR 0

FIBRE 2g

SODIUM 5mg

SERVES 4
PREPARATION TIME: 25 minutes
COOKING TIME: 2 minutes

8oz (225g) fine green beans, trimmed and halved
1 tablespoon virgin olive oil
1 clove garlic, peeled and crushed
½ level teaspoon dried tarragon
Freshly ground black pepper
1 medium courgette, cut into matchstick strips
1 small red onion, peeled and chopped
1½ teaspoons tarragon-flavoured vinegar

1 Cook the beans, in just enough unsalted boiling water to cover, for 2-3 minutes, until slightly softened but still crisp. Pour into a colander, rinse with cold water, then drain.

2 Mix the oil, garlic and tarragon, and season with pepper. Stir in the beans, courgette and onion, and turn until coated. Serve at once sprinkled with the vinegar or, if you prefer, cover and chill in the refrigerator for 1 hour; toss the salad and sprinkle with the vinegar just before serving.

Mixed bean salad

Beans are versatile ingredients for salads. Fresh green beans are tossed with courgettes in tarragon dressing (left), while dried beans make a colourful mix with celery, red pepper and firm button mushrooms.

SERVES 4
PREPARATION TIME: 10 minutes
COOKING TIME: 5-8 minutes

1 large red pepper
2oz (60g) fine green beans, trimmed and halved
1 small red onion, peeled and thinly sliced,
or 2 spring onions, trimmed and thinly sliced
3oz (85g) cooked cannellini beans or black-eyed beans (see p.17)
3oz (85g) cooked flageolet beans (see p.17)
3oz (85g) cooked red kidney beans (see p.17)
2 sticks celery, trimmed and thinly sliced
2oz (60g) button mushrooms, wiped and sliced
1 tablespoon virgin olive oil
1 tablespoon lemon juice
1 level tablespoon chopped fresh parsley
Freshly ground black pepper

1 Grill the red pepper under a moderate heat, turning often, for 5-8 minutes, until the skin blisters. Put the pepper in a bowl, cover with a damp cloth and leave for about 5 minutes.

2 Meanwhile, cook the green beans, in just enough unsalted boiling water to cover, for 2-3 minutes, or until slightly softened but still crisp. Rinse with cold water and drain.

3 Peel and de-seed the pepper, working over a bowl to catch any juices. Slice the pepper lengthways into strips.

4 Mix all the ingredients, including the pepper juice, and season with black pepper. Serve at once, or cover and chill in the refrigerator for 2 hours if preferred; mix again before serving.

Bean sprout salad

SERVES 4
PREPARATION TIME: 10 minutes, plus 1 hour
to refrigerate

ONE SERVING	
CALORIES 60	
TOTAL FAT 4g	
SATURATED FAT 0	
CARBOHYDRATES 4g	
ADDED SUGAR 0	
FIBRE 1g	
SODIUM 10mg	

1 tablespoon sesame or peanut oil
2 spring onions, trimmed and chopped
1 level teaspoon tomato purée (see p.16)
1 clove garlic, peeled and crushed
2 level teaspoons peeled and grated root ginger
8oz (225g) bean sprouts, rinsed and drained
1 small red pepper, de-seeded and thinly sliced
1½ teaspoons lemon juice
1½ teaspoons rice vinegar or white wine vinegar

1 Combine the oil, onions, tomato purée, garlic and ginger in a small saucepan, and stir over a low heat for about 1 minute, or until the mixture starts to bubble. Remove from the heat and leave the dressing until cold.

2 Mix the bean sprouts and red pepper, stir in the dressing and toss well. Cover and chill in the refrigerator for 1 hour, tossing occasionally.

3 Just before serving, stir in the lemon juice and vinegar, toss again and spoon the salad into a serving bowl.

Pickled beetroot salad

ONE SERVING	
CALORIES 70	
TOTAL FAT 0	
SATURATED FAT 0	
CARBOHYDRATES 14g	
ADDED SUGAR 0	
FIBRE 4g	
SODIUM 160mg	

SERVES 4
PREPARATION TIME: 20 minutes, plus 2 hours
to refrigerate
COOKING TIME: 1 hour 30 minutes

6 medium beetroots, about 1½ lb (680g) together,
washed and with tops trimmed to 1in (25mm)
4fl oz (115ml) water
4fl oz (115ml) cider vinegar
2 level teaspoons freshly grated horseradish
1 level teaspoon Dijon mustard
6 black peppercorns
4 cloves
1 bay leaf
2 spring onions, trimmed and chopped
1 level tablespoon chopped fresh dill or fennel fronds

1 Put the beetroots in a large, uncovered saucepan of unsalted boiling water and simmer them for 1 hour 30 minutes, or until tender. Drain and leave to cool. Top and tail and peel the beetroots. Cut them into slices and arrange the slices in a heatproof dish.

2 Bring the water, vinegar, horseradish, mustard, peppercorns, cloves and bay leaf to the boil. Pour the mixture over the beetroot slices and leave to cool. Cover and chill in the refrigerator for 2 hours.

3 Just before serving, remove the bay leaf and cloves, and sprinkle the salad with the spring onions and dill or fennel.

TIP
Pick beetroots with undamaged skin and avoid damage while washing and trimming, or colour will bleed out.

Italian-style bread and tomato salad

ONE SERVING	
CALORIES 260	
TOTAL FAT 13g	
SATURATED FAT 2g	
CARBOHYDRATES 30g	
ADDED SUGAR 0	
FIBRE 5g	
SODIUM 340mg	

SERVES 4
PREPARATION TIME: 20 minutes, plus 2-3 hours
to refrigerate

8oz (225g) stale wholemeal or white bread,
with crusts cut off
4 tablespoons water
4 large ripe tomatoes, skinned, de-seeded and diced
1 small cucumber, peeled and sliced
1 stick celery, trimmed and chopped
1 small onion, peeled and finely chopped
1 level teaspoon capers, rinsed and drained

1 large sprig fresh basil leaves, finely shredded
Freshly ground black pepper
3 tablespoons virgin olive oil
1 tablespoon lemon juice or wine vinegar
1 level tablespoon chopped celery leaves

1 Cut the bread into thick slices and spread them in a wide dish. Sprinkle with the water and leave to stand for 5-10 minutes.

2 Tear the bread into small pieces. Mix in the tomatoes, cucumber, celery, onion, capers and

Beetroot slices in a pungent mustard and horseradish marinade create a sweet and sour salad of vibrant colour. An Italian salad of bread and tomatoes (top), sharpened with capers and basil, makes unusual and delicious use of stale bread. Bean sprouts match the sweetness of red pepper in a low-calorie salad dressed in an Oriental style.

basil. Season with pepper and pour on the oil. Cover and put in the refrigerator for 2-3 hours for the bread to absorb the dressing.

3 Sprinkle the lemon juice or vinegar over the salad and spoon into a serving dish. Stir in the celery leaves just before serving.

Broccoli and sesame salad

ONE SERVING

CALORIES 105

TOTAL FAT 6g

SATURATED FAT 1g

CARBOHYDRATES 4g

ADDED SUGAR 1g

FIBRE 5g

SODIUM 200mg

SERVES 4
PREPARATION TIME: 15 minutes
COOKING TIME: 5 minutes

1½ lb (680g) broccoli, cut into small florets and
thick stems cut off, peeled and coarsely chopped
2 teaspoons soy sauce
2 tablespoons white wine vinegar
2 teaspoons sesame oil or peanut oil
½ teaspoon clear honey
1 level tablespoon sesame seeds, lightly toasted

1 Steam the broccoli for 5 minutes, or
until cooked through but still firm. Turn it
into a serving dish.

2 Mix the soy sauce, vinegar, oil and honey,
pour the mixture over the broccoli and
toss well. Sprinkle the sesame seeds over the
broccoli and serve.

Marinated carrots

ONE SERVING

CALORIES 70

TOTAL FAT 4g

SATURATED FAT 1g

CARBOHYDRATES 8g

ADDED SUGAR 0

FIBRE 2g

SODIUM 30mg

SERVES 4
PREPARATION TIME: 10 minutes, plus 24 hours
to marinate
COOKING TIME: 10 minutes

12oz (340g) young carrots, peeled and cut
into quarters lengthways
7fl oz (200ml) white wine vinegar
4fl oz (115ml) water
1 tablespoon virgin olive oil
2 garlic cloves, peeled and finely chopped
2 level tablespoons chopped fresh oregano,
or 1 level teaspoon dried oregano
Finely chopped carrot leaves or parsley to garnish

1 Cook the carrots in enough unsalted boiling
water to cover them, for about 8 minutes or
until cooked through but still firm. Drain, turn
into a heatproof bowl and set aside.

2 Meanwhile, pour the vinegar and water into
a small stainless steel or enamel saucepan and
bring to the boil. Boil rapidly, uncovered, until
the mixture is reduced by about a half.

3 Mix the oil, garlic and oregano into the
carrots, then stir in the vinegar. Leave until
cool, then cover and put in the refrigerator
for 24 hours.

4 Spoon the carrots into a serving dish
and scatter on the carrot leaves or parsley
before serving.

This sweet and sour dish is a good partner for
cold roast beef or pork.

> **TIP**
> *To give the
> marinade the
> best flavour, be
> sure to boil
> the vinegar. This
> gives it a much
> mellower taste.*

Cauliflower and mushroom salad

ONE SERVING

CALORIES 150

TOTAL FAT 13g

SATURATED FAT 2g

CARBOHYDRATES 4g

ADDED SUGAR 0

FIBRE 3g

SODIUM 20mg

SERVES 4
PREPARATION TIME: 25 minutes

8oz (225g) firm white cauliflower, divided
into florets
Chinese cabbage heart, washed, dried and
finely sliced
8 button mushrooms, wiped and thinly sliced
6 walnut halves, roughly chopped

3 level tablespoons low-fat natural yoghurt
1 teaspoon lemon juice
1½ level tablespoons chopped fresh chervil
or parsley
1 level teaspoon mustard seeds, crushed
1 tablespoon virgin olive oil
2 tablespoons water
Freshly ground black pepper

1 Wash the cauliflower and dry it thoroughly with kitchen paper. Cut the florets lengthways into thin slices.

2 Put the cauliflower, cabbage, mushrooms and walnuts in a salad bowl.

3 Whisk together the yoghurt, lemon juice, chervil or parsley, mustard seeds, oil and water, and season with pepper.

4 Pour the dressing over the salad, mix gently to coat everything lightly, and serve.

Long marination allows tender carrots to absorb the tangy oregano and vinegar dressing. Tart mustard yoghurt gives a light coating to firm cauliflower and mushroom slices topped with walnuts (top). Broccoli is tossed in honeyed soy sauce and scattered with sesame seeds.

Celeriac salad

ONE SERVING

CALORIES 40

TOTAL FAT 2g

SATURATED FAT 1g

CARBOHYDRATES 4g

ADDED SUGAR 0

FIBRE 4g

SODIUM 90mg

SERVES 4
PREPARATION TIME: 15 minutes

Juice of ½ lemon
4 level tablespoons Greek yoghurt
½ level teaspoon mustard powder
¼ level teaspoon caster sugar
12oz (340g) celeriac, peeled and shredded
or coarsely grated
1 small lettuce, washed, drained and chilled

1 Put the lemon juice, yoghurt, mustard and sugar into a large bowl and whisk to combine into a smooth dressing.

2 Mix the celeriac into the dressing, stirring well to coat it.

3 Line four individual salad bowls with lettuce leaves. Spoon the celeriac into the centre and serve at once.

TIP
Do not peel and shred the celeriac until the dressing is ready. Add it immediately to the dressing and stir frequently to avoid discoloration.

A creamy-textured mustard dressing makes a fiery companion for mildly peppery celeriac in a refreshing salad that is easy to prepare.

Citrus fruit and watercress salad

ONE SERVING

CALORIES 170

TOTAL FAT 11g

SATURATED FAT 1g

CARBOHYDRATES 12g

ADDED SUGAR 0

FIBRE 5g

SODIUM 30mg

SERVES 4
PREPARATION TIME: 30 minutes

2 pink grapefruits
2 oranges
1 small cos or iceberg lettuce, trimmed and washed
8oz (225g) watercress, washed and thick
stems removed
1 tablespoon red wine vinegar
2 teaspoons virgin olive oil
6 walnut halves, lightly toasted and
coarsely chopped

1 Using a small sharp knife, remove the peel and all the white pith from the grapefruits and oranges. Hold the fruit over a bowl to catch the juice while you slice between the membrane and the flesh at each side of every segment to cut it free.

2 Put the lettuce leaves into a salad bowl with the watercress. Drain the juice from the grapefruit and orange segments and set it aside. Add the segments to the lettuce and watercress and mix gently.

3 Mix the vinegar and oil with 2 tablespoons of the grapefruit and orange juice. Pour it over the lettuce and watercress, and toss well. Sprinkle on the walnuts and serve at once.

Coleslaw

TIP
*Give the coleslaw
2-3 hours to develop
and mingle the
flavours but do not
leave it longer. The
cabbages lose their
crispness and
release a rather
bitter juice into the
dressing.*

SERVES 4
PREPARATION TIME: 15 minutes,
plus 2-3 hours to refrigerate

6 level tablespoons low-fat natural yoghurt
½ small onion, peeled and grated
2 level teaspoons mustard powder mixed with water
¼ level teaspoon caraway seeds
⅛ level teaspoon dried dill weed
Freshly ground black pepper
4oz (115g) white cabbage, finely shredded
4oz (115g) red cabbage, finely shredded
1 small carrot, peeled and coarsely grated

*¼ small green pepper, de-seeded and sliced
lengthways into thin strips*
*¼ small red pepper, de-seeded, and sliced
lengthways into thin strips*

1 Combine the yoghurt, onion, mustard,
caraway and dill in a large dish, and season with
pepper. Mix in the white and red cabbage, the
carrot and the peppers, stirring thoroughly to
coat everything with the dressing.

2 Cover the dish and chill in the refrigerator
for 2-3 hours, stirring occasionally.

*Sweet oranges and sharper grapefruits refresh
a green salad and add to the zesty dressing,
while mustard and caraway flavour a coleslaw.*

Cottage cheese and fruit salad

SERVES 4
PREPARATION TIME: 30 minutes, plus 1 hour
to refrigerate

2 level teaspoons cornflour
2 level teaspoons paprika
1 tablespoon lemon juice
Juice of 3 large oranges
1lb (450g) fresh pineapple, skin, core and
woody eyes removed, flesh cut into cubes
2 oranges, peeled, pith removed, cut into chunks
2 kiwi fruits, peeled and thinly sliced
8oz (225g) fresh strawberries, hulled and sliced
12 small cos lettuce leaves, washed and chilled
10oz (275g) cottage cheese

ONE SERVING

CALORIES 215

TOTAL FAT 3g

SATURATED FAT 2g

CARBOHYDRATES 35g

ADDED SUGAR 0

FIBRE 3g

SODIUM 280mg

1 In a stainless steel or enamel saucepan, blend the cornflour and paprika to a smooth cream with the lemon juice, then stir in the orange juice. Stir the mixture as you bring it to the boil over a moderate heat. Simmer the sauce for 2-3 minutes, still continuing to stir, until it has thickened slightly.

2 Pour the sauce into a bowl, leave it to cool, then cover and refrigerate for about 1 hour.

3 Meanwhile, put the pineapple, oranges, kiwi fruits and strawberries into a large bowl, cover and refrigerate.

4 Pour the cold orange sauce over the chilled fruit and mix gently. Line individual salad bowls with the lettuce leaves, spoon cottage cheese into the middle of each bowl and encircle it with fruit and sauce.

The sweetness and fragrance of fresh fruit is balanced by the slight acidity of cottage cheese to make a light and colourful summer salad.

Crisp, cool cucumber, juicy melon and fragrant strawberries glisten in a lemon dressing, perfumed with the mild citrus scent of coriander.

Cucumber and fruit salad

ONE SERVING	
CALORIES	80
TOTAL FAT	4g
SATURATED FAT	1g
CARBOHYDRATES	9g
ADDED SUGAR	0
FIBRE	1g
SODIUM	20mg

SERVES 4
PREPARATION TIME: 15 minutes

1 small honeydew melon, halved and de-seeded
1 medium cucumber, scored lengthways with a fork
and thinly sliced
5oz (150g) strawberries, hulled and quartered
2 tablespoons lemon juice
1 tablespoon virgin olive oil
⅛ level teaspoon cayenne pepper
2 level tablespoons chopped fresh coriander,
or ½ level teaspoon ground coriander
Sprigs of fresh mint or coriander to garnish

1 Slice the melon into wedges and cut the flesh away from the skin. Cut the flesh into cubes and mix it with the cucumber and strawberries in a salad bowl.

2 Combine the lemon juice and oil with the cayenne pepper and chopped or ground coriander. Pour the dressing over the fruits and turn to coat everything. Garnish with the mint or coriander sprigs.

You can use any other small ripe melon to make this refreshing dish.

317

Spicy cucumber and red pepper salad

SERVES 4
PREPARATION TIME: 10 minutes

ONE SERVING	
CALORIES	45
TOTAL FAT	3g
SATURATED FAT	0
CARBOHYDRATES	3g
ADDED SUGAR	0
FIBRE	1g
SODIUM	20mg

4 level tablespoons low-fat natural or Greek yoghurt
2 teaspoons sesame or peanut oil
1 tablespoon cider vinegar
½ level teaspoon peeled and grated root ginger,
or ¼ level teaspoon ground ginger
¼ level teaspoon ground coriander
1 large cucumber, halved, quartered lengthways,
de-seeded and cut into thin strips
1 small red pepper, de-seeded and cut into strips
¼ level teaspoon cumin seeds

1 Blend the yoghurt, oil, vinegar, ginger and coriander to make the dressing.

2 Mix the cucumber with the pepper in a salad bowl, spoon on the dressing, sprinkle with the cumin seeds and serve at once. If you prefer, mix the salad thoroughly and chill for 1-2 hours in the refrigerator before serving.

Fennel and cabbage salad

SERVES 4
PREPARATION TIME: 20 minutes,
plus 15 minutes to stand

ONE SERVING	
CALORIES	65
TOTAL FAT	5g
SATURATED FAT	1g
CARBOHYDRATES	5g
ADDED SUGAR	0
FIBRE	4g
SODIUM	15mg

2 tablespoons cider vinegar
1 tablespoon virgin olive oil
1 tablespoon white wine
1 level tablespoon cumin seeds, crushed
2 level tablespoons chopped fresh parsley
Freshly ground black pepper
1 medium bulb fennel
12oz (340g) white cabbage, trimmed and
finely shredded
Fennel or dill fronds to garnish

1 Whisk the vinegar, oil and white wine with the cumin seeds and parsley in a salad bowl.

2 Trim off the top and root from the fennel bulb. Discard the outer fennel leaves and cut the bulb in half lengthways. Cut across the halves to give fine slices and put the slices into the dressing.

3 Add the cabbage to the salad, season with pepper and toss the salad thoroughly to combine everything.

4 Cover the salad and leave it to stand for 15 minutes. Garnish it with the fennel or dill fronds just before serving.

This crunchy salad with its slight flavour of aniseed goes particularly well with fish and pasta dishes.

> **TIP**
> *Put the fennel slices into the dressing as you cut them so they do not discolour.*

Fusilli salad with peppers and basil

SERVES 4
PREPARATION TIME: 15 minutes,
plus 30 minutes to stand
COOKING TIME: 10 minutes

ONE SERVING	
CALORIES	225
TOTAL FAT	4g
SATURATED FAT	2g
CARBOHYDRATES	40g
ADDED SUGAR	0
FIBRE	3g
SODIUM	210mg

6oz (175g) fusilli
1 large red pepper
1 large yellow pepper
1 clove garlic, peeled and finely chopped
10 basil leaves, finely shredded
½ level teaspoon finely chopped fresh thyme
2 level teaspoons capers, rinsed and drained
1oz (30g) Parmesan cheese, finely chopped
or grated
2 level tablespoons Greek yoghurt
1 level tablespoon seedless raisins
½ level teaspoon paprika
1 level tablespoon snipped chives
Basil sprigs and whole chive stems to garnish

1 Cook the fusilli (see p.18), and rinse with cold water. Drain thoroughly and set aside.

TIP
*If you have time,
soak the raisins
in 2 tablespoons of
cold water for
1 hour before
adding them to the
salad. Soaking
makes them plump
and juicy.*

2 Grill the peppers under a moderate heat for 10 minutes, turning them frequently until all sides are blistered. Put the peppers in a small bowl, cover with a clean damp cloth and leave for 5 minutes.

3 Peel and de-seed the peppers, working over a bowl to catch the juices. Blend the peppers and their juices into a purée, using a food processor or food mill.

4 Mix the garlic, shredded basil, thyme, capers and Parmesan into the purée, then stir in the yoghurt and raisins.

5 Put the fusilli into a serving bowl, pour on the dressing and mix well until all the spirals are coated with dressing. Sprinkle with the paprika and chives, and garnish with the basil sprigs and chive stems. Cover and leave to stand for 30 minutes before serving.

Aniseed-scented fennel offers a contrasting flavour to the cabbage but matches its texture in a crisp salad (below left). Fusilli — spirals of pasta — add body and raisins sweeten a well-seasoned red pepper purée. Spiced yoghurt with high notes of ginger, coriander and cumin tops colourful strips of cucumber and red pepper.

Greek salad

ONE SERVING
CALORIES 120
TOTAL FAT 8g
  SATURATED FAT 3g
CARBOHYDRATES 4g
ADDED SUGAR 0
FIBRE 2g
SODIUM 400mg

SERVES 4
PREPARATION TIME: 20 minutes

½ cos lettuce, trimmed and washed
8oz (225g) young spinach leaves, trimmed
and washed
½ small cucumber, diced
2oz (60g) cottage cheese
2oz (60g) fetta cheese, rinsed with cold water
and cut into small pieces
2 level tablespoons chopped fresh mint,
or 1½ level teaspoons dried mint
1 teaspoon virgin olive oil

1 teaspoon lemon juice
1 clove garlic, peeled and crushed
2 medium black olives, stoned and sliced
Freshly ground black pepper

1 Dry the lettuce and spinach leaves gently with kitchen paper and tear them into small pieces. Mix with the cucumber, cottage cheese, fetta and mint in a salad bowl.

2 Blend the oil with the lemon juice and garlic, mix in the olives and season with pepper. Pour the dressing over the salad, toss and serve.

Lamb's lettuce and beetroot salad

ONE SERVING
CALORIES 65
TOTAL FAT 4g
  SATURATED FAT 1g
CARBOHYDRATES 5g
ADDED SUGAR 0
FIBRE 2g
SODIUM 40mg

SERVES 4
PREPARATION TIME: 15 minutes

8oz (225g) cooked beetroots, peeled and sliced
3 tablespoons red wine vinegar
1 tablespoon virgin olive oil
1 clove garlic, peeled and finely chopped
Freshly ground black pepper
8oz (225g) lamb's lettuce, trimmed and washed

1 Put the beetroot in a glass bowl, sprinkle the vinegar on it, cover and leave to stand for 10 minutes. Drain off and discard the vinegar.

2 Combine the oil and garlic in a salad bowl and season with pepper. Mix in the lamb's lettuce and beetroot, and serve immediately.

Serve with striped Italian bread for colour.

Oriental mushroom salad

ONE SERVING
CALORIES 50
TOTAL FAT 4g
  SATURATED FAT 0
CARBOHYDRATES 3g
  ADDED SUGAR 2g
FIBRE 1g
SODIUM 190mg

SERVES 4
PREPARATION TIME: 10 minutes,
plus 20 minutes to refrigerate

1 clove garlic, cut in half
1 teaspoon clear honey
2 teaspoons soy sauce
¼ level teaspoon ground ginger
2 teaspoons red wine vinegar
2 teaspoons sesame or peanut oil
8oz (225g) button mushrooms, wiped and trimmed
1 small yellow pepper, de-seeded and diced
8 radishes, trimmed, washed and sliced
2 level teaspoons chopped fresh coriander or parsley
1 level teaspoon sesame seeds

1 Rub the inside of a large bowl with the half-cloves of garlic. Whisk the honey, soy sauce, ginger, vinegar and oil in the bowl.

2 Slice the mushrooms very thinly and add to the dressing with the pepper and radishes. Toss well, cover and refrigerate for 20 minutes.

3 Spoon the salad onto a serving plate, sprinkle with the coriander or parsley and the sesame seeds, and serve at once.

The slight bitterness of lamb's lettuce makes it a perfect foil for crimson slices of sweet beetroot. Spinach and lettuce form a leafy base for mild cheeses mixed with salty olives (far right). Honey, ginger and soy sauce give a taste of the East to crisp sliced and diced vegetables.

Pasta salad with salmon and spinach

ONE SERVING

CALORIES 375

TOTAL FAT 14g

SATURATED FAT 3g

CARBOHYDRATES 43g

ADDED SUGAR 0

FIBRE 3g

SODIUM 265mg

TIP
Use only fresh, young and tender spinach leaves as they have the sweetest flavour. The bitterness of larger leaves would dominate the flavour of the salmon.

SERVES 4
PREPARATION TIME: 25 minutes
COOKING TIME: 10 minutes

7oz (200g) fusilli
2 pints (1.15 litres) water
1 small onion, peeled and chopped
½ lemon, quartered
1 sprig parsley
10oz (275g) salmon steaks
1 clove garlic, peeled and crushed
1 level tablespoon snipped chives
½ level teaspoon fennel seeds, crushed
4oz (115g) low-fat natural yoghurt
1 tablespoon virgin olive oil
½ level teaspoon paprika
7oz (200g) tender young spinach leaves, washed, patted dry and finely shredded
1 medium courgette, trimmed and thinly sliced

1 Cook the fusilli (see p.18), rinse with cold water and drain well.

2 Pour the water into a large frying pan with the onion, lemon and parsley. Bring to a simmer then put in the salmon and poach gently for about 5 minutes, or until the fish flakes easily and is opaque all through. Lift the salmon out of the pan, remove the skin and bones and flake the flesh coarsely. Leave to cool for 15 minutes.

3 Meanwhile, combine the garlic, chives, fennel seeds, yoghurt, oil and paprika in a salad bowl.

4 Mix the pasta with the spinach and courgette. Gently fold in the cold salmon, top with the yoghurt dressing and serve.

Lightly poached salmon makes an elegant contrast to crunchy courgette and tender young spinach. Spirals of pasta add body to this eye-catching salad, topped with a creamy yoghurt, chive and fennel dressing.

Pasta shells are the heart of this simple salad, which is flavoured with red onion and black olives and piled on a lacy base of frisée leaves.

Summer pasta salad

ONE SERVING

CALORIES 210

TOTAL FAT 5g

SATURATED FAT 1g

CARBOHYDRATES 37g

ADDED SUGAR 0

FIBRE 3g

SODIUM 175mg

SERVES 4
PREPARATION TIME: 15 minutes

6oz (175g) miniature pasta shells or macaroni
1 tablespoon virgin olive oil
4 level tablespoons chopped fresh basil or parsley
1 small red onion, peeled and finely chopped
Freshly ground black pepper
½ medium cucumber, cut into cubes
1 large beef tomato, skinned, de-seeded and chopped
4 black olives, stoned and thinly sliced
Small frisée lettuce, washed and dried

1 Cook the pasta (see p.18), rinse with cold water and drain well.

2 Combine the oil, basil or parsley and onion in a salad bowl, and season with pepper. Stir in the pasta until lightly coated.

3 Stir the cucumber and tomato into the pasta mixture and scatter on the olives.

4 Line four individual salad plates with the lettuce leaves and spoon a share of the pasta mixture onto each one.

Pineapple salad

SERVES 4
PREPARATION TIME: 25 minutes

ONE SERVING	
CALORIES 85	
TOTAL FAT 4g	
SATURATED FAT 1g	
CARBOHYDRATES 11g	
ADDED SUGAR 0	
FIBRE 2g	
SODIUM 10mg	

Mouthwatering chunks of pineapple add their unique sweet but tangy juiciness to a tomato and green pepper salad and create a refreshing, vividly coloured medley.

1 clove garlic, peeled and crushed
1 level teaspoon English mustard powder
1 tablespoon lemon juice
Freshly ground black pepper
1 tablespoon virgin olive oil
4 medium tomatoes
1 medium green pepper, quartered and de-seeded
½ medium pineapple
4 small sprigs mint or watercress to garnish

1 Blend the garlic and mustard, stir in the lemon juice and season with black pepper. Whisk in the oil vigorously until the dressing thickens slightly.

2 Drop the tomatoes and green pepper into boiling water for 1 minute, then rinse with cold water and drain.

3 Skin the tomatoes and cut them into thin wedges. Slice the pepper thinly. Turn the tomatoes and pepper gently in the dressing until coated.

4 Slice the pineapple into thick rings, cut off all the hard skin and prise out the woody 'eyes' with the tip of a knife. Cut the rings in half, trim out the hard centre and slice the flesh into chunks.

5 Mix the pineapple in with the tomatoes and pepper and garnish the dish with the sprigs of mint or watercress. Serve at once.

This sweet but sharp salad goes particularly well with ham and cold pork. You can use unsweetened tinned pineapple chunks instead of fresh pineapple, but the chunks need to be drained well on kitchen paper before being added to the salad.

TIP
Cut the pineapple and mix it into the salad just before serving. If added earlier, it releases too much juice and dilutes the dressing.

Potato, artichoke and red pepper salad

SERVES 4
PREPARATION TIME: 30 minutes,
plus 30 minutes to stand
COOKING TIME: 20 minutes

2 large globe artichokes
4 tablespoons fresh lemon juice
12oz (340g) new potatoes, scrubbed and
thickly sliced
1 large red pepper, halved and de-seeded
3½ oz (100g) set low-fat natural yoghurt
1 level teaspoon Dijon mustard
2 level tablespoons chopped fresh coriander
2 level teaspoons poppy seeds
Freshly ground black pepper
Coriander leaves to garnish

1 Break off the stalk from each artichoke,
flush with the base. Pull off the outer layers of
leaves, starting from the bottom, until you
reach the pale inner leaves, pulling each leaf
outwards and downwards until it snaps off.

2 Cut off the pointed top of each artichoke
about 1½ in (40mm) above the base, then trim
off the dark part from each artichoke base and
brush the bases with lemon juice.

3 Using a teaspoon or grapefruit knife, scrape
out and discard the hairy choke from the centre
of each artichoke. Trim off any remaining dark
green parts from the tops and brush the tops
with lemon juice.

4 Set aside two teaspoons of the lemon juice
and add the remainder to a saucepan of
unsalted boiling water. Cook the artichoke
hearts in it for about 15 minutes, or until
tender, then drain.

5 Meanwhile, steam the potato slices for
about 10 minutes, until tender, then cool.

6 While the potatoes cook, grill the pepper
halves, skin side up, under a moderate heat for
5-6 minutes, until they blister. Put them in a
bowl and cover with a clean damp cloth.

7 Combine the yoghurt, mustard, chopped
coriander, poppy seeds and reserved lemon
juice, and season with pepper. Slice the
artichoke hearts, mix with the potato slices
and pour the dressing over them.

8 Peel the skin off the pepper, slice the flesh
into strips and scatter on top of the salad.
Cover and stand in a cool place for 30 minutes.
Garnish with the coriander leaves to serve.

ONE SERVING	
CALORIES	95
TOTAL FAT	2g
SATURATED FAT	1g
CARBOHYDRATES	20g
ADDED SUGAR	0
FIBRE	2g
SODIUM	90mg

Tender slices of artichoke and potato served with an
aromatic mustard and coriander dressing are topped
with brilliant strips of smoky grilled pepper.

Prawn and fetta salad

SERVES 4
PREPARATION TIME: 20 minutes
COOKING TIME: 5 minutes

ONE SERVING	
CALORIES	165
TOTAL FAT	7g
SATURATED FAT	2g
CARBOHYDRATES	7g
ADDED SUGAR	0
FIBRE	2g
SODIUM	235mg

TIP
Always rinse fetta cheese well under cold running water before using it. This mild sheep's-milk cheese is preserved in brine – which greatly increases its salt content if not rinsed off.

1 large red pepper, halved and de-seeded
1lb (450g) frozen uncooked freshwater prawns, thawed, shelled and de-veined
3 spring onions, trimmed and thinly sliced
½ medium cucumber, peeled and chopped
2 level tablespoons chopped fresh dill or parsley
1oz (30g) fetta cheese, rinsed and crumbled
2 tablespoons lemon juice
1 tablespoon virgin olive oil
1 tablespoon white wine vinegar
1 level teaspoon Dijon mustard
1 clove garlic, peeled and crushed
Freshly ground black pepper
8oz (225g) frisée lettuce, washed and dried
Lemon wedges to garnish

1 Grill the pepper halves, skin side up, under a moderate heat for 5-6 minutes until blistered all over. Put the halves in a small bowl and cover with a clean damp cloth.

2 Bring 2 pints (1.15 litres) of unsalted water to the boil in a large saucepan and cook the prawns in it over a moderate heat, stirring continuously, for about 2 minutes, until they are just firm. Rinse the prawns in a colander under cold running water, drain them and pat dry with kitchen paper.

3 Mix the prawns with the onions, cucumber, dill or parsley and fetta.

4 Pull the skin off the pepper, working over a bowl to catch any juices. Slice the pepper flesh thinly and add it to the prawn mixture.

5 Whisk together the lemon juice, oil, vinegar, juice from the pepper, mustard and garlic until the mixture thickens slightly, then season with black pepper. Pour the dressing over the prawn mixture and toss gently to coat everything.

6 Line a salad bowl with lettuce leaves and spoon in the prawn mixture. Serve with lemon wedges to squeeze over the salad.

If you cannot get uncooked freshwater prawns, you can thaw 8oz (225g) frozen cooked peeled prawns to mix into the salad, but these will have a higher salt content.

Young spinach leaves make a simple and colourful foil for plump and tender Dublin Bay prawns, sharpened with a wine and lemon dressing. Smaller freshwater prawns (far right) partner fetta cheese and grilled red pepper on a bed of frilled lettuce leaves flavoured with dill and spring onion.

Prawn and spinach salad

SERVES 4
PREPARATION TIME: 15 minutes

16 large uncooked freshwater prawns, shelled and
de-veined
1lb (450g) young spinach leaves, trimmed
and washed
2 tablespoons lemon juice
2 tablespoons dry white wine
Freshly ground black pepper
1 tablespoon virgin olive oil

ONE SERVING

CALORIES 140

TOTAL FAT 5g

SATURATED FAT 1g

CARBOHYDRATES 2g

ADDED SUGAR 0

FIBRE 2g

SODIUM 315mg

1 Boil the prawns for 2-3 minutes in unsalted
water. Rinse with cold water, drain and pat dry.

2 Dry the spinach leaves gently but thoroughly
with kitchen paper or a clean cloth. Tear
the leaves into small pieces put them in a salad
bowl and mix in the prawns.

3 Pour the lemon juice and white wine into
a bowl, season with pepper and whisk in the oil.
Pour the dressing over the salad and serve.

Rice, orange and walnut salad

SERVES 4
PREPARATION TIME: 15 minutes
COOKING TIME: 35 minutes

8oz (225g) brown rice
2 large oranges, gently scrubbed under warm water
1 tablespoon cider vinegar
1 level teaspoon Dijon mustard
1 tablespoon walnut oil
1 tablespoon virgin olive oil
1 level tablespoon chopped fresh chervil
1 level tablespoon chopped fresh tarragon
Freshly ground black pepper
5 spring onions, trimmed and chopped
3oz (85g) walnuts, chopped
4oz (115g) small strawberries, hulled and cut in half
Chervil sprigs to garnish

ONE SERVING	
CALORIES 415	
TOTAL FAT 20g	
SATURATED FAT 2g	
CARBOHYDRATES 55g	
ADDED SUGAR 0	
FIBRE 3g	
SODIUM 70mg	

1   Cook the rice (see p.17).

2   Finely grate the rind from one orange into a large bowl. Stir in the vinegar, mustard, walnut oil, olive oil, chopped chervil and tarragon. Season with the pepper, then mix in the rice and spring onions. Cover and leave until cold.

3   Peel and segment the oranges, and cut each segment into four, discarding any pips. Stir the oranges, walnuts and strawberries into the rice. Turn the salad into a serving bowl and garnish with the chervil sprigs.

You can use 3 clementines in place of the oranges. Add the grated rind of 2 clementines to the dressing, and cut the segments in half. Use wild strawberries when they are in season.

Spinach and bacon salad

SERVES 4
PREPARATION TIME: 10 minutes
COOKING TIME: 10 minutes

1lb (450g) fresh young spinach leaves, trimmed and washed
1 lean rasher unsmoked back bacon
2 teaspoons olive oil
1 medium red or yellow pepper, de-seeded and cut into strips
1 small red onion, peeled and finely chopped
1 clove garlic, peeled and finely chopped
4 tablespoons dry white wine
4 tablespoons cider vinegar
Freshly ground black pepper

ONE SERVING	
CALORIES 85	
TOTAL FAT 4g	
SATURATED FAT 1g	
CARBOHYDRATES 5g	
ADDED SUGAR 0	
FIBRE 3g	
SODIUM 280mg	

1   Dry the spinach gently but thoroughly with kitchen paper or a clean cloth. Tear the leaves into small pieces and spread them in a large heatproof serving bowl.

2   Grill the bacon under a moderate heat for 5-6 minutes, or until crisp. Drain it on kitchen paper and set aside.

3   Heat the oil in a small saucepan and cook the pepper strips, onion and garlic in it over a moderate heat, stirring, for 2 minutes. Pour in the wine and vinegar, and season with black pepper. Bring to the boil, then reduce the heat and simmer, uncovered, for 1 minute. Pour the dressing over the spinach while still hot, and toss well.

4   Trim all the fat off the bacon. Cut the meat into fine strips, scatter them over the spinach and serve the salad at once.

To vary the taste of the salad, you can use crisp lettuce leaves or lamb's lettuce to replace all the spinach, or part of it.

Chopped walnuts add crunch and a rich flavour to a brown rice and orange salad (top), while strawberries give a fragrant and unusual touch, as well as extra juiciness. Bacon makes a delicious savoury contrast with peppery young spinach leaves just wilting to a delicious tenderness in a hot and sharp dressing.

Spinach and orange salad

SERVES 4
PREPARATION TIME: 20 minutes, plus 1 hour
to refrigerate

1 level teaspoon chopped fresh marjoram,
or ¹/₂ level teaspoon dried marjoram
¹/₈ level teaspoon freshly grated nutmeg
1 tablespoon virgin olive oil

Freshly ground black pepper
1 small orange, skin and pith removed,
flesh cut into small pieces
4 radishes, trimmed and sliced
1 small onion, peeled and finely chopped
8oz (225g) young spinach leaves, trimmed
and washed
¹/₂ tablespoon red wine vinegar

1 Mix the marjoram and nutmeg with the oil in a bowl. Season with pepper and stir in the orange, radishes and onion. Cover and place in the refrigerator for 1 hour, stirring occasionally.

2 Dry the spinach leaves gently but thoroughly with kitchen paper or a clean cloth. Tear them into small pieces and put in a salad bowl.

3 Sprinkle the vinegar over the spinach, then pour on the orange and radish mixture and toss the salad gently before serving.

You can vary the salad by using lamb's lettuce or cos lettuce in place of the spinach. When not using spinach, leave out the nutmeg and use cayenne pepper instead.

The contrasting flavours of sweet, succulent fresh orange, crisp, peppery radish and pungent raw onion equal the assertive flavour of the spinach and create a strikingly colourful combination.

Syrian herb and wheat salad

SERVES 4
PREPARATION TIME: 10 minutes, plus 30 minutes
soaking time and 30 minutes to stand

6oz (175g) medium-ground bulgur wheat
¹/₂ pint (285ml) vegetable stock (see p.19) or water
1 tablespoon lemon juice
2 teaspoons virgin olive oil
¹/₂ level teaspoon ground coriander

¹/₂ level teaspoon ground cumin
¹/₂ teaspoon Tabasco
3 level tablespoons chopped fresh mint,
or 1 level tablespoon crumbled dried mint
3 level tablespoons chopped fresh parsley
2 level tablespoons chopped fresh coriander
1 small red onion, peeled and sliced
2 spring onions, trimmed and chopped
2 medium tomatoes, de-seeded and roughly chopped

Wheat salad, the 'tabouleh' that is so popular in Syria, is generously flavoured with fresh herbs, and usually scooped up with flatbread.

1 Put the bulgur wheat into a heatproof bowl. Bring the stock or water to the boil and pour it over the bulgur. Cover and leave to soak for 30 minutes. Drain away any liquid which has not been absorbed.

2 Blend the lemon juice and oil in a salad bowl and mix in the ground coriander, cumin and

Tabasco. Stir in the mint, parsley, chopped coriander and onions.

3 Stir the bulgur into the dressing until it is well coated and the herbs are evenly distributed, then gently mix in the tomatoes. Cover and leave to stand for 30 minutes for the flavour to develop before serving.

Roasted vegetable salad

ONE SERVING

CALORIES 125

TOTAL FAT 8g

SATURATED FAT 1g

CARBOHYDRATES 11g

ADDED SUGAR 0

FIBRE 3g

SODIUM 10mg

Roasting the peppers intensifies their flavour, and garlic, herbs and citrus juice heighten the savoury appeal of this unusual salad.

SERVES 4
PREPARATION TIME: 15 minutes, plus 1 hour to cool
COOKING TIME: 30 minutes
OVEN: Preheat to 200°C (400°F, gas mark 6)

1 whole bulb garlic
3 medium peppers, red, green and yellow, de-seeded and sliced lengthways into strips
1 large onion, peeled and thickly sliced
2 tablespoons virgin olive oil
1 level teaspoon dried oregano
½ level teaspoon ground cumin
Freshly ground black pepper
1 large tomato, de-seeded and cut into squares
1 tablespoon lime or lemon juice
2 level tablespoons chopped fresh parsley or basil

1 Separate the garlic bulb into individual cloves and peel each clove. Put the garlic, red, green and yellow peppers, onion, oil, oregano and cumin in a large ovenproof dish. Season with black pepper, and stir gently to coat the vegetables with the oil.

2 Cook the vegetables in the heated oven, uncovered, for 15 minutes, stirring them occasionally. Mix in the tomato and cook for a further 15 minutes, stirring two or three times to prevent sticking at the bottom.

3 Spoon the vegetables into a serving dish, stir in the lime or lemon juice, and leave until cold. Sprinkle the chopped parsley or basil over the salad just before serving.

> **TIP**
> **To enjoy the full character of this dish, use the whole bulb of garlic without hesitation. Roasted garlic has a mild, nutty taste quite different from that of raw garlic.**

Waldorf salad

ONE SERVING

CALORIES 155

TOTAL FAT 9g

SATURATED FAT 1g

CARBOHYDRATES 17g

ADDED SUGAR 0

FIBRE 2g

SODIUM 100mg

SERVES 4
PREPARATION TIME: 20 minutes

3 medium dessert apples, cored and cut into chunks
6oz (175g) seedless green grapes
2 sticks celery, trimmed and finely sliced
2 spring onions, trimmed and finely chopped
1 tablespoon virgin olive oil

1 level teaspoon Dijon mustard
1 tablespoon lemon juice
¼ teaspoon celery seeds
Freshly ground black pepper
12 large radicchio leaves, washed and dried
2 bunches watercress, washed, thick stems removed
2 level tablespoons chopped walnuts
Sage sprigs to garnish

TIP
To make watercress crisp, rinse it under a cold tap, shake and put into a polythene bag. Tie the top and keep the bag in the bottom of the refrigerator. Use within 48 hours.

1 Mix the apples with the grapes, celery and spring onions.

2 Whisk the oil with the mustard, lemon juice and celery seeds until the mixture thickens slightly. Season with pepper, pour over the apple mixture and toss gently.

3 Arrange the radicchio leaves in cup shapes on a serving plate or in individual salad bowls.

Half fill with the watercress and spoon on the apple mixture. Sprinkle the walnuts on top and garnish with sage.

Crisp apples such as Granny Smiths or Sturmers give this salad a pleasing variety of textures, and if you can get purple sage it will complement the radicchio's colour. For a creamier dressing, use Greek yoghurt in place of the olive oil.

This variation of the salad first created at New York's Waldorf-Astoria hotel, uses grapes to sweeten and spring onions to sharpen the usual blend of apple, celery and walnuts. A mustard and lemon dressing replaces the mayonnaise, adding piquancy and reducing calories. Radicchio leaves make the glowing salad bowls.

DESSERTS

Ices and gâteaux, puddings and pies end a meal with a touch of luxury. When the fat and sugar have been carefully controlled, a moderate portion does no harm in a generally healthy diet. This selection of desserts makes the most of fresh fruits in season for the fibre they contribute and offers simple rhubarb crumble or gooseberry pancakes, airy orange soufflé or tingling peach sorbet, and spicy strudel or raspberry meringue for glamorous party pieces.

Almond and raspberry meringue

SERVES 8
PREPARATION TIME: 30 minutes,
plus 1 hour to cool
COOKING TIME: 1 hour 30 minutes–2 hours
OVEN: Preheat to 140°C (275°F, gas mark 1)

1¹⁄₂ oz (45g) blanched almonds, finely chopped
and lightly toasted
3¹⁄₂ oz (100g) caster sugar
1 level tablespoon cornflour
4 egg whites, size 2
¹⁄₈ level teaspoon cream of tartar
12oz (340g) fresh raspberries, or frozen
raspberries, thawed
5oz (150g) Greek yoghurt

1 Line two baking sheets with 12in (30cm) squares of nonstick baking paper.

2 Reserve a quarter of the almonds. Mix the rest with 1 tablespoon of the sugar and the cornflour. Whisk the egg whites until frothy. Add the cream of tartar and 1 tablespoon of sugar and whisk until the mixture forms soft peaks. Keep whisking, adding 1 tablespoon of sugar at a time, until the meringue is stiff and shiny. Whisk in the cornflour mixture.

3 Divide the meringue between the two lined baking sheets and spread with a palette knife into rounds 9¹⁄₂ in (24cm) in diameter. Mark swirls on the top of the meringues. Sprinkle the reserved almonds over one meringue.

4 Bake the meringues in the heated oven for 1¹⁄₂-2 hours, or until dry but slightly soft in the centre so that they give when gently pressed. Leave to cool on the baking sheets for 1 hour.

5 Press 4oz (115g) of the raspberries through a nylon sieve to make a purée.

6 Peel the baking paper off the meringues. Place the meringue without nuts flat-side up on a serving plate and spread the yoghurt on it. Arrange all but 2 tablespoons of the fruit over the yoghurt, and trickle the purée over it. Place the second meringue on top, nut side up, and decorate with the remaining raspberries. Refrigerate until serving time.

You can use hulled loganberries or strawberries in place of the raspberries.

ONE SERVING

CALORIES 125

TOTAL FAT 5g

SATURATED FAT 1g

CARBOHYDRATES 17g

ADDED SUGAR 13g

FIBRE 1g

SODIUM 50mg

TIP
As a guide for spreading out the meringue mixture, pencil a circle firmly on each of the squares of baking paper, drawing it round an upturned plate. Turn the paper over so that the circle is on the underside but still visible.

A slightly tart filling of thick yoghurt and whole and puréed raspberries is sandwiched between meringues lightly flavoured with almonds.

Apple and raisin crisp

SERVES 6
PREPARATION TIME: 25 minutes
COOKING TIME: 30 minutes
OVEN: Preheat to 150°C (300°F, gas mark 2)

3 medium cooking apples, peeled, cored
and thinly sliced
1 tablespoon lemon juice
3oz (85g) seedless raisins
1½ oz (45g) soft dark brown sugar
1 level teaspoon ground cinnamon

For the topping:
3oz (85g) wholemeal breadcrumbs
1oz (30g) polyunsaturated margarine, melted
1 level tablespoon soft brown sugar
½ level teaspoon ground cinnamon

1 Toss the apples with the lemon juice, then mix them with the raisins, sugar and cinnamon.

Spoon the mixture into an oval ovenproof dish about 9in (23cm) long.

2 To prepare the topping, spread out the breadcrumbs on a baking tray and bake in the heated oven, stirring occasionally, for 15 minutes or until they are dry. Put them in a small bowl and mix in the margarine, sugar and the cinnamon. Increase the oven temperature to 190°C (375°F, gas mark 5).

3 Sprinkle the topping over the apples and bake in the heated oven for 30 minutes. If the topping is browning too fast, cover it loosely with greaseproof or baking paper.

The acidity of apples and bite of cinnamon are sweetened by raisins under a top layer of crunchy wholemeal breadcrumbs and brown sugar.

ONE SERVING	
CALORIES	165
TOTAL FAT	4g
SATURATED FAT	1g
CARBOHYDRATES	32g
ADDED SUGAR	10g
FIBRE	2g
SODIUM	125mg

Blending a selection of summer berries and yoghurt before, during and after freezing creates a deliciously fresh, smooth, soft ice cream.

TIP
To make blending easier, cut the frozen ice cream into cubes before putting it into the food processor.

Mixed berry ice cream

SERVES 4
PREPARATION TIME: 20 minutes,
plus 4 hours to freeze

4oz (115g) each fresh raspberries, strawberries and blackberries, hulled
2oz (60g) caster sugar
2 teaspoons lemon juice
8oz (225g) low-fat natural yoghurt
4 raspberries and pansies, violets or other edible flowers for decoration

1 Blend the raspberries, strawberries and blackberries with the sugar in a food processor for 60 seconds to make a smooth purée. Rub the purée into a bowl through a fine nylon sieve to remove the seeds. Mix in the lemon juice and yoghurt. Pour the fruit mixture into a shallow plastic container, cover and freeze for about 1 hour, or until almost solid.

2 Blend the mixture in a food processor again for 1-2 minutes, or until smooth. Freeze for 3 hours or until just frozen. Blend the ice cream again in the food processor until smooth and creamy. Spoon into glasses, top with the raspberries and flowers and serve at once.

You can use frozen fruits in place of fresh. Thaw them before blending to a purée.

Black Forest gâteau

SERVES 12
PREPARATION TIME: 40 minutes,
plus 1 hour to cool
COOKING TIME: 20 minutes
OVEN: Preheat to 180°C (350°F, gas mark 4)

ONE SERVING	
CALORIES 175	
TOTAL FAT 6g	
SATURATED FAT 3g	
CARBOHYDRATES 27g	
ADDED SUGAR 16g	
FIBRE 1g	
SODIUM 95mg	

1oz (30g) cocoa
2oz (60g) plain flour
6oz (175g) caster sugar
8 egg whites, size 2
1 level teaspoon cream of tartar
1½ teaspoons vanilla extract
2 tablespoons cold water
1 level teaspoon gelatine
2 level teaspoons soft dark brown sugar
1 level tablespoon cornflour
Finely grated rind of ½ lemon and 1 teaspoon juice
15oz (425g) tinned stoned black cherries in
unsweetened juice, drained and juice reserved
4fl oz (115ml) double cream
4fl oz (115ml) evaporated milk, well chilled
Fresh cherries for decoration

1 Line the bases of two nonstick sponge cake tins, 8½ in (21cm) in diameter, with nonstick baking paper. Sift the cocoa, flour and 5oz (150g) of the caster sugar into a large bowl.

2 Beat the egg whites with an electric or rotary hand whisk until they will hold soft peaks. While whisking, add the cream of tartar, the remaining caster sugar and 1 teaspoon of the vanilla extract.

3 Fold the cocoa mixture gently into the egg whites, a third at a time, using a spatula. Divide the mixture between the two sponge cake tins and spread evenly.

4 Bake the sponges in the heated oven for about 20 minutes, or until they are risen and springy to the touch when lightly pressed at the centre. Leave to cool, then run a spatula round the edge of each sponge and turn out onto a wire rack. Remove the baking paper.

5 Pour the water into a small basin, sprinkle the gelatine evenly over the water and leave for 5 minutes for the gelatine to swell.

6 Blend the brown sugar, cornflour and lemon rind in a saucepan with the reserved juice from the cherries. Bring to the boil, stirring continuously. Reduce the heat and simmer for 1 minute, still stirring, until the sauce becomes thick and clear. Remove from the heat.

7 Check the cherries to make sure there are no stones in them, then stir into the sauce and leave to cool.

8 Stand the bowl of gelatine in a saucepan of hot water until the gelatine dissolves. Leave to cool. Whisk the cream and remaining vanilla extract until the cream forms soft peaks. Whisk the evaporated milk and lemon juice until the mixture becomes very thick, then whisk in the cooled gelatine. Gently fold in the whipped cream.

9 Put one sponge onto a serving plate, top side down. Spread with the cherry filling and then cover with half the whipped cream. Place the other sponge on it, top side up. Pipe rosettes of the remaining cream on top of the cake and decorate with fresh cherries. Refrigerate until 30 minutes before serving time.

TIP
For a delicate vanilla flavour, use vanilla sugar instead of caster sugar and vanilla extract. Keep a vanilla pod in a storage jar of caster sugar to flavour it. Top up the jar each time you use some of the sugar.

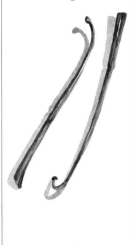

In this skilful adaptation of the originally indulgent German gâteau, the fragrant, juicy cherry filling and thick whipped cream are still sandwiched between feather-light cakes of chocolate sponge to make a special-occasion dessert. But the usually high calorie and fat content has been significantly reduced by leaving out the egg yolks and whisking up a delicate, creamy vanilla mousse for the filling and topping.

Juicy raspberries and crunchy almonds layered with pleasantly tart chocolate-flavoured yoghurt make this a perfect cooling summer treat.

Chocolate berry parfait

ONE SERVING

CALORIES 205

TOTAL FAT 10g

SATURATED FAT 2g

CARBOHYDRATES 15g

ADDED SUGAR 5g

FIBRE 3g

SODIUM 115mg

SERVES 4
PREPARATION TIME: 15 minutes,
plus 1-2 hours to chill

12oz (340g) low-fat natural yoghurt
2 level tablespoons cocoa, sifted
1 level tablespoon icing sugar, sifted
8oz (225g) fresh raspberries, or frozen
raspberries, thawed
2oz (60g) blanched almonds, finely chopped
and lightly toasted
4 mint sprigs for decoration

1 Whisk the yoghurt, cocoa and icing sugar
until blended.

2 Set aside 4 of the raspberries. Spoon one
third of the yoghurt mixture into 4 tall glasses,
put half the raspberries on top, and sprinkle
on half the toasted almonds.

3 Repeat these layers in each glass, then finish
with the remaining yoghurt mixture. Put in the
refrigerator to chill for 1-2 hours. Garnish each
parfait with a raspberry and sprig of mint just
before serving.

You can use strawberries or loganberries in
place of raspberries. For a richer mixture, use
half and half low-fat and Greek yoghurt, or
replace the yoghurt entirely with fromage frais.

Chocolate pudding

SERVES 4
PREPARATION TIME: 5 minutes,
plus 3-4 hours to cool and chill
COOKING TIME: 10 minutes

3 level tablespoons cocoa
1oz (30g) soft light brown sugar
3 level tablespoons cornflour
14fl oz (400ml) skimmed milk
1 teaspoon vanilla extract
Dark chocolate curls for decoration
4 large strawberries, washed and dried

1 Mix the cocoa, sugar and cornflour in a heavy-based saucepan and, using a wire whisk, gradually blend in the milk. Bring the mixture to the boil over a moderate heat, stirring continuously with a wooden spoon. Reduce the heat to low and continue stirring for about 3 minutes, until the cornflour is cooked and the mixture is thickened and smooth.

2 Remove from the heat, stir in the vanilla extract and pour into 4 small individual dishes. Cover with wetted greaseproof paper and when they are cool, put them, still covered, in the refrigerator to chill for about 3 hours. Just before serving, decorate each pudding with chocolate curls and a strawberry.

You can use finely grated orange rind instead of, or in addition to, the vanilla extract.

ONE SERVING	
CALORIES	125
TOTAL FAT	2g
SATURATED FAT	1g
CARBOHYDRATES	23g
ADDED SUGAR	8g
FIBRE	1g
SODIUM	135mg

TIP
To make chocolate curls, spread 2-3 squares of melted dark chocolate thinly on a clean marble slab or laminated plastic surface. As soon as the chocolate is dry to the touch, push a knife blade against it to lift it in curls.

Luscious strawberries give these little pots of smooth dark chocolate a fresh finish in a luxury dessert that is surprisingly low in calories and simplicity itself to prepare.

Crème brûlée

SERVES 4
PREPARATION TIME: 15 minutes,
plus 2 hours to cool and chill
COOKING TIME: 20 minutes

3 egg yolks, size 2
½ oz (15g) cornflour
½ oz (15g) caster sugar
14fl oz (400ml) skimmed milk
2 level tablespoons Greek yoghurt
1 teaspoon vanilla extract
1 small banana
6oz (175g) fresh raspberries
1oz (30g) demerara sugar

ONE SERVING

CALORIES 180

TOTAL FAT 6g

SATURATED FAT 2g

CARBOHYDRATES 27g

ADDED SUGAR 12g

FIBRE 1g

SODIUM 70mg

1 Whisk the egg yolks, cornflour and caster sugar in a bowl.

2 Heat the milk until it is hot but not boiling, and whisk it into the egg yolk mixture. Place the bowl over a saucepan of gently simmering water and stir continuously with a wooden spoon for about 20 minutes, or until the custard has thickened sufficiently to coat the back of the spoon.

3 Remove the bowl of custard from the saucepan and stir in the yoghurt and vanilla.

4 Peel and slice the banana and mix it with the raspberries. Divide the fruit between four ¼ pint (150ml) ramekin dishes. Pour a share of the custard into each dish, leave to cool, then put in the refrigerator for about 1½ hours, until very cold.

5 Sprinkle the demerara sugar evenly over the top of the four dishes, leave to stand for 5 minutes, then put under a hot grill for only about 20 seconds to melt and brown the sugar. Serve immediately, or return to the refrigerator to keep chilled until serving time.

Raspberries and banana nestle under the crème brûlée, 'burnt cream', in this reduced-fat adaptation of a rich pudding. As in the traditional version, the smooth vanilla custard is topped by a crackly, toffee-flavoured crust.

Fruit salad

SERVES 4
PREPARATION TIME: 20 minutes,
plus 1-2 hours to refrigerate

1 medium, ripe melon, about 1½ lb (680g)
2 medium oranges with peel and pith
pared off, segments cut from membranes
and any pips removed

8oz (225g) strawberries, hulled and sliced
6oz (175g) seedless green grapes, peeled
and halved
1½ level teaspoons finely grated orange rind
4fl oz (115ml) freshly squeezed and strained
orange juice
2 medium bananas
Fresh mint sprigs for decoration

A medley of colourful fresh fruits, full of natural sweetness and refreshed with real orange juice, makes an enjoyably light end to a meal.

TIP
Do not peel and slice the bananas until there is plenty of juice in the salad to coat them. The flesh quickly goes brown when exposed to air.

1 Halve and de-seed the melon, take out the flesh with a melon scoop and put the balls into a large bowl. Mix in the orange segments.

2 Stir the strawberries, grapes and orange rind into the salad and pour on the orange juice.

3 Peel and slice the bananas and mix them gently into the salad. Cover and refrigerate for 1-2 hours, until 30 minutes before serving.

4 Just before serving, spoon the salad into a serving bowl and decorate it with the mint.

You may prefer to serve the fruit salad in individual serving bowls and top each with a sprig of mint. For a sweeter fruit salad, you can add 1 level tablespoon of golden sultanas. For a special occasion you can hand round a small bowl of Greek yoghurt for each diner to have a spoonful with the salad.

Gooseberry pancakes

ONE SERVING

CALORIES 245

TOTAL FAT 5g

SATURATED FAT 2g

CARBOHYDRATES 43g

ADDED SUGAR 11g

FIBRE 4g

SODIUM 65mg

SERVES 4
PREPARATION TIME: 20 minutes
COOKING TIME: 35 minutes
OVEN: Preheat to 190°C (375°F, gas mark 5)

Finely grated rind and juice of ½ orange
1oz (30g) soft light brown sugar
1lb (450g) ripe dessert gooseberries, topped and tailed
4oz (115g) plain wholemeal flour

1 egg, size 2, beaten
½ pint (285ml) semi-skimmed milk
2 teaspoons corn oil
Squares of greaseproof paper for stacking
1 level tablespoon demerara sugar

1 Gently heat the orange rind and juice with the light brown sugar in a saucepan, stirring to dissolve the sugar. Put in the gooseberries and simmer for about 10 minutes, stirring occasionally, until they are soft and the juice is slightly thickened. Leave to cool.

2 Put the flour in a mixing bowl, make a well in the centre and pour in the egg and half the milk. Stir well with a wooden spoon until the ingredients are combined, then beat until smooth. Stir in the remaining milk and pour the batter into a measuring jug.

3 Smear a little oil over the base of a nonstick frying pan 6in (15cm) in diameter. Heat it over a moderate heat until it gives off a slight haze. Pour one-eighth of the batter into the pan and quickly tilt the pan until the base is coated thinly. Cook until the top of the batter is set and the underside golden brown. Turn or toss the pancake over and cook the other side. Slide out onto a plate. Make seven more pancakes in the same way and put greaseproof paper between them as you stack them on the plate.

4 Lay the pancakes with the side cooked first down on the work surface. Divide the filling between the pancakes and spread evenly. Fold each one in half, then in half again to make a fan shape and overlap the fans in an ovenproof dish. Sprinkle the demerara sugar over the top.

5 Place in the heated oven for 15 minutes, until heated through and crisp round the edges. Serve immediately.

When you cannot get dessert gooseberries, use a cooking variety, but you might need to add more sugar. You can make the pancakes a day ahead, let them cool and keep them in the refrigerator in a polythene bag.

Dessert gooseberries with their full flavour and slightly acid tang make a refreshing filling for fans of pancakes with a crisp, sweet demerara topping.

Lime and ginger cheesecake

SERVES 8
PREPARATION TIME: 20 minutes,
plus 5 hours to refrigerate

ONE SERVING	
CALORIES	140
TOTAL FAT	3g
SATURATED FAT	2g
CARBOHYDRATES	21g
ADDED SUGAR	11g
FIBRE	0
SODIUM	95mg

*Cool, sharp lime and
hot, spicy ginger flavour
the feather-light,
low-fat cheese and
yoghurt topping and
also the sweetened
breadcrumb base that
adds crunch and texture
to this zesty cheesecake.*

¾ oz (20g) unsalted butter
2oz (60g) fine breadcrumbs, lightly toasted
3oz (85g) caster sugar
Grated rind and juice of 3 limes
1½ level teaspoons ground ginger
3 tablespoons cold water
1 level tablespoon powdered gelatine
11oz (300g) quark or low-fat fromage frais
7oz (200g) low-fat natural yoghurt
6 tablespoons skimmed milk
Slices of lime, cut into quarters, for decoration

1 Line the bottom of a spring-clip cake tin,
8½ in (21cm) in diameter, with nonstick baking
paper. To prepare the cheesecake base, melt the
butter in a saucepan over a low heat. Take it off
the heat and mix in the breadcrumbs, 1 level
teaspoon of the sugar, ½ level teaspoon of the
lime rind and ½ level teaspoon of the ginger.
Spread the mixture evenly over the bottom of

the tin, pressing it down firmly. Chill in the
refrigerator while preparing the filling.

2 Put the water in a small saucepan and
sprinkle the gelatine evenly on top. Leave for
5 minutes to let the gelatine swell, then stir
over a low heat until the gelatine dissolves.

3 Mix the quark or fromage frais with the
yoghurt, milk and remaining sugar in a bowl.
Add the remaining lime rind, the lime juice,
the remaining ginger and the dissolved gelatine,
and stir until thoroughly combined. Cover and
leave until the mixture begins to thicken.

4 Pour the mixture onto the bread base
without disturbing it, then refrigerate for
at least 5 hours until firmly set.

5 Run a knife round the cheesecake and take
off the side of the tin. Carefully lift the
cheesecake with fish slices or palette knives
onto a flat plate, then ease out the baking
paper. Decorate with slices of lime to serve.

Mango choux ring

SERVES 6
PREPARATION TIME: 40 minutes,
plus 1-2 hours to refrigerate
COOKING TIME: 40 minutes
OVEN: Preheat to 220°C (425°F, gas mark 7)

ONE SERVING	
CALORIES	265
TOTAL FAT	13g
SATURATED FAT	3g
CARBOHYDRATES	33g
ADDED SUGAR	8g
FIBRE	2g
SODIUM	125mg

TIP
To ensure that the choux pastry is light and crisp, add only about 2 teaspoons of egg to the paste at a time and beat vigorously before adding any more.

For the filling:
1½ oz (45g) cornflour
1½ oz (45g) caster sugar
¾ pint (425ml) semi-skimmed milk
2 tablespoons rum, or 1 teaspoon vanilla extract
1½ oz (45g) blanched almonds
6 level tablespoons Greek yoghurt
1 large ripe mango, peeled, stoned and thinly sliced

For the choux pastry:
¼ pint (150ml) water
2oz (60g) polyunsaturated margarine
2½ oz (70g) plain flour
1 egg, plus 1 egg white, size 2

1 Blend the cornflour and ½ oz (15g) of the sugar with the milk in a saucepan, and slowly bring to the boil, stirring continuously. Cook for 2-3 minutes, still stirring all the time.

2 Remove from the heat and beat in the rum or vanilla extract. Pour the custard into a bowl and put a disc of wetted nonstick baking paper directly on the custard to cover it completely. Leave to cool, then refrigerate for 1-2 hours.

3 Pencil a circle 7in (18cm) in diameter firmly on a sheet of nonstick baking paper, using an upturned plate as a guide. Turn the paper over and lay it on a baking sheet.

4 To prepare the choux pastry ring, slowly heat the water and the margarine in a saucepan, until the margarine has melted. Bring to the boil, tip in all the flour and quickly stir it in. Beat over the heat until the mixture forms a ball of stiff paste. Remove from the heat and cool for 3-4 minutes.

5 Whisk the whole egg and the egg white and beat little by little into the cooled paste, using a hand-held electric mixer or a wooden spoon. Beat well between each addition of egg.

6 Put spoonfuls of the choux paste barely touching one another in a ring on the baking sheet, placing them just inside the pencilled circle. Alternatively, pipe the choux paste through a large, plain nozzle to form a thick ring just inside the pencilled circle.

7 Bake in the heated oven for 30 minutes until well risen, golden brown and firm to the touch. Remove from the oven and pierce with a knife in several places round the side of the ring, to let out the steam. Put the ring back in the oven for a further 10 minutes.

8 Lift the choux ring onto a wire rack and cut in half horizontally. Carefully separate the two halves and scoop out and discard any uncooked pastry from the centre. Leave the ring halves to cool completely.

9 Put the remaining caster sugar and the almonds in a small saucepan, set over a very low heat and stir until the sugar dissolves and turns to a golden brown caramel; watch all the time, as it quickly burns and goes bitter. Pour onto a plate lined with nonstick baking paper, and leave to cool. When cold, grind finely in a food processor, or put between sheets of nonstick paper and crush firmly with a rolling pin on a sturdy surface to make a praline.

10 Remove the chilled custard from the refrigerator and whisk until smooth. Whisk in the yoghurt and all but two teaspoons of the praline mixture.

11 Just before serving time, put the bottom half of the choux ring on a flat serving plate and fill with the custard. Arrange the mango slices on top, then cover with the top half of the choux ring. Sprinkle on the remaining praline.

Puffs of airy choux pastry, sprinkled with a golden almond praline, form a ring filled with a creamy, rum-flavoured custard and slices of mellow mango. An intriguing acid-sweet flavour and silky texture make this tropical fruit an ideal, although unusual, partner for such a crisp, light pastry. You can put a few pansies, primroses or nasturtiums in the centre for a particularly festive presentation.

Melba summer pudding

ONE SERVING

CALORIES 190

TOTAL FAT 1g

SATURATED FAT 0

CARBOHYDRATES 43g

ADDED SUGAR 15g

FIBRE 6g

SODIUM 180mg

SERVES 4
PREPARATION TIME: 20 minutes,
plus 30 minutes to cool, and overnight standing
COOKING TIME: 10 minutes

1lb (450g) ripe apricots, halved, stoned
and quartered
8oz (225g) peaches or nectarines, skinned,
halved, stoned and sliced

2oz (60g) soft light brown sugar
2 tablespoons water
4oz (115g) redcurrants, topped and tailed
4oz (115g) raspberries
6 slices wholemeal bread, ¼ in (6mm) thick,
crusts removed
Sprigs of mint to decorate

1 Put the apricots and peaches or nectarines
in a saucepan with the sugar and water. Cook,
covered, over a moderate heat for 5 minutes,
until the fruit begins to soften. Gently stir in
the redcurrants and the raspberries and cook
until the juice turns red, but the fruit remains
whole. Leave to cool for 30 minutes.

2 Cut one slice of bread into a round and fit
it in the bottom of a 1½ pint (850ml) pudding
basin. Line the sides of the basin with bread,
trimming the slices with clean kitchen scissors
once in place to fit snugly together. Trim the
top edges of the bread level with the basin rim.

3 Set aside 5 tablespoons of the fruit juice.
Spoon the fruit and remaining juice into the
basin without disturbing the bread. Fill up to
½ in (13mm) from the top. Cover the fruit with
bread, trimming it to fit inside the lined sides.
Spoon a little of the reserved juice over the top
covering of bread to colour it. Cover the bowl
of juice and put it in the refrigerator.

4 Cover the bread with nonstick baking paper.
Place on top a small plate that fits inside the
rim of the basin. Weight the plate and stand
the basin in a wide dish to catch any juice that
overflows. Refrigerate the pudding overnight.

5 Uncover the pudding and run a knife round
to loosen it from the basin. Turn out the
pudding onto a serving dish. Spoon the
reserved fruit juice over any patches of bread
not saturated with juice. Decorate with mint
sprigs and serve.

*A gentle poaching of raspberries, redcurrants,
peaches and apricots extracts their delicious juices,
which overnight transform slices of wholemeal bread
into a moist, sweetened cover melting as any pastry.*

A generous dash of orange liqueur accentuates the warm citrus flavour of this light, frothy soufflé, which is particularly low in calories yet brings a touch of luxury to the end of a meal.

TIP
Citrus fruits are often coated with a wax that deters fungus growth. Unless you are sure your oranges are wax-free, do not grate the rind before scrubbing well with a new or boiled nylon pan-scrubber under cold running water.

ONE SERVING	
CALORIES 80	
TOTAL FAT 1g	
SATURATED FAT 0	
CARBOHYDRATES 15g	
ADDED SUGAR 10g	
FIBRE 0	
SODIUM 65mg	

Orange soufflé

SERVES 6
PREPARATION TIME: *20 minutes, plus 1 hour to cool*
COOKING TIME: *30 minutes*
OVEN: *Preheat to 180°C (350°F, gas mark 4)*

2oz (60g) granulated sugar
1½ level tablespoons cornflour
4fl oz (115ml) skimmed milk
1 egg, separated, plus 3 egg whites, size 2
2 tablespoons orange liqueur
Finely grated rind of 2 oranges
½ teaspoon vanilla extract

1 Mix the sugar and cornflour in a saucepan, then stir in the milk little by little. Bring to the boil over a moderate heat, stirring continuously. Reduce the heat to low and simmer, stirring, for 30 seconds.

2 Remove from the heat and cool slightly. Beat in the egg yolk, orange liqueur, orange rind and vanilla extract. Pour the custard into a bowl and lay a disc of wetted nonstick baking paper directly on it to prevent a skin from forming on top. Leave the custard for about 1 hour to cool to room temperature.

3 Whisk the egg whites until they hold soft peaks. Fold 1 tablespoon of the egg white into the orange mixture to lighten it, then gently fold in the rest of the egg white. Spoon the mixture into a deep soufflé dish 7in (18cm) in diameter. Bake in the heated oven for about 30 minutes, or until the soufflé is well risen and lightly browned on top. Serve immediately.

Use Seville oranges when they are in season, for a particularly zesty soufflé.

Orange and strawberry flan

SERVES 6
PREPARATION TIME: 25 minutes,
plus 30 minutes to cool
COOKING TIME: 20 minutes
OVEN: Preheat to 200°C (400°F, gas mark 6)

½ teaspoon corn oil
2 eggs, size 2
1½ oz (45g) caster sugar
2oz (60g) plain flour
6oz (175g) curd cheese
Finely grated rind and juice of 1 orange
4oz (115g) strawberries, washed, dried well
and halved
2 oranges, peel and white pith removed, cut
into thin slices

1 Lightly rub the oil over a nonstick sponge flan tin 8½ in (21cm) in diameter, and line the base with nonstick baking paper.

2 Whisk the eggs and caster sugar in a bowl, using an electric or a rotary hand whisk. Continue until the mixture is very fluffy and so thick that a ribbon of the mixture trailed onto it from the whisk stays on the surface.

3 Sift the flour lightly over the egg mixture, and fold in carefully with a large metal spoon. Pour into the flan tin and spread evenly to the edges. Bake in the centre of the heated oven for about 20 minutes, or until well risen, lightly browned and springy to the touch.

4 Gently ease the sponge from the edges of the tin with a palette knife and turn out onto a wire rack to cool for 30 minutes. Remove the baking paper.

5 Mix the curd cheese with the orange rind and juice until smooth.

6 Place the flan case flat side down and fill the central hollow with the curd cheese mixture, spreading it evenly. Decorate the top with the strawberry halves and orange slices.

ONE SERVING

CALORIES 170

TOTAL FAT 6g

  SATURATED FAT 3g

CARBOHYDRATES 22g

  ADDED SUGAR 8g

FIBRE 1g

SODIUM 145mg

A smooth but lively orange-curd filling is sandwiched between a light and golden sponge base and a fragrant pairing of strawberry halves and orange slices, achieving a perfect balance between the sweet and the tart in this fresh-fruit flan.

Peach and almond strudel

SERVES 6
PREPARATION TIME: 30 minutes
COOKING TIME: 45 minutes
OVEN: Preheat to 200°C (400°F, gas mark 6)

TIP
If the peach skins will not pull off easily, put the fruit in a heatproof bowl, pour boiling water over them, leave for 1 minute then rinse with cold water. The skin will come away easily.

1½ oz (45g) ground almonds
1 level tablespoon caster sugar
1 level teaspoon ground mixed spice
Finely grated rind of 1 lemon
1½ oz (45g) wholemeal breadcrumbs
6oz (175g) filo pastry sheets
1oz (30g) polyunsaturated margarine, melted
4 large ripe peaches, skinned, stoned and sliced

1 Mix the almonds, sugar, spice and lemon rind with 1oz (30g) of the breadcrumbs.

2 On a large clean teacloth, lay half the sheets of pastry, trimmed as necessary and with edges overlapping, to form a rectangle about 20×16in (51×40cm). Arrange the rectangle so that one of its long sides is nearest to you. Brush lightly with melted margarine. Arrange a second layer of pastry sheets on top in the same way and brush with a little more margarine.

3 Spread the ground almond mixture in a 4in (10cm) strip along the side nearest to you, setting it in 2in (50mm) from the edge. Arrange the peach slices on top of the mixture.

4 Fold the two short sides in by 1in (25mm), and fold the clear 2in (50mm) strip of pastry over the peaches. Lift the edge of the teacloth nearest to you so that the strudel begins to roll away from you. Keep lifting until the strudel is completely rolled. Carefully lay the strudel, seam side down, on a nonstick baking sheet.

5 Brush the remaining margarine over the strudel and sprinkle with the remaining breadcrumbs. Bake in the heated oven for about 45 minutes, or until the pastry is golden brown and crisp. Serve the strudel warm.

When fresh peaches are unavailable use 1¾ lb (800g) of unsweetened tinned peach halves, drained, dried with kitchen paper and sliced. For a special occasion, sift 1 level teaspoon of icing sugar over the strudel and put a teaspoon of Greek yoghurt beside each serving.

Melting, spiced almond paste and fresh peach slices in a wafer-thin wrapping create this tempting variation of the Viennese apple strudel.

Peach sorbet

SERVES 4
PREPARATION TIME: 20 minutes, plus 5 hours
to chill and freeze

$3\frac{1}{2}$ oz (100g) granulated sugar
7fl oz (200ml) water
4 large ripe peaches, skinned, halved and stoned,
and sliced
2 tablespoons lemon or lime juice
1 small ripe peach, sliced, for decoration

ONE SERVING

CALORIES 145

TOTAL FAT 0

SATURATED FAT 0

CARBOHYDRATES 37g

ADDED SUGAR 26g

FIBRE 2g

SODIUM 0

1 Put the sugar and water in a saucepan and stir over a low heat until the sugar dissolves, then bring to the boil and boil for 1 minute. Take the syrup off the heat and let it cool for 30 minutes. Pour it into a bowl, cover and refrigerate for $1\frac{1}{2}$ hours.

2 Blend the peach slices in a food processor for 1 minute, then add the syrup and the lemon or lime juice, and blend for 30 seconds more. Pour the mixture into a plastic box, cover and freeze for about 3 hours or until hard.

3 Peel and slice the small peach. Cut the frozen peach mixture into large pieces and blend in a food processor for 10 seconds, until soft. Spoon the sorbet into individual dishes and decorate each serving with some peach slices. Serve at once.

The luscious crushed flesh of ripe peaches, mingled with a syrup and enlivened with citrus juice, makes a tingling-fresh, ice-cold pudding for summer days.

Plump, silky-smooth pears poached in wine laced with liqueur and cinnamon are translucent and glossy; toasted hazelnuts give a crunchy finish.

Pears in white wine

ONE SERVING	
CALORIES	145
TOTAL FAT	3g
SATURATED FAT	0
CARBOHYDRATES	30g
ADDED SUGAR	0
FIBRE	4g
SODIUM	20mg

TIP
After peeling the pears, cut a thin sliver from the base of each one. This ensures that the pears will stand upright for serving.

SERVES 6
PREPARATION TIME: 15 minutes, plus 30 minutes to cool
COOKING TIME: 50 minutes

1 pint (570ml) sweet white wine
2 tablespoons concentrated pear juice
½ in (13mm) piece cinnamon stick
6 firm but ripe Comice pears
2 level teaspoons arrowroot blended with 1 tablespoon cold water
1 tablespoon pear brandy or orange liqueur
1oz (30g) chopped hazelnuts, lightly toasted

1 Pour the wine and pear juice into a stainless steel or enamel saucepan, put in the cinnamon stick and bring to the boil.

2 Meanwhile, peel the pears, leaving their stalks on. Put the pears in the saucepan and spoon the liquid over them to prevent discoloration. Cover the pan and simmer the pears for about 25 minutes, turning them from time to time and spooning the liquid over, until they are cooked through and translucent. Leave the pears to cool in the wine.

3 Lift the pears out of the liquid with a slotted spoon, and stand them up in a serving bowl.

4 Remove the cinnamon stick and boil the cooking liquid briskly until it is reduced to ½ pint (285ml). Remove from the heat and stir in the arrowroot mixture. Bring back to the boil, stirring until the sauce is thickened and clear. Remove from the heat and leave to cool.

5 Stir the liqueur into the sauce, then pour it over the pears. Cover and refrigerate until 30 minutes before serving time. Sprinkle the hazelnuts on top at the last moment.

For a more colourful dish, cook the pears in red wine instead of white.

Plum cobbler

ONE SERVING

CALORIES 280

TOTAL FAT 8g

SATURATED FAT 1g

CARBOHYDRATES 48g

ADDED SUGAR 8g

FIBRE 4g

SODIUM 245mg

SERVES 6
PREPARATION TIME: 30 minutes
COOKING TIME: 45 minutes
OVEN: Preheat to 200°C (400°F, gas mark 6)

1½ lb (680g) ripe Victoria plums or Spanish dessert plums, halved and stoned
1½ oz (45g) soft light brown sugar
1oz (30g) ground almonds
6 tablespoons water

For the topping:
6oz (175g) self-raising flour
2oz (60g) plain wholemeal flour
1 level teaspoon baking powder
1oz (30g) polyunsaturated margarine
1 egg, size 2, lightly beaten
7 tablespoons skimmed milk
1 teaspoon caster sugar

Mellow dessert plums, their juice thickened by ground almonds, are baked beneath thick rounds of low-fat scone pastry in this warming family pudding for autumn days.

1 Mix the plums with the brown sugar, ground almonds and water. Spread the mixture in an ovenproof dish 8in (20cm) in diameter.

2 To make the topping, combine the flours and baking powder in a bowl, and rub in the margarine. Pour in the egg and 6 tablespoons of the milk, and mix to form a soft dough. Knead to an even texture on a lightly floured surface.

3 Roll out the dough on a lightly floured surface to ½ in (13mm) thick. Use a fluted 2½ in (65mm) cutter to cut rounds from the dough. Knead and roll the trimmings and cut out more rounds to make 12 in all. Lay them,

slightly overlapping, in a circle round the dish and brush with the remaining milk.

4 Bake in the heated oven for 45 minutes, or until the rounds are golden and the plums soft. Cover with greaseproof paper after 30 minutes so the top does not brown too much. Sprinkle the cobbler with the caster sugar and serve hot.

If you like, you can add 1 teaspoon of vanilla extract to the dough. A spoonful of Greek yoghurt on each serving would add a touch of luxury. If you cannot get ripe Victoria or Spanish dessert plums you can use a cooking variety, but you might have to add more sugar.

Rhubarb and date crumble

SERVES 6
PREPARATION TIME: 15 minutes,
plus 1 hour to stand
COOKING TIME: 35 minutes
OVEN: Preheat to 190°C (375°F, gas mark 5)

1¼ lb (550g) rhubarb, trimmed and cut into short lengths
3oz (85g) stoned dates, chopped
Finely grated rind of 1 orange
1oz (30g) soft brown sugar

For the topping:
4oz (115g) rolled oats
2oz (60g) wholemeal flour
2 level tablespoons soft brown sugar
4 tablespoons corn oil

ONE SERVING	
CALORIES	250
TOTAL FAT	10g
SATURATED FAT	2g
CARBOHYDRATES	39g
ADDED SUGAR	10g
FIBRE	4g
SODIUM	5mg

1 To prepare the filling, mix the rhubarb with the dates, orange rind and sugar, and leave to stand for 1 hour.

2 Stir the rhubarb mixture and turn it into a deep oval ovenproof dish 9in (23cm) long.

3 To make the topping, mix the oats, flour and sugar in a bowl, then stir in the oil with a fork until the oats are completely coated.

4 Spoon the oat mixture over the fruit and spread to the edges, pressing it down lightly. Stand the dish on a baking tray and bake in the heated oven for about 35 minutes, or until the rhubarb is tender and the crumble is crisp and golden brown on top.

Under the oat topping, orange rind highlights the rhubarb's sharp taste, while dates add sweetness and absorb some of the plentiful juice.

Strawberry charlotte

SERVES 8
PREPARATION TIME: 50 minutes, plus 3 hours
to refrigerate
COOKING TIME: 10 minutes
OVEN: Preheat to 220°C (425°F, gas mark 7)

3 eggs, size 2
4oz (115g) caster sugar
3oz (85g) plain flour
1½ lb (680g) strawberries, hulled, washed
and dried
7oz (200g) Greek yoghurt
7oz (200g) low-fat natural yoghurt
6 tablespoons cold water
1oz (30g) powdered gelatine
Sprigs of mint and whole strawberries for decoration

1 Line a swiss-roll tin, 15×12in (38×30cm), with nonstick baking paper.

2 Whisk the eggs and half the sugar in a bowl with an electric or rotary hand whisk until fluffy and so thick that a ribbon of mixture trailed on it from the whisk stays on the surface. Sift the flour over the mixture and fold it in gently with a large metal spoon. Pour into the swiss-roll tin and spread evenly. Bake in the heated oven for about 8 minutes, or until well risen, very lightly coloured and springy to the touch. Turn onto a wire rack, remove the baking paper and leave to cool.

3 Meanwhile blend two-thirds of the hulled strawberries with the yoghurts and the rest of the sugar in a food processor until smooth, and pour into a bowl. Roughly chop the remaining third of the strawberries and fold into the strawberry and yoghurt mixture.

4 Pour the water into a small saucepan and sprinkle the gelatine evenly over the surface. Leave to stand for 5 minutes until the gelatine swells and becomes opaque, then stir over a low heat until dissolved. Quickly stir the hot gelatine into the strawberry and yoghurt

ONE SERVING
CALORIES 205
TOTAL FAT 5g
SATURATED FAT 2g
CARBOHYDRATES 30g
ADDED SUGAR 15g
FIBRE 1g
SODIUM 75mg

TIP
Be sure to pat the strawberries thoroughly dry with kitchen paper before blending with the yoghurts. If the mixture is too watery, the gelatine will not set it.

This low-fat variation of a special-occasion dessert has crushed fresh strawberries whisked to a pink cream with thick yoghurt and encased in a delicate sponge. Gelatine firms up the filling, holding it in shape without affecting its refreshing lightness.

mixture, then refrigerate the mixture for 5-10 minutes, until it is thickened but not set.

5 Meanwhile, cut across the sponge cake to make four strips and trim them to fit the bottom, sides and ends of a nonstick loaf tin 10×4½ in (25×12cm). Arrange the sponge with the unbrowned sides against the tin. Spoon in the strawberry and yoghurt mixture

and spread evenly. Cover the charlotte and put it in the refrigerator for 3 hours, or overnight, until the filling is firmly set.

6 If necessary, trim the sponge so that it is level with the top of the strawberry filling. Turn the charlotte onto a flat serving plate and decorate with sprigs of fresh mint and strawberries cut into thin slices.

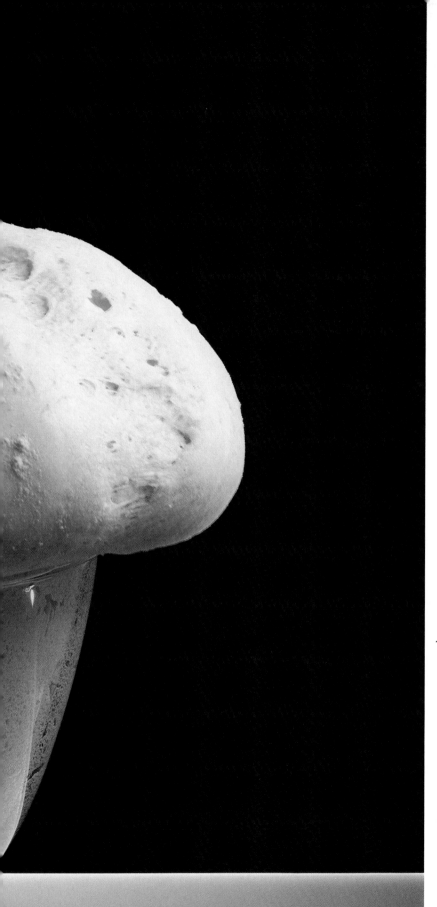

BREADS, CAKES AND BISCUITS

Nothing has a more tempting aroma than home-baked bread, a food heartily recommended now for its starch, fibre, minerals and vitamins. Whether you choose to make wholemeal loaves, Italian-style focaccia or Greek pitta bread, the recipes are here, along with those for the sweeter date and walnut tea-bread, banana spice loaf, sesame snaps and many others. All have been adapted to form a healthy part of your daily menu without compromising on taste.

Cheese and onion bread

ONE SERVING	
CALORIES 150	
TOTAL FAT 3g	
SATURATED FAT 1g	
CARBOHYDRATES 26g	
ADDED SUGAR 0	
FIBRE 2g	
SODIUM 90mg	

TIP
To speed up the rising, stand the bowl of dough in a warm airing cupboard or near a hot radiator.

MAKES 10 servings (20 slices)
PREPARATION TIME: 25 minutes,
plus 2 hours to rise
COOKING TIME: 25 minutes
OVEN: Preheat to 220°C (425°F, gas mark 7)

1 tablespoon olive oil
1 large onion, peeled and chopped
4fl oz (115ml) lukewarm water
¼ level teaspoon caster sugar
1 level teaspoon dried yeast
6oz (175g) plain wholemeal flour
6oz (175g) strong unbleached plain flour
1 level teaspoon mustard powder
¼ level teaspoon salt
1 level teaspoon dried oregano
1oz (30g) grated Parmesan cheese
4fl oz (115ml) lukewarm skimmed milk

1 Heat the oil in a frying pan and cook the onion in it over a moderate heat for about 10 minutes, stirring occasionally, until golden. Remove from the heat and leave to cool.

2 Pour the water into a small bowl, stir in the sugar until dissolved, and whisk in the yeast. Cover and leave to stand in a warm place for 10 minutes until the yeast becomes frothy.

3 Sift the flours into a mixing bowl, tipping in the bran left in the sieve. Stir in the mustard, salt, oregano and all but 1 tablespoon of the Parmesan. Make a well in the centre, pour in the yeast liquid and milk, and add the onion with its cooking oil. Mix to a soft dough, using a little extra lukewarm water if necessary. Turn the dough onto a floured surface and knead for 5 minutes, until even-textured and springy, then put it in a clean, lightly floured bowl. Cover with a clean, damp teacloth and leave in a warm place until doubled in size.

4 Turn the dough onto a floured surface, knock out the bubbles and knead again for 2 minutes, until springy. Roll with your hands into a sausage shape about 15in (38cm) long. Lift onto a greased baking sheet and cut across the top with diagonal slashes. Brush with water and sprinkle with the remaining Parmesan. Cover loosely with a clean teacloth and leave in a warm place for about 1 hour, or until the dough doubles in size, and retains a slight dent when lightly pressed with a fingertip.

5 Bake in the heated oven for 10 minutes, then turn the oven to 200°C (400°F, gas mark 6) and cook for 15 minutes more, until the loaf is golden brown and sounds hollow when tapped underneath. Cool on a wire rack.

A light-textured loaf flavoured with onion, cheese, mustard and oregano is given a crisp, savoury crust with a sprinkling of Parmesan.

Crumpets

ONE CRUMPET	
CALORIES 140	
TOTAL FAT 1g	
SATURATED FAT 0	
CARBOHYDRATES 30g	
ADDED SUGAR 0	
FIBRE 1g	
SODIUM 215mg	

MAKES 6
PREPARATION TIME: 25 minutes,
plus 1 hour to rise
COOKING TIME: 15 minutes

¼ pint (150ml) lukewarm water
½ level teaspoon caster sugar

1½ level teaspoons dried yeast
8oz (225g) strong unbleached plain flour
¼ level teaspoon salt
¼ pint (150ml) lukewarm skimmed milk
½ level teaspoon bicarbonate of soda
6 tablespoons cold water

1 Pour the lukewarm water into a small bowl with the sugar, and stir until the sugar has dissolved. Whisk in the yeast, cover and leave in a warm place for 10 minutes until frothy.

2 Sift the flour and salt into a bowl and make a well in the centre. Whisk the milk into the yeast liquid and pour into the flour. Beat vigorously with a wooden spoon for 5 minutes to make a smooth batter.

3 Cover the bowl with a clean, damp teacloth and put in a warm place for 30 minutes, until the batter doubles in volume then starts to drop.

4 Dissolve the bicarbonate of soda in the cold water and beat into the batter. Cover and leave to stand for 5 minutes.

5 Heat a griddle or a heavy-based frying pan on a low heat. Lightly grease the griddle or pan and put in 3 greased crumpet rings 4in (10cm) in diameter.

6 Fill each ring to half its depth with batter and cook for about 5 minutes, or until the top is covered with holes and no longer wet, and the underside is lightly browned.

7 Loosen the crumpets at the bottom with a palette knife, turn over and cook the other side for 30 seconds, until lightly browned. Cool on a wire rack while making 3 more crumpets with the remaining batter.

Serve the crumpets toasted and spread with reduced sugar conserve or cottage cheese.

Bubbles which form as the batter cooks and burst over the surface of crumpets give them the characteristic honeycomb structure that is such a delight to bite into.

Crusty breads and rolls

MAKES 2 large loaves, or 4 small loaves,
or 1 large loaf and 18 rolls, or 36 rolls
PREPARATION TIME: About 30 minutes,
plus up to 2 hours to rise
COOKING TIME: 25–40 minutes for loaves,
depending on size; 15 minutes for rolls
OVEN: Preheat to 230°C (450°F, gas mark 8)

½ pint (285ml) lukewarm water
½ level teaspoon caster sugar
2 level tablespoons dried yeast
3lb (1.4kg) plain wholemeal or strong unbleached
plain flour, or a mixture of the two
2 level teaspoons salt
3oz (85g) polyunsaturated margarine
1 pint (570ml) lukewarm skimmed milk

ONE ROLL	
CALORIES 145	
TOTAL FAT 3g	
SATURATED FAT 0	
CARBOHYDRATES 26g	
ADDED SUGAR 0	
FIBRE 4g	
SODIUM 135mg	

TIP
For the lukewarm water, pour ¼ pint (150ml) of boiling water into a measuring jug, then add cold water until the jug feels comfortably warm when you touch it with the inside of your wrist. Pour off excess water. The milk should be heated until the pan feels comfortably warm to your wrist.

1 Pour the water into a bowl, stir in the sugar to dissolve it, and whisk in the yeast. Cover and put in a warm place for 10 minutes until frothy.

2 Sift the flour and salt into a large mixing bowl, tipping in any bran left in the sieve. Rub in the margarine and make a well in the centre.

3 Whisk the yeast liquid with the milk, pour it into the flour and mix to form a soft dough.

4 Knead the dough on a lightly floured surface by folding it towards you, then pushing it down and away with the palm of your hand. Give the dough a quarter turn and repeat. Continue for about 10 minutes, until the dough is even-textured, springy and no longer sticky.

5 Put the dough in a clean, lightly floured bowl and cover with a clean, damp teacloth. Leave in a warm place (by a radiator or in an airing cupboard, for example) for 1–1½ hours, until the dough has doubled in size and springs back when pressed with a finger.

6 Turn the dough onto a lightly floured work surface and beat with clenched fists to knock out the air bubbles. Knead again until even-textured, then shape into loaves or rolls.

7 For two large tin loaves, grease two 2lb (900g) loaf tins. Divide the dough into two halves and roll each piece under your hands to form a smooth roll the same length as the loaf tin. For four small loaves, divide and shape the dough to fit 1lb (450g) loaf tins. Fit the dough into the tins, cover loosely with a clean teacloth and put in a warm place for about 45 minutes, or until the dough has risen to the top of the tins. Make 3 or 4 slashes across the top of each loaf before baking.

For two large cottage loaves, cut the dough in half, then cut a third off each piece. Roll the pieces under your hands to form rounds. Place the larger rounds on greased baking sheets, and set the smaller rounds on top. Flour the handle of a large wooden spoon, push it down through the centre of each loaf and pull it out again, to make the pieces join. Cover loosely with clean teacloths and put in a warm place to rise for about 1 hour, or until doubled in size.

To make four cob loaves, cut the dough into quarters. Shape each piece with your hands into a neat round. Place the loaves well apart on two greased baking sheets, cover loosely with clean teacloths and put in a warm place to rise for about 45 minutes, until doubled in size. Cut a deep cross in the top of each loaf before baking.

To make two large plaited loaves, cut the dough in half and cut each half into three equal pieces. Cover three pieces with an upturned bowl and roll the others under your hands into strands 18in (46cm) long. Lay the strands together end on to you and, working from the centre, plait them towards you, right strand over the centre, left strand over the new centre, and so on. Pinch the ends firmly together to seal. Turn the loaf over and away from you so that the loose ends are towards you. Plait these in the same way. Make up the second loaf, then place the loaves on greased baking sheets and cover loosely with clean teacloths and put the loaves in a warm place to rise for about 1 hour, or until doubled in size.

To make 36 rolls, weigh the dough into 2oz (60g) pieces and roll each one under your cupped palm into a smooth ball. If you like, you can then roll out each ball with a rolling pin to a 3in (85mm) disc to make baps. Alternatively, you can shape the pieces into mini-plaits or cottage loaves, or roll them into strands and tie each into a knot. Place the rolls well apart on greased baking sheets, cover loosely with clean teacloths and put in a warm place to rise for about 45 minutes, or until doubled in size.

Large or small, plaited, plain or cottage-style, floured, glazed or sprinkled with seeds or oats, homemade crusty loaves and rolls are welcome at any meal from family breakfast to festive dinner party.

8 When the loaves or rolls have risen, and will retain a slight dent if pressed lightly with a fingertip, brush the tops with salty water to give an extra crisp crust. If you prefer a softer crust, leave them plain or dust very lightly with flour. To give the tops a sheen, brush lightly with milk, and for a shiny glaze, brush with an egg beaten with 2 tablespoons of milk. After brushing, you can finish with a sprinkling of poppy seeds, sesame seeds or rolled oats.

9 Bake the bread in the heated oven. Large loaves will take about 40 minutes, small loaves about 25 minutes, and rolls about 15 minutes.

10 Turn the bread over on the baking sheet, or turn out of the tin and rap with a knuckle. It sounds hollow when cooked. If it does not, bake it for a few minutes longer. As soon as the bread is cooked, take it off the baking sheet or out of the tin and put on a wire rack to cool.

Wholemeal muffins

MAKES 10
PREPARATION TIME: 35 minutes,
plus 1 hour 40 minutes to rise
COOKING TIME: 25 minutes

7½ fl oz (215ml) lukewarm water
½ level teaspoon caster sugar
1½ level teaspoons dried yeast
5oz (150g) plain wholemeal flour, warmed
5oz (150g) strong unbleached plain flour, warmed
¼ level teaspoon salt
1 tablespoon olive oil

1 Pour half the water into a bowl and stir in the sugar until it dissolves. Whisk in the yeast, cover and leave in a warm place for 10 minutes until frothy.

2 Sift both flours and the salt into a bowl, tipping in the bran left in the sieve. Make a well in the centre of the flour. Pour in the yeast liquid, oil and remaining water, and mix to form a very soft dough, adding a little more water if necessary. The softer the dough, the more difficult it is to handle, but the better the muffins it makes.

3 Knead the dough on a well-floured surface until even-textured and springy. Put the dough into a lightly oiled bowl, cover with a clean, damp teacloth and put in a warm place to rise for about 1 hour, or until doubled in size.

4 Turn the dough onto a floured surface and knead for 2 minutes. Divide it into 10 equal pieces and shape each into a ball by rolling under the cupped palm of your hand. Heavily flour a board, place the balls of dough on it and sift flour over them. Cover loosely with a clean teacloth and put in a warm place to rise for about 40 minutes, until the dough keeps a slight dent if pressed lightly with a fingertip.

5 Heat a griddle, or a heavy-based frying pan, and oil it lightly. Lift in half the muffins and cook over a moderate heat for about 5 minutes, until lightly browned. Turn the muffins over and cook the other side for 6-7 minutes. Remove from the griddle and fold in a napkin to keep warm while you cook the rest.

Serve the muffins warm with fromage frais and fresh fruit, or with a savoury spread.

ONE MUFFIN

CALORIES 105

TOTAL FAT 2g

SATURATED FAT 0

CARBOHYDRATES 20g

ADDED SUGAR 0

FIBRE 2g

SODIUM 50mg

These soft, light little cakes of bread were once so popular that muffin men sold them warm in city streets. Now they are an all-too-rare treat, still most enjoyable warm from the oven, either just as they are or torn open and spread with a sweet or savoury filling.

TIP
Weigh out the flours in advance into warm bowls, cover and put on the boiler or in the airing cupboard for 30 minutes. This helps to keep this very soft mixture warm and to start the rising more quickly.

Olive and tomato focaccia

ONE PIECE	
CALORIES	165
TOTAL FAT	5g
SATURATED FAT	1g
CARBOHYDRATES	27g
ADDED SUGAR	0
FIBRE	3g
SODIUM	155mg

MAKES 2 loaves, each to give 6 pieces
PREPARATION TIME: 30 minutes,
plus 1 hour to rise
COOKING TIME: 20 minutes
OVEN: Preheat to 230°C (450°F, gas mark 8)

½ pint (285ml) lukewarm water
¼ level teaspoon caster sugar
2 level teaspoons dried yeast

8oz (225g) strong unbleached plain flour
8oz (225g) plain wholemeal flour
¼ level teaspoon salt
1 level teaspoon dried basil
3 tablespoons olive oil
2oz (60g) black olives, stoned and chopped
2oz (60g) sun-dried tomatoes, drained on kitchen paper and chopped
1 level teaspoon dried mixed herbs

This Italian bread, Genoa's version of the southern pizza, is full of the savoury tang of olives and the intense fruitiness of sun-dried tomatoes. Eat it newly baked, with cottage cheese or a salad, or pack it up to give a Mediterranean flavour to a picnic.

1 Pour half the water into a small bowl, stir in the sugar to dissolve it and whisk in the yeast. Cover and put in a warm place for 10 minutes, until frothy. Whisk in the remaining water.

2 Sift both flours and the salt into a mixing bowl, tipping the bran remaining in the sieve into the bowl. Mix in the basil and make a well in the centre.

3 Stir 2 tablespoons of the oil into the yeast liquid and pour into the well. Mix to a soft dough, then knead for 5 minutes on a floured surface, until even-textured and springy.

4 Put the dough in a lightly floured bowl, cover with a clean, damp teacloth and put in a warm place for 1 hour, or until doubled in size.

5 Turn the dough onto a floured surface and knead for 2 minutes. Slightly flatten the dough, spread the olives and tomatoes on it, then knead until they are well mixed in.

6 Divide the dough in half and roll out each piece to an oval about 12in (30cm) long. Place on a lightly greased baking sheet.

7 Make small dents all over the dough with your fingertips, brush it with the remaining oil and sprinkle with the mixed herbs. Bake in the heated oven for about 20 minutes, or until golden brown. Cool on a wire rack. Tear or cut the bread into 12 even pieces and serve.

If you prefer, you can add olives to one half of the risen dough and tomatoes to the other.

Pitta breads

MAKES 10
PREPARATION TIME: 40 minutes,
plus 1 hour 20 minutes to rise
COOKING TIME: 10 minutes
OVEN: Preheat to 240°C (475°F, gas mark 9)

½ pint (285ml) lukewarm water
¼ level teaspoon sugar
2 level teaspoons dried yeast
1lb (450g) strong unbleached plain flour
¼ level teaspoon salt
2 tablespoons olive oil

ONE PITTA BREAD	
CALORIES	180
TOTAL FAT	4g
SATURATED FAT	0
CARBOHYDRATES	34g
ADDED SUGAR	0
FIBRE	1g
SODIUM	50mg

TIP
Be sure to heat the baking sheets thoroughly. This is what makes the pitta breads become hollow in the middle as they cook.

1 Pour half the water into a bowl, stir in the sugar until it dissolves, then whisk in the yeast. Cover, leave to stand in a warm place for 10 minutes until frothy, then whisk in the rest of the water.

2 Sift the flour and salt into a bowl, make a well in the centre and pour in the yeast liquid and oil. Mix to a soft dough, then knead on a lightly floured surface for about 5 minutes, or until even in texture and springy.

3 Put the dough in a lightly floured bowl and cover with a clean, damp teacloth. Leave in a warm place for 1 hour, or until doubled in size.

4 Turn the dough onto a floured surface and knead for 2 minutes. Divide into 10 equal pieces, shape each into a ball by rolling under your cupped palm, then roll with a rolling pin into very thin ovals about ⅛ in (3mm) thick.

5 Spread out the ovals on two clean, floured teacloths, cover with more teacloths and leave to rise for 20 minutes. Halfway through the rising time, put two lightly greased baking sheets into the heated oven.

6 Quickly put the ovals on the hot baking sheets and bake for about 10 minutes, or until puffed and golden brown. Serve warm.

Slit the pitta breads along one side or cut across into halves and pack with hot savouries such as falafel (see p.245) or spicy beans, or cold fillings such as cheese or salads.

Very high heat puffs up these Balkan flatbreads, which can then be opened up to provide pockets for filling.

Pretzels with cumin seeds

MAKES 12
PREPARATION TIME: 40 minutes,
plus 1 hour 30 minutes to rise
COOKING TIME: 10 minutes
OVEN: Preheat to 230°C (450°F, gas mark 8)

½ pint (285ml) lukewarm water
¼ level teaspoon caster sugar
2 level teaspoons dried yeast
1lb (450g) strong unbleached plain flour
¼ level teaspoon salt
1oz (30g) polyunsaturated margarine
1 egg, size 3, beaten with 1 teaspoon water
2 level teaspoons cumin seeds

1 Pour half the water into a small bowl and stir in the sugar until it dissolves. Whisk in the yeast, cover and leave to stand in a warm place for 10 minutes, until frothy.

2 Sift the flour and salt into a bowl, rub in the margarine and make a well in the centre. Mix the remaining water into the yeast liquid and pour into the well. Mix to form a soft dough, then turn onto a lightly floured surface and knead for about 10 minutes, or until even in texture, springy and no longer sticky. Put the dough into a clean, lightly floured bowl, cover with a clean, damp teacloth and leave in a warm place for 1 hour, or until doubled in size.

3 Turn the dough onto a floured surface, knock out the air, then knead for 2 minutes. Divide the dough into 12 pieces. Take one piece of the dough for shaping, keeping the rest covered to prevent them from drying out.

4 To shape a pretzel, roll the dough under your hands into a sausage shape 20in (50cm) long. Bring the ends round until they cross and then take them up to the top of the circle, spacing them about 1½ in (40mm) apart, and press in position. Alternatively, roll the ends of the sausage thinner than the centre and twist them together before pressing down. Place on a baking sheet lined with nonstick baking paper, and cover loosely with a clean teacloth. Shape the other 11 pretzels in the same way, cover them loosely and put in a warm place again for 30 minutes, or until they have doubled in size.

5 Brush the pretzels with the beaten egg and sprinkle with cumin seeds. Bake in the heated oven for about 10 minutes, or until well risen, golden brown and hollow sounding when tapped underneath. Cool on wire racks.

For smaller, crisper pretzels, divide the dough into 24 pieces, roll and curve like horseshoes, brush with salty water and mark with cuts.

ONE LARGE PRETZEL	
CALORIES 155	
TOTAL FAT 3g	
SATURATED FAT 0	
CARBOHYDRATES 28g	
ADDED SUGAR 0	
FIBRE 1g	
SODIUM 70mg	

Cumin gives its distinctive spicy edge to these glossy-topped loose knots of bread.

This country bread, raised with bicarbonate of soda instead of yeast, is quick to make and at its soft, crumbly best when it is freshly baked.

Soda bread

MAKES 2 loaves, each to serve 6
PREPARATION TIME: 15 minutes
COOKING TIME: 25 minutes
OVEN: Preheat to 230°C (450°F, gas mark 8)

8oz (225g) unbleached plain flour
8oz (225g) plain wholemeal flour
¼ level teaspoon salt
1 level teaspoon bicarbonate of soda
1oz (30g) polyunsaturated margarine
½ pint (285ml) buttermilk, or 10oz (275g)
low-fat natural yoghurt

1 Sift both flours, the salt and the bicarbonate of soda into a bowl, reserving the bran remaining in the sieve. Rub in the margarine, then add the buttermilk or yoghurt and mix to form a soft dough.

2 Turn onto a lightly floured surface and knead for 1-2 minutes, until even-textured. Cut in half and shape each piece into a round.

3 Roll out the rounds to 1in (25mm) thick and place on separate greased baking sheets. Score each one deeply with a sharp knife to mark into six wedges. Sprinkle lightly with the reserved bran and bake in the heated oven for about 25 minutes, or until the loaves are well risen, golden brown and sound hollow when tapped underneath. Cool on wire racks.

Semi-skimmed milk can replace the buttermilk, but you will need to add 1 level teaspoon of cream of tartar to the flour. To vary the flavour, add 2 teaspoons of cumin seeds or caraway seeds, or 2 tablespoons of sultanas.

Banana spice loaf

MAKES 16 slices
PREPARATION TIME: 10 minutes
COOKING TIME: 40 minutes
OVEN: Preheat to 180°C (350°F, gas mark 4)

4oz (115g) unbleached plain flour
4oz (115g) plain wholemeal flour
2 level tablespoons muscovado sugar

2 level teaspoons bicarbonate of soda
1 level teaspoon each ground cinnamon and nutmeg
2oz (60g) polyunsaturated margarine
4oz (115g) low-fat natural yoghurt,
or 4fl oz (115ml) buttermilk
2 ripe medium bananas, mashed
1 egg, size 2, lightly beaten
1 teaspoon vanilla extract

Flavours from the tropics are blended into this country-kitchen tea-bread. A slice or two would be a welcome addition to a packed lunch.

> **TIP**
> *If using a nonstick loaf tin, there is no need to line the tin with baking paper. Simply grease the tin very lightly with margarine.*

1 Line a loaf tin 10×5in (25×13cm) with nonstick baking paper.

2 Sift both flours, the sugar, bicarbonate of soda, cinnamon and nutmeg into a mixing bowl, tipping the bran remaining in the sieve into the bowl.

3 Melt the margarine in a small saucepan, remove from the heat and mix in the yoghurt or buttermilk, the bananas, egg and vanilla extract. Pour into the flour and mix well to make a smooth batter.

4 Pour into the loaf tin and bake in the heated oven for 40 minutes, or until a skewer inserted into the centre of the loaf comes out clean. Leave the loaf in the tin for 10 minutes, then turn out onto a wire rack to cool completely before storing in an airtight container.

Date and walnut tea-bread

ONE SLICE

CALORIES	115
TOTAL FAT	3g
SATURATED FAT	0
CARBOHYDRATES	20g
ADDED SUGAR	4g
FIBRE	2g
SODIUM	65mg

MAKES 24 slices
PREPARATION TIME: 20 minutes,
plus 4 hours to stand
COOKING TIME: 1 hour 10 minutes
OVEN: Preheat to 180°C (350°F, gas mark 4)

½ pint (285ml) warm tea, strained
3oz (85g) demerara sugar

8oz (225g) stoned dates, chopped
8oz (225g) cooking apples
4½ oz (130g) walnuts, chopped
10oz (275g) malted wheat flour
2½ level teaspoons baking powder
1 egg, size 2, beaten
2 red-skinned dessert apples, washed with warm
water and dried
Juice of ½ a lemon
2 teaspoons clear honey

1 Pour the tea into a mixing bowl and stir in half the sugar and all the dates. Cover and leave to stand for 4 hours.

2 Line a cake tin 8in (20cm) square with nonstick baking paper.

3 Peel, core and coarsely grate the cooking apples and mix into the dates. Set aside 2 tablespoons of the walnuts and stir the rest into the dates.

4 Sift the flour and baking powder into the date mixture, and tip in the grains remaining in the sieve. Add the egg and mix well.

5 Spoon the mixture into the prepared tin and spread evenly. Core the dessert apples, slice them thinly into rings and overlap them on top of the mixture. Brush with the lemon juice and sprinkle with the remaining sugar. Bake in the heated oven for 1 hour 10 minutes, or until a skewer inserted in the centre comes out clean.

6 Take the tin out of the oven, brush the honey over the apples and sprinkle the reserved walnuts on top. Cool the bread in the tin for 20 minutes, then take it out and stand it on a wire rack to cool completely.

This tea-bread keeps well for up to a week in an airtight tin. For serving, cut it in half and cut each half into 12 slices.

Tea and grated apple soften the dates and make this tea-bread dark and moist. A light brushing with honey on the oven-hot loaf gives a glistening finish to the attractive topping of apples and walnuts.

High in fibre and in flavour, this spiced tea-bread offers the concentrated taste of dried fruits and the perfumed sweetness of maple syrup.

Spicy maple tea-bread

ONE SLICE	
CALORIES	112
TOTAL FAT	1g
SATURATED FAT	0
CARBOHYDRATES	25g
ADDED SUGAR	3g
FIBRE	3g
SODIUM	180mg

TIP
Keep the tea-bread in an airtight tin for 2-3 days before eating. It improves in flavour with keeping and also becomes moister.

MAKES 24 slices
PREPARATION TIME: 20 minutes, plus 3 hours to stand
COOKING TIME: 1 hour 15 minutes
OVEN: Preheat to 180°C (350°F, gas mark 4)

4oz (115g) ready-to-use dried apricots, chopped
4oz (115g) ready-to-use stoned prunes, chopped
4oz (115g) dried figs, stalk ends removed, chopped
3oz (85g) chopped mixed candied peel
4oz (115g) All-bran
¾ pint (425ml) buttermilk, or 15oz (425g) low-fat natural yoghurt
7fl oz (200ml) skimmed milk
4fl oz (115ml) maple syrup
8oz (225g) plain wholemeal flour
4oz (115g) unbleached plain flour
3 level teaspoons baking powder
2 level teaspoons ground mixed spice

1   Put the apricots, prunes, figs and mixed peel into a large bowl with the All-bran, buttermilk or yoghurt, skimmed milk and maple syrup. Mix well, cover and leave to stand for 3 hours, stirring occasionally.

2   Line a loaf tin 11½ ×4in (29×10cm) with nonstick baking paper.

3   Sift the flours, baking powder and spice into the bowl containing the fruit, and tip in the bran left in the sieve. Mix well.

4   Spoon the mixture into the loaf tin and spread evenly. Bake in the heated oven for 1 hour 15 minutes, or until a skewer inserted in the centre of the loaf comes out clean.

5   Take the bread out of the oven. Cool in the tin for 20 minutes, then remove from the tin and leave on a wire rack to cool completely.

You could use sultanas, raisins and currants instead of the apricots, prunes and figs.

Prune tea-bread

MAKES 16 slices
PREPARATION TIME: 10 minutes
COOKING TIME: 40 minutes
OVEN: Preheat to 190°C (375°F, gas mark 5)

4oz (115g) unbleached plain flour
2oz (60g) plain wholemeal flour
½ level teaspoon bicarbonate of soda
½ level teaspoon ground cinnamon
½ level teaspoon freshly grated nutmeg
or ground nutmeg
1 egg, size 2
2oz (60g) soft dark brown sugar
7fl oz (200ml) buttermilk, or 7oz (200g) low-fat
natural yoghurt
1 tablespoon corn oil
3oz (85g) ready-to-use stoned prunes, roughly
chopped or snipped with kitchen scissors

ONE SLICE	
CALORIES	75
TOTAL FAT	2g
SATURATED FAT	0
CARBOHYDRATES	14g
ADDED SUGAR	4g
FIBRE	1g
SODIUM	22mg

1 Line a loaf tin 10×5in (25×13cm) with nonstick baking paper.

2 Sift the flours, bicarbonate of soda, cinnamon and nutmeg into a mixing bowl and tip in the bran remaining in the sieve.

3 Beat the egg and sugar in a bowl with a fork, then mix in the buttermilk or yoghurt and the oil. Stir the mixture into the flour to make a smooth, thick batter. Stir in the prunes.

4 Pour the batter into the loaf tin and cook in the heated oven for 40 minutes, or until a skewer pushed into the centre of the bread comes out clean. Cool in the tin for 5 minutes, then turn out onto a wire rack, and leave until cold before storing in an airtight tin.

This open-textured, spiced loaf, studded with sweet, dark prunes and lightened with buttermilk or yoghurt will stay fresh and soft for several days – and its flavour improves with keeping.

Fruit and nut cake

ONE PIECE	
CALORIES	285
TOTAL FAT	12g
SATURATED FAT	2g
CARBOHYDRATES	41g
ADDED SUGAR	0
FIBRE	2g
SODIUM	105mg

MAKES 12 pieces
PREPARATION TIME: 25 minutes
COOKING TIME: 1 hour 15 minutes
OVEN: Preheat to 180°C (350°F, gas mark 4)

4oz (115g) plain wholemeal flour
4oz (115g) unbleached plain flour
2 level teaspoons baking powder
2 level teaspoons ground mixed spice

4oz (115g) stoned dates, chopped
4oz (115g) sultanas
4oz (115g) seedless raisins
3oz (85g) malt extract
2 eggs, size 3, lightly beaten
2 dessert apples, peeled, cored and grated
4fl oz (115ml) unsweetened apple juice
4fl oz (115ml) corn oil
1oz (30g) blanched almonds, split into halves

1 Line a cake tin 8in (20cm) in diameter with nonstick baking paper.

2 Sift the flours, baking powder and spice into a mixing bowl, and tip in the bran left in the sieve. Mix in the dates, sultanas and raisins. Make a well in the centre and put in the malt extract, eggs, apples, apple juice and oil. Mix until all the ingredients are combined.

3 Spoon the mixture into the cake tin, smooth the top and arrange the almonds on the top in concentric circles. Bake in the heated oven for about 1 hour 15 minutes, or until a skewer inserted into the centre comes out clean.

4 Cool the cake in the tin for 5 minutes, then turn it onto a wire rack to cool completely before storing it in an airtight tin.

Not quite a traditional fruit cake but equally satisfying, this teatime treat has malt extract and apple juice to enrich its flavour, and it becomes moister if you can wait for a few days before cutting into it.

Swiss roll

TIP
If you are using a balloon or other hand whisk, set the bowl of eggs and sugar on a saucepan of hot water and whisk. When the mixture is thick, lift the bowl off the pan and keep whisking until the mixture has cooled.

SERVES 8
PREPARATION TIME: 25 minutes,
plus 30 minutes to cool
COOKING TIME: 10 minutes
OVEN: Preheat to 200°C (400°F, gas mark 6)

3 eggs, size 2
3oz (85g) caster sugar
3oz (85g) plain flour
7oz (200g) fresh or frozen blueberries
Strained juice of 1 small lemon
1 level teaspoon arrowroot
1 tablespoon water
4oz (115g) Greek yoghurt
1 level tablespoon pistachio nuts, skinned and chopped

1 Grease a swiss-roll tin 13×9in (33×23cm) and line it with nonstick baking paper.

2 Whisk the eggs and 2oz (60g) of the sugar with an electric or hand whisk until the mixture is pale, very fluffy and so thick that a ribbon of mixture trailed onto it from the whisk stays on the surface.

3 Sift the flour over the mixture and gently fold it in, using a metal tablespoon. Pour the mixture into the tin and gently spread it out with a palette knife. Bake for about 10 minutes, until well risen, firm to the touch and golden.

4 Meanwhile, place a sheet of nonstick baking paper on a damp teacloth and sprinkle with 1 teaspoon of the remaining sugar.

5 Quickly turn the sponge onto the paper, with a short side towards you, and peel off the cooking paper. Trim off the crisp edges with a sharp knife. Carefully roll the sponge away from you, rolling sponge and paper together. Place seam side down on a wire rack to cool.

6 Gently heat the blueberries with the remaining sugar and the lemon juice in a small, covered saucepan until the juices begin to run.

Remove from the heat. Blend the arrowroot with the water, then stir into the fruit. Return to the heat and continue cooking, stirring gently, until the liquid thickens and clears. Pour into a wide bowl to cool.

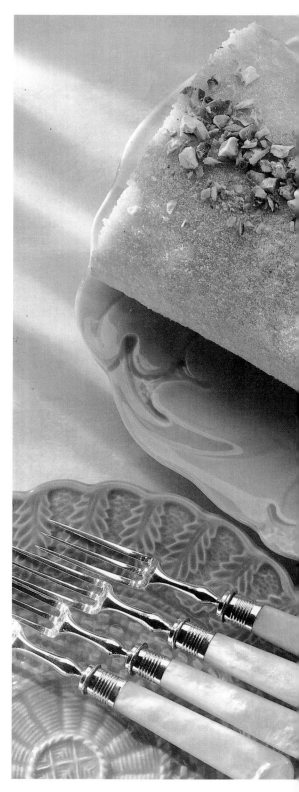

A cup of tea and a slice of cake for friends on leisurely summer Sunday afternoons are all the more enjoyable with a light treat such as this. Thick yoghurt and deep crimson blueberries make a fresh, slightly sharp filling for the delicate sponge roll.

7 When both roll and blueberry filling are cold, carefully unroll the sponge. Spread the yoghurt over it, then cover with the blueberry mixture, leaving a narrow border all round. Roll up from the other short edge. Scatter the nuts in a line along the top. Lift the swiss roll onto a serving dish, cover with an upturned plastic box and put in a cool place until serving time.

If this is more than an hour away, put the roll, covered, in the refrigerator, taking it out 30 minutes before serving.

You can use blackcurrants or bilberries instead of blueberries, but they will need a little more sugar. You can also fill the roll with raspberries, which need no sugar or cooking.

Chocolate cookies

MAKES 36
PREPARATION TIME: 15 minutes
COOKING TIME: 15 minutes
OVEN: Preheat to 190°C (375°F, gas mark 5)

2oz (60g) polyunsaturated margarine
1½ oz (45g) caster sugar
1½ oz (45g) soft light brown sugar
2 eggs, size 2, lightly beaten
1 teaspoon vanilla extract
4oz (115g) plain white flour
1oz (30g) plain wholemeal flour
½ level teaspoon bicarbonate of soda
1oz (30g) plain chocolate, coarsely grated

ONE COOKIE	
CALORIES	45
TOTAL FAT	2g
SATURATED FAT	1g
CARBOHYDRATES	6g
ADDED SUGAR	3g
FIBRE	0
SODIUM	40mg

1 Beat the margarine, caster sugar and brown sugar until the mixture is light and fluffy.

2 Add the eggs a little at a time, beating the mixture well after each addition. Beat in the vanilla extract.

3 Sift the plain and wholemeal flour and the bicarbonate of soda into the mixture, tipping in the bran remaining in the sieve. Sprinkle in the chocolate and mix together gently but thoroughly with a metal spoon until the ingredients are combined.

4 Put half-tablespoons of the mixture onto baking sheets lined with nonstick baking paper, spacing them well apart. Bake in the heated oven for about 15 minutes, or until lightly browned. Cool on wire racks and store in an airtight container.

These American-style cookies, speckled with flakes of chocolate, are at their crisp, light best when just cooled from the oven.

Crunchy-topped slices, chewy with sticky dates, flakes of oats and malt extract, make satisfying snacks to enjoy at home or to pack for munching at work or school.

TIP
Use cooking dates to make the slices. You can snip them up very quickly with kitchen scissors.

ONE SLICE	
CALORIES	105
TOTAL FAT	4g
SATURATED FAT	1g
CARBOHYDRATES	17g
ADDED SUGAR	0
FIBRE	1g
SODIUM	28mg

Date and oat slices

MAKES 18
PREPARATION TIME: 15 minutes
COOKING TIME: 20 minutes
OVEN: Preheat to 200°C (400°F, gas mark 4)

2oz (60g) polyunsaturated margarine
4oz (115g) malt extract
6oz (175g) stoned dates, chopped
6oz (175g) rolled oats

1 Melt the margarine and malt extract in a large saucepan over a low heat, stirring. Mix in the dates and oats until everything is thoroughly combined.

2 Spread the mixture evenly in a shallow nonstick baking tin 11×7in (28×18cm). Bake in the heated oven for about 20 minutes, or until golden brown.

3 Remove from the oven and immediately score the top deeply with a sharp knife, marking in half lengthways, and then marking each half across into 9 equal sections. Leave in the tin until completely cold.

4 Carefully turn out onto a board and divide into slices by cutting through the marked divisions with a sharp knife.

Savoury biscuits

MAKES 24
PREPARATION TIME: 1 hour,
plus 15 minutes to rise
COOKING TIME: 15 minutes
OVEN: Preheat to 180°C (350°F, gas mark 4)

4fl oz (115ml) lukewarm skimmed milk
¼ level teaspoon caster sugar
1 level teaspoon dried yeast
8oz (225g) plain flour
⅛ level teaspoon salt
1oz (30g) polyunsaturated margarine, melted
2 level teaspoons each sesame seeds and poppy seeds

1 Pour the milk into a bowl, stir in the sugar until it dissolves, then whisk in the yeast. Cover and leave in a warm place for about 10 minutes until frothy.

2 Sift the flour and salt into a bowl and make a well in the centre. Pour in the yeast liquid and the melted margarine. Mix to form a slightly dry dough; do not add any extra liquid.

3 Turn the dough onto a lightly floured surface and knead for about 6 minutes, until smooth and springy. Put the dough in a clean bowl, cover with a clean, damp teacloth and leave to rise in a warm place for 15 minutes.

4 Roll the dough out to form an oblong about 18×6in (46×15cm) long. Working from a narrow end, fold the bottom third of the dough up and over the centre third, then bring the top third down over it. Press the edges firmly together with the rolling pin.

5 Give the dough a quarter turn and roll it out to the large oblong again, then fold as before. Repeat seven more times.

6 Roll the pastry out to ⅛ in (3mm) thick and prick with a fork, pricking at close intervals all over the dough. Cut out rounds with a 3in (75mm) plain biscuit cutter. Place the rounds on ungreased baking sheets.

7 Put together the trimmings, overlapping them to form an oblong, then roll out to ⅛ in (3mm) thick and cut out more rounds.

8 Lightly brush the rounds with cold water. Sprinkle one half with sesame seeds and the other with poppy seeds, pressing the seeds down lightly with the back of a spoon. Bake in the heated oven for 15 minutes, or until lightly browned. Remove the biscuits from the oven and immediately cool on wire racks. They will keep well in an airtight container.

ONE BISCUIT
CALORIES 45
TOTAL FAT 2g
SATURATED FAT 0
CARBOHYDRATES 6g
ADDED SUGAR 0
FIBRE 0
SODIUM 25mg

Sesame snaps

MAKES 30
PREPARATION TIME: 20 minutes
COOKING TIME: 15 minutes
OVEN: Preheat to 180°C (350°F, gas mark 4)

8oz (225g) plain wholemeal flour
⅛ level teaspoon salt
½ level teaspoon baking powder
2oz (60g) polyunsaturated margarine
1oz (30g) sesame seeds
4 tablespoons skimmed milk
1 egg white, size 2
1 level teaspoon paprika

1 Sift the flour, salt and baking powder into a bowl, tipping in the bran left in the sieve. Rub in the margarine, stir in half the sesame seeds and make a well in the centre.

2 Set aside ½ tablespoon of the milk. Lightly beat the rest with the egg white and pour into the well. Mix to a firm, even-textured dough.

3 Roll out on a lightly floured surface until ⅛ in (3mm) thick. Cut with a sharp knife into 3×1½ in (75×40mm) oblongs.

4 Arrange well spaced out on lightly greased baking sheets. Knead and roll out the pastry trimmings to cut into more oblongs.

5 Brush the biscuits with the reserved milk and sprinkle the remaining sesame seeds and the paprika on top. Bake in the heated oven for about 15 minutes, or until lightly browned. Put the biscuits on wire racks to cool before storing in an airtight tin.

ONE BISCUIT
CALORIES 40
TOTAL FAT 2g
SATURATED FAT 0
CARBOHYDRATES 4g
ADDED SUGAR 0
FIBRE 1g
SODIUM 30mg

Home-baked flaky and wholemeal biscuits offer a crisp and light alternative to bread. Enjoy them with cheese, pâtés, dips and spreads.

COCKTAIL SNACKS AND DRINKS

Light bites and imaginative drinks set parties and celebratory dinners off with a swing. This selection has something for every season and social occasion – and all, from spicy toasted nuts and savoury dips to turkey bouchées and stuffed tomatoes, have been vetted for sugar and fat. There is redcurrant punch to take the chill off winter evenings, an icy spritzer to refresh in the summer sun, and hot chocolate with a difference to make a soothing pick-me-up.

Chickpea and rosemary dip

MAKES 18 level tablespoons
PREPARATION TIME: 20 minutes,
plus 1 hour to refrigerate

7oz (200g) cooked chickpeas (see p.17)
1 level teaspoon chopped fresh rosemary,
or ½ level teaspoon dried rosemary
2 level teaspoons chopped fresh parsley
1 small clove garlic, peeled and crushed
1 small red onion, peeled and finely chopped
2 teaspoons lime juice
1-4 tablespoons vegetable stock (see p.19)
Freshly ground black pepper
¼ level teaspoon paprika
Sprigs of fresh rosemary to garnish

LEVEL TABLESPOON	
CALORIES 15	
TOTAL FAT 0	
SATURATED FAT 0	
CARBOHYDRATES 2g	
ADDED SUGAR 0	
FIBRE 1g	
SODIUM 0	

1 Blend the chickpeas, rosemary, parsley and garlic in a food processor for 30 seconds to make a smooth purée.

2 Mix in the onion and lime juice and stir in enough stock to give the dip the consistency of thick whipped cream. Season with pepper.

3 Turn the dip into a serving bowl, sprinkle with paprika and garnish with the rosemary sprigs. Cover and refrigerate for 1 hour, or up to 3 hours, before serving.

Serve with fingers of toast, pitta bread triangles, savoury biscuits (see p.382), or raw vegetables.

Cottage cheese and basil dip

MAKES 18 level tablespoons
PREPARATION TIME: 15 minutes,
plus 1 hour to refrigerate

10oz (275g) cottage cheese, drained
6 medium radishes, trimmed and finely chopped
2 level tablespoons chopped fresh basil,
or 1 level teaspoon dried basil
1 clove garlic, peeled and crushed
½ level teaspoon finely grated lemon rind
Basil leaves and 2-3 radish flowers to garnish

LEVEL TABLESPOON	
CALORIES 15	
TOTAL FAT 0	
SATURATED FAT 0	
CARBOHYDRATES 1g	
ADDED SUGAR 0	
FIBRE 0	
SODIUM 60mg	

1 Blend the cheese in a food processor for 20 seconds, or pass it through a nylon sieve.

2 Stir the chopped radishes, basil, garlic and lemon rind into the cheese. Spoon the mixture into a serving bowl, cover and refrigerate for 1 hour, or up to 3 hours, before serving.

3 Garnish the dip with the basil leaves and radish flowers, and serve with warm muffins (see p.368), toast or raw vegetables.

Guacamole

MAKES 18 level tablespoons
PREPARATION TIME: 20 minutes

1 large ripe avocado, halved, stoned and peeled
2 level tablespoons low-fat natural yoghurt
2 medium tomatoes, skinned, de-seeded and chopped
2 level tablespoons chopped fresh parsley
or coriander
½ level teaspoon ground coriander
1 small red onion, peeled and finely chopped
4 teaspoons lime or lemon juice
1 clove garlic, peeled and crushed
Coriander leaves to garnish

LEVEL TABLESPOON	
CALORIES 25	
TOTAL FAT 2g	
SATURATED FAT 0	
CARBOHYDRATES 1g	
ADDED SUGAR 0	
FIBRE 1g	
SODIUM 5mg	

1 Mash the avocado with a fork in a bowl, until it becomes smooth and creamy. Stir in all the other ingredients gently but thoroughly.

2 Spoon the guacamole into a serving bowl, garnish with coriander leaves and serve at once, or cover and refrigerate for up to 30 minutes. Do not keep the dip any longer or it will start to blacken.

You can serve savoury biscuits or Melba toast with the guacamole, or pack it into short lengths of celery.

An assortment of crudités provides edible scoops for three delicious dips: coriander, onion and tomato add flavour and body to guacamole (near right); the mild, nutty flavour of chickpeas is sharpened with lime and rosemary (centre); and cottage cheese is given a peppery bite by chopped radishes and a seasoning of fresh basil.

TIP
To make a radish flower, slice off the stalk end, stand the radish cut end down and trim off the tip. Make rows of deep cuts round the radish, cutting downwards. Put it in iced water in the refrigerator for 30 minutes and the cuts will open up.

Courgette and cheese wheels

MAKES 30 wheels
PREPARATION TIME: 15 minutes,
plus 1 hour to refrigerate

2oz (60g) low-fat cottage cheese, drained and passed through a nylon sieve
2oz (60g) ricotta cheese
1 level teaspoon each chopped fresh basil, chives and thyme
2 large courgettes, each about 4oz (115g), washed and trimmed
Whole mixed peppercorns (pink, green, white and black)
Thyme or parsley to garnish

1 Mix the cottage cheese and ricotta cheese with the basil, chives and thyme. Using a potato peeler, cut the courgettes lengthways into thin slices. Discard the narrow first and last slices of each courgette.

2 Spread each courgette slice with cheese mixture and roll up neatly. Lay them close together in a shallow dish, cover and refrigerate for at least 1 hour and up to 3 hours.

3 Arrange the wheels on a serving plate. Grind the pepper over them, garnish with thyme or parsley and serve.

THREE WHEELS	
CALORIES 15	
TOTAL FAT 1g	
SATURATED FAT 0	
CARBOHYDRATES 1g	
ADDED SUGAR 0	
FIBRE 0	
SODIUM 25mg	

Mushrooms with watercress stuffing

MAKES 12
PREPARATION TIME: 20 minutes
COOKING TIME: 10 minutes
OVEN: Preheat to 200°C (400°F, gas mark 6)

12 medium open-cap mushrooms, wiped and trimmed
2 tablespoons olive oil
2 cloves garlic, peeled and crushed
2 bunches watercress, trimmed, washed and chopped
½ level teaspoon dried oregano
1 tablespoon lemon juice
1½ oz (45g) wholemeal breadcrumbs
3 slices wholemeal bread
1 level tablespoon chopped fresh thyme or chives

1 Separate the stalks from the mushrooms and chop them, leaving the cups whole. Heat half the oil in a frying pan and cook half the garlic in it over a moderate heat for 30 seconds. Stir in the mushroom stalks and cook for about 5 minutes, until lightly coloured.

2 Mix in the watercress and oregano, and cook for about 1 minute, until the watercress wilts. Sprinkle in the lemon juice and remove the pan from the heat.

3 Fill the mushrooms with the stuffing and top with the breadcrumbs. Arrange the mushrooms on a nonstick baking tray and cook in the heated oven for about 10 minutes, or until the breadcrumbs are lightly browned and the mushrooms softened.

4 Meanwhile, mix the remaining oil and garlic with the thyme or chives. Toast the bread on one side under the grill, then brush the oil mixture over the other side and toast until lightly coloured.

5 Using a plain round biscuit cutter about the same size as the mushrooms, stamp out 12 small rounds from the toast. Set a mushroom on each and serve immediately.

ONE MUSHROOM	
CALORIES 45	
TOTAL FAT 2g	
SATURATED FAT 0	
CARBOHYDRATES 5g	
ADDED SUGAR 0	
FIBRE 1g	
SODIUM 60mg	

Spicy toasted nuts

MAKES 15 level tablespoons
PREPARATION TIME: 20 minutes

3½ oz (100g) shelled almonds
6 cardamom pods

¾ level teaspoon ground cumin
¾ level teaspoon ground coriander
⅛ level teaspoon cayenne pepper
1 teaspoon olive oil
3½ oz (100g) unsalted cashew nuts

LEVEL TABLESPOON	
CALORIES 80	
TOTAL FAT 7g	
SATURATED FAT 1g	
CARBOHYDRATES 1g	
ADDED SUGAR 0	
FIBRE 1g	
SODIUM 5mg	

TIP
To crush a few small seeds, such as cardamom or fennel, put them in one spoon and press the bowl of another down on them.

1 Put the almonds into a saucepan, cover with cold water, bring to the boil and drain immediately. Slide off and discard the skins.

2 Take the cardamom seeds from their pods and crush them. Mix in the cumin, coriander and cayenne pepper.

3 Heat the oil in a frying pan and stir-fry the nuts in it over a moderate heat for about 3 minutes, until golden, as if lightly toasted.

4 Mix in the spices and stir over the heat for 30 seconds. Turn into a heatproof dish and leave until cold before serving.

Colourful spirals of paper-thin courgette slices holding soft cheese make an attractive show on party platters; baked mushrooms filled with hot watercress and oregano have a crisp crumb topping and sit on discs of toast; almonds and cashew nuts take on a richer colour and flavour when tossed with a coating of spices.

Freshwater prawns in spiced dressing

ONE PRAWN

CALORIES 20

TOTAL FAT 1g

SATURATED FAT 0

CARBOHYDRATES 1g

ADDED SUGAR 0

FIBRE 0

SODIUM 25mg

TIP
To de-vein a prawn, make a shallow cut along its back and lift out the fine black vein with the tip of the knife.

MAKES 24
PREPARATION TIME: 30 minutes, plus 2-3 hours to cool and refrigerate
COOKING TIME: 20 minutes

12 whole black peppercorns
12 coriander seeds
4 cloves
1 bay leaf
½ level teaspoon mustard seeds
½ level teaspoon dried thyme
1 medium onion, peeled and chopped
1 stick celery, trimmed and chopped
3 slices lemon
3 cloves garlic, peeled and chopped
2 tablespoons white wine vinegar
24 large raw freshwater prawns, about 1¼ lb (550g) together, peeled, de-veined, tails left on
2 tablespoons lemon juice
1 tablespoon virgin olive oil
⅛ level teaspoon cayenne pepper
Lemon and lime slices and dill fronds to garnish

1 Put the peppercorns, coriander seeds, cloves, bay leaf, mustard seeds and thyme in a small square of muslin or white cotton fabric, gather the sides together and tie securely with clean thread.

2 Bring 1¼ pints (725ml) of unsalted water to the boil in a large stainless steel or enamel saucepan and add the onion, celery, lemon slices, garlic, vinegar and the bag of spices. Reduce the heat and simmer, uncovered, for 15 minutes.

3 Pour in the prawns and cook, uncovered, for 2-3 minutes, stirring frequently, until they turn pink. Remove from the heat and leave to cool in the pan, then cover and refrigerate for 2 hours.

4 Drain the prawns and discard the lemon slices and spices. Gently toss the prawns, onion and celery with the lemon juice, oil and cayenne. Turn into a serving dish and garnish with slices of lemon, lime and dill.

Remember to put a supply of cocktail sticks on the table beside the prawns.

Stuffed radishes

THREE RADISHES

CALORIES 15

TOTAL FAT 0

SATURATED FAT 0

CARBOHYDRATES 1g

ADDED SUGAR 0

FIBRE 0

SODIUM 10mg

MAKES about 30
PREPARATION TIME: 15 minutes, plus 30 minutes to refrigerate

2 bunches radishes, washed and trimmed, leaving a little stalk on each
4oz (115g) quark or low-fat cottage cheese
⅛ level teaspoon cayenne pepper, or 1 level teaspoon celery seeds
1 level teaspoon poppy seeds

1 Cut downwards through the centre tip of each radish three times, making a star pattern and cutting almost to the stalk. Put the radishes in iced water in the refrigerator for 30 minutes, or until they open into a flower shape.

2 Mix the cheese with the cayenne pepper or celery seeds; if using cottage cheese, pass it through a sieve first. Pipe the mixture through a small star nozzle into the centre of each radish, or press it in with a knife.

3 Sprinkle the radishes with poppy seeds and arrange on a serving dish. Serve them at once, or keep in the refrigerator, covered, for up to 2 hours. Take them out about 30 minutes before serving time.

Meaty prawns are flavoured with a subtle infusion of herbs, spices and vegetables while they cook, and then given a hot cayenne dressing; pretty radishes opened like tulips and filled with a spicy cream cheese stuffing, make eye-catching party appetisers.

Sardine and rice parcels

ONE PARCEL

CALORIES 40

TOTAL FAT 1g

SATURATED FAT 0

CARBOHYDRATES 3g

ADDED SUGAR 0

FIBRE 0

SODIUM 30mg

MAKES 24
PREPARATION TIME: 30 minutes,
plus 15 minutes to cool
COOKING TIME: 10 minutes

2½ oz (70g) long-grain rice
1 tablespoon white wine vinegar
28 large, undamaged spinach leaves
8 small fresh or frozen and thawed sardines, scaled
(see p.96), cleaned, gutted and boned
2 small spring onions, finely chopped
Lemon wedges to garnish
2 level tablespoons English mustard powder mixed
with 4 teaspoons water

1 Cook the rice (see p.17). Mix the vinegar into the rice while it is still warm, then leave the mixture to cool.

2 Meanwhile, spread 4 spinach leaves in a steamer basket and place the sardines on top. Put the basket in the steamer pan over 1in (25mm) of boiling water, cover and steam for

about 6 minutes, until the sardines flake readily when tested with a fork. Take the basket out of the steamer and carefully lift the sardines onto a plate. Divide each sardine into three pieces and leave to cool. Discard the spinach.

3 Put the remaining spinach leaves in the steamer basket and steam them for 1 minute. Remove the basket from the steamer, rinse the leaves with cold water and lift them out carefully onto kitchen paper to pat dry.

4 Put a rounded teaspoon of rice at the stem end of a spinach leaf. Set one piece of sardine on top and sprinkle some onion on it. Fold the sides of the leaf over the filling, then roll up to make a neat parcel. Fill the rest of the leaves, arrange the parcels on a serving plate and garnish them with the lemon wedges. Put the mustard beside them to dab on the parcels.

Serve the parcels at once, or cover them and refrigerate for up to 3 hours before serving.

> **TIP**
> *To prepare each sardine, cut off its head and tail, slit it along the belly, gut it and lay it flat, skin side down. Lift the backbone from the tail end with the knife tip and pull towards the head; all the bones will come away with it.*

Spinach soufflé squares

ONE PIECE

CALORIES 45

TOTAL FAT 2g

SATURATED FAT 1g

CARBOHYDRATES 2g

ADDED SUGAR 0

FIBRE 1g

SODIUM 105mg

MAKES 25 pieces
PREPARATION TIME: 15 minutes
COOKING TIME: 25 minutes
OVEN: Preheat to 200°C (400°F, gas mark 6)

2lb (900g) fresh spinach, trimmed, washed
and chopped
⅛ level teaspoon freshly grated nutmeg
8oz (225g) low-fat cottage cheese, drained
2 level teaspoons plain flour
2 level tablespoons grated Parmesan cheese
3 eggs, size 2, separated
⅛ level teaspoon cayenne pepper
Freshly ground black pepper
Red or yellow cherry tomatoes to garnish

1 Put the spinach in a saucepan with only the water that clings to it and sprinkle with the nutmeg. Cook, uncovered, over a moderate heat for about 5 minutes, stirring several times, until the spinach is tender. Drain thoroughly and leave to cool.

2 Blend the cottage cheese in a food processor for 30 seconds or pass it through a nylon sieve. Add the flour, Parmesan, egg yolks, cayenne and black pepper, and blend for a further 30 seconds, or beat with a wooden spoon. Mix with the spinach in a large bowl.

3 Line a baking tin 7½ in (18cm) square with nonstick baking paper.

4 Whisk the egg whites until they hold soft peaks and fold into the spinach mixture, using a large metal spoon. Pour into the tin, smooth the top and bake in the heated oven for about 20 minutes, until set.

5 Cool on a wire rack for 5 minutes, then turn out of the tin, peel off the paper and cut the soufflé into 1½ in (40mm) squares.

Serve at once, garnished with the tomatoes, or cover and refrigerate for up to 24 hours.

Hidden in each of these neat, bite-sized parcels of lightly steamed spinach (right, bottom) is a portion of rice and a morsel of sardine. Spinach is also the vital ingredient in the soufflé squares; there it mingles with cottage cheese, nutmeg and Parmesan to make light, savoury party pieces.

Tomatoes with prawn stuffing

MAKES 24
PREPARATION TIME: 20 minutes,
plus 20 minutes to cool
COOKING TIME: 4 minutes

4oz (115g) raw freshwater prawns
2 level tablespoons chopped fresh parsley
1 clove garlic, peeled and crushed
1 tablespoon lemon juice
1 tablespoon olive oil
1/8 level teaspoon cayenne pepper
24 cherry tomatoes, washed, stalks left on

1 Put the prawns in a saucepan, cover with unsalted cold water and bring to the boil. Cook, uncovered, for 2 minutes, or until the prawns turn pink. Drain and leave for about 20 minutes, until cool enough to handle.

2 Peel and de-vein the prawns (see p.390), then chop them finely. Mix them in a bowl with the parsley, garlic, lemon juice, oil and cayenne pepper. Cover and chill the mixture in the refrigerator while you are preparing the tomatoes.

3 Slice the top off each tomato and set aside. Scoop out the core and seeds carefully with a small teaspoon and place the shells upside-down on pieces of kitchen paper until any liquid has drained out.

4 Fill the tomatoes with the prawn mixture and place the reserved tops back on them. Arrange on a serving plate and serve at once or cover the tomatoes and refrigerate them for up to 3 hours before serving.

You can use 3oz (85g) of cooked, peeled prawns in place of the freshwater prawns, but the salt content will be higher. Use yellow tomatoes, when you can get them, as well as red ones.

THREE TOMATOES

CALORIES 32

TOTAL FAT 2g

SATURATED FAT 0

CARBOHYDRATES 2g

ADDED SUGAR 0

FIBRE 1g

SODIUM 15mg

TIP
For the best proportion of filling to cucumber, use thin cucumbers and leave a shell about 1/2 in (13mm) thick. Do not cut the slices too thin; thicker slices hold the filling more securely.

Tuna and cucumber rings

MAKES 30 rings
PREPARATION TIME: 20 minutes,
plus 1-3 hours to refrigerate

3 1/2 oz (100g) tinned tuna in oil, drained and flaked
1/2 oz (15g) fresh wholemeal breadcrumbs
1 small stick celery, trimmed and finely chopped
2 spring onions, trimmed and finely chopped
4 level tablespoons Greek yoghurt
2 level teaspoons chopped fresh parsley
1 level teaspoon chopped fresh tarragon
2 teaspoons lemon juice
1/2 level teaspoon Dijon mustard
Freshly ground black pepper
1/2 red pepper, de-seeded and finely chopped
2 cucumbers, each about 12oz (340g), washed
Parsley or watercress leaves to garnish

1 Mix the tuna with the breadcrumbs, celery, onions and yoghurt. Stir in the parsley, tarragon, lemon juice and mustard, and season with black pepper. Mix in half the red pepper, then cover the rest and refrigerate.

2 Trim off the narrow ends of the cucumbers, then run a cannelle knife or the prongs of a fork down the length of the cucumbers at regular intervals to score the skin and give the cucumbers a green-and-white striped look. Cut each cucumber into four equal lengths and, using an apple corer or a small teaspoon, carefully hollow out the centre of each one.

3 Fill the hollows with the tuna mixture, pressing it in with a wooden spoon handle. Put the cucumbers in a dish, cover and refrigerate for 1 hour for the filling to firm up.

4 Cut the cucumbers into slices about 1/2 in (13mm) thick. Garnish each slice with a sprinkling of the reserved red pepper and a parsley or watercress leaf. Arrange the rings on a plate or tray.

You can prepare and fill the cucumbers up to 3 hours in advance. Keep them covered in the refrigerator, taking them out and slicing them 30 minutes before serving.

THREE RINGS

CALORIES 35

TOTAL FAT 2g

SATURATED FAT 0

CARBOHYDRATES 2g

ADDED SUGAR 0

FIBRE 0

SODIUM 55mg

Rows of brilliant cherry tomatoes filled with prawns, and cucumber rings packed with tuna make a cheerful display for a buffet party.

Turkey bouchées

ONE BOUCHÉE

CALORIES 50

TOTAL FAT 2g

SATURATED FAT 1g

CARBOHYDRATES 2g

ADDED SUGAR 0

FIBRE 0

SODIUM 45mg

MAKES 24
PREPARATION TIME: 25 minutes
COOKING TIME: 20 minutes
OVEN: Preheat to 180°C (350°F, gas mark 4)

1 tablespoon olive oil
2 small carrots, peeled and finely diced
1 medium onion, peeled and finely chopped
½ small green pepper, de-seeded and finely chopped
½ small red pepper, de-seeded and finely chopped

1 level teaspoon dried rubbed sage
1 egg, size 2, lightly beaten
1lb (450g) minced uncooked turkey
2oz (60g) wholemeal breadcrumbs
2 tablespoons tomato purée (see p.16)
2oz (60g) grated Gruyère cheese
Freshly ground black pepper
24 unsalted pistachio nuts, shelled and skinned
½ level teaspoon paprika

Attractive little bouchées, or mouthfuls, of turkey, speckled and moistened with carrot, onion and pepper, are given extra flavour by Gruyère and pistachios.

1 Heat the oil in a heavy-based saucepan and cook the carrots, onion, green and red pepper and sage in it, covered, over a low heat for 10 minutes, stirring occasionally.

2 Turn into a large bowl and mix in the egg, turkey, breadcrumbs, tomato purée and Gruyère. Season with pepper.

3 Spoon the mixture into small-cup nonstick bun trays, half-filling each cup. Place a

pistachio nut on each bouchée. Cook in the heated oven for about 20 minutes, or until the bouchées are golden and firm, and there is no trace of pink in the juice that oozes out when they are tested with a fine skewer or a fork.

4 Leave to cool slightly, then lift out the bouchées carefully. Serve them immediately while hot, or cool and refrigerate for up to 4 hours. Sprinkle lightly with the paprika just before serving.

Iced apple-mint tea

MAKES 4 GLASSES
PREPARATION TIME: 5 minutes,
plus 20 minutes to infuse

1 pint (570ml) boiling water
2 Ceylon tea bags
3 level tablespoons chopped fresh apple-mint leaves
1 wide strip lemon rind
¾ pint (425ml) dry cider, well chilled
1 tablespoon lemon juice
12-20 ice cubes
4 sprigs mint and 4 lemon slices for decoration

1 Pour the boiling water into a warmed teapot with the tea bags, mint and lemon rind. Cover and leave to infuse for 20 minutes, then remove and discard the tea bags.

2 Strain the tea into a large jug and stir in the cider, lemon juice and half the ice.

3 Share the remaining ice between four tumblers and pour equal amounts of mint tea into each glass. Stir briskly and garnish each glass with a mint sprig and a slice of lemon.

ONE GLASS	
CALORIES	40
TOTAL FAT	0
SATURATED FAT	0
CARBOHYDRATES	0
ADDED SUGAR	0
FIBRE	0
SODIUM	10mg

TIP
You can make decorative ice cubes for this drink by adding mint leaves to the cubes before freezing.

Mint and lemon, among the freshest of all tastes, combine with fragrant tea and cider to create a long, cooling drink for sunny summer days.

Banana milk shake

ONE GLASS	
CALORIES	120
TOTAL FAT	2g
SATURATED FAT	1g
CARBOHYDRATES	21g
ADDED SUGAR	0
FIBRE	0
SODIUM	80mg

MAKES 4 GLASSES
PREPARATION TIME: 5 minutes

8 ice cubes
1 pint (570ml) semi-skimmed milk
2 large ripe bananas, peeled and sliced
1 teaspoon vanilla extract

1 Blend the ice cubes and milk in a food processor for 1 minute, or until smooth.

2 Add the bananas and vanilla extract and blend for 1 minute more, or until foamy. Pour into tall glasses and serve.

Make this milk shake immediately before serving so that there is no danger that the bananas will discolour. You can also make fruit milk shakes with 8oz (225g) of hulled ripe strawberries or raspberries, adding 2 level teaspoons of caster sugar, if necessary.

Hot chocolate and banana

MAKES 4 CUPS
PREPARATION TIME: 15 minutes

2 level tablespoons cocoa
4 tablespoons cold water
1¼ pints (725ml) skimmed milk
1 vanilla bean, split lengthways
½ level teaspoon ground cinnamon
1 medium, ripe banana, peeled and chopped
2 level tablespoons Greek yoghurt
1 level teaspoon grated plain chocolate

1 Blend the cocoa and water to a paste in a saucepan. Gradually whisk in half the milk.

2 Stir in the vanilla bean and cinnamon and bring to the boil, then simmer for 2-3 minutes, stirring. Discard the vanilla bean.

3 Blend the bananas and remaining milk in a food processor until smooth. Stir into the chocolate milk and bring to the boil.

4 Take off the heat, whisk in the yoghurt, then pour into cups or mugs, and sprinkle with the grated chocolate. Serve immediately.

ONE CUP	
CALORIES	110
TOTAL FAT	2g
SATURATED FAT	1g
CARBOHYDRATES	16g
ADDED SUGAR	0
FIBRE	1g
SODIUM	150mg

Milky drinks are wonderfully refreshing when ice-cold and comforting when hot. A summer afternoon is the time for serving tall glasses of iced coffee to the grown-ups and a pale froth of banana milk shake to the children. Young and old alike will enjoy cups of hot chocolate flavoured with banana and vanilla, and given a spicy edge with cinnamon.

Iced coffee

ONE GLASS
....
CALORIES 60
....
TOTAL FAT 1g
....
SATURATED FAT 0
....
CARBOHYDRATES 1g
....
ADDED SUGAR 0
....
FIBRE 0
....
SODIUM 105mg
....

MAKES 4 GLASSES
PREPARATION TIME: 10 minutes

1 level tablespoon cocoa
1 tablespoon cold water
4 level tablespoons ground coffee
6fl oz (175ml) boiling water
1 pint (570ml) skimmed milk, well chilled
½ teaspoon vanilla extract
6 ice cubes

1 Mix the cocoa to a smooth paste in a cup with the cold water.

2 Stir the coffee with the boiling water in a small bowl and leave to stand for 5 minutes.

3 Strain the coffee through a sieve lined with kitchen paper into a blender or food processor. Add the cocoa, milk, vanilla and ice, and blend for 1 minute. Serve at once in tall glasses.

Mulled cider

ONE GLASS

CALORIES 95

TOTAL FAT 0

SATURATED FAT 0

CARBOHYDRATES 8g

ADDED SUGAR 0

FIBRE 0

SODIUM 20mg

MAKES 4 GLASSES
PREPARATION TIME: 10 minutes

1¾ pints (1 litre) dry cider
2 cinnamon sticks, crumbled
8 allspice berries
6 cloves
Thinly pared rind of 1 orange
4 orange wedges

1 Pour the cider into a stainless steel
or enamel saucepan, and stir in the crumbled
cinnamon sticks, allspice, cloves and orange
rind. Bring to the boil, then turn down
the heat and leave the cider to simmer,
uncovered, for 5 minutes.

2 Strain the hot cider into heatproof glasses
and put an orange wedge in each drink.

Bittersweet cider is mellowed by warming and spicing into an aromatic winter beverage for enjoying at the fireside – or round a bonfire.

Shrub is a name borrowed from the Arabs' fruit sherbet drinks. This one is irresistible – deep, glowing pink, ice-cold and refreshingly tart.

Spiced cranberry shrub

ONE GLASS	
CALORIES	45
TOTAL FAT	0
SATURATED FAT	0
CARBOHYDRATES	8g
ADDED SUGAR	2g
FIBRE	1g
SODIUM	5mg

MAKES 4 GLASSES
PREPARATION TIME: 5 minutes, plus 1 hour to cool

½ pint (285ml) cranberry juice (see p.16)
8fl oz (225ml) dry cider
1 tablespoon cider vinegar
1 cinnamon stick
2 cloves
2 strips lemon rind
12 ice cubes
1 pint (570ml) mineral water, chilled
4 orange slices
Small red-skinned apple

1 Pour the cranberry juice into a stainless steel or enamel saucepan with the cider, vinegar, cinnamon, cloves and lemon rind. Bring to the boil, then take off the heat. Cover and leave for about 1 hour, until cooled.

2 Strain the shrub into a jug and add the ice, mineral water and orange slices. At the last moment slice and add the apple. Serve in chilled glasses.

For a slightly sweeter drink, use half and half cranberry and raspberry juice.

Gingered lemon and lime fizz

ONE GLASS
CALORIES	40
TOTAL FAT	0
SATURATED FAT	0
CARBOHYDRATES	10g
ADDED SUGAR	10g
FIBRE	0
SODIUM	0

TIP
For a frosty appearance, chill the serving glasses in the refrigerator for 1 hour before using.

MAKES 6 GLASSES
PREPARATION TIME: 5 minutes, plus 1 hour to infuse

3 lemons
1 pint (570ml) boiling water
2 level tablespoons peeled and grated root ginger
2oz (60g) sugar
Strained juice of 2 limes
6 slices lemon
6 slices lime
8 ice cubes
1 pint (570ml) soda water or sparkling mineral water, chilled

1 Pare the rind thinly from one lemon. Put the rind into a heatproof jug, pour the boiling water on it and add the ginger and sugar. Stir well, cover and leave to infuse for 1 hour.

2 Squeeze the juice from all three lemons and strain into a serving jug. Add the lime juice, then strain in the liquid from the ginger mixture and stir.

3 Add the lemon and lime slices and the ice to the jug. Top up with the soda water or mineral water. Stir again and serve in tall glasses.

Ginger tea punch

ONE GLASS
CALORIES	10
TOTAL FAT	0
SATURATED FAT	0
CARBOHYDRATES	2g
ADDED SUGAR	2g
FIBRE	0
SODIUM	0

MAKES 10 GLASSES
PREPARATION TIME: 10 minutes, plus 1-2 hours to cool and chill

1½ pints (850ml) boiling water
8 Assam, Darjeeling or Ceylon tea bags
1 level tablespoon caster sugar
3 level tablespoons peeled and grated root ginger, or 1½ level teaspoons ground ginger
1¾ pints (1 litre) soda water or sparkling mineral water
20 ice cubes
Slivers of peeled root ginger for decoration

1 Pour the water into a large heatproof jug and stir in the tea bags, sugar and ginger. Leave the mixture to infuse for 8 minutes, then take out the tea bags. Leave the tea to cool before covering and putting it in the refrigerator for 1-2 hours.

2 Strain the tea through a coffee filter, or a sieve lined with kitchen paper, into a serving jug or punch bowl. Stir in the soda water or mineral water, and serve in long glasses with two ice cubes and a sliver or two of fresh ginger in each glass.

Grapefruit and mint spritzer

ONE GLASS
CALORIES	35
TOTAL FAT	0
SATURATED FAT	0
CARBOHYDRATES	9g
ADDED SUGAR	3g
FIBRE	0
SODIUM	5mg

MAKES 4 GLASSES
PREPARATION TIME: 10 minutes

Strained juice of two large pink grapefruits
Strained juice of 1 lemon
2 level teaspoons caster sugar
4 sprigs mint
24 ice cubes
½ pint (285ml) soda water or sparkling mineral water, chilled
Mint sprigs for decoration

1 Mix the grapefruit juice with the lemon juice in a jug.

2 Put ½ teaspoon of the sugar and a sprig of mint into each of four glasses. Using the back of a spoon, crush the mint into the sugar.

3 Put 6 ice cubes into each glass and pour in a share of the juice. Top up with the soda water or mineral water. Stir, decorate with mint sprigs and serve.

Drinks are more fun when they gently prickle the palate. The grapefruit spritzer (near right) prickles with sparkling water, while the tea punch and jug of lemon and lime make doubly certain by adding ginger as well.

A steaming glass of this herb tea spreads a tantalising scent of mint, sage and verbena, and makes a thirst-quenching after-dinner drink.

Herb tea

MAKES 4 GLASSES
PREPARATION TIME: 5 minutes,
plus 5 minutes to infuse

2 level tablespoons dried mint
1 level tablespoon dried sage
1 level tablespoon dried verbena
1¾ pints (1 litre) boiling water
2 teaspoons clear honey
2 teaspoons lemon juice
2 lemon slices, quartered, and fresh sage sprigs
for decoration

1 Spoon the mint, sage and verbena into a large, warmed teapot. Pour on the boiling water and stir quickly, then cover and leave to infuse for 5 minutes.

2 Put ½ teaspoon of honey and ½ teaspoon of lemon juice into each of four tea glasses, then pour in the tea through a strainer. Drop two quarter-slices of lemon into each glass and decorate with a sprig of sage.

You can use thyme or borage instead of verbena.

Amber orange-tea punch

MAKES 12 CUPS
PREPARATION TIME: 15 minutes,
plus overnight refrigeration

ONE CUP	
CALORIES 40	
TOTAL FAT 0	
SATURATED FAT 0	
CARBOHYDRATES 6g	
ADDED SUGAR 0	
FIBRE 0	
SODIUM 5mg	

An icy cup of spiced fresh orange juice hisses gently with the bubbles of mineral water and wine. Assam tea gives the drink perfumed depths, but devotees of Earl Grey may prefer its smoky delicacy.

4 Assam or Earl Grey tea bags
¾ pint (425ml) boiling water
¾ pint (425ml) freshly squeezed orange juice (about 5 large oranges)
2 cinnamon sticks, cracked
12 cloves
½ pint (285ml) sparkling mineral water, chilled
½ pint (285ml) sparkling dry white wine, chilled
Slices of orange and sprigs of mint for decoration

1 Put the tea bags into a large, heatproof jug, pour on the boiling water and leave to infuse for 8 minutes. Remove and discard the tea bags.

2 Pour half the orange juice into a small, stainless steel or enamel saucepan with the cinnamon sticks and cloves. Bring to the boil, then turn down the heat, cover and leave to simmer for 1 minute.

3 Pour the hot, spiced orange juice into the jug with the tea, then stir in the remaining juice. Cover and, when cool enough, put in the refrigerator and leave overnight.

4 Just before serving, strain the mixture into a punchbowl and pour in the mineral water and wine. Float the slices of orange and sprigs of mint on the punch and serve immediately, ladling it into silver or glass punch cups, or into small tumblers.

Orange and pineapple crush

MAKES 4 GLASSES
PREPARATION TIME: 25 minutes

1 pineapple, about 2lb (900g), sliced, skin, core
and woody eyes removed, flesh chopped
½ pint (285ml) freshly squeezed orange juice
(about 4 medium oranges), strained
2 tablespoons lemon juice, strained
12 ice cubes
½ pint (285ml) soda water or sparkling mineral water
2 orange slices, halved, and 4 pineapple chunks
for decoration

1 Blend the pineapple in a food processor for
1-2 minutes, then strain through a nylon sieve,
pressing with a spoon to extract all the juice.
Discard the remaining pulp.

2 Mix the pineapple juice, orange juice and
lemon juice in a jug.

3 Put 3 ice cubes into each of four tall glasses
and pour a share of the fruit juice into each
glass. Top up with the soda water or mineral
water and stir well. Decorate with the halved
orange slices and the pineapple chunks,
threaded on cocktail sticks, and serve at once.

ONE GLASS	
CALORIES	80
TOTAL FAT	0
SATURATED FAT	0
CARBOHYDRATES	20g
ADDED SUGAR	0
FIBRE	0
SODIUM	10mg

Orange-yoghurt drink

MAKES 4 GLASSES
PREPARATION TIME: 10 minutes

14 oz (400g) low-fat natural yoghurt
¾ pint (425ml) skimmed milk, well chilled
12fl oz (340ml) freshly squeezed orange juice,
(about 4 large oranges), strained
2 teaspoons clear honey
½ level teaspoon ground ginger
Orange slices for decoration

1 Blend the yoghurt, milk, orange juice, honey
and ginger in a food processor for 1 minute.

2 Pour into four glasses, decorate with the
orange slices, and serve immediately.

ONE GLASS	
CALORIES	140
TOTAL FAT	1g
SATURATED FAT	1g
CARBOHYDRATES	26g
ADDED SUGAR	3g
FIBRE	0
SODIUM	150mg

Freshly squeezed orange juice whips to a cool froth with yoghurt (left), and effervesces when mixed with pineapple juice and soda (right).

Passion fruit citrus sodas

ONE GLASS	
CALORIES	25
TOTAL FAT	0
SATURATED FAT	0
CARBOHYDRATES	5g
ADDED SUGAR	3g
FIBRE	0
SODIUM	5mg

TIP
Choose passion fruits with wrinkled skin, or keep them until the skin wrinkles. The wrinkling is a sign that the fruit is ripe.

MAKES 4 GLASSES
PREPARATION TIME: 20 minutes, plus 2 hours to cool and chill

Thinly pared rind of 1 gently scrubbed lemon
¼ pint (150ml) water
2 level teaspoons granulated sugar
10 ripe passion fruits
Strained juice of 1 lemon
Strained juice of ½ lime
12 ice cubes
4 thin slices lemon
4 thin slices lime
1½ pints (850ml) soda water, chilled

1 Put the lemon rind, water and sugar into a stainless steel or enamel saucepan. Bring to the boil, stirring to dissolve the sugar, and boil for 1 minute. Remove from the heat and leave to cool for about 30 minutes, then cover and refrigerate for about 1 hour, or until the mixture is very cold.

2 Meanwhile, cut each passion fruit in half and scoop the seeds out with a teaspoon into a nylon sieve placed over a bowl. Rub the seeds firmly in the sieve with the back of a stainless steel spoon to squeeze out all the juice, then discard the seeds.

3 Strain the chilled lemon syrup into the bowl with the passion fruit juice, then strain in the lemon juice and the lime juice and stir the mixture well.

4 Put 3 ice cubes into each of four tall glasses. Ladle a quarter of the fruit juice mixture into each glass and drop a slice of lemon and lime into each one. Top up the glasses with the soda water, stir quickly and serve immediately while still fizzing.

You can prepare the passion fruit and lemon mixture up to 6 hours in advance, if this is more convenient. Cover the bowl and keep it in the refrigerator. Mix it with the ice and soda water just before serving. You can make up the passion fruit mixture into a hot drink; just dilute it with hot water instead of soda water, remembering to use heatproof glasses. Passion fruits can be very tart before they are ripe. If you cannot wait for them to ripen completely, you may need to add a little more sugar.

Pineapple-mint yoghurt drink

ONE GLASS	
CALORIES	100
TOTAL FAT	1g
SATURATED FAT	0
CARBOHYDRATES	20g
ADDED SUGAR	3g
FIBRE	0
SODIUM	90mg

MAKES 4 GLASSES
PREPARATION TIME: 10 minutes

1½ lb (680g) fresh pineapple, sliced, skin, core and woody eyes removed, flesh chopped
8oz (225g) low-fat natural yoghurt
8fl oz (225ml) chilled skimmed milk
2 level teaspoons caster sugar
3 level tablespoons chopped fresh mint
Mint sprigs for decoration

1 Put the pineapple flesh with the yoghurt, milk, sugar and chopped mint in a food processor and blend for 1-2 minutes until the mixture has an even, creamy texture.

2 Strain the pineapple drink into four tumblers, decorate each with a mint sprig and serve immediately.

The coolest, palest shade of cream and a heady scent promise smooth and fruity refreshment, a promise that is fulfilled when you taste pineapple-mint yoghurt drink (near right), while the exotic flavours in a jug of passion fruit citrus soda (far right) make a blend just sharp enough to quench the fiercest thirst.

Its warm ruby colour and sharp spicy flavour make this drink popular at outdoor parties – and especially in summer when the evenings can be cool and strings of fruit are hanging on the redcurrant bushes.

TIP
Prepare the redcurrant juice the day before you need it and store in the refrigerator. Or make the juice when redcurrants are in season and freeze it.

Hot redcurrant punch

MAKES 4 CUPS
PREPARATION TIME: 25 minutes

1 pint (570ml) dry cider
1 cinnamon stick, crumbled
4 cloves
4 allspice berries
1 strip of lemon rind
7fl oz (200ml) boiling water
1 tea bag
7fl oz (200ml) redcurrant juice (see p.16)
Redcurrants for decoration

1 Pour the cider into a stainless steel or enamel saucepan. Stir in the cinnamon, cloves, allspice and lemon rind, and bring to the boil. Lower the heat and simmer for 10 minutes.

2 Meanwhile, pour the boiling water on the tea bag in a teapot, cover and leave to infuse for 5 minutes, then discard the tea bag.

3 Pour the tea and the redcurrant juice in with the cider. Heat for 2-3 minutes, until the liquid is hot but not boiling, then strain it into a punchbowl.

4 To serve, ladle the punch into cups or heatproof glasses, and decorate each serving with redcurrants.

ONE CUP	
CALORIES 75	
TOTAL FAT 0	
SATURATED FAT 0	
CARBOHYDRATES 9g	
ADDED SUGAR 2g	
FIBRE 0	
SODIUM 10mg	

Mixed vegetable juice

MAKES 6 GLASSES
PREPARATION TIME: 10 minutes

8oz (225g) ripe tomatoes, skinned and chopped
2 sticks celery, trimmed and chopped
6oz (175g) cucumber, peeled and sliced
2oz (60g) red pepper, de-seeded and chopped
1 tablespoon lemon juice
1 level teaspoon grated fresh horseradish
3-4 drops Tabasco
4 frozen tomato purée cubes (see p.16)
24 ice cubes
¼ pint (150ml) water
⅛ level teaspoon salt
Celery sticks and cucumber slices to garnish

ONE GLASS	
CALORIES	20
TOTAL FAT	0
SATURATED FAT	0
CARBOHYDRATES	4g
ADDED SUGAR	0
FIBRE	1g
SODIUM	80mg

1 Put the tomatoes, celery, cucumber and pepper in a liquidiser with the lemon juice, horseradish, Tabasco, tomato purée cubes and 6 of the ice cubes. Add the water and salt, and blend for 2 minutes, until an even texture.

2 Put three ice cubes in each of six glasses and pour in the vegetable juice. Garnish each glass with a celery stick and a cucumber slice and serve immediately.

A cool blend of cucumber and tomato with a hot dash of horseradish makes a long drink in a short time, and each serving has its own swizzle stick of celery.

INDEX

alfalfa sprouts 25
All-bran 375
almond(s)
 cabbage noodle casserole 237
 and raspberry meringue 336
 spicy toasted nuts 388
 strudel, peach and 354
apple(s)
 and cabbage, pheasant casserole
 with 146
 and carrot soup 52
 duck and, with orange dressing 73
 and raisin crisp 338
 sweet potatoes with 301
apple-mint tea, iced 397
apricot(s)
 chicken, sweet and sour 134
 Chinese noodles with nuts and
 208
 melba summer pudding 350
 spicy maple tea bread 375
 stuffed escalopes of veal 173
artichoke(s)
 broccoli and cheese salad 306
 with creamed bean filling 70
 hearts, preparing 325
 Jerusalem, braised in wine 283
 polenta with tomatoes and 220
 potato and red pepper salad 325
 preventing discoloration 283
 stuffing, peppers with 259
asparagus
 baked in white wine 270
 lamb and, stir-fry 174
 and mushroom omelettes 71
 plaice and vegetable parcels 93
 potato peeler for 270
 salmon ramekins 79
aubergine(s)
 bean and, moussaka 234
 and cheese gratin 232
 lamb in 174
 and pumpkin gratin 270
 salad 307
 stuffed 232
 and sweet pepper soup 53
 and tomato slices 271
avocado(s)
 bean and cucumber salad 308
 filled, with strawberry dressing 22
 guacamole 386
 making halves stand 22
 preparing 308

bacon
 and mushrooms, fusilli with 203

potato cakes with 41
 southern, and beans 195
baguettes, hot vegetable 47
baked cabbage wedges with cheese
277
baked monkfish 90
baked tuna tomatoes 82
balloon whisk 166, 378
bamboo shoots 174
banana(s)
 Caribbean lime chicken 122
 crème brûlée 344
 fruit salad 345
 hot chocolate and 398
 milk shake 398
 spice loaf 373
barley, pearl 62, 150, 176
basil
 beef stew with tomatoes and 165
 dip, cottage cheese and 386
 fusilli salad with peppers and 318
 quiche, cottage cheese and 242
 sauce, broccoli and 274
 sauce, sirloin steak with 168
baton loaf 30
bay leaves, grinding 193
bean(s)
 and aubergine moussaka 234
 black-eyed, bacon and 195
 bobby 308
 borlotti 23, 158
 broad 70, 236, 260, 272, 308
 butter 236, 264
 cannellini 60, 309
 dried, cooking method 17
 fine green 228, 272, 309
 flageolet 179, 309
 kidney 227, 309
 mixed, salad 309
 risotto 227
 runner 137, 177, 272
 spicy, on toast 23
 topping and tailing 272
bean sprout(s) 163, 194
 salad 310
beef 158-171
 minimising fat 162
 potted 24
 slicing when raw 163
 stock 19
beetroot(s)
 beefburgers, Scandinavian 158
 choosing 310
 with horseradish sauce 274
 lamb's lettuce salad 320
 pickled 310
Black Forest gâteau 340

black peppercorns, crushing 171
bouquet garni, fresh 218
braised
 fennel and potatoes 282
 lamb chops 179
 pigeons with orange and rice 148
 quail with mushrooms 150
 red cabbage with cranberries 278
breadcrumbs, making 132
breads 364-82
 lukewarm water for 366
 rising 364
breakfast and brunch 22-49
bream, sea, in parcels 26
broccoli
 artichoke and cheese salad 306
 with basil sauce 274
 and cheddar soufflé 235
 cooking, stems 275
 farfalle with, and nuts 202
 peeling stems 275
 and sesame salad 312
 with sweet pepper 275
broth, chicken and Chinese leaves 54
brussels sprouts with garlic crumbs
276
bulgur
 Armenian, pilau 216
 and lentils with pepper sauce 218
 type for pilau 217
butter-bean hotpot 236

cabbage
 beef wrapped in 158
 chicken and vegetable curry 123
 coleslaw 315
 and fennel salad 318
 leaves, rolling 159
 noodle casserole 237
 red, braised with cranberries 278
 red, pheasant casserole with 146
 red, pork casserole and 192
 roast venison parcel 154
 savoy 158, 237, 277
 spiced 249
 wedges, cooking 277
Californian seafood stew 116
calories 11, 12
cannelloni
 with chicken and walnuts 200
 filling 200
 with ricotta and spinach 200
carbohydrates 10, 11, 12
cardamom pods 22, 388
carrot(s)
 glazed with orange and ginger 278

lamb stew with 177
mangetout and red pepper 285
marinated 312
and peppers in onion sauce 278
quiche, courgette and 243
and rice terrine 238
soup, apple and 52
swede, and potato purée 300
casserole
 cabbage noodle 237
 pheasant 146
 pork and red cabbage 192
cauliflower
 and mushroom salad 312
 in red pepper sauce 280
 in spicy tomato sauce 280
celeriac
 creamed, with scallops 114
 preparing 314
 salad 314
charlotte, strawberry 360
cheese
 and basil quiche 242
 Blue Stilton 47, 76
 and broccoli soufflé 235
 cocktail snacks 386, 388
 cottage 47, 242, 316
 fetta 326
 fromage frais 24, 30, 76, 108, 173
 goat's 88, 232
 Gruyère 239, 240
 haddock soufflé 88
 and onion bread 364
 piquant filling for pears 76
 and potato pie 239
 quark 347
 rarebit 42
 ricotta 200, 232, 239
 salad in pitta bread 25
 and vegetable pudding 240
chestnut mushrooms 166, 195
chestnuts
 peeling 160
 purée 79
 sweet 160
 water 110, 148, 174, 299
chicken 120-37
 broth, and Chinese leaves 54
 cannelloni with 200
 and courgette soup 55
 jambalaya 225
 lemon marinade for 135
 liver 72, 78, 221
 minted soup 56
 paella 222
 poussin 128
 skinning with kitchen shears 126

stock 19
chickpeas
  chilli with rice 241
  cooking method 17
  falafel in pitta bread 245
  and rosemary dip 386
  stew, pork and 187
  vegetable stew with couscous 265
chilled cream of tomato soup 67
chilled cucumber and walnut soup 57
chilli with rice 241
Chinese noodles with nuts and apricots 208
chive vichyssoise 69
chocolate
  berry parfait 342
  cookies 380
  curls 343
  pudding 343
cholesterol 13
choux pastry ring
  mango 348
  savoury, with ratatouille 246
citrus and mango salad 26
citrus fruit and watercress salad 314
cobbler, plum 358
cocktail snacks and drinks 386-411
cocoa 340, 342, 343, 398, 399
coleslaw 315
coley 90
cooking times 15
cottage cheese
  and basil dip 386
  and basil quiche 242
  salad with fruit 316
courgette(s)
  beef kebabs with 161
  and carrot quiche 243
  and cheese wheels 388
  and cherry tomatoes 281
  risotto, lamb and 226
  salad, green bean and 308
  soup, chicken and 55
  and tomato omelette 27
couscous 173, 219, 265
crab
  devilled 111
  getting out meat 112
  seafood gumbo 116
  souffléed Brixham 112
  soup 58
crème brûlée 344
crumble, rhubarb and date 359
crumpets 364
cucumber
  avocado and bean salad 308
  de-seeding 133
  and fruit salad 317
  pan-fried chicken with 133
  and red pepper salad 318
  tuna-filled rings 394
  and walnut soup, chilled 57
  and yoghurt sauce 244

curried
  potatoes 293
  tuna and fruit 110
  vegetables with cucumber sauce 244
curry
  chicken and vegetable 123
  lamb 178

date and oat slices 381
desserts 336-60
dressings
  dill 272
  orange 73
  spiced 390
  strawberry 22
  vinaigrette 16
  yoghurt 17
dried fruit compote 40
duck(ling) 138-40
  and apple with orange dressing 73
  roast, with lime sauce 138
  satay 139
  stir-fried, and vegetables 140

egg(s)
  asparagus and mushroom omelettes 70
  Benedict 28
  courgette and tomato omelette 27
  nutty brown rice with 228
  orange French toast 29
  and prawns, rice with 224
  scrambled 28
  tortilla, two-layer 267
  vegetable paella with 254
escalopes
  turkey with sherry sauce 144
  veal, stuffed 173

falafel in pitta bread 245
farfalle with broccoli and nuts 202
fats
  monounsaturated 11
  polyunsaturated 11
  saturated 11, 12
fennel
  braised 282
  and cabbage salad 318
  and potato hotpot 246
  preventing discoloration 318
fibre 11, 12
fig, rice and thyme stuffing, roast chicken with 124
filo pastry 74, 152, 354
fish 86-116
  cakes, coating 102
  filleting 86
  pie 90
  rarebit 43
  scaling 96

slice 101
  stock 19
food safety 14-15
French-style peas 290
fresh vegetable soup 69
fruit
  blackberries 339
  blending 360
  blueberries 36, 378
  cherries 36, 340
  cranberries 278, 401
  dates 359, 374, 381
  dried, compote 40
  figs 124, 375
  gooseberries 346
  grapefruit 26, 129, 402
  grapes 34, 110, 332, 345
  juice 16
  lemon 94, 105, 298, 402
  lime 122, 136, 138, 347, 402
  mangoes 26, 164, 348
  melon 34, 317, 345
  and nut cake 376
  olives 32, 46, 369
  orange 29, 73, 108, 148, 183, 278, 328, 330, 351, 352, 405, 406
  orange, grating 352
  pancakes 36
  passion fruit 408
  peaches 350, 354, 356
  pears 41, 76, 357
  plums 196, 358
  prunes 147, 376
  raspberries 336
  redcurrants 350, 410
  rhubarb 359
  salad 345
  strawberries 22, 352, 360
  sultanas 377
  washing 15
  wax on citrus fruit 15
fusilli
  with bacon and mushrooms 203
  salad with peppers and basil 318

game 146-55
gammon
  and lentil loaf 196
  grilling 197
  in plum sauce 196
garlic
  baked potatoes 292
  crumbs for brussels sprouts 276
  poussins with 128
  roasted 332
  sautéed spinach with 298
ginger(ed)
  carrots glazed with orange and 278
  cheesecake, lime and 347
  lemon and lime fizz 402
  steamed cod with 86
  lime and, cheesecake 347

marrow with 286
  swordfish steaks 106
  tea punch 402
gooseberry pancakes 346
gougère ring with ratatouille 246
grains 11, 216-28
grapefruit
  chicken with pink 129
  and mint spritzer 402
Greek salad 320
grilled
  beef kebabs 161
  gammon 196
  halibut 89
  lamb cutlets 180
  mackerel 99
  peppers 77
  pork loin 193
  poussins 128
  rabbit 152
  red mullet 100
  salmon 104
  sardines 105
  sole 94
guacamole 386

haddock
  fish rarebit 43
  and goat's cheese soufflé 88
  kedgeree, double 30
  seafood stew, Californian 116
ham, boiled 28
ham, pea and noodle gratin 208
herb(s)
  chopping 227
  lamb cutlets 180
  and onion stuffing, chicken with 130
  sauce, onions in 289
  tea 404
  and wine jelly, trout in 107
herrings
  oatmeal 97
  soused 98
horseradish 104, 274, 411
hotpot
  butter-bean 236
  chicken and mushroom 130
  fennel and potato 246
  Lancashire 181
hummous savoury slices 30

ice cream
  blending 339
  mixed berry 339
iced apple-mint tea 397
iced coffee 399
Italian bread and tomato salad 310

jambalaya 225
Jerusalem artichokes

braised in wine 283
broccoli and cheese salad 306

kedgeree, double haddock 31
kidney bean risotto 227
kidneys
    creole 182
    removing core 182
    in tomatoes 32
kitchen paper, absorbing fat 131
kneading 366

lamb 174-86
    and courgette risotto 226
    leg of, stuffing 184
    liver with orange and onion 183
    liver, removing membrane 183
    quick browning 178
lamb's lettuce and beetroot salad 320
leek(s) 100, 195, 207
    stir-fry with herb croutons 284
lemon sole with sesame seeds 94
lentil(s)
    and bulgur, with pepper sauce 218
    cleaning 248
    cooking method 17
    cottage pie 248
    dhal and spiced cabbage 249
    loaf, gammon and 196
    and potato stew 251
    shepherd's pie, lamb and 186
    soup 59
    split pea and nut rissoles 250
lettuce, crisping 245
lime
    Caribbean chicken 122
    and ginger cheesecake 347
    gingered lemon and, fizz 402
    roast duckling with, sauce 138
    smoked mackerel pâté 33
    twist 33
linguine
    with peas and tuna 205
    and tomato pie 206
listeria 15
lobster 228
lukewarm water for breadmaking 366

macaroni with leeks and tarragon 207
mackerel
    fisherman's 99
    with hot sour sauce 100
    smoked, pâté 33
malt extract 376, 381
mangetout 140, 285
mango
    choux ring 348
    salad, citrus and 26

marinading 122
marinated
    carrots 312
    sardines 105
    scallop brochettes 80
    tuna and tomato sandwiches 46
marrow with ginger and almonds 286
melba summer pudding 350
melon 34, 317, 345
meringue
    almond and raspberry 336
    guide for spreading 336
minerals 12, 14
minestrone 60
mint
    creamy sauce, new potatoes 294
    grapefruit spritzer 402
    leaves, keeping green 143
    pineapple, yoghurt drink 408
    rolled turkey with 142
    stuffing, trout with 108
minted chicken soup 56
mixed bean salad 309
mixed berry ice cream 339
mixed vegetable juice 411
moussaka
    bean and aubergine 234
    fluffy topping 234
muesli 35
muffins, wholemeal
    making 368
    pizza 37
mulled cider 400
mulligatawny soup 62
mushroom(s)
    and asparagus omelettes 71
    and bean filling, in peppers 260
    chestnut 166, 195
    chicken hotpot 130
    and chicken stuffing for pasta 212
    dried, cleaning 187
    fusilli with 203
    gravy, with roast beef 166
    quail with 150
    in red wine 287
    salad, oriental 320
    sauce, with escalopes of veal 173
    soup, with barley 63
    with watercress stuffing 388
    wild 74,169
    with yoghurt and dill sauce 288
mussel(s)
    Californian seafood stew 116
    cleaning 91
    fish pie 90,
    paella 222
    salad 75
mustard-glazed turnips 303

nonstick loaf tin 373
noodle(s)
    Chinese 18, 252

gratin 208
nutrition charts 12
nut(s)
    almonds 253, 286, 336, 354, 377
    almonds, blanching 286
    almonds, decoration 377
    cashews 208, 253
    hazelnuts 250, 253
    peanut satay for duck 139
    peanut skins 209
    peanuts, shelled 208, 253
    pine 148, 174, 202
    rissoles 250
    roast 253
    spicy toasted 388
    walnuts 57, 328, 374
nutty brown rice with eggs 228

oatmeal 40, 97
okra 116, 178
olive and tomato foccacia 369
onions
    fricaseed chicken with 126
    in herb sauce 289
    and herb stuffing 130
    peeling 289
    red, in raisin sauce 290
    sauce 278
    spring, how to curl 256
orange(s)
    citrus and mango salad 26
    cottage cheese salad 316
    curried tuna 110
    dressing 73
    French toast 29
    and onion, liver with 183
    and pineapple crush 406
    rice salad 328
    sauce, leg of lamb with 184
    soufflé 351
    spinach salad 314
    and strawberry flan 352
    watercress salad 314
    yoghurt drink 406
oriental mushroom salad 320

paella 222, 254
pancakes
    fruit 36
    gooseberry 346
    making in advance 346
    Mexican stuffing 254
    oriental style 256
parcels
    beef in cabbage leaves 158
    beef with chestnuts and red wine 160
    plaice and vegetable 93
    roast venison 154
    sardine and rice in spinach 392
    sea bream and vegetable 86
parsley, snipping 203

passion fruit citrus sodas 408
pasta 200-16
    cannelloni 200
    cooking guide 18
    farfalle 202
    fusilli 203, 318
    homemade fresh 18
    lasagne 202
    linguine 205-6
    macaroni 207, 259
    noodles 18, 208, 237, 252
    penne 210
    salad with salmon and spinach 320
    shells 211, 212, 214, 322
    small for soups 60
    spaghetti 215
    summer salad 323
    tagliatelle 208, 216
peach(es)
    and almond strudel 354
    melba summer pudding 350
    removing skin 354
    sorbet 356
peanuts, removing skins 209
pear(s)
    with piquant cheese filling 76
    standing upright 357
    in white wine 357
Peas
    dried, cooking method 17
    French-style 290
    linguine with tuna and 205
    noodle gratin, ham and 208
    purée 290
pease pudding, layered 258
penne with spinach and cheese 210
peppers
    with artichoke stuffing 259
    and aubergine soup 53
    with bean and mushroom filling 260
    broccoli with 275
    fusilli salad 318
    grilled 77
    mangetout with carrots and red 285
    in onion sauce, carrots and 278
    pizza with 262
    pork with roasted 191
    potato and artichoke salad 325
    roasted vegetable salad 332
    sauce, with cauliflower 280
    sauce, with halibut 89
    spicy cucumber salad 318
pheasant
    casserole with apple and cabbage 146
    pie, pork and 38
    roast, with prunes 147
    terrine 78
pickled beetroot salad 310
pies
    cheese and potato 239

fish 90
lamb and lentil shepherd's 186
lentil cottage 248
linguine and tomato 206
pork and pheasant 38
rabbit 153
pigeon braised with orange and rice 148
pine nuts, toasting 148
pineapple
cottage cheese and fruit salad 316
curried tuna and fruit 110
mint yoghurt drink 408
orange crush 406
preparing 324
salad 324
pitta breads
cheese salad in 24
falafel in 245
hot baking sheets 370
making 370
pizza
muffins 37
with three-pepper topping 262
plaice
stuffed, with nutmeg sauce 92
and vegetable parcels 93
plum cobbler 358
polenta with tomatoes and artichokes 220
pork 187-195
and bean tacos 44
loin, how to stuff 189
and pheasant pie 38
porridge and dried fruit compote 40
potato(es)
artichoke and red pepper salad 325
baked garlic 292
cakes with bacon 41
coating with sesame seeds 295
curried 293
hotpot, fennel and 246
new 127, 151, 294, 325
pie, cheese and 239
preventing discoloration 295
purée, swede, carrot and 300
sesame 295
slices 295
soup, split pea and 64
stew, lentil and 251
sweet 296, 301
two-potato cake 296
potted beef 24
prawn(s)
de-veining 390
Dublin Bay 327
and fetta salad 326
freshwater 113, 116, 326, 390, 394
spiced 113, 390
and spinach salad 327
tiger 228
preparation times 15

pretzels with cumin seeds 371
protein 11, 13
Provençal
chicken breasts 134
soup 65

quick acting yeast 262
quail, braised with mushrooms 150

rabbit
Calabrian 151
couscous 219
farmed or wild 151
grilled 152
pie 152
radicchio 81, 332
raisins
apple crisp 388
chicken and vegetable curry 123
fruit and nut cake 376
sauce, red onions in 290
soaking 319
ratatouille 246
red mullet with leeks and tomatoes 100
rhubarb and date crumble 359
rice
arborio 220, 243
basmati 229
brown 228, 328
carrot terrine 238
cooking method 17
with egg and prawn 224
long-grain 31, 148, 195, 224, 299
long-grain brown 124, 227
orange and walnut salad 328
quiche base 243
risotto 226
saffron 222
tofu and vegetable stir-fry with 266
Valencia 254
wild mixture 31, 238
rising of bread dough 364, 366
risotto
best rice for 226
chicken liver 221
kidney bean 227
lamb and courgette 226
roast
beef with Yorkshire puddings 166
chicken with fig, rice and thyme stuffing 124
duckling with lime sauce 138
leg of lamb 184
pheasant with prunes 147
stuffed loin of pork 188
turkey with sweet potato stuffing 144
venison parcel 154
roasted
peppers, pork with 191

vegetable salad 332
rolled oats 35, 381
rolls, bread and 366

salmon 102-4
and asparagus ramekins 79
with cucumber and dill sauce 102
fish cakes 102
with horseradish sauce 104
pasta salad with spinach 322
salt, safe amount 12, 14
sardine(s)
lemon marinated 105
pasta shells pesto 214
and rice parcels 392
using tinned 214
saffron, use 222
salads 75, 306-32, 345
sauces
basil 168, 274
creamy mint 294
cucumber 244
cucumber and dill 102
herb 289
horseradish 274
hot sour 100
lime 138
mushroom 173
nutmeg 92
orange 184
parsley 272
pear 49
pepper 89, 218, 280
plum 196
raisin 290
sherry 144
spicy tomato 280
tomato 16, 37, 297
watercress 212
white bean 264
yoghurt 278
yoghurt and dill 288
savoury biscuits 382
scallops
Californian seafood stew 116
with creamed celeriac 114
marinated, brochettes 80
spiced seafood pilau 228
scrambled eggs Benedict 28
sea bream and vegetable parcels 86
seafood gumbo 116
seeds, crushing 389
sesame seeds, lemon sole with 94
sesame snaps 382
side salads 306-332
skate vinaigrette 94
skate wings, preparing 94
skewered
beef kebabs 161
duck satay 139
pork kebabs, Indonesian style 188
scallops, marinated 80
smoked mackerel pâté 33

smoked trout pâté 81
soda bread 372
sodium 12, 14
soufflé
Brixham crab 112
broccoli and Cheddar 235
good rise 88
haddock and goat's cheese 88
orange 351
spinach squares 392
soups 52-69
soured cream 142, 158
spaghetti with prawns and capers 215
spiced
beef 162
cabbage 249
cranberry shrub 401
prawns 113, 390
seafood and coconut pilau 228
vegetable stew with couscous 265
spicy
beans on toast 23
cucumber and red pepper salad 318
pork loin 193
toasted nuts 388
tomato sauce with cauliflower 280
spinach
and bacon salad 328
balls in tomato sauce 297
cannelloni with ricotta 200
orange salad 330
penne with 210
pheasant terrine 78
and rice cakes 299
ring with white bean sauce 264
salmon and pasta salad 320
sardine and rice parcels 392
sautéed 298
soufflé squares 392
split pea(s)
cooking method 17
and potato soup 64
pudding 258
purée 290
rissoles 250
squid 114, 222
starch 11
starters 70-82
steak(s)
fillet with wild mushrooms 169
oriental 170
peppered sirloin 171
sirloin, with basil sauce 168
steamed cod with ginger 86
stew
beef, with tomatoes and basil 165
chicken and vegetable 137
lamb and barley 176
lamb, with carrots and runner beans 177
pork and chickpea 187

seafood, Californian 116
venison 155
stir-fry
beef 163
duck and vegetables 140
lamb and asparagus 174
leek, with herb croutons 284
noodle and tofu 252
pork and vegetable 194
squid and vegetable 114
tofu and vegetable 266
stocks 18-19
strawberry
charlotte 360
dressing with avocado 22
flan, orange and 352
strudel, peach and almond 354
stuffed
aubergines 232
escalopes of veal 173
leg of lamb 184
loin of pork 188
pasta shells and watercress sauce 212
peppers 259, 260
plaice with nutmeg sauce 92
radishes 390
turkey 144
whiting 96
swede, carrot and potato purée 300
sweet potatoes with apples 301
sweetcorn chowder 66
swiss roll 378
swordfish steaks, gingered 106

tacos, filling and folding 44
tagliatelle bolognese 216
tarragon 82, 207
tea-breads
banana spice-loaf 373
date and walnut 374
prune 376
spicy maple 375
thyme
fig and rice stuffing 124
with rabbit 151
toast
French 29
rarebit 42, 43
spicy beans on 23
tofu 252, 256, 266
tomato(es)
aubergine slices 271
baked, tuna-filled 82
beef kebabs 32
courgettes with 281
gratin 302
kidneys in 32
marinated tuna sandwiches 46
polenta with 220
with prawn stuffing 394
purée, homemade 16
runner beans with 272

salads 310, 324
sauce, homemade 16
soup, chilled cream of 67
sun-dried 369
tortilla, two-layer 267
trout
in herb and wine jelly 107
with orange and mint stuffing 108
smoked, paté 81
tuna 46, 82, 110, 206, 394
turkey 141-45
balsamico 141
boucheés 396
burgers with soured cream 142
escalopes with sherry sauce 144
rolled with mint 142
with sweet potato stuffing 144
and tarragon loaf 82

vanilla sugar 340
veal
osso bucco 172
stock 19
stuffed escalopes 173
vegetable(s)
curried, with cucumber sauce 244
curry, chicken and 123
hot, baguettes 47
lasagne 204
mixed, juice 411
paella with eggs 254
pudding, cheese and 240
side dishes 270-303
soup, fresh 68
stir-fried duck and 140
stock 19
vegetarian main dishes 232-67
venison
roast 154
stew 155
vitamins 12, 14

waffles with Stilton topping 48
Waldorf salad 332
walnuts
cannelloni with chicken and 200
rice salad 328
watercress 33, 212, 332, 388
wheat salad, and herbs 330
whisking 166, 378
wholemeal muffins 368
wild mushroom tartlets 74

yoghurt
cucumber sauce 244
dill sauce 288
dressing 17
homemade 48
mint sauce 294
onion sauce 278
Yorkshire puddings, with beef 166

Acknowledgments

Some of the photographs in this book were taken from 'Le Ricette della Buona Salute', published 1991 by Selezione dal Reader's Digest, Sp.A. Milano: *Photographer* Giandomenico Frazzi; *Home Economist* Alessandra Avallone; *Stylist* Stella Rustioni.

Other photographs were taken from 'Grand Recipes de Bonne Santé', published 1992 by Sélection de Reader's Digest, Paris: *Photographer* Christine Fleurent; *Home Economist and Stylist* Danièle Schnapp.

All the photographs in this book are Reader's Digest copyright. The photographer of each picture is listed below.

Martin Brigdale 22, 23, 30, 31, 34, 35, 39 42, 43, 48, 49, 52, 53, 58, 59, 62, 63, 68, 69, 70, 71, 74, 75, 83, 88, 89, 97, 98, 99, 107, 108-9, 121, 122, 127, 143, 147, 148-9, 151, 155, 158, 159, 177, 202, 203, 208, 209, 211, 212-13, 214, 217, 221, 225, 226, 228, 239, 273, 279, 280, 281, 292, 293, 300, 301, 313, 326-7, 331, 336-7, 344, 346, 347, 354-5, 370, 371, 383, 393, 398-9, 403, 410, 411.

Gerrit Buntrock 1, 2-3, 4-5, 6-7, 8-9, 20-21, 50-51, 84-85, 118-19, 156-7, 198-9, 230-1, 268-9, 304-5, 334-5, 362-3, 384-5.

Laurie Evans 24, 25, 32, 33, 45, 46, 47, 54, 55, 64, 65, 78, 79, 80, 81, 91, 105, 111, 112, 113, 114, 115, 123, 125, 132, 137, 140, 141, 142, 146, 150, 172, 173, 176, 200, 201, 204, 205, 206, 207, 215, 216, 219, 220, 222-3, 224, 227, 229, 276, 277, 284, 285, 291, 294, 295, 298, 299, 306, 307, 314, 315, 319, 324, 325, 329, 338, 339, 349, 356, 357, 368, 369, 374, 380, 391, 395, 404, 405, 409.

Christine Fleurent 90, 94, 138, 152, 218.

Giandomenico Frazzi 86, 92, 102, 120, 252.

Vernon Morgan 26, 27, 28-29, 36, 37, 56, 57, 76, 77, 82, 93, 101, 104, 106, 117, 126, 130, 131, 133, 135, 154, 160, 161, 163, 164, 169, 170, 178, 182, 185, 187, 188, 189, 192, 193, 194, 195, 210, 232, 233, 236, 237, 240, 241, 244, 245, 248, 249, 254, 255, 257, 264, 265, 270, 271, 282, 283, 286, 287, 296, 297, 308, 309, 316, 317, 321, 332, 333, 341, 345, 350, 351, 360-1, 367, 375, 378-9, 389, 396, 397, 406-7.

Clive Streeter 40, 41, 60-61, 66, 67, 72, 73, 87, 95, 96, 100, 103, 110, 116, 128, 129, 134, 136, 139, 144, 145, 153, 162, 165, 167, 168, 171, 174, 175, 179, 180, 181, 183, 186, 190, 191, 196, 197, 234, 235, 238, 242, 243, 246, 247, 250, 251, 253, 258, 259, 260-1, 263, 266, 267, 274, 275, 288, 289, 302, 303, 311, 322, 323, 330, 342, 343, 352-3, 358, 359, 364, 365, 372, 373, 376, 377, 381, 387, 400, 401.

Cover photograph Vernon Morgan
Home Economist Kathy Man; *Stylist* Anne Fleming

Typesetting Apex Computersetting, London, England

Separations Scantrans Ltd, Singapore

Paper Townsend Hook Ltd, Snodland, Kent, England

Printing and binding Fabrieken Brepols n.v., Turnhout, Belgium